New Opportunities for Sentiment Analysis and Information Processing

Aakanksha Sharaff
National Institute of Technology, Raipur, India

G. R. Sinha
Myanmar Institute of Information Technology, Mandalay, Myanmar

Surbhi Bhatia
King Faisal University, Saudi Arabia

IGI Global
PUBLISHER of TIMELY KNOWLEDGE

A volume in the Advances in Data Mining and
Database Management (ADMDM) Book Series

Published in the United States of America by
IGI Global
Engineering Science Reference (an imprint of IGI Global)
701 E. Chocolate Avenue
Hershey PA, USA 17033
Tel: 717-533-8845
Fax: 717-533-8661
E-mail: cust@igi-global.com
Web site: http://www.igi-global.com

Library of Congress Cataloging-in-Publication Data

Names: Sharaff, Aakanksha, 1989- editor. I Sinha, G. R., 1975- editor. I
  Bhatia, Surbhi, 1988- editor.
Title: New opportunities for sentiment analysis and information processing
  / Aakanksha Sharaff, G.R. Ram Sinha, and Surbhi Bhatia, editors.
Description: Hershey, PA : Engineering Science Reference, [2021] I Includes
  bibliographical references and index. I Summary: "This book provides a
  unique contribution to the various interdisciplinary fields of
  information retrieval and sentiment analysis, which are fueling the
  revolutionary growth of digital marketing and changes in the market game
  but also presents new opportunities for skilled professional skilled and
  expertise"-- Provided by publisher.
Identifiers: LCCN 2021017693 (print) I LCCN 2021017694 (ebook) I ISBN
  9781799880615 (hardcover) I ISBN 9781799880622 (paperback) I ISBN
  9781799880639 (ebook)
Subjects: LCSH: Data mining--Industrial applications. I Sentiment analysis.
  I Internet marketing.
Classification: LCC QA76.9.D343 N4855 2021 (print) I LCC QA76.9.D343
  (ebook) I DDC 006.3/12--dc23
LC record available at https://lccn.loc.gov/2021017693
LC ebook record available at https://lccn.loc.gov/2021017694

This book is published in the IGI Global book series Advances in Data Mining and Database Management (ADMDM) (ISSN: 2327-1981; eISSN: 2327-199X)

British Cataloguing in Publication Data
A Cataloguing in Publication record for this book is available from the British Library.

For electronic access to this publication, please contact: eresources@igi-global.com.

Advances in Data Mining and Database Management (ADMDM) Book Series

David Taniar
Monash University, Australia

ISSN:2327-1981
EISSN:2327-199X

MISSION

With the large amounts of information available to organizations in today's digital world, there is a need for continual research surrounding emerging methods and tools for collecting, analyzing, and storing data.

The **Advances in Data Mining & Database Management (ADMDM)** series aims to bring together research in information retrieval, data analysis, data warehousing, and related areas in order to become an ideal resource for those working and studying in these fields. IT professionals, software engineers, academicians and upper-level students will find titles within the ADMDM book series particularly useful for staying up-to-date on emerging research, theories, and applications in the fields of data mining and database management.

COVERAGE

- Decision Support Systems
- Educational Data Mining
- Data Mining
- Profiling Practices
- Neural Networks
- Data Quality
- Data Analysis
- Information Extraction
- Web-based information systems
- Text Mining

IGI Global is currently accepting manuscripts for publication within this series. To submit a proposal for a volume in this series, please contact our Acquisition Editors at Acquisitions@igi-global.com or visit: http://www.igi-global.com/publish/.

Titles in this Series

For a list of additional titles in this series, please visit:
http://www.igi-global.com/book-series/advances-data-mining-database-management/37146

Transforming Scholarly Publishing With Blockchain Technologies and AI
Darrell Wayne Gunter (Gunter Media Group, USA)
Information Science Reference • © 2021 • 336pp • H/C (ISBN: 9781799855897) • US $205.00

Political and Economic Implications of Blockchain Technology in Business and Healthcare
Dário de Oliveira Rodrigues (Instituto Politécnico de Santarém, Portugal)
Business Science Reference • © 2021 • 389pp • H/C (ISBN: 9781799873631) • US $225.00

Data Preprocessing, Active Learning, and Cost Perceptive Approaches for Resolving Data Imbalance
Dipti P. Rana (Sardar Vallabhbhai National Institute of Technology, Surat, India) and Rupa G. Mehta (Sardar Vallabhbhai National Institute of Technology, Surat, India)
Engineering Science Reference • © 2021 • 309pp • H/C (ISBN: 9781799873716) • US $225.00

Data Science Advancements in Pandemic and Outbreak Management
Eleana Asimakopoulou (Independent Researcher, Greece) and Nik Bessis (Edge Hill University, UK)
Engineering Science Reference • © 2021 • 255pp • H/C (ISBN: 9781799867364) • US $225.00

Industry Use Cases on Blockchain Technology Applications in IoT and the Financial Sector
Zaigham Mahmood (University of Northampton, UK & Shijiazhuang Tiedao University, China)
Engineering Science Reference • © 2021 • 400pp • H/C (ISBN: 9781799866503) • US $245.00

Analyzing Data Through Probabilistic Modeling in Statistics
Dariusz Jacek Jakóbczak (Koszalin University of Technology, Poland)
Engineering Science Reference • © 2021 • 331pp • H/C (ISBN: 9781799847069) • US $225.00

Applications of Big Data in Large- and Small-Scale Systems
Sam Goundar (British University Vietnam, Vietnam) and Praveen Kumar Rayani (National Institute of Technology, Durgapur, India)
Engineering Science Reference • © 2021 • 377pp • H/C (ISBN: 9781799866732) • US $245.00

Developing a Keyword Extractor and Document Classifier Emerging Research and Opportunities
Dimple Valayil Paul (Department of Computer Science, Dnyanprassarak Mandal's College and Research Centre, Goa University, Goa, India)
Engineering Science Reference • © 2021 • 229pp • H/C (ISBN: 9781799837725) • US $195.00

701 East Chocolate Avenue, Hershey, PA 17033, USA
Tel: 717-533-8845 x100 • Fax: 717-533-8661
E-Mail: cust@igi-global.com • www.igi-global.com

Table of Contents

Detailed Table of Contents

Chapter 1

    Aakanksha Sharaff, National Institute of Technology, Raipur, India
    Ramya Allenki, UnitedHealth Group, India
    Rakhi Seth, National Institute of Technology, Raipur, India

Sentiment analysis works on the principle of categorizing and identifying the text-based content and the process of classifying documents into one of the predefined classes commonly known as text classification. Hackers deploy a strategy by sending malicious content as an advertisement link and attack the user system to gain information. For protecting the system from this type of phishing attack, one needs to classify the spam data. This chapter is based on a discussion and comparison of various classification models that are used for phishing SMS detection through sentiment analysis. In this chapter, SMS data is collected from Kaggle, which is classified as ham or spam; while implementing the deep learning techniques like Convolutional Neural Network (CNN), CNN with 7 layers, and CNN with 11 layers, different results are generated. For evaluating these results, different machine learning techniques are used as a baseline algorithm like Naive Bayes, Decision Trees, Support Vector Machine (SVM), and Artificial Neural Network (ANN). After evaluation, CNN showed the highest accuracy of 99.47% as a classification model.

Chapter 2

    Shikha Jain, Banasthali University, India
    Shubham Jain, ZEE Entertainment Ltd, India
    Ajit Kumar Jain, Banasthali Vidyapith, India

With the meteoric development of the big data, internet of things (IoT), the very first question is about how to scout the massive volume of data from heterogeneous data sources. The modern tools and techniques commonly used in successful transmuting of well-structured data into business intelligence (BI) clearly don't work when started on unlabeled data. It is needed to have effective and efficient mapping processes to transform unstructured text data to structured text data with assigned categories to make rapid decisions. With the support of modern automatic text mining tools, the decision-making process can now be done efficiently and cost-effectively. The deep learning concept has attained state-of-the-art results. The mapping operation of unstructured text data to classified structured text data will symbolize unstructured data as renewable assets that are well arranged, useful, and meaningful to serve organizational operations. This chapter presented a comparison of conventional and deep learning methods for unstructured text data classification and its challenges.

Chapter 3
Shakeel Ahmed, King Faisal University, Saudi Arabia
Shubham Sharma, Tata Consultancy Services, India
Saneh Lata Yadav, K. R. Mangalam University, India

Information retrieval is finding material of unstructured nature within large collections stored on computers. Surface web consists of indexed content accessible by traditional browsers whereas deep or hidden web content cannot be found with traditional search engines and requires a password or network permissions. In deep web, dark web is also growing as new tools make it easier to navigate hidden content and accessible with special software like Tor. According to a study by Nature, Google indexes no more than 16% of the surface web and misses all of the deep web. Any given search turns up just 0.03% of information that exists online. So, the key part of the hidden web remains inaccessible to the users. This chapter deals with positing some questions about this research. Detailed definitions, analogies are explained, and the chapter discusses related work and puts forward all the advantages and limitations of the existing work proposed by researchers. The chapter identifies the need for a system that will process the surface and hidden web data and return integrated results to the users.

Chapter 4
Puneet Misra, University of Lucknow, India
Arun Singh Yadav, University of Lucknow, India
Siddharth Chaurasia, University of Lucknow, India

Technological advancements and their adaptation have made social media one of the most used platforms for sharing ideas and expressing views and experiences. Fields like finance and retail have mined and used information on social platforms to a good effect. The healthcare domain too can leverage social forums in various ways, and it has just started its journey by taking baby steps. Events like the COVID-19 pandemic have accelerated the adaptation to increase the pace and breadth of information outreach. The chapter discusses social media usage in healthcare. The chapter highlights challenges, opportunities, and issues encountered so far and the way forward.

Chapter 5
Arabela Briciu, Transilvania University of Brasov, Romania
*Cristian-Laurenţiu RomanCristian-Laurenţiu RomanCristian-Laurenţiu Roman, Transilvania
    University of Brasov, Romania*
Victor-Alexandru Briciu, Transilvania University of Brasov, Romania

This chapter aims to present the process of selecting and analyzing a number of reviews using a software solution (an online application) created specifically for text analysis and extracting user sentiment. This software measures the level of user satisfaction, analyzing product reviews and taking into account the qualitative part of the content generated by users. Analyzing online customer reviews with the help of specialized software can help both companies and other users. The software can also help us reach a conclusion regarding the analysis of reviews and customer feedback on products or services. This study can also be useful for customers or buyers who want to know the opinion of others about a product, having the opportunity to differentiate between positive and negative reviews.

Chapter 6
Fredrick Ishengoma, The University of Dodoma, Tanzania

Recently, the Tanzanian government has started making m-government initiatives. However, little is known about the factors and conditions surrounding m-government adoption in Tanzania. Consequently, some m-government services have been successfully adopted while others are still struggling (having a low level of adoption). This study investigates critical success factors (CSFs) that led m-government services belonging to the same family to have varying degrees of adoption level. The study employs a set of web analytics tools that monitored and analyzed the traffic data of the selected three m-government services. The results show that inspecting the web analytics data from multiple viewpoints and varying levels of detail gives insights on the CSFs towards the adoption of m-government services. The findings suggest that perceived usefulness, user needs, and usability favor the adoption of one m-government service over the other.

Chapter 7
Supriya Gupta, National Institute of Technology, Raipur, India
Aakanksha Sharaff, National Institute of Technology, Raipur, India
Naresh Kumar Nagwani, National Institute of Technology, Raipur, India

The expanding amount of text-based biomedical information has prompted mining valuable or intriguing frequent patterns (words/terms) from extremely massive content, which is still a very challenging task. In the chapter, the authors have conceived a practical methodology for text mining dependent on the frequent item sets. This chapter presents a strategy utilizing item set mining graph-based summarization for summing up biomedical literature. They address the difficulties of recognizing important subjects or concepts in the given biomedical document text and display the relations between the strings by choosing the high pertinent lines from biomedical literature using apriori itemset mining algorithm. This method utilizes essential criteria to distinguish the significant concepts, events, for example, the fundamental subjects of the input record. These sentences are determined as exceptionally educational, applicable, and chosen to create the final summary.

Chapter 8
Saman Qureshi, Maulana Azad National Institute of Technology, India
Sri Khetwat Saritha, Maulana Azad National Institute of Technology, India
D. Kishan, Maulana Azad National Institute of Technology, India

Websites like Quora, Yahoo! Answers, and Reddit are examples of community question answering (CQA) systems that enable users to ask questions as well as to answer questions. Answer selection is the most challenging task in CQA systems to get the good and relevant answer for the user questions. The shortcomings in the current approaches are lexical gap between text pairs, dependency on external sources, and manual features which lead to lack of generalization ability. These shortcomings are resolved by already proposed work, but they lack generalization, and their performance is not satisfying. Whereas to focus on rich quality answers, attention mechanism can be integrates with neural network. This chapter proposes two models BLSTM and BLSTM with attention mechanism. Attention mechanism aligns question to the answer with the answer's more informative part. So, when it is applied in the model, BLSTM with attention mechanism model surpasses the top approaches.

Chapter 9

Lalitha T. B., Hindustan Institute of Technology and Science, Chennai, India
Sreeja P. S., Hindustan Institute of Technology and Science, Chennai, India

Education provides a predominant source of worldly knowledge around us and changes the perspective of the living society as a global village. However, education has revealed fragmentary remains in the professional competence and personal growth of the learners without the involvement of online learning. E-learning brings out a broader vision of sources to the learners available over the web with the holistic approach to learning from anywhere without cost and minimal effort. The proposed theoretical framework analyses the long-term evolution of e-learning and its effect on mankind. The various methods, technologies, and approaches of e-learning that exist in various forms were discussed exponentially according to the range of necessities among the learners. The recommendation system plays a pivotal role in referring contents and enhancing the learning environment. The education promoted to the learners through the recommendations system over their personal preferences were explored here in detail.

Chapter 10

Victor-Alexandru Briciu, Transilvania University of Brasov, Romania
Cristian-Laurenţiu RomanCristian-Laurenţiu RomanCristian-Laurenţiu Roman, Transilvania University of Brasov, Romania
Arabela Briciu, Transilvania University of Brasov, Romania

This chapter aims to present the issue of manipulation of online reviews, behind which there is always an interest, whether it is about increasing sales, promoting a product, degrading the image of a competing brand or product. Such reviews can influence the purchase decision or the sales of a company. Combining users' text with their behavior has yielded the best results in identifying fake reviews, and this remains probably the most effective method to date. The chapter proposes, as a novelty factor, a methodological solution before analyzing reviews through specialized software (e.g., SmartMunk, Revuze, Aspectiva, SentiGeek, etc.), a filter for identifying fake reviews by introducing them into a fake review application called Fakespot. Moreover, the idea that these false reviews can influence the purchase decision of customers in any field is emphasized, so it is very important that large companies develop programs or systems that detect them.

Sentiment analysis, stance detection, and intent detection on social media texts are all significant research problems with several application opportunities. In this chapter, the authors explore the possible contribution of sentiment and intent information to machine learning-based stance detection on tweets. They first annotate a Turkish tweet dataset with sentiment and proprietary intent labels, where the dataset was already annotated with stance labels. Next, they perform stance detection experiments on the dataset using sentiment and intent labels as additional features. The experiments with SVM classifiers show that using sentiment and intent labels as additional features improves stance detection performance considerably. The final form of the dataset is made publicly available for research purposes. The findings reveal the contribution of sentiment and intent information to the solution of stance detection task on the Turkish tweet dataset employed. Yet, further studies on other datasets are needed to confirm that our findings are generalizable to other languages and on other topics.

In the present scenario, social media platforms have become more accessible sources for news. Social media posts need not always be truthful information. These posts are widely disseminated with little regard for the truth. It is necessary to realize the evolution and origins of false news patterns in order to improve the progression of quality news and combat fake news on social media. This chapter discusses the most frequently used social media (Facebook) and the type of information exchanged to solve this issue. This chapter proposes a novel framework based on the "Fake News Detection Network – Long Short-Term Memory" (FNDN-LSTM) model to discriminate between fake news and real news. The social media news dataset is to be taken and preprocessed using the TF BERT model (technique). The preprocessed data will be passed through a feature selection model, which will select the significant features for classification. The selected features will be passed through the FNDN-LSTM classification model for identifying fake news.

Chapter 13

Sentiment analysis is perceived to be a multi-disciplinary research domain composed of machine learning, artificial intelligence, deep learning, image processing, and social networks. Sentiment analysis can be used to determine opinions of the public about products and to find the customers' interest and their feedback through social networks. To perform any natural language processing task, the input text/comments should be represented in a numerical form. Word embeddings represent the given text/sentences/words as a vector that can be employed in performing subsequent natural language processing tasks. In this chapter, the authors discuss different techniques that can improve the performance of sentiment analysis using concepts and techniques like traditional word embeddings, sentiment embeddings, emoticons, lexicons, and neural networks. This chapter also traces the evolution of word embedding techniques with a chronological discussion of the recent research advancements in word embedding techniques.

Chapter 14

Vikas Kumar, Maulana Azad National Institute of Technology, India
Sri Khetwat Saritha, Maulana Azad National Institute of Technology, India

In the internet world we will have a lot of information, public opinions, and researchers' comments on the economy of a country, but it will be very difficult to analyze these opinions. Analysis of these opinions is very important to know how the economy of a country does change and to predict the economy of the country. Sentiment analysis does analysis of public opinion in the textual form, and it provides either of positive, neutral or negative sentiments of the textual comment given on the economy. Sometimes, sentiment analysis may not develop a model for better prediction and judgement of public opinion. In this chapter, the authors proposed a method that integrates sentiment analysis with the time series. They proposed a method to create a domain-specific lexicon to calculate the sentiment of the textual opinions over the economic dataset. This chapter implements the sentiment time series model on economic news by using the lexicon-based approach based on built-in lexicons and domain-specific lexicon.

Preface

Sentiment analysis, also known as opinion mining, is a machine learning and natural language processing technique. Information processing is the new area with intend to retrieve relevant information using different algorithms. Both lie at the crossroads of information retrieval, natural language processing and data mining. This book focusses on both theoretical and practical contributions to the related literature. The findings of the current study can readily be used by future work on determining the interrelationships between these three significant areas in the applications of multiple areas.

Mining sentiments from review comments or textual data is the main task of Sentiment Analysis. Several multinational organizations realize that sentiment mining plays an important role for decision making and market strategy. The revolutionary growth of digital marketing not only changes the market game but also results new opportunities for skilled professional and expertise. Nowadays the technologies are rapidly changing and the artificial intelligence (AI) and the machine learning are contributing as game changer technologies which are not only trending but also very popular among the data scientist and data analyst. Sentiment Analysis and Information Retrieval can be applied to almost every analytical field for predicting and analysis. The affective computation applications are very popular and widely used by the industries. Mining information by analyzing the sentiments has become one of the most interesting field of research. Sentiment Analysis is one of major research area in Data Science. There exists various technique of Sentiment Analysis like affective computing, machine learning, linear regression, decision trees, logistic regression, principal component analysis, Naïve Bayesian classifier, neural networks, deep learning, predictive modelling, text analysis, survival analysis, and many more, all of which allow using the data in such a way so that better and intelligent decisions are made. As we all know data is exponentially increasing day by day and for the analysis of this large data become a competition among data scientist and data analysis industries. This book will provide a unique effort in the various interdisciplinary field of information retrieval and sentiment analysis.

Sentiment analysis, stance detection, and intent detection have a variety of significant application areas. These areas include recommender systems, personalized advertising, market analysis, information retrieval, and predictions for elections, among others etc. With the exploration of opinions and reviews with the trend of being online, social media analytics have opened new opportunities for researchers to conduct studies in these avenues. This book will play a significant role by opening new areas towards exploring recent advances by deploying novel methodologies in sentiment analysis and information processing services and applications. It is ideally designed for researchers and industrialists. This book consists of fourteen chapters in total, focusing on several domains using computational techniques to explore sentiment analysis for phishing SMS detection, identifying novel and efficient solutions for online fake reviews in the research process, ways to retrieve relevant and correct information using hidden web, presenting analysis of online customer Reviews on Face Masks, performing web analytics study on critical reviews related to government and policy makers, data analytics related to mining and opinion summarization, novelties and innovations in question answering systems and recommendation systems. It also deals with posting some questions about this research done in several domains including healthcare.

THE CHALLENGES

The current books available do not focus extensive scope of Sentiment analysis in social media mining, Sentiment Visualization, Emotion Detection, Real time sentiment analysis etc. Especially handing and managing the Data in Several Applications. Case Studies and Research Directions will be Unique Contributions in the Proposed Book.

The introduction and overview of sentiment analysis, emotion detection, opinion mining and related terminologies is what is expected in the chapters. Feature extraction, data visualization and numerous tools will be discussed and introduced so that the same can be used in further data management and handling methods and applications of sentiment analysis. The highlights on the importance of the data handling and managements related issues in sentiment analysis while implementing and solving real time problems is needed. The discussion related to the necessary mathematical modelling, hypothesis concepts and statistical data analysis in textual mining. Suitable mathematical models that are used in analysis of textual data analysis related problems should be discussed. Natural language processing based opinion mining and sentiment analysis needed to be discussed. The discussion on various text pre-processing techniques namely removing stop words, stemming, lemmatization, tokenization, text representation techniques etc. Feature selection using n-grams, regular expression, evolutionary approaches etc. is the needed solution. The description on various machine learning techniques used in sentiment analysis related issues and problems especially for dimensionality reduction challenges and clustering techniques should be presented. The various deep learning techniques currently used in related area of sentiment analysis such as Long Short-Term Memory, Generative Adversarial Network, Restricted Boltzmann Machine, Deep Belief Network etc. related to various aspects of opinion mining should be presented. The highlights on various clustering methods used in related area of sentiment analysis e.g. analyzing customer satisfaction responses, priority urgency detection, customer review diagnosis etc. using AI should be also the matter of discussion. How fuzzy convolutional neural network will be explored for textual data analysis in related area of sentiment analysis can be the target too. In the current scenario, communication media email, SMS, e-newspaper, plays a vital role in professional and personal commitments. The impact and challenges of sentiment analysis in communication network should be the matter of discussion. Since, Social media has widespread usage and effect in almost all of us and the usage is so huge that data handling and management become essential for such applications and thus the chapter to discuss analysis tools and services for social media and business applications is needed. The highlights provides few important applications of how and why sentiment analysis are used in social networking media in their analysis and content based retrieval. The few important examples of how and why sentiment analysis are used in healthcare systems in their analysis and content based retrieval. The applications discussing biomedical as well as other medical imaging modalities and their computer-aided-diagnosis (CAD) especially utilizing emotion detection concepts must be there. How security and encryption methods for big data applications and how the sentiment analysis concepts are useful in simplifying the big data challenges are the need of the society. Also the few important applications of how and why sentiment analysis are used in e-commerce in their analysis and content based retrieval are the emergent topics in this domain. The set of performance measures and evaluation tools for assessing how the data handling or reduction methods work efficiently should be explored. The summarization of textual data and visualization of large scale text data Word Cloud, Tag Cloud sentiment values (positive, negative or neutral). Moreover, neural network concepts for sentiment analysis applications should be there as the trend of data analytics is taking up space. Case studies where text analytics is applied and benefited and applications of text mining in various domains such as software engineering, web analytics, document content etc. The important case studies on data handling and management problems on sentiment analysis applications from various application domains such as cognitive, computer vision, AI. The Future applications and open challenges in handling large volume unstructured and structured text data in sentiment analysis. The sentiment analysis study has become very important and emerging area of study as well as research and thus should highlight what would be future research directions and scope in the area of sentiment analysis applications.

Searching for a Solution

Sentiment Analysis has become an essential part of all modern advancements in several applications areas such as Automation, Economy, IT/ITES, Big Data, Affective Computation etc. The data handling and management, not done properly poses big challenge in various implementations and thus this book highlights major case studies, real time applications, implementation strategies, challenges, and future research directions. It requires an in-depth understanding of sentiment analysis and data manipulation. The in-depth understanding of supervised and unsupervised learning models such as linear regression, logistic regression, clustering, dimensionality reduction, etc. mathematical modeling of the problem, explaining the different components of the data manipulation related to research in information retrieval and sentiment analysis, presenting regression models and classification techniques for data analysis, concepts of time series modeling and gain practical mastery over principles, algorithms, and applications of machine learning/deep learning, learning to analyze data and become proficient in analyzing the data is necessary.

The objective of the book completes study of extracting sentiments from textual data. Performing sentiment visualization-based dimensionality reduction for multiple features. Used state-of-art machine learning and deep learning-based multi-domain sentiment extraction, discussed several optimization techniques used for sentiment identification and explained varied applications of sentiment analysis and emotion detection. It also deals with several chapters focusing on the existing usage of social media in the field of healthcare and how modern-day technology innovations are finding new ways to pace up the cycle of inception to delivery in various fields. It discusses the potential aspects that can be extended in each field. The innovative usage of applications of sentiment analysis and information processing with the technological impacts in different domains are explained. Detailed definitions, analogies are explained with an intent to focus on domains and applications related to sentiment analysis. The book will be useful to industrial sector, health care, engineers and researcher in addition to academics. Knowledge of fundamentals of data science, emerging applications and case studies will be emphasized. Learning outcomes to be highlighted along with future research directions of data science study and research.

ORGANIZATION OF THE BOOK

The book is organized into 14 chapters. A brief description of each of the chapters follows:

Chapter 1 discussed and compared various classification models that are used for phishing SMS detection through sentiment analysis. The chapter used Kaggle dataset for classifying the documents into spam and ham using deep learning methods and compared the proposed work using visualization tools. CNN reported the best results of SMS classification with the highest accuracy of 99.47% as a classification model. The results were also evaluated using different machine learning techniques as a baseline algorithm like naïve bayes, decision trees, SVM, and ANN.

Chapter 2 explained the problems and existing solutions for text analytic issues. The chapter well outlined the in-depth problems the researchers are facing to collect a large amount of quality data for DNN's training. This paper presented the outcomes of both proposed models with an imbalanced and small dataset. The chapter also explained the optimal solutions for businesses, as they cannot rely only on traditional models as they can work with structured data only which is not acceptable for the current scenario. The conversion process of unstructured text data to classified structured text data is detailed and are well listed to be informed, useful, and meaningful to carry out organizational operations.

Chapter 3 discussed the different types of information retrieval models that are used in retrieving hidden information from the web. Also, the strategies used to assess the recovery execution. In the Information Retrieval frameworks are also presented. The varied types of crawlers that are used to extract hidden information has been presented in detail. All this is important as the key part of the hidden web remains inaccessible to the users. This chapter deals with posting some questions about this research. Detailed definitions, analogies are explained and discusses related work and puts forward all the advantages and limitations of the existing work proposed by researchers. The proposed work identifies the need for a system that will process the surface and hidden web data and returns integrated results to the users pertaining to information extracting and processing the hidden information from the dark web and articulate methods of thinking through various concerns.

Chapter 4 reviews the existing usage of social media in the field of healthcare and how modern-day technology innovations are finding new ways to pace up the cycle of inception to delivery in various fields. It discusses the potential aspects that can be extended in each field. The paper listed that with innovative usage of this immensely powerful technological concept in one of the most important domains for humans. The potential areas where social media can be pivotal at achieving better and faster results are discussed and presented in detail with the comprehensive related work in the related domain.

Chapter 5 presents an analysis of issues and concerns in Online Customer Reviews on Face Masks. The main objectives of this chapter are suggested by the online reviews, putting the focus on the importance of the reviews in the user purchase decision, which are the most important elements of a review and what users take into account when writing a review. Also, in the study provided, the interest is to reveal if there are differences between the online shops (e.g. Amazon and Walmart), in terms of reviews and the attitude towards the stores. This chapter discusses the framework and the process of selecting and analyzing a number of reviews, using a software solution (an online application) created specifically for text analysis and extracting users' sentiments.

Chapter 6 investigates investigate the CSFs for the adoption of m-Government services in Tanzania by employing a web analytics approach. The chapter examines user behavior and the whys and wherefores that led to different levels of adoption among m-Government services belonging to the same family. The findings prove that web analytics methodology is suitable for exploring the system and the user's behavior of m-Government sites. The study enlightens developers and designers about the critical nature of adhering to international accessibility and usability standards for websites. The authors ground their work by contextualizing as qualitative and quantitative research.

Chapter 7 presents an extractive document summarization system that is based upon graph and item-set mining methodology. The strategy utilizing item set mining graph-based summarization for summing up biomedical literature is explained in detail. The challenges and the solutions for recognizing important subjects in the biomedical document text has been addressed. The proposed summarizer can distinguish the item-sets which would be able to measure as the majority significant ones. The outcome of experiments is demonstrated using the hybrid method that can upgrade the summary created for biomedical literature.

Chapter 8 discusses the shortcomings in the current approaches in the current question answering systems (CQA) which are lexical gap between text pairs, dependency on external sources and manual features which leads to lack of generalization ability. This chapter focus on the previous limitations and removes the dependency of manual features and external resources with the help of deep learning methods as compared to other methods which based on machine learning and also on grammatical analysis. It proposes two models based on deep learning which uses similarity calculation method to evaluate semantically matching of question and its comments and then classify the comments as good, potential and bad on the dataset having CQA-QL corpus. The results shows improvement in the performance of community question answering system and can effectively classify the answers/comments in the three classes.

Chapter 9 discusses generic concepts on how online learning has entirely modified how efficient teaching and revolutionized learning is imparted to the learners in contrast to traditional learning reviews. It concentrates majorly on the latest trends evolving in the e-learning domain globally. The integral part of the chapter depicts a greater view of trends in the e-learning recommendation system which will pave a positive path for society's growth. The key purpose of this chapter revolves over non-formal education which majorly involves e-learning for the development of professional and organizational growth focusing on the application and implementation of artificial intelligence, machine learning methodologies for the future benefits of human race.

Chapter 10 presents the notion that Fake reviews are the most dangerous element that can affect the purchase decision, having the power to create a false image of a product or service by spreading false information through reviews, whether positive or negative. This chapter proposes a methodological solution before analyzing reviews through specialized software (e.g., SmartMunk, Revuze, Aspectiva, SentiGeek, etc.), a filter for identifying fake reviews by introducing them into a fake review application called Fakespot.

Chapter 11 gives descriptive information about the tweet dataset which has sentiment, stance, and intent annotations, all at once. The dataset which is further annotated within the context of the current book chapter is made publicly available for research purposes at github. The experiments are performed on the three stance detection experiments by training a separate SVM for each dataset. All the possible contribution of sentiment and intent information to stance detection in Turkish tweets has been explained with experiments in this chapter.

Chapter 12 concludes and presents principles necessary on fake news detection on social media platforms using machine learning techniques and deep learning techniques. The proposed novel techniques introduce the combination of BERT and LSTM, which boost the performance of the fake news detection method. By developing this false information detecting system, the problems behind the imitated text will be controlled and rumors will be blocked. This research proposes a novel FNDN-LSTM model of fake information and real information from the social media news datasets. Thus, this chapter proposes a model that can classify efficiently, conserve memory usage and consume less time for training. Thus, the study assists appropriate guidelines on the fake news detection model (FNDN-LSTM) on social media.

Chapter 13 presented a survey on various embedding techniques that can be employed for constructing better models for sentiment analysis like basic word embedding techniques, sentiment embedding techniques, and emoticon space embedding techniques and also traces the evolution of word embedding techniques in a chronological order.

Chapter 14 consists of the sentiment analysis of the textual data on the US economic news with time series to build sentiment prediction models. The chapter proposes a method to create domain-specific lexicon and used the economic based lexicon to experiment the system. The design and implementation related to a sentiment judgment model based on real data of the US economic news has been shown. The results claims that the logistic binomial regression model gives the best result or accuracy among the different regression models experimented in the chapter.

Aakanksha Sharaff
National Institute of Technology, Raipur, India

G. R. Sinha
Myanmar Institute of Information Technology, Mandalay, Myanmar

Surbhi Bhatia
King Faisal University, Saudi Arabia

Chapter 1
Deep Learning Based Sentiment Analysis for Phishing SMS Detection

Aakanksha Sharaff

National Institute of Technology, Raipur, India

Ramya Allenki

UnitedHealth Group, India

Rakhi Seth

National Institute of Technology, Raipur, India

ABSTRACT

Sentiment analysis works on the principle of categorizing and identifying the text-based content and the process of classifying documents into one of the predefined classes commonly known as text classification. Hackers deploy a strategy by sending malicious content as an advertisement link and attack the user system to gain information. For protecting the system from this type of phishing attack, one needs to classify the spam data. This chapter is based on a discussion and comparison of various classification models that are used for phishing SMS detection through sentiment analysis. In this chapter, SMS data is collected from Kaggle, which is classified as ham or spam; while implementing the deep learning techniques like Convolutional Neural Network (CNN), CNN with 7 layers, and CNN with 11 layers, different results are generated. For evaluating these results, different machine learning techniques are used as a baseline algorithm like Naive Bayes, Decision Trees, Support Vector Machine (SVM), and Artificial Neural Network (ANN). After evaluation, CNN showed the highest accuracy of 99.47% as a classification model.

DOI: 10.4018/978-1-7998-8061-5.ch001

INTRODUCTION

Text Classification

Text classification is one of the most important parts of text analysis. It is defined as the process of interpreting and extracting important information from the present textual data this data can be of any type like SMS, Twitter data, emoji, and short messages while talking about classification which is one of the major parts of sentiment analysis; which occurs to be the measuring people's attitude from the piece of text through which they are sharing their views. Views can be of different types based on user intent this can be understood through various examples, we saw over the internet sometimes inappropriate like abusive language and pornographic content; sentiment analysis also deals with classifying those data which helps the policymaker to understand the trend that is running in a market that solely depends on users' reviews, feedbacks, and ratings. From a research point of view, some of the major challenges that could be solved through sentiment analysis like spam filtering, phishing attack, categorization, and summarization well over the decades, spamming and phishing based classification has been some of the most researched topics based on techniques like machine learning and deep learning. A good text classifier is a classifier that efficiently categorizes large sets of text documents in a reasonable amount of time with acceptable accuracy. Many techniques and algorithms for automatic text categorization have been devised.

Applications

There are various applications of text classification:

1. **Document Organization:** Document organization is also known as Document classification. (Rinaldi et al., 2021) discuss the documents that were collected through the different platform in huge amount, but from the information retrieval point of view, not all the data was always relevant, so sometimes the issue of information overloading may generate, for solving this issue the new concept of document classification is introduced while using the text present in the document, we illustrate it through an example given below; here document belongs to a different class (class 1, class 2 and class 3) in the training set as given in Table 1 and associated feature is retrieved from each document class and vector is created from these words of class in Table 2. As we can see "Some" belongs to one class, "Yellow" belong to another based on the specified documents, while testing the new data this labeling helps to understand which word vector belongs to which class.

Table 1. Documents

Document Class 1	Document Class 2	Document Class 3
Some Lion live in the jungle	Yellow is a color	Go to Manhattan city

Table 2. Classes of each word

Some	Lion	Live	In	the	jungle	Yellow	is	A	color	Go	To	Manhattan	City	Class
1	1	1	1	1	1	0	0	0	0	0	0	0	0	Class 1
0	0	0	0	0	0	1	1	1	1	0	0	0	0	Class 2
0	0	0	0	0	0	0	0	0	0	1	1	1	1	Class 3

Now when any unlabelled data came, like "Blue is a color" then a new word vector will be created by taking labeled data from the previous table and match it as we see that some word vector matched with class 2 word vector of *Table 2* so we assign unlabelled data with an unknown class as well as 1 as an assigned value for the matched word vector as shown in *Table 3*;

Table 3. Test Data classification

Some	Lion	Live	In	the	jungle	Yellow	is	A	color	Go	To	Manhattan	City	Class
0	0	0	0	0	0	0	1	1	1	0	0	0	0	Unknown

2. **Spam Filtering:** Spam is more likely related to malicious content or comes with suspicious intent mainly through mails and most of the time without the receiver's consent. Initially, this spam comes as a promotion or advertising mail but soon after hackers used it as a mask for attacking a system because it is one of the cheapest ways to get through the user's system. So different researchers after doing rigorous study gave the approach called spam filtering, (Chetty et al., 2019) proposes the idea of detecting and classifying spam mails by using deep learning models, and this model was used to learn the features of text documents, not only deep neural model has been used for spam detection there are various other models like (Jain et al., 2020) suggested the machine learning model which used for smishing attack with a combination of SMS and phishing attack; (Jain et al., 2020) goes one step ahead i.e., by classifying smishing messages from spam messages.

3. **Filtering non-suitable content:** The Internet is a very vast and different type of data move all around over the internet some of these data are harmful for an organization like marketing policies used by different companies is completely confidential, some data comes with an intent to harm society like pornographic content (Garcia et al., 2018) gives the approach to remove or suspend this type of source from the internet; some data is for harming the economy of a country like false message spreading about person or government. So this type of data needs constant monitoring and sometimes the government takes legal policies for stopping such type of content like; recently JIO reliance for its users restrict the pornographic content to access over the network because a large no. of users are using the internet amongst these small aged children are present for them this type of content is inappropriate, also; YouTube is monitoring the content and it is done through YouTube users only when you are seeing any video in YouTube and you don't find that content suitable then you can report that video and if too many reports are there then the server will block owners uploaded a video in similar way twitter suspend the ids for spreading false messages. The

server uses the filtering technique while training the model and uses the classification model for a specific type of text or visuals to get restricted.

4. **Summarization Evaluation:** This is nothing but extracting the content from the various informatics source and presents the most important content in a very precise way to the user while understanding summarization most important part is data which is sensitive towards the information on a user, topic, and query asked by the user. So it aims at user-specific classification. In summarization, there is another concept called evaluation which deals with the serious issues of doing automation in summarization. (Lloret et al., 2018) handles the evaluation issues like output that comes using summarization is either correct or incorrect it hard to arrive the conclusion because it completely depends on the user. Another issue is compression, in which evaluation of compression rates increases the complexity of evaluation

5. **Web Page Prediction:** Web page prediction is an area of web mining and this prediction works in the recommendation system. While understanding the prediction (Rajeswari & Nisha, 2018) focuses on weblog files which were generated whenever user access the internet over the network and approach behind this prediction is the previous navigation data to understand the owner's access behavior and is based on the access pattern. This approach works on various parameters like session, time, and frequency of visiting the same page again and again this prediction use for classifying patterns which helps the algorithm to provide the next suggestion to the user. (Rajeswari & Nisha, 2018) provides the different ML models like SVM, Adaboost, c4.5 as well as also suggested the other advanced techniques that can be used for prediction.

6. **Mobile SMS Classification:** While ago, the researcher thought spam messages is associated with e-mails only and can be deployed through promotional advertisements while sent through e-mails but nowadays, a message is passed from one person to another in seconds through mobile. Mobile is a mode through which anyone can send false or obscene messages to someone without understanding the consequences. Several riots and other illegal work take place through messaging only and this type of attack is known as SMS spam and for this monitoring is done through various detection methods. Some detection methods are (Marsault et al., 2020) implemented by using the feature engineering on the lexical extracted text or words, and put the classifier to train the model so that prediction can be done by the model.

Spamming

Initially spamming is an unwanted digital communication that mostly takes place through emails, mostly it is a marketing strategy like a promotion of a product but with time it becomes a weapon for hackers with malicious intent. Hackers take over the ISPs (Internet Service Provider) and send cheating/malicious emails to the users over the network.

There are different types of Spamming is there which are as follows:

1. **Bulking Message:** A message sent to a group of people over a very small period. For example, a Google job offering message in the year 2006 was an example of spam messages spread over mass. There is some other advertising malware is present over the system.

2. **Spreading Malicious links:** When the user's device gets damaged through a malicious link opened by him/her. This malware takes the personal information of the victim and uses it in a harmful way.

3. **Fraudulent reviews:** Today many reviews that you see on youtube, on Twitter fake reviews of products through fake ids that are also one type of spam and comes under fraudulent reviews but in our country for online platforms there are no strict rules for this type of forgery.
4. **Sharing undesired or excessive content:** Insults, threats, and other important, as well as confidential information that is shared by a hacker or sent by a hacker to others, are threatening and it comes under spamming.

Phishing

Phishing is a process of making people visit a duplicitous website and tell them to enter their personal information. These types of websites are not new rather it is some of the known organization's mocked website. Hacker injects these fake websites into the user's system. Phishing is spread through technical teams and send through false mails generally forged by attackers to gain the information of user's system mostly sensitive data, credential data, and some of the highly confidential data. Phishing is one of the most common types of attack as well as a cheaper way to enter one's system but sometimes this phishing attack becomes a ransomware attack. The phishing attack is not something that attacker sends a file and attacks to the user system rather when a phishing attack happens then at that point, the attacker runs the whole life cycle of the attack and when a user came to know about the attack, the damage has been already done. The steps of the lifecycle for Phishing attacks as shown in Figure 1.

Step1: Proper Planning with Setup: In this step, an attacker or hacker finds his/her target organization there is no specific reason for attacking a particular target but most of the time money as well as accessing confidential information is the prominent reason for the attack. Also, the phisher makes some technical strategies to get confidential information.

Step2: Construction of Phishing/false Site: Phisher creates a false website that looks similar to the official website; several tools are available for creating the replica of well-known websites. Once the site is developed, the phisher uploads the files to a web-hosting server.

Step3: Phishing Deployment: The proper distribution method is used to deploy the link of the phishing website.

Step4: Installation: It is a process where a fake link redirects to the fake website created by the phisher and after this; malicious software has been installed to the user system.

Step5: Data Collection: The information filled in by the user over the internet is available to the phisher.

Step6: Breaking-away: After getting all the information from the user, the phisher deletes all the traces or web footprints that work as evidence like phisher accounts, websites, and all other files.

Figure 1. Lifecycle of phishing attack

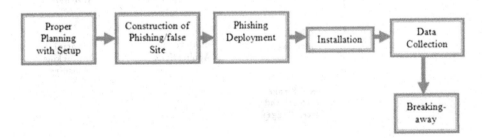

Now we need to understand, various motivations for a phisher to attack the user; some of them are as follows:

1. **Financial Gain:** A ransomware attack is an example of a phishing attack while entering the user's system and corrupt all the data and ask for ransom; nowadays cryptocurrency is one of the ways to give the amount to a phisher or attacker.
2. **Identity Theft:** By taking another person's identity you can do any illegal task like accessing a user bank account, also you can send mails to other users as a valid sender.
3. **Internet Sensation:** Some people did it to become famous and some did it for recognition but it is a serious offense and one can go to jail for it.

Taxonomy of Phishing Attacks

The phishing attack has two environments, which are as follows:

1. Desktop
2. Mobile

First, we need to discuss the desktop environment, (Jain & Gupta, 2021) tells about the phisher who uses the social engineering and technical evasion technique. By using a malicious website that appears

Figure 2. Taxonomy of Phishing Attacks

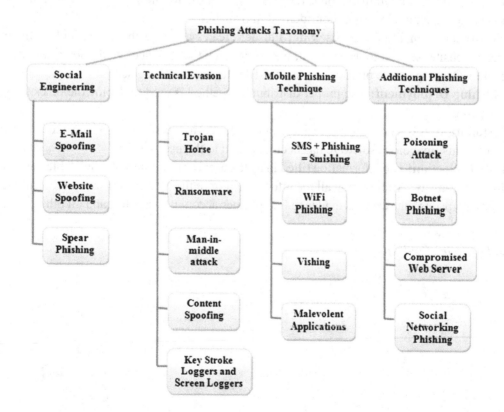

legitimate, accessing the whole system became much easier. The technical evasion method does the installation of malware and gains the information from the user's system. The second one, the mobile environment is very vulnerable to a phishing attack in mobiles this attack is done through SMS and WiFi. For a brief understanding of the taxonomy of phishing attacks, one requires knowledge of each area as shown in Figure 2, where these attacks do the major damage.

1. **Social Engineering:** A psychological control over user so that user discloses the secret information. A forged mail looks like a real one and the user relies on and gives all the credentials that are known as Social Engineering.
2. **E-Mail Spoofing:** The fake URL redirects the user to the malicious web page and does the attack.
3. **Website Spoofing:** The attacker doesn't create the whole website because it can be detected by the anti-phishing software. So phisher creates only a login page and embeds the legal contents in the frame of a malicious webpage to avoid the anti-phishing technique.
4. **Spear phishing:** This attack works on the target individuals and sent emails. The attacker regularly monitors the user's activities on the websites or on WhatsApp to acquire the user's information. After collecting the information, the attacker writes an email, which looks like the real mail that comes from any legitimate source like the manager, and takes the organizational details and other personal information.
5. **Trojan horse:** The attack happens from the backdoor and deploys the victim's malicious code and installs the applications like worms to the user's device.
6. **Ransomware:** Ransomware is software or malware which is considered to be a kind of malicious. The concept of Ransomware is that the attacker demands from the victim a particular amount (it can be a different form like Bitcoin is one of the examples.) to restore access to the data upon payment.
7. **Man-in-middle Attack:** An attack that doesn't manipulate it just does observing and monitoring the traffic between the sender and receiver. Sometimes the whole network is controlled by an attacker and the user doesn't know about it.
8. **Content Spoofing:** Content injection is also used for this attack. There are two types of spoofing used:
    a. **Text Injection:** A vulnerable web application in which URLs get modified. The fake page request link is sent to the attacker server.
    b. **HTML Injection:** The attacker sends the modified URL to the user by any means, by clicking on the URL user is navigated to the attacker's webpage, which looks like a legitimate one.
9. **Keystroke Logger and Screen Logger:** Key logger is malicious software through which attackers can observe the keystroke of the user's system. This is used for getting the password and through that confidential data.
10. **Smishing:** Through phone-text messaging using SMS phishing is performed. Through SMS the user gets the link and if the user accesses the link and shares his personal information with the attacker.
11. **Wi-Fi Phishing:** The associated vulnerable hotspot, the authenticated interface presented to users looks like a genuine one used by the legitimate access point. Creating an authentication interface that looks legitimate may increase the chances of the attack.

12. **Vishing:** "Voice+Phishing" has been more successful over other networks. It is an attack over the phone where someone calls and tells the user that he is from this bank and there is some account details required for updating and user gives the detail of his/her bank account.

13. **Poisoning Attack:** It is the attack where the genuine website is diverted from a fake website. An attacker takes the control to change the data in the DNS cache. Once the cache is poisoned, the data is sent to a malicious URL.

14. **Botnet Phishing:** Botnet word comes from the combination of words i.e. "robot" and "network" and it takes the whole control of the network it uses for various scams and cyberattacks. It works on the steps

    a. **Preparation:** The hijacker uses the malware to exploit the victim.

    b. **Infection:** Once the malware damage the system or hacker takes control through a botnet.

    c. **Activate:** Hacker prepares the infected devices to do further attacks.

15. **Compromised Web Server:** It means that a hacker hijacks the server and sends the fake web pages to the user through the server.

16. **Social Networking Phishing:** This type of phishing can be done through social networking site and sharing the fake URL, this type of URL usually comes through fake advertisement or fake invitation link. Another way of phishing is Masquerading through URLs it can be done by asking on behalf of social networking site ask for a login id and password through a false link. Fake profile creation and asking for credentials is one of the most common types of social networking phishing sometimes the people create a fake profile and ask for money from the friends of that person through messenger and in this way sometimes people got trapped.

Figure 3. Phishing Attack Features

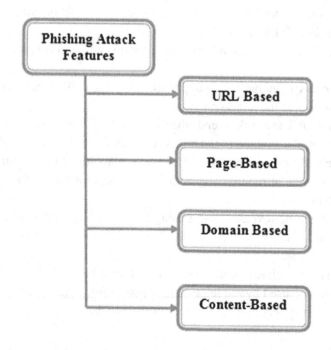

RELATIVE STUDY

In this section, we discuss the different ML (Jupin et al., 2019) & DL (Annareddy & Tammina, 2019) techniques that are used for detecting phishing attacks. Now for detecting an attack, one needs to know

Table 4. Summary of existing phishing & spam techniques

References	Level	Technique Used	Application	Dataset
(Rinaldi et al., 2021)	Semantic-Based	1. Semantic textual analysis	It helps in textual topic detection	DMOZ a multimedia dataset.
(Chetty et al., 2019)	Document-Based	1. CNN	E-mail filtering, movie reviews, Twitter message classification	UCI repository.
(Yerima et al., 2021)	Application Based	1. CNN 2. DNN 3. Long Short Term Memory (LSTM) 4. Gated Recurrent Units (GRU) 5. CNN-LSTM 6. CNN-GRU	Android device apps	ISCX botnet dataset
(Zhu et al., 2020)	URL based	1. Decision Tree 2. ANN	Spam filtering and fake emails with malicious content	UCI Library, Phishtank, and Alexa records.
(Jain et al., 2020)	SMS Based(Text Level)	1. Naïve Bayes 2. Neural Network 3. Logistic Regression	WhatsApp message system, messenger applications any fake information does not get spread.	SMS dataset contains 5574 messages
(Garcia et al., 2018)	Image(or video) based	1. Segmentation 2. Texture Filtering 3. For classifying confusion matrix is used	A measure for stopping inappropriate content through different platforms.	Multimedia files data set (1239, Images=986, Videos=253)
(Kalaharsha & Mehtre, 2021)	Site Based	1. ML techniques 2. DL techniques	URL based emails, In banking application,	UCI repository
(Shirazi et al., 2017)	Site-based	1. SVM with stratified K-fold	Helps in detecting fake websites, a measure for blacklisting some sites, fake E-mails	From the Alexa database, 6000 online phishing sites were collected.
(Arshey & Angel, 2020)	E-mail Based	1. Classification: Deep belief network(DBN) 2. Training: Earthworm optimization algorithm.	For SMS, spam emails, spoofing	Enron Dataset
(Saha et al., 2020)	Webpage based	1. Feed Forward network	Detecting the fake pages asking for money(mostly in health care)	Kaggle dataset
(Soykan et al., 2021)	EV charging based	1. SMS attack was done through EV charging by using the power grid by creating the testing simulation tool	Helps in the future where EV charging becomes the tool and attack detection is necessary when power grid collapse	IEEE European Low Voltage Feeder Test System.
(Gupta et al., 2021)	SMS based	1. TF-IDF vectorizer algorithm	SPAM SMS detection, spam mails detection, spam with phishing detection	Kaggle repository
(Zhang et al., 2017)	Semantic-based	1. Adaboost 2. Bagging 3. Random forest	Word-based helps in detecting copyright text, URLs, and contents.	Legitimate URLs taken from DirectIndustry web guides a search engine.

Table 5. Methods advantages and disadvantages of ML & DL techniques

Methods	Advantages	Disadvantages
ANN	1. ANN works in distributed memory and benefits in parallel processing. 2. ANN generates the precise model by taking experimental data only 3. ANN can work with incomplete knowledge and with noise. 4. ANN allows defining the attribute as well as types of learning.	1. The result may alter the order of data attributes. 2. ANN is very slow in learning rate. 3. It is difficult to understand the result produced by ANN. 4. Hard to predict the model.
Decision Tree(DT)	1. The classification process takes less time. 2. It is easy to implement. 3. It is simple to interpret the feature relationships.	1. It is low as compared to another ML technique. 2. When no of features increased then DT implementation becomes more complex. 3. Each time a new sample came, the tree rebuilding for each sample becomes quite complex.
RF	1. The efficiency of RF is very high 2. The overfitting problem is handled by RF.	1. A large no of trees is quite a problem of processing. 2. It works only for predictive modeling, not for descriptive modeling. 3. The result produced by RF is not consistent.
Naive Bayes	1. A less no of data required for the feature classification process. 2. NB handles the missing values. 3. It is a direct method	1. A large amount of data is necessary for higher accuracy. 2. Due to its instance-based nature, NB requires a large space to store the data. 3. Regarding data, NB is not sensitive.
SVM	1. It handles the high-dimensional data better than the other algorithms. 2. It is known for higher accuracy. 3. It handles a large amount of data 4. It helps in finding the optimum solution and memory efficiency. 5. It maximizes the margin and therefore it is one of the robust models.	1. The classification process is time-consuming. 2. Interpretation is difficult. 3. It works for binary classifiers and for other types it needs some modifications. 4. Each set should be correct because SVM is sensitive to the data.
CNN	1. CNN doesn't require feature engineering 2. It works well with complex background.	1. It takes a long time to train a model. 2. Poor labeling is one of the problems. 3. While using pre-trained models and small datasets optimization issues may be generated.
LSTM	1. It dealt with larger data 2. It is efficient and faster 3. No need for a finite number of states 4. It handles the vanishing gradient problem.	1. The sample size is quite small 2. LSTM needs high memory and bandwidth. 3. Past information is not taken for a larger time. 4. The overfitting problem is not solved by LSTM.
GRU	1. For long sequencing training samples. 2. It is more efficient. 3. With less training data GRU works faster. 4. It is simple and modification is easy.	1. Efficiency is very less. 2. Accuracy is very less

a phishing attack with its features; so there are mainly 4 features in phishing attack as shown in Figure 3. Feature 1 is based on URL, Feature 2 is based on Page-based, Feature 3 Domain-based, and Feature 4 relies on Content-Based.

While discussing the existing spam and phishing-related applications as shown in Table 4 we understand the different levels in which we can detect phishing as well as which algorithm provides the appropriate classification for phishing and spam detection.

Table 6. Comparative Analysis of existing algorithms

Authors	ML technique	DL technique	Spam Detection	Phishing Detection	Classification Algorithm	Accuracy Achieved
(Mishra & Soni, 2020)	✓	✗	✗	✓	Naïve Bayes Classifier	96.29
(Bagui et al., 2019)	✓	✓	✗	✓	Naïve Bayes, SVM, DT, LSTM, CNN, Word Embedding	98.89
(Popovac et al., 2018)	✗	✓	✓	✗	CNN	98.4
(Sonowal, 2020)	✓	✗	✗	✓	The ranking algorithm, AdaBoost, RF, DT, SVM	98.4
(Maurya & Jain, 2020)	✗	✓	✗	✓	Adam, Deep learning algorithms.	97.51
(Makkar & Kumar, 2020)	✗	✓	✓	✗	LSTM	95.21
(Zhu et al., 2020)	✓	✗	✓	✗	Decision Tree and optimal features based ANN	97.5
(Chakraborty et al., 2020)	✗	✓	✗	✗	Gaussian membership function based fuzzy rule	81%
(Basheer et al., 2021)	✗	✓	✗	✗	CNN with RELU activation and also Squash a special type of activation function used for capsule network	92.39%

After studying a while on classification; we came to know about different methods that are used with a specific purpose and we try to understand it through Table 5 with all utilities and shortcomings of different method that comes under ML & DL technique.

As per the further discussion through an algorithmic point of view as shown in Table 6, gives the comparison of a different technique with different accuracy this helps in understanding which classifier approach works better for which detection technique.

RESEARCH METHODOLOGY

In a follow-up experiment, we will study the implementation in different stages for understanding the role of different classifiers that came under the ML and DL technique and also, which classifier works better and give a higher performance for phishing detection. So through the architecture of this paper as shown in Figure 4 first we analyze the SMS corpus and then classify the message by using different models; it also measures the performance of different algorithms.

Data Collection

The ham and spam SMS messages were collected from the "SMS-spam-collection" dataset from Kaggle. It consists of 5574 messages of which 4287 are ham messages and 747 are spam messages. The dataset was collected in a CSV file where each line represents one message and a label has been presented for

Figure 4. Architecture of this paper

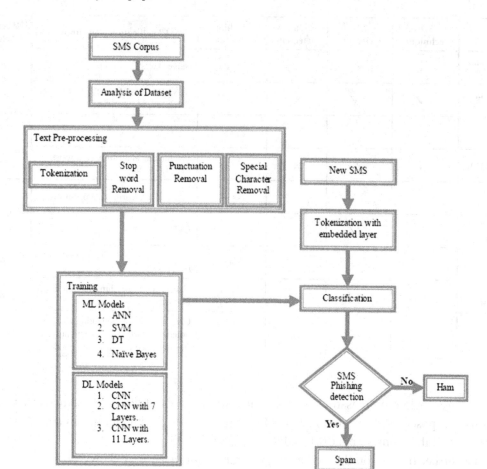

each message as either spam or ham. The initial steps of preprocessing is very similar in text mining as we can see for finding positive, negative and neutral tweets for better sentiment analysis.

Pre-Processing

1. **Removal of Punctuation:** It splits the word and checks if it contains any punctuation characters. If yes, it replaces with a blank or else does nothing.
2. **Word Tokenization:** To tokenize the sentences into words based on whitespaces and put them in a list for applying further process.
3. **Converting Words to lowercase:** Converting all the upper, lower, proper case words into lowercase. This reduces the duplicity of words in the corpus.
4. **Stop Word Removal:** To remove the words that do not carry much weight in understanding the sentence. They are mostly used as connecting words.
5. **Keeping Words of At least Three:** To remove words having a length less than 3. These words don't have much meaning to carry.

6. **Stemming Words:** To stem the extra suffixes from the word.
7. **POS Tagging:** pos tag function return the parts of speech for each word. There are four formats for nouns and six formats for the verb.
8. **Lemmatization of Words:** It is the process of grouping together the different inflected forms of a word to analyze as a single item.

Tf-IDF Conversion

The input to any neural network is in the format of numbers. So the conversion of the text into vector format is very important. So, tf-idf conversion is used here. Tf-IDF stands for "**Term frequency-inverse document frequency**". Firstly the sentences will be converted into tokens and the frequency of each word is found and divided with the number of words in that document for normalization. This is the term frequency. Idf is the logarithm of the ratio of the number of documents to the no of documents containing that word. We multiply tf and idf to find the weight of each word. This gives weights to each word that explains the importance of word in document.

Tf (t,d) = frequency of term / number of words in document
Idf(t,d) = $\log_2$ total no of documents / no of documents containing that word.

MACHINE LEARNING TECHNIQUES

For detecting all these features various techniques are used. First is Machine learning; ML is one of the study areas that belong to artificial intelligence.ML works on the principle of computation that can be done directly from the data, by identifying a pattern and make decisions from observed data. ML trains a model by taking known input and predicting the data as output. In phishing attack ML model is useful; as we can see the attack is based on features these features can be trained through ML models because ML converts the detection problem into classification, once the classification task is completed then detection of attack can be done easily. For detecting the attack, ML uses different models which comprise of;

1. Artificial Neural Network (ANN)
2. Decision Tree
3. Naïve Bayes
4. Random Forest
5. Support Vector Machine(SVM)

1. Artificial Neural Network

ANN is a simulated model as shown in Figure 5 of the biological human brain and it works in layers, each layer represents the artificial neurons that are connected. In Figure 5, X1, X2,……, Xn is the input vector of the neuron, W1, W2,…….., Wn represented weights which represents the neuron of the input layer. Σ represents the sum of all input with the bias (b), and Activation Function (ƒ) and output (Y) is used in the model.

Figure 5. Basic elements of ANN

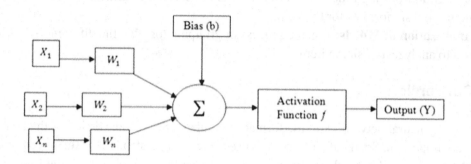

2. Decision Tree (DT)

A Decision Tree is a type of supervised learning algorithm. It works on the root node and leaf node. It is a classification algorithm categorized into two types:

1. Categorical Variable DT
2. Continuous Variable DT

Decision trees classify data from the root node to the leaf node in sorting order. Based on the type of target variable DT algorithm suggested other two algorithms which are as follows:

1. Iterative Dichotomiser(ID3)
2. C4.5

ID3 works on the "top-down" approach and creates the decision tree. C4.5 is also a DT that handles the problem of missing, large and continuous data. The DT algorithm works on expressions given below (1) to (6) which are as follows

$$E(S) = -\sum_{i=1}^{m} p_i log_2 p_i. \tag{1}$$

$$E(T,X) = \sum_{c=X} P(C) E(S). \tag{2}$$

$$Information\, Gain(T,X) = E(T) - E(T,X). \tag{3}$$

$$Information\,Gain = E\left(before\right) - \sum_{j=1}^{k} E\left(j, after\right). \tag{4}$$

$$Gini\,Index = 1 - \sum_{i=1}^{m} \left(p_i\right)^2. \tag{5}$$

$$Gain\,Ratio = \frac{Information\,Gain}{SplitInfo} = \frac{E\left(before\right) - \sum_{j=1}^{k} E\left(j, after\right)}{\sum_{j=1}^{k} w_j log_2 w_j}. \tag{6}$$

Now here E(S) is entropy to measure the randomness, Information Gain (IG) is defined as how correctly a given attribute splits the training example to the corresponding target classification. Gini Index is a cost function that evaluates the split in the data set. Gain Ratio is used to reduce the bias.

3. Naïve Bayes Algorithm

An NB algorithm works on the Bayes theorem. Bayes Theorem approach is on probabilistic classification and every character is being independent when classified. The equation (7) is

$$P\left(a|B\right) = \frac{P\left(B|a\right)P\left(a\right)}{P\left(B\right)}. \tag{7}$$

Here, P (a|B) is an independent probability of a prior probability; P (B) is an independent probability of B, P (B|a) is a conditional probability of a given B. Naïve Bayes is widely used for spam detection in e-mails by computing the probability of e-mails that e-mails are spam or not based on words used in spam and non-spam emails.

4. Random Forest Algorithm (RF)

Random forest is related to a decision tree, it means that RF generates the individual DT at training and then the prediction is done by combining all trees to make the final output of prediction. Through equations (8) to (11), we understand the basic principle of RF.

$$ni_j = w_j C_j - w_{left(j)} C_{left(j)} - w_{right(j)} C_{right(j)}. \tag{8}$$

$$fi_i = \frac{\sum_{j:\text{node } j \text{ splits on feature } i} ni_j}{\sum_{k \in \text{all nodes}} ni_k}. \tag{9}$$

$$normfi_i = \frac{fi_i}{\sum_{j \in \text{all features}} fi_j}. \tag{10}$$

$$RFfi_i = \frac{\sum_{j \in \text{all trees}} normfi_{ij}}{T}. \tag{11}$$

Here in equation (8) to (10), ni_j is the importance of node j, w_j weighted samples reached node j, $C_{left(j)}$ impurity value of left split child node j and similarly $C_{right(j)}$ is impurity value of right node j. Normalization is the process of converting any value into a range of 0 to 1.

5. Support Vector Machine Algorithm (SVM)

SVM is a type of supervised learning method and helps in classification, outlier detection, and regression techniques. SVM uses specific methods for a specific problem like Support Vector Classifier (SVC) and Support Vector Regression (SVR). For understanding these methods; we need to know the working principle of SVM. So SVM works on few hyperparameters like kernel, hyperplane, and decision boundary. Kernel helps to identify the hyperplane in higher dimensional space without elevating the cost. Sometimes it is difficult to identify the separating hyperplane when there is an increase in dimension so at that point higher dimension space is needed. Now, a hyperplane is nothing but a separating line between two data classes in SVM but for SVR it derives the continuous output for regression. Decision Boundary is defined as the simplification of classes through which positive and negative data class can be distinguished. In SVM optimization the concept of hard margin, and the soft margin is highly popular. Soft margin is flexible and it also handles the large value through regularization; this margin is one of the most useable methods for a dataset with a large no. of values.

DEEP LEARNING TECHNIQUES

In previous sections, we talk about the ML models like SVM, RF, Decision tree, and ANN. In this entire model of ML, the first step is feature extraction and the next step is classification but the feature extraction process is quite complex because it needs the whole knowledge of the problem domain and tested again and again for the better and optimized result. So researcher suggested the new approach called a Deep learning technique which is a subset of ML techniques but with the difference that here feature extraction and classification is combined and gives more abstract and compressed data than the classical ML techniques previously used. DL is quite fast to implement and because a combined version of testing or training requires less cycle while implementing it became one of the widely used approach.

Different models are defined under DL.;
In Supervised;

1. Convolutional Neural Network (CNN)
2. Recurrent Neural Network (RNN)
3. Classical Neural Networks (Multilayer Perceptron)

In Unsupervised;

1. Self-organizing maps
2. Boltzmann Machine
3. AutoEncoders

1. Convolutional Neural Network (CNN)

CNN works on two major components i.e. Feature extraction and another one is classification. CNN works in layers, for example, an image of animals or birds needs to classify through CNN, then in the first layer, the pattern and edges get defined and sent to the next layer where shape, size, and color get defined and all this data go to the next layer which is final layer tries to classify the image. The overall structure is given in Figure 6. So these layers are as expressed from equation (12) to (23)

a. **Layer 1:** Convolutional Layer: In this layer, kernel or filter is used to convert the input matrix to an output matrix which is known as convolution. For this, a mathematical equation is there;

$$conv\left(o^{(l-1)}, K^{(n)}\right)_{x,y} = \psi^{[l]}\left(\sum_{i=1}^{n_H^{[l-1]}}\sum_{j=1}^{n_W^{[l-1]}}\sum_{k=1}^{n_C^{[l-1]}} K_{i,j,k}^{(n)} o_{x+i-1,y+j-1,k}^{[l-1]} + b_n^l\right). \tag{12}$$

$$\dim\left(conv\left(o^{[l-1]}, K^{(n)}\right)\right) = \left(n_H^l, n_W^l\right). \tag{13}$$

Output;

$$o^{[l]} = \left[\psi^{[l]}\left(conv\left(o^{[l-1]}, K^{(1)}\right)\right), \psi^{[l]}\left(conv\left(o^{[l-1]}, K^{(2)}\right)\right), \dots, \psi^{[l]}\left(conv\left(o^{[l-1]}, K^{\left(n_C^{[l]}\right)}\right)\right)\right]. \tag{14}$$

$$\dim\left(o^{[l]}\right) = \left(n_H^l, n_W^l, n_C^l\right). \tag{15}$$

Here, $\psi^{[l]}$ .is activation function, $o^{[l]}$ .is output with size $\left(n_H^l, n_W^l, n_C^l\right)$. n_C^l .represents the no of filters where each K has dimensions. With:

$$n_{H/W}^l = \begin{cases} \dfrac{n_{H/W}^{[l-1]} + 2p^l - f^l}{s^l} + 1; s > 0 \\ n_{H/W}^{[l-1]} + 2p^l - f^l; s = 0 \end{cases}.$$ (16)

b. **Layer 2:** Pooling Layer; Downsampling of features has been done in this layer we observe through equation

$$o_{x,y,z}^l = pool\left(o^{[l-1]}\right)_{x,y,z} = \Big|^{[l]}\left(\left(o_{x+i-1,y+j-1,z}^{[l-1]}\right)_{(i,j)\in\left[1,2,\dots,f^{[l]}\right]^2}\right).$$ (17)

$$\dim\left(o^{[l]}\right) = \left(n_H^l, n_W^l, n_C^l\right).$$ (18)

$$n_{H/W}^l = \begin{cases} \dfrac{n_{H/W}^{[l-1]} + 2p^l - f^l}{s^l} + 1; s > 0 \\ n_{H/W}^{[l-1]} + 2p^l - f^l; s = 0 \end{cases}.$$ (19)

$$n_C^l = n_C^{[l-1]}.$$ (20)

Where, $\Phi^{[l]}$ .epresents the pooling function.

c. **Fully Connected Layer:** It takes a finite no of neurons as an input vector and returns another vector.

$$z_j^i = \sum_{l=1}^{n_{i-1}} w_{j,l}^{[i]} o_l^{[i-1]} + b_j^{[i]}.$$ (21)

$$o_j^i = .\psi^{[i]}\left(z_j^i\right). \tag{22}$$

After this we need to seal it with a fully connected layer we have to use flatten function by converting it into 1-dimension

$$n_{i-1} = n_H^{i-1} \times n_W^{i-1} \times n_C^{i-1}. \tag{23}$$

CNN is majorly used for phishing detection because of fast implementation as we discussed above in advantages and disadvantages.

2. Recurrent Neural Network (RNN)

RNN is one of the variants of neural networks and one of the main features of RNN is that it can memorize the previous layer and also helps to train the model with better and more precise output. One of the similar working models is a feed-forward network in which every output is dependent on the spe-

Figure 6. Workflow of CNN algorithm

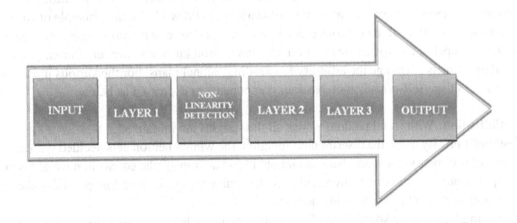

cific input. RNN takes input x= (x1,x2,…,xt), the RNN contains the hidden layer h=(h1,h2,….,ht) and the output sequence y=(y1,y2,…,yt) as expressed in equation (24) to (25) where; f(.) and g(.) is an activation function and W_{hx} .is input hidden weight, W_{hh} .is hidden-hidden weight, W_{yh} .is hidden-output weight, b_h .s a hidden bias, b_y .is output bias, h_t .is hidden state to recall over the network over the time step t.

$$h_t = f\left(W_{hx}x_t + W_{hh}x_{t-1} + b_h\right). \tag{24}$$

$$y_t = g\left(W_{yh}h_t + b_y\right).$$

(25)

3. Multilayer Perceptron(MP)

Perceptron defines as a linear classifier in which two categories are present, and are linearly separable through a margin which is mathematically formulated as y=wx+b, where w is the weighted value that may affect the two classes directly. Also, perceptron works with the single output with a single layer but in real life, with real data, this implementation doesn't go too far and as a solution, the next suggested approach is multilayer perceptron which comes under the deep neural network, MP composed of two perceptrons in which one as input and the other as output to take decisions. It comes under the supervised learning technique via a correlation between inputs and outputs. It works in two ways, Forward pass when the signal flows from the input to the output layer, and backward pass, in which bias is backpropagated through the multilayer perceptron.

4. Self Organizing Maps

In previous sections, we saw supervised learning now we have to understand deep learning models in unsupervised learning. So as we know that in unsupervised networks learning is done through their classification no class labels are present in this type of learning. SOM works on the principle of competitive neuron, which means that all the neurons that came as output does competition to get activated and the result of this competition activates one neuron and that neuron known as winner neuron. The purpose of SOM algorithms is to change the arbitrary to two-dimensional maps. For the various input patterns, neurons get selective. Self-organization has four components as expressed as below;

1. **Initialization:** With small random values all the weights are initialized.
2. **Competition:** By using the discriminant function, the winner neuron gets decided with an x input vector of n-dimensional space, between input "i" and neuron "j" the connection weight is present.
3. **Cooperation:** The winning neuron is used to determine the spatial location, providing the basis of cooperation with other neighboring neurons.
4. **Adjusting Neighbors/Adaptation:** The exciting neurons decrement its value of the discriminant functions and adjust the other values associated with that neuron.

5. Boltzmann Machine (BM)

The BM is also unsupervised learning. It is used for an optimization problem; here fixed weights are present that's why we can't train the model. We test the network by using a function called Consensus Function (CF). Boltzmann has a fixed unit called with a bidirectional connection between them.

6. Autoencoders

An auto-encoder is used to copy the input to its output. It works in two parts one is the encoder and the other is the decoder. When we talk about autoencoder then stochastic mapping (a probability space between functions from X to Y as elementary events) is the concept which prominently works. It is a type of unsupervised learning but more it is called self-supervised learning because Auto Encoder requires small information to encode the data.

RESULTS & DISCUSSION

In this section, as we showed the % distribution of the dataset in Figure 7; also find the frequency of words in spam and ham messages helps to count the overall occurrence of each word as shown in Figure

Figure 7. (A) % wise Distribution of Spam & Ham Message, (B) frequently occurring words graph form,

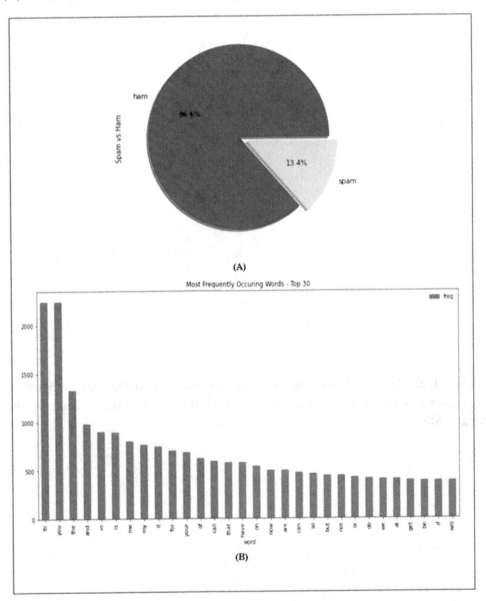

Figure 8. (A) Frequency of Spam word occurrence, (B) Frequency of ham word occurrence

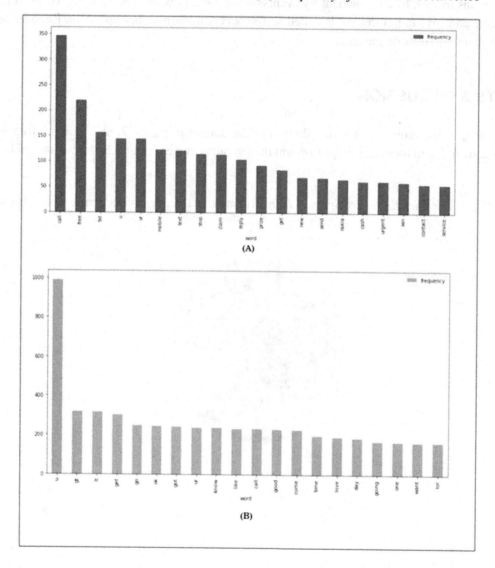

8, and message length of ham and spam with punctuation count is evaluated in Figure 9 we also classify the text that comes under spam and ham in Figure 10 this is the very first step of detecting the phishing attack through SMS.

Figure 9. (A) Message Length ham & spam, (B) Punctuation count in ham & spam

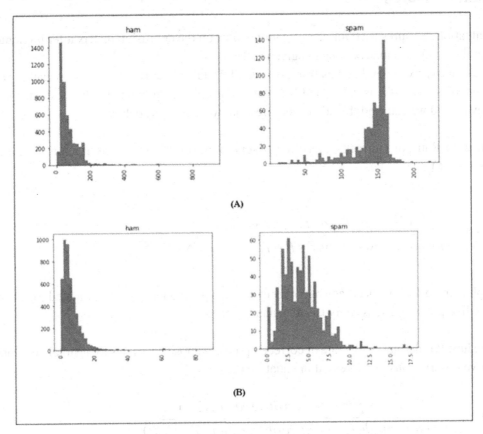

(A)

(B)

Figure 10. (A) Classified as Spam, (B) Classified as Ham.

Testing Sample:
    The message [Thanks for your Ringtone Order, Reference T56.   ] has been classified as spam

(A)

    The message [Can you say what happen] has been classified as ham

(B)

Table 7. Confusion Matrix

		Predicted	
		spam	**ham**
Actual	spam	957	6
	ham	9	143

Evaluation Measures

All the evaluation measures used for classification works on the confusion matrix after implementation we also get the confusion matrix which is given in Table 7.

A confusion matrix generalized as true positive (TP), false positive (FP), false negative (FN), and true negative (TN), and this is calculated between the actual and predicted value and once confusion matrix is evaluated we can find the other measures that we discussed below.

1. **Accuracy:** Ratio of Correctly predicted observation to total no of observation as expressed in equation (26)

$$Accuracy = \frac{Correctly\ Predicted\left(TP + TN\right)}{Total\ no.of\ observations\left(TP + TN + FP + FN\right)}. \tag{26}$$

We implemented the only accuracy but other evaluation parameters can be computed based on confusion matrix-like precision, sensitivity (recall), and f1 score

2. **Precision:** It is defined as the rate of correctly predicted positive values to the total no of predictive positive observations as expressed in equation (27)

$$precision = \frac{Correctly\ predicted\ positive\ values\left(TP\right)}{total\ no\ of\ predicted\ positive\ observation\left(TP + FP\right)}. \tag{27}$$

3. **Sensitivity:** Ratio of predicted observations to the actual observations as expressed in equation (28)

$$Sensitivity = \frac{Correctly\ predicted\ positive\ obsevations\left(TP\right)}{Actual\ observations\left(TP + FN\right)}. \tag{28}$$

4. **F1 Score:** A weighted average of precision and sensitivity as expressed in equation (29)

$$F1Score = \frac{2*\left(Sensitivity * Precision\right)}{Sensitivity + Precision}. \tag{29}$$

Training

Various training algorithms are implemented in which SVM, Decision tree, Naïve Bayes, ANN, Convolutional Neural Networks (CNN), 7-layer CNN, 11-layer CNN. The architecture of a CNN has an input layer, hidden layers, and the output layer. The number of hidden depends on each shallow and deep CNN.

1. **Convolution:** The hidden layers in CNN are generally used for pooling and convolution. In each convolution layer, we take a small filter and move that filter across the input matrix or the image and convolution operations will be done. These operations are nothing but the multiplication of the filter values with the matrix values and summing up those values. The filter values will be adjusted as the iterations on the corpus increase. As the epochs increase they start recognizing better features.
2. **Pooling:** It helps in reducing the number of parameters thereby reducing the computation. It prevents the problem of overfitting. There are two types of pooling functions. They are:
    a.   Max pooling function – selects the maximum values.
    b.   Average pooling function – an average of all the values
3.   Activation Functions:
    a.   **ReLU:** The activation used at hidden layers is the ReLU (Rectified Linear Unit) activation. This is a widely used activation in deep learning techniques nowadays.

$$f(x) = \begin{cases} 0 \ for \ x < 0 \\ x \ for \ x \geq 0 \end{cases}. \tag{30}$$

    b.   **Softmax:** This activation is used at the output layer. This is a wonderful activation that outputs a vector that represents the probabilities of the list of possible outcomes. The probabilities always sum to 1.

$$f(z_i) = \frac{e^{z_i}}{\sum_{j=1}^{K} e^{z_j}}. \tag{31}$$

Table 8. Comparative Analysis of ML & DL technique over accuracy

Technique	Classifier Used	Accuracy
ML techniques	ANN	**97.36**
	Decision Tree	96.42
	SVM	92.14
	Naiye Bayes	90.07
DL Techniques	CNN	**99.47**
	CNN with 7 Layers	97.64
	CNN with 11 Layers	92.14

c. **Dropout:** It is a technique of regularization. In each iteration, it drops out some neurons randomly and doesn't use these neurons either in forwarding or backpropagation. That is the reason it forces the learning algorithm to spread the weights rather than focusing on specific features.

d. **Flatten:** It flattens the input.

As per the above discussion and implementation of all the training algorithms; we compared these models by using a measure called accuracy as shown in Table 8, for both ML and DL techniques. ANN gave higher accuracy of 97.36% among all ML models. On the other hand, CNN of the DL technique gave an accuracy of 99.47%.

CONCLUSION AND FUTURE DIRECTION

The proposed work demonstrates that the deep learning method using CNN can get the best results of SMS classification. This deep learning model not only learns high dimensional representations but also performs efficient classification tasks. The test comes about on SMS spam dataset demonstrates that CNN can learn a better generative model and perform well on SMS spam recognition task. The deep learning algorithms provide new design ideas and strategies for future research on SMS phishing discovery. In the future, other deep learning algorithms like Recurrent Neural Networks, LSTM, and GRU can be used in the detection of SMS phishing messages.

ACKNOWLEDGMENT

This research received no specific grant from any funding agency in the public, commercial, or not-for-profit sectors.

REFERENCES

Annareddy, S., & Tammina, S. (2019, December). A Comparative Study of Deep Learning Methods for Spam Detection. In *2019 Third International conference on I-SMAC (IoT in Social, Mobile, Analytics and Cloud)(I-SMAC)* (pp. 66-72). IEEE. 10.1109/I-SMAC47947.2019.9032627

Arshey, M., & KS, A. V. (2020). An optimization-based deep belief network for the detection of phishing e-mails. *Data Technologies and Applications*.

Bagui, S., Nandi, D., Bagui, S., & White, R. J. (2019, June). Classifying phishing email using machine learning and deep learning. In *2019 International Conference on Cyber Security and Protection of Digital Services (Cyber Security)* (pp. 1-2). IEEE. 10.1109/CyberSecPODS.2019.8885143

Basheer, S., Bhatia, S., & Sakri, S. B. (2021). Computational Modeling of Dementia Prediction Using Deep Neural Network: Analysis on OASIS Dataset. *IEEE Access: Practical Innovations, Open Solutions*, 9, 42449–42462. doi:10.1109/ACCESS.2021.3066213

Chakraborty, K., Bhatia, S., Bhattacharyya, S., Platos, J., Bag, R., & Hassanien, A. E. (2020). Sentiment Analysis of COVID-19 tweets by Deep Learning Classifiers—A study to show how popularity is affecting accuracy in social media. *Applied Soft Computing*, *97*, 106754. doi:10.1016/j.asoc.2020.106754 PMID:33013254

Chetty, G., Bui, H., & White, M. (2019, December). Deep learning based spam detection system. In *2019 International Conference on Machine Learning and Data Engineering (iCMLDE)* (pp. 91-96). IEEE. 10.1109/iCMLDE49015.2019.00027

Garcia, M. B., Revano, T. F., Habal, B. G. M., Contreras, J. O., & Enriquez, J. B. R. (2018, November). A pornographic image and video filtering application using optimized nudity recognition and detection algorithm. In *2018 IEEE 10th International Conference on Humanoid, Nanotechnology, Information Technology, Communication and Control, Environment and Management (HNICEM)* (pp. 1-5). IEEE. 10.1109/HNICEM.2018.8666227

Gupta, S. D., Saha, S., & Das, S. K. (2021, February). SMS Spam Detection Using Machine Learning. *Journal of Physics: Conference Series*, *1797*(1), 012017. doi:10.1088/1742-6596/1797/1/012017

Jain, A. K., & Gupta, B. B. (2021). A survey of phishing attack techniques, defence mechanisms and open research challenges. *Enterprise Information Systems*, 1–39. doi:10.1080/17517575.2021.1896786

Jain, A. K., Yadav, S. K., & Choudhary, N. (2020). A Novel Approach to Detect Spam and Smishing SMS using Machine Learning Techniques. *International Journal of E-Services and Mobile Applications*, *12*(1), 21–38. doi:10.4018/IJESMA.2020010102

Jupin, J. A., Sutikno, T., Ismail, M. A., Mohamad, M. S., Kasim, S., & Stiawan, D. (2019). Review of the machine learning methods in the classification of phishing attack. *Bulletin of Electrical Engineering and Informatics*, *8*(4), 1545–1555. doi:10.11591/eei.v8i4.1344

Kalaharsha, P., & Mehtre, B. M. (2021). *Detecting Phishing Sites—An Overview*. arXiv preprint arXiv:2103.12739.

Lloret, E., Plaza, L., & Aker, A. (2018). The challenging task of summary evaluation: An overview. *Language Resources and Evaluation*, *52*(1), 101–148. doi:10.100710579-017-9399-2

Makkar, A., & Kumar, N. (2020). An efficient deep learning-based scheme for web spam detection in IoT environment. *Future Generation Computer Systems*, *108*, 467–487. doi:10.1016/j.future.2020.03.004

Marsault, B., Gigot, F., & Jagorel, G. (2020). *Sms Spam Detection*. Text Analysis And Retrieval 2020 Course Project Reports, 42.

Maurya, S., & Jain, A. (2020). Deep learning to combat phishing. *Journal of Statistics and Management Systems*, *23*(6), 945–957. doi:10.1080/09720510.2020.1799496

Mishra, S., & Soni, D. (2020). Smishing Detector: A security model to detect smishing through SMS content analysis and URL behavior analysis. *Future Generation Computer Systems*, *108*, 803–815. doi:10.1016/j.future.2020.03.021

Popovac, M., Karanovic, M., Sladojevic, S., Arsenovic, M., & Anderla, A. (2018, November). Convolutional neural network based SMS spam detection. In *2018 26th Telecommunications Forum (TELFOR)* (pp. 1-4). IEEE. 10.1109/TELFOR.2018.8611916

Rajeswari, B., & Nisha, S. S. (2018). *Web Page Prediction Using Web Mining*. Academic Press.

Rinaldi, A. M., Russo, C., & Tommasino, C. (2021). A semantic approach for document classification using deep neural networks and multimedia knowledge graph. *Expert Systems with Applications*, *169*, 114320. doi:10.1016/j.eswa.2020.114320

Saha, I., Sarma, D., Chakma, R. J., Alam, M. N., Sultana, A., & Hossain, S. (2020, August). Phishing Attacks Detection using Deep Learning Approach. In *2020 Third International Conference on Smart Systems and Inventive Technology (ICSSIT)* (pp. 1180-1185). IEEE. 10.1109/ICSSIT48917.2020.9214132

Shirazi, H., Haefner, K., & Ray, I. (2017, August). Fresh-phish: a framework for auto-detection of phishing websites. In 2017 IEEE international conference on information reuse and integration (IRI) (pp. 137-143). IEEE. doi:10.1109/IRI.2017.40

Sonowal, G. (2020). Detecting Phishing SMS Based on Multiple Correlation Algorithms. *SN Computer Science*, *1*(6), 1–9. doi:10.100742979-020-00377-8 PMID:33163974

Soykan, E. U., Bagriyanik, M., & Soykan, G. (2021). Disrupting the power grid via EV charging: The impact of the SMS Phishing attacks. *Sustainable Energy, Grids and Networks*, 100477.

Yerima, S. Y., Alzaylaee, M. K., Shajan, A., & P, V. (2021). Deep Learning Techniques for Android Botnet Detection. *Electronics (Basel)*, *2021*(10), 519. doi:10.3390/electronics10040519

Zhang, X., Zeng, Y., Jin, X. B., Yan, Z. W., & Geng, G. G. (2017, December). *Boosting the phishing detection performance by semantic analysis. In 2017 IEEE international conference on big data (big data)*. IEEE.

Zhu, E., Ju, Y., Chen, Z., Liu, F., & Fang, X. (2020). DTOF-ANN: An Artificial Neural Network phishing detection model based on Decision Tree and Optimal Features. *Applied Soft Computing*, *95*, 106505. doi:10.1016/j.asoc.2020.106505

KEY TERMS AND DEFINITIONS

Activation Function: It is one of the important functions in the neural network through which the output of the network is decided. Different activation functions present for a different type of network.

Frequency: Occurrence of no of times word appear during the text processing.

Gated Recurrent Unit: It is an advanced version of RNN. GRU uses the Gates for the information flow, and it is a two-step process with the Reset and Update gate.

Long Short-Term Memory: It comes under the field of deep learning and works on the feedback connection and especially of this network is the whole sequence of data.

Message Length: It shows no. of messages present in ham as well as spam messages which later helpful for finding maximum length.

Pooling: It is used to decrease the resolution of the feature map while preserving the features that are required for classification.

Punctuation Count: It is used to find the total no of punctuation present in ham and spam messages.

Chapter 2
Deep Learning Approach Towards Unstructured Text Data Utilization:
Development, Opportunities, and Challenges

Shikha Jain
Banasthali University, India

Shubham Jain
ZEE Entertainment Ltd, India

Ajit Kumar Jain
Banasthali Vidyapith, India

ABSTRACT

With the meteoric development of the big data, internet of things (IoT), the very first question is about how to scout the massive volume of data from heterogeneous data sources. The modern tools and techniques commonly used in successful transmuting of well-structured data into business intelligence (BI) clearly don't work when started on unlabeled data. It is needed to have effective and efficient mapping processes to transform unstructured text data to structured text data with assigned categories to make rapid decisions. With the support of modern automatic text mining tools, the decision-making process can now be done efficiently and cost-effectively. The deep learning concept has attained state-of-the-art results. The mapping operation of unstructured text data to classified structured text data will symbolize unstructured data as renewable assets that are well arranged, useful, and meaningful to serve organizational operations. This chapter presented a comparison of conventional and deep learning methods for unstructured text data classification and its challenges.

DOI: 10.4018/978-1-7998-8061-5.ch002

INTRODUCTION

National Security Agency reported that 1.8 PB data is sparking off on the web every day (Oussous et al., 2018) This growth brings various opportunities in the field of medical, agricultural systems, commercial industries, and social media. Google is the place of origin of about 20,000 TB of data and 3.6 TB of data is brought into being by flicker (Oussous et al., 2018). Unfortunately, an estimated only 20% of data is ready for analysis, and the rest 80% of data is neglected because of its complex and unstructured format (salminena et al., 2019).

Unstructured data does not have any predefined format and it is very difficult to understand the textual data which is coming from various heterogeneous data sources (logs, reports, news, articles, social media, etc.) (Abdullah & Ahmed, 2013).

One way to manage the textual documents is to categorize them into fix set of categories. This cataloguing arrangement of the available data is a key module of knowledge management Systems. But the problem is that today data is available in large quantity and it is a challenging task to learn the text features with statistic-based models.

Since 2010, researchers gradually started switching from shallow networks to deep neural networks. Deep Neural Network (DNN) consists of hidden layers and these deep architectures are capable to learn feature representations directly from raw or unstructured data. Statistics-based methods and other conventional methods are competent for text analytics despite that a lot of possible improvements are possible to scout. Deep learning technology does not need any prior knowledge and manual intervention, but it needs enormous data to gain good performance. Many text classifiers brush up the accuracy index of various text categorization pieces of work, but they suffer to indicate whether the model cognizes the text on the same level as human beings.

A paradigm shift started in 2010 when a deep learning (DL) based model Alexnet won the image net competition by a large margin (Melnyk et al., 2020). Since then, deep learning systems have been implemented to a extensive range of tasks in computer vision and NLP improving the state-of-the-art. DL based models do not need manually extracted features as it is capable to provide semantic representation automatically. DNNs avoid designing rules by a human. Most of the primary issues with DNNs are that they stand in a need of high computational complexity and enormous data. Few Researchers are still focusing on traditional methods and trying to root out the solution for the unstructured data and computational limitations.

LITERATURE SURVEY

This paper presented an overview of the existing solutions for text analytic issues. These are:

Unstructured Text Data

Raw data that is been generated on the web and contains a lot of noise such as website links, unnecessary characters, and words with numbers. It creates a hindrance in drawing various inferences from text (Khanna et al., 2020). Majorly every business needs this data to strategize via predictions and analysis. Unfortunately, Machine learning (ML) systems have shown their potential for knowledge discovery with structured and quality data, but they get failed when it comes to unstructured data (Salminena et al., 2019). It is indeed a need today to remove all these hindrances by utilizing modern practices of text pre-processing like improving feature generation as well as selection procedures.

Text Classification and Knowledge Discovery Systems

Decision-making industries are switching from traditional rule-based methods to automatic knowledge discovery systems to attain fast and more effective results (Salminena et al., 2019). A review of 85 academic publications was conducted by the authors that focused on text mining techniques and unstructured document organization. From 1998 to 2009, the Research trend was heavily skewed towards the technical aspects of text mining systems, but later researchers moved towards the field of data analytics (Melnyk et al., 2020). Automatic text mining models create potential in modern-day jobs that were initially expensive and time-consuming (Hsu et al., 2020).

Text classification is one of the prime research disciplines and named as the classical problem in text analytics and natural language processing (NLP). It assigns labels or tags to textual data and units such as queries, documents, sentences, paragraphs. Here, data can come from different sources, for example, web data, email, chat, social media, ticket insurance claims, questions, and answers from customer services, and many more (Melnyk et al., 2020)

Data Pre-Processing

The very first step is to make sense of available unstructured or raw data. Before model development, data processed with Standard statistics and NLP methods. It includes text cleaning, tokenization, stopwords removal, Lemmatization, stemming, and many more. Statistics technique makes the input text data ready for learning. Data pre-processing minimizes information loss and makes it easy to understand the raw text data. The performance of a model is resultant from quality text input.

Conventional Text Representation Methods

TF-IDF Encoding

When a model reads input data it provides higher weight to more frequent words than rarely occurring words. Tf-Idf methods provide a better text encoding instead of using only frequency parameter, It is the weighted frequency measure calculated as the product of term frequency (Tf) and inverse document frequency (IDF) (Khanna et al., 2020).

Bag-of words

Most of the text analysis techniques rely on the Bag-of words technique to acquire domain knowledge. A paper presented this fact clearly stated that many models are still dependent on human work and specific to a single task (Melnyk et al., 2020). We need a generalized mechanism that can be used in multiple disciplines. According to (Fromm et al., 2019), text mining models need to explore all relevant features and researchers need to extend their work across different domains.

Text Encoding Techniques for Neural Networks

A different approach is adopted in the deep learning framework for feature extraction. Traditional ML models used word frequency attribute to encode text data. But for DL, it stands in a need to convert text data or sequence of words into a fixed dimensional vector space.

Fasttext

This is an open-source library created by Facebook. It is developed by the Tomas Markov team to obtain vectors for unknown words. It resolved this issue by considering words as a sequence of characters. This method is the best choice for a smaller dataset. It used either skip-gram or CBOW method to obtain the contextual information about text.

Word2vec

This is a sophisticated embedding technique that considers the word as the smallest unit for text data. It is an elastic solution that has shown its usefulness in various NLP tasks (Mikolov et al., 2013). The quality of word vectors is influenced by the size of the training data set, the algorithm used in training, and the required vector size. But it fails to understand the morphological structure of a sentence and considers a word as a single entity. This is the reason it fails to generate a vector for unknown words. Two architectures that are used in word embedding are skip-gram and CBOW where skip-gram performs well for infrequent and rare words and CBOW on the other hand is faster than skip-gram. Training algorithms used are hierarchical softmax and negative sampling. Hierarchical softmax is good to understand infrequent words while negative sampling is used with low dimensional vector size and performs more accurately for frequent words. The problem occurs when enormous data emerged on the web and it becomes a tedious task to collect and encode this vast amount of data. Google provided its solution with pre-trained vectors to assist deep learning frameworks. These are easily accessible vectors available at Google's official site. These vectors are generated from the news dataset in 300 dimensions (Semberecki & Maciejewski., 2017). These vectors are trained with 100 billion English words and provide very accurate word representations.

Glove

This is proposed in 2014. Glove used an unsupervised learning method and came up with a pre-trained vector of Wikipedia text data. If we have large corpora this training may be very expensive still it is efficient for text mining. The reason is that it is a one-time process to generate relevant vectors. It calculates word vectors based on co-occurrence probability. Word2vec and glove both learn with the unsupervised method and are based on distribution. But Word2vec considers local individual word context. On the other hand, global level word context considers (Pennington et al., 2014).

These methods categorized the text data based on a predefined rule. The issue with this approach is that it requires deep domain knowledge and that's why these models needed much effort to maintain.

Machine Learning Methods

ML methods are capable enough to uncover hidden patterns from text data and relatively more scalable. ML gain a lot of popularity in recent years because it can learn the inherent associations between text segments. The only disadvantage is that feature engineering is a tedious task.

Support Vector Machine (SVM)

SVMs were initially developed for binary classification in 1963. This method learns from example specifically tackle the pattern reorganization tasks. Joachims used this algorithm first time for text classification.

Probabilistic Graphical Models

Bayesian Network, Hidden Markov Network, and Naïve Bayes (NB) are well-liked probabilistic graphical models. The NB method has a very simple structure, and it performs well for text classification on smaller categories. To settle the different distribution of datasets, the researcher proposed a NB transfer classification method.

Decision Trees (DT)

This group of algorithms uses a supervised learning method. DT algorithms follow the divide and conquer strategy during the learning phase. This technique extracts the correlations between classes and their attribute at the first phase. After the Tree construction phase, the next step is tree pruning. The pruning phase helps out to reduce noise influence. C4.5 algorithms create a map index from attribute to classes which help to find out the category for unknown data. The only disadvantage of Dt based method is the high computational cost. The fast decision tree has been resolved this issue. It also provides a solution of imbalance classes by generating multiple decision trees with the pre-selected feature set. In the end, the data fusion technique is used to combine all trees and obtain an outcome.

k- Nearest Neighbour (KNN) Algorithm

This method is very simple to understand and uses a supervised learning approach during training. KNN algorithm store all available data and calculate the similarity of a new case with the existing datasets. Based on the similarity result, this method assigns the most suitable category to unlabeled input data. It is a non-parametric algorithm. KNN algorithms are designed to decrease the number of features. It finds out the most relevant subset of features based on their inter-dependencies. To improve classification performance for imbalanced data. Neighbour-weighted KNN deals with the upcoming challenges with vast data, few researchers suggested enhanced versions of the KNN method. A scalable KNN algorithm is introduced to tackle high-dimensional data. The clustering based KNN classification method is suggested for large-scale data with neural code representation. Another approach is to design efficient KNN classification algorithms with the different number of nearest neighbors (Jain et al., 2020).

Deep Learning

Many researchers are moving towards DL models for better performance and to achieve higher accuracy for different NLP applications. The DL model simulates the human brain to automatically learn features from data. Several deep neural networks have been proposed in the last few years to process the available data and to extract valuable information from it. Text mining plays a vital role to understand the text data that is coming from heterogeneous platforms. Convolutional neural networks (CNN) and attention mechanism have shown their usefulness for text mining. But the feed-forward network, recurrent neural network, and recursive neural networks are well-liked choices for text processing. The recently proposed advanced models such as BERT, XLNet, transformer achieves good performance and led to quick progress than the predefined models. DL models are more transferable frameworks from one NLP domain to other. Several advanced neural networks, datasets, and evaluation metrics have been proposed over the past decade to improve the accuracy and performance of basic models. These are explained below:

Recursive Neural Network (ReNN)

In most cases, a tree-type structure is required to understand the sentence formation and its semantics. ReNN doesn't need any structural tree as it is capable to predict semantically distributions automatically (Kowsari et al., 2019). Matrix vector recursive neural network recognizes the phrase representation in the input sentence. One advanced version of Renn is a Recursive Neural Transfer model that is conscious of sentence semantics. The major challenge with RNTN is to attain good performance because the time complexity for building the textual tree is high. Therefore, the one proposed solution is the deep recursive neural network (DeepReNN). This network stakes multiple recursive layers (Irsoy et al., 2014).

Feed-forward network

These are the simplest neural networks that recognize input text as a bag of words. The model calculates the average of word embedding for text representation. One solution is the doc2vec method(Le & Mikolov, 2014). It follows an unsupervised learning approach to convert variable-length features to a fixed dimension representation. Doc2vec method is a very successful technique for many text mining applications. It produced better text representations as compare to other conventional techniques.

Multilayer Perceptron (MLP) Network

MLP is a simple neural network and popularly known as a "Vanilla" neural network it is used to capture the text features automatically.

Recurrent Neural Networks (RNN)

The most famous network for text analysis is the RNN. RNN are specifically used for text processing because they deduce text as a sequence of words and capable to understand text structure and word dependencies. It allows recurrent computation and captures long-range dependencies among the words. Feed-forward neural networks outperform vanilla RNN to solve several NLP problems. RNN has many advanced variants such as long short term memory (LSTM) and gated recurrent unit (GRU) which are proficient to learn historical information and produce better results (Semberecki & Maciejewski., 2017). LSTM is the most suitable neural network as it is specifically designed to capture long-term dependencies (Hochreiter & Schmidhuber, 1997). Hence it alleviates the vanishing gradient problem, frequently comes up with basic RNN. LSTM network consists of a memory cell composed of three gates to control the information flow. LSTM is the popular choice for text classification because of this special feature. According to the author, LSTM provides more accuracy as compared to CNN networks and the GRU is almost the same effect as LSTM. Many researchers proposed enhanced versions of LSTM to capture the richer information more effectively. A tree-LSTM generalized the LSTM network to the tree structure (Tai et al., 2015). It helps the framework to understand the semantic representations more accurately. Chain LSTM networks underperform than Tree LSTM because they lack to extract phrase-level information (Zhu et al., 2015). This is the reason Tree LSTM naturally validates its effectiveness for sentiment analysis and text classification. One other variant is introduced by Zhu et al. (2015) that utilize memory cell to capture global semantic structure but lacks to account word order in the given document. Therefore, TopicRNN was introduced to combine the merits of both concepts (Deing et al., 2020). This the best network for sentiment analysis tasks and topic modeling. This network explores the latest topics in the input document or text and finds out the global semantic dependencies. One other proposed is the capsule network comprised of a group of neurons in a single layer. This model finds out the relationship among the text features using dynamic routing between capsules. This enhanced model structure is composed of three gates, input gate, forget gates, and output gate. The information flow is controlled by these gates. These networks improve the total captioning ability of a text classifier.

Convolutional Neural Networks (CNN)

CNN was initially proposed for image classification but later they have shown their effectiveness for many NLP tasks including text classification. CNN architectures are trained to recognize patterns in text, such as key phrases, for classification. Dynamic CNN (DCNN) is one of the introductory CNN models and it applies dynamic k-max pooling for text classification (Kalchbrenner et al., 2014). This parameter depends on the sentence size and convolutional hierarchy level. Later, a simpler method was introduced with only one convolutional layer on top of the word vectors. Word vectors are supplied into a matrix because the text needs to be present in the same way as the image. This input is further fed to network filters with different dimensions. In the end, it needs to apply a pooling layer and predict the final vector representation of the text category. Word embedding is an unsupervised learning approach. Four different word embedding methods are introduced to find out their impact on the performance of CNN architecture like CNN-rand, CNN-static, CNN-non-static, and CNN-multichannel (Kim, 2014). Here, CNN rand initialized word embedding randomly, and these vectors modified during training. The next approach is CNN-static that uses pre-trained word vectors. CNN-non-static models fine-tuned the word embedding for each piece of work. The fourth type of design which is CNN-multichannel utilizes both fixed and dynamic word embedding techniques. These models are specifically developed for sentiment analysis and classification tasks. One other kind of model presented is based on character level encoding (Zhang et al., 2015). This character level CNN takes character level one-hot encoding as input and fed them to deep CNN architecture (Kim et al., 2016). Very deep CNN (VDCNN) (Conneau et al., 2017) was inspired by ResNets(He et al., 2016) and VGG(Simonyan & Zisserman, 2015). The information that we achieved with the above study is that max-pooling performs better than the other pooling methods with non-static word embedding techniques such as word2vec and Glove. TextCNN is specifically proposed for text classification (Kim, 2014). A good model may not rely only on labeled data. Many researchers switched to unlabelled data for their groundwork. A two-view semi-supervised learning model has been introduced by which is a CNN-based text classifier. This model makes use of both labeled and unlabelled data. A more specific version called deep pyramid convolutional neural network (DPCNN) was introduced with increased network depth (HE et al., 2016). It results in more computational accuracy which is directly proportional to network depth. Text embedding can be done in three ways, character-level embedding, word-level embedding, sentence-level embedding. By considering these approaches three learning models were developed. An author motivated with word embedding concept and introduced a dictionary-based deep learning method. On the other hand, the multilingual text classification method centered on character level CNN, known as MGTC (Adams & Mckenziel, 2018). TransCap framework is come up with sentence-level semantic representations. CNN-based models are different from RNN models because RNN acquires a knowledge of the word dependencies while CNN models extract the relevant features. Many models are the combination of both strategies. For example, the BiLSTM-2DCNN method is the fusion of a bidirectional LSTM with 2D max-pooling (Tai et al., 2015). Another approach, MTNA proposed to join BiLSTM and CNN layers for category classification (Xue et al., 2017).

Transformer-Based Methods

These models use global semantic representations to facilitate NLP tasks. Elmo (Peters et al. 2018), BERT (Devlin et al., 2019), and OpenAI GPT (Kowsari et al., 2019) are trained transformer-based methods that have significantly shown their usefulness in many NLP tasks such as sentiment analysis, machine translation, topic analysis, and so on. Elmo model learns word representations according to the context words by using the LSTM network. Bert and OpenAIGPT follow fine-tuning approach. BERT model outperforms as compare to Elmo and OpenAI. These models are very efficient for NLP applications because allow parallel computations using the GPU platform. Robert (Liu et al., 2019)and Albert(Lan et al., 2020) are two other versions of the BERT method. Generally, transformer-based methods go along with an unsupervised learning approach for training.

Hybrid Models

Many researchers developed hybrid models for text processing which are based on the fusion of LSTM and CNN architectures. Convolutional LSTM (CLSTM) was proposed to learn the phrase-level features in document classification (Zhou et., 2015). Here, CNN is used to extract phrase-level features while LSTM obtains sentence representations. Similarly, RCNN leverages the advantage of both networks to learn long-range contextual information. Dependency Sensitive CNN (DSCNN) hierarchical model design is different from CLSTM because it first employs LSTM for feature extraction then CNN for document modeling (Zhou et., 2015). It uses a max-pooling strategy for document representation. CNN-RNN model used for multi-label text categorization (Chen et al., 2017). This model is capable enough to extract both local and global textual semantics. A framework is designed with CNN and gated RNN that can understand sentence-level representations as well as document-level encoding. It extracts the relationship between sentences. One more proposal came to view a text document as the sequence of characters. This model uses character-level encoding to obtain document representation instead of word embeddings (Xiao & Cho, 2016). This model has shown comparable results as compare to other models which extracted word-level features. an enhanced version of existing deep learning networks has been developed by combining MLP, RNN, and CNN to achieve each level of understanding. It implemented stacks of different hybrid networks to provide an understanding of the document hierarchy. The other successful models are Deep Belief Network (DBN), Hierarchical Attention Network (HAN), RMDL, and HDLTex (Kowsari et al., 2017).

Other Methods

Another task-specific algorithm for text mining is the conditional random field algorithm for structure prediction. Pointwise mutual information algorithm used to measure associations and has been extended to classify text data based on phrase sematic orientation. Porter stemmer algorithm first converts word to its root then allows word grouping (Salminena et al., 2019). Lots of methods are inspired by the integration approach. These models integrate multiple algorithms for better understanding. For example, Random Forest, AdaBoost, and XG boost.

Deep neural network training needs a robust and high computational resource which is now possible with the use of Graphical Processor Units (GPUs). It makes authors feasible to utilize existing deep learning libraries such as TensorFlow and Keras (Schlegel, 2015).

DATASETS

A labelled dataset is the prime driving force that encourages authors towards the data classification. In this paper, a summarize table for the available dataset and their related NLP areas has been mentioned (Table 1).

EVALUATION MODEL

Lots of evaluation metrics and performance measures are available to compare the performance of word embedding models and various classifiers. Evaluator that has been proposed to measure the performance of word embedding models are word analogy, cosine similarity, outlier detection, and concept categorization. To train the deep learning model, we use loss functions (the variation between the actual value and expected value). Some common loss functions are root mean square error (RMSE), cross-entropy, kullback-leibler (KL), mean square error (MSE), hinge loss, mean absolute error (MAE), micro average, macro average, precision, recall, f-measure, accuracy, etc. These metrics may vary according to the information they are going to deal with and we need to choose the measure according to what exactly it represents. The well-known functions that are widely used in text classification model training and testing are cross-entropy and confusion metrics (Tharwat, 2020). Cross entropy estimates the performance of the machine learning system as it predicts the divergence probability from the actual tag. Other techniques are based on the confusion matrix. It includes false positives (Fp., true negatives (Tn., false negatives (Fn., and true positives (Tp.. Metrics are accuracy, recall, precision, and f-measure.

The accuracy metric computes the frequency. Here, Y_{true} match up Y_{pred} function requires taking both values as parameters and generate a tensor value. This frequency or return value is eventually known as

Table 1.Summary and statistics for the datasets

Domain Name	Explanation	Datasets	description
Sentiment Analysis	Analysing the content within the emotional colour	Movie Review (MR)	5331 positive data and 5331 negative data
		Standford Sentiment Treebank (SST)	8544 training data and 2210 test data with 5 classes
		The Multi-Perspective Question Answering (MPQA)	10606 extracted news sentences with 3311 texts of positive category and 7293 texts of negative category
		IMDB reviews	25000 comments of both positive and negative class
		Yelp reviews	Yelp5: 650000 training and 50000 test texts with positive and negative emotions category
		Amazon Reviews (AM)	Amazon-2: two classes and 3600000 training and 400000 testing sets. Amazon-5: 5 classes with 3000000 comments for training and 650000 comments for testing
News Classification	NC system facilitates to recognizing news topics and improve news recommended system	20 Newsgroups (20NG)	18846 texts with 20 categories
		AG News (AG)	120000 training texts and 7600 test texts with four target classes
		R8 and R52	R8: 5485 training courses and 2189 test files with 8 categories, R52: 6532 training and 2568 test files with 52 categories.
		Sogou News (Sogou)	Combination of two news datasets: SogouCA and SogouCS. Labels / domain name for each text is presented in the URL
Topic Labeling (TL)	Assign one or more label/ subject to a text document	DBpedia	560000 training data and 70000 test data with 14 classes
		Ohsumed	Medline database with, 7400 text instances and 23 disease categories
		Yahoo answers (YahooA)	140,000 training data and 5,000 test data with 10 classes
Question Answering (QA)	Extractive QA: select the most appropriate answer for a given question. Generative QA: generate answers for the questions with no answer or wrong answer	Stanford Question Answering Dataset (SQuAD)	536 pairs of 107,785 QA
		MS MARCO	extracted QA from the web by Bing search engine
		TREC-QA	5452 training and 500 testing sets
		WikiQA	Questions with wrong answers
Natural Language Inference (NLI)	Predict the meaning of one text from another with semantic similarity	The Stanford Natural Language Inference (SNLI)	570,152 human-annotated sentence pairs with neutral, contradiction, and entailment labels
		Multi-Genre Natural Language Inference (MNLI).	4333000 sentence pairs annotated with textual entailment label
		Sentences Involving Compositional Knowledge (SICK)	10,000 English sentences (consists of 3 labels: neutral, entailment, and contradictory)
		Microsoft Research Paraphrase (MSRP)	1725 training and 4076 test sets

binary accuracy, where Y_{true} - true labels, Y_{pred} - predictions. In other words, accuracy will be calculated as the fraction of accurate predictions over total predictions.

Where positive predictive value (or precision) is the fraction of relevant instances among the retrieved instances and sensitivity (or recall) is the fraction of the entire number of relevant instances that were retrieved.

$$accuracy = \frac{(Tp + Tn)}{(Tp + Fp + Fn + Tn)} \cdot precision = \frac{\sum_{l=1}^{L}(Tp_l)}{\sum_{l=1}^{L}(Tp_l + Fp_l)} \cdot$$

$$recall = \frac{\sum_{l=1}^{L}(Tp_l)}{\sum_{l=1}^{L}(Tp_l + Fn_l)} \cdot F1 - Score = \frac{\sum_{l=1}^{L}(2Tp_l)}{\sum_{l=1}^{L}(2Tp_l + Fp_l + Fn_l)} \cdot$$

For multi-class classification, the precision and recall can be calculated separately for each class, and then divide the sum with the number of classes. It will give the approximate calculation of precision and recall.

RESEARCH WORK

To compare conventional systems with newly proposed deep learning frameworks, we designed two machine learning models for multiclass text classification. Two strategies applied in our research work, are the old approach Bag of words with Td-IDF and the well-known cutting edge word2vec model. This research work aims to classify available text data according to its content. The first proposed model used a popular Naïve Bayes text classifier and other approach to train deep neural network (bidirectional LSTM). This study reached to the conclusion that which framework is more suitable for text processing.

Dataset and Setup

The dataset collect for research is a semi-structured news corpus of 80MB which contains 202,372 records with 41 categories. It is a very time-consuming task to train a deep learning model. That's why we have done this execution on Google Colab notebook. It provides a facility to imports and installs all dependencies without any specific hardware requirements. Figure 1 visualizes the data instances and their category distribution. It has been clear that data is imbalanced and difficult to achieve high accuracy. This paper has shown the classification results with imbalanced data to prove that why researchers are facing problems with low-quality data. Also, another experiment is to train the same model for 3 classes which are "business", "comedy" and "sports". These have almost the same number of instances as shown in Figure 2. That's why the model results are more accurate.

Figure 1. Visualization of News Data Distribution According to Its Assigned Categories

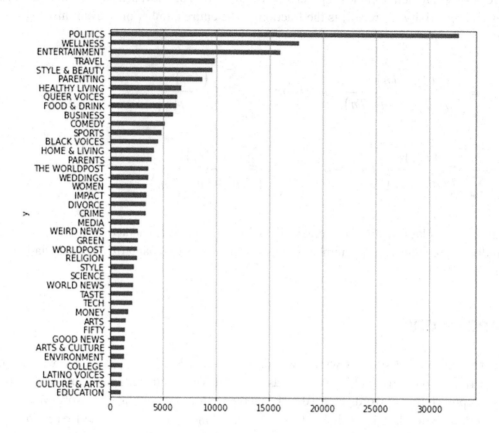

Text Pre-processing:

This is the very first step to understand the data composition. It avoids the situation of imbalanced classes. Once we acquired knowledge about the input dataset, we have applied text pre-processing techniques. This includes text cleaning, stopword removal, and lemmatization. In the end, the dataset is partitioned into a training set (80%) and target set(20%) for training and evaluation.

Framework I

Here, Bag-of-words is applied for feature engineering and the very famous Naïve Bayes algorithm for classification. The bag-of-words model considers words as features and the text document is represented by a vector. The designed model used an advanced variant of Bag-of-words which is the term frequency-inverse document frequency (TD-IDF). It effectively deals with the frequency of common words and rare words in the text corpora.

Figure 2.Visualisation Of News Data Distribution For Balanced Data Of 3 Categories

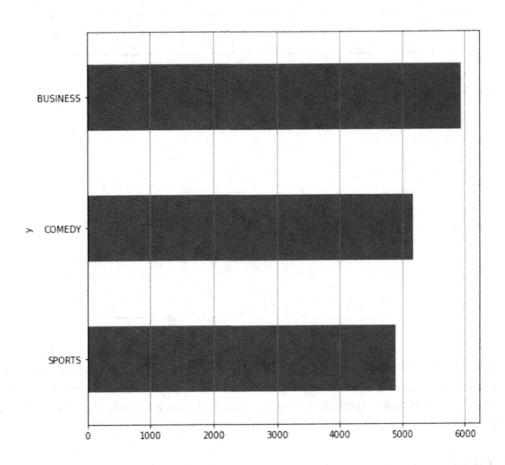

After feature engineering, the next step is feature selection. It is a necessary step to reduce matrix dimensionality. Also, a classifier performs better with more relevant features instead of all attributes. The feature selection method produces a shorter vocabulary and a smaller feature matrix.

The next phase is to build a classifier. This model used probabilistic classification algorithm Naïve Bayes. Naïve bayes considers each feature different from the other and calculates the probabilities of

Table 2. Precision, recall, and f2 score results for balance text data categorization with naive bayes classification model

	precision	recall	f1-score	
accuracy				.85
Business	.82	.89	.85	
comedy	.87	.78	.82	
sports	.87	.87	.87	

Table 3. Evaluation results of naive bayes text classification model with all categories

	precision	recall	f1-score	
accuracy				.48
macro avg	.65	.22	.24	
weighted avg	.57	.48	.40	

Figure 3. Deep learning text classification model for multi-class classification

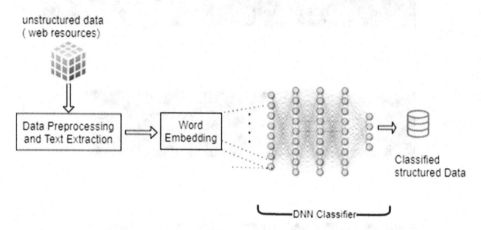

each class. The output will be the category with the highest frequency. The confusion matrix is used here for performance evaluation. The results have shown that Naïve Bayes-based classifier work outstanding with a balanced text dataset but fails to recognize categories for an imbalanced dataset explained in Table 2 and Table 3.

Framework II

The next procedure is to design a deep learning model with word2vec and LSTM architecture (shown in Figure 3). We can use Google's pre-trained word vectors to map the words into the vectors of the real number. It is an unsupervised approach with contextually same words appear together and close in the vector space. But For our research, we have trained our corpus with genism instead of using Google's

Table 4. Precision, recall and f2 score results for balance text data categorization with deep neural network (bilstm)

	precision	recall	f1-score	
accuracy				.78
Business	.77	.85	.81	
comedy	.78	.72	.74	
sports	.80	.76	.78	

Table 5. Evaluation results of deep learning model with all categories

	precision	recall	f1-score	
accuracy				.42
macro avg	.38	.24	.25	
weighted avg	.42	.42	.38	

word vectors. Data transformed to the list of n-grams before fitting to the word2vec model. The dimensions used are 300.

and the training algorithm selected is skip-gram. To reduce dimensionality, the TSNE algorithm has been used. Finally, we build a DNN as a text classifier that makes use of embedding vector matrix as input. Two layers of bidirectional LSTM network have been designed for classification. The final dense layers predicted the probability of each news category. Deep Neural Networks need an enormous amount of data for training. Hence, traditional methods perform better for small datasets. However, the problem of imbalanced data remains the same here. Evaluation results have shown in Table 4 and Table 5.

Figure 4 and Figure 5 visualize the LSTM performance and training graph.

CHALLENGES

With the evolution of IoT, social media content, and big data, information processing becomes an essential module to support knowledge discovery systems. The generated text doesn't have any precise structure and it is extremely complex to analyse the unstructured text data. Many advanced ML algorithms

Figure 4. DNN performance for news text data classification

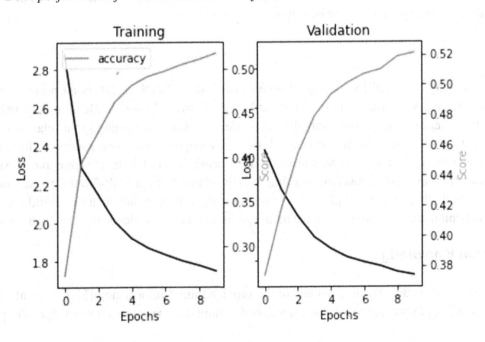

Figure 5. DNN performance for text classification with balanced data of 3 categories

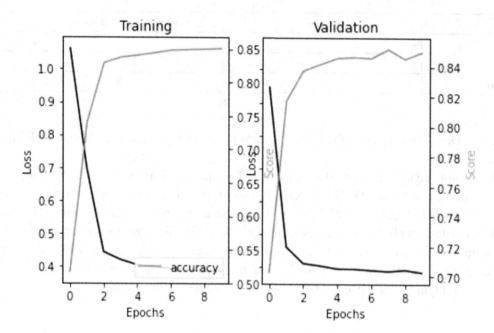

and mechanisms have been proposed to accelerate this process, but they are lacking in accuracy and performance as the volume of digital documents increases. Statistics-based methods design rules that need a lot of human effort. Neural networks automatically provide semantic representations of text. This feature extraction and model development trigger high computational complexity. Researchers working on deep learning models must face many obstacles during their research. Many novel ideas such as attention mechanism, self-attention, neural embedding, BERT have been proposed for fast progress, but many challenges exist ahead of us to be solved. These are:

Data

The first necessity for a DNN's training is the enormous data. DNN models don't perform well with a small dataset and we cannot rely on them until they are trained enough. Dealing with imbalanced classes is the other existing problem with data. A model performs outstanding for the classes with more instances but fails to analyse the text of other classes. To recognize and process messy online content is very critical. Media also require a deep learning monitoring system for social web content. Automatic feature extraction: in existing machine learning models, features are provided to the classifiers. On the other hand, methods extract this information automatically to reduce human effort. But the problem is that it is difficult to understand whether the model gains semantic knowledge like a human being or not.

Additional Knowledge

DNN performance is directly proportional to the provided input information (Melnyk et al., 2020). If the input is lacking to provide these insides, we need to impart some external knowledge to improve the accuracy measures. common sense knowledge, conceptual knowledge, and knowledge base information promote model performance effectively.

Architecture Design

After collecting enough volume of data, quality improvement, the next challenge that come up in this discovery system is to design training procedures. How to select a suitable ML algorithm or neural network according to the target, computational resources, and the existing dataset is worth studying.

Performance

Calculating the neural network's performance is a technical challenge. Many text classifications are in existence, but the difficulty is to compare them based on suitable evaluation metrics and other parameters. If data is lacking in quality, the model performance decreases. In recent years, this is a hot research topic to refine the model's robustness and accuracy index with available data.

Interpretability

Deep learning models produce semantic knowledge from data on their own and it is difficult to explain their intelligence level to understand the text like humans. If they output poor interpretability, optimization is required for improvement. This is a black-box system, where explain the improvements, as well as information loss, is near to impossible. The major challenge for deep learning comes during the feature extraction phase, the external issues are high complexity, robust platform requirements, and data amount.

FUTURE RESEARCH OPPORTUNITIES

In the earliest history of artificial intelligence (AI), document and text categorization find use in information retrieval systems. As technology emerged over time, it is globally used in healthcare, phycology, law, social sciences, and many other domains [22]. Text analytics helps to analyse text data which applies to many industries. The process of dealing with raw web data is recognized as one of the prime unsolved issues in the information technology (IT) domain. Machine learning methods have attained supreme results in NLP. But it is a big challenge to design an architecture to classify unstructured data that itself doesn't have any format. Traditional architectures and data mining algorithms are lacking in performance and accuracy. They require a large training time which is not admissible in the current scenario.

Deep learning and scaling up ML techniques has become a prime subject for research, nowadays, that can tackle large datasets and automate the practice of knowledge discovery. This technology has the potential for future advancement. But researchers are facing the problem to collect a large amount of quality data for DNN's training. This paper presented the outcomes of both proposed models with an imbalanced and small dataset. Here, the traditional model performs better than the DL model because of the data problem. But businesses cannot rely only on traditional models as they can work with structured data only which is not acceptable for the current scenario.

The conversion process of unstructured text data to classified structured text data is urgently needed as it symbolizes unstructured data as sustainable assets that are well informed, useful, and meaningful to carry out organizational operations.

REFERENCES

Abdullah, M. F., & Ahmad, K. (2013). The mapping process of unstructured data to structured data. In *International Conference on Research and Innovation in Information Systems (ICRIIS)*. IEEE. 10.1109/ICRIIS.2013.6716700

Adams, B., & Mckenzie, G. (2018). Crowdsourcing the character of a place: Character-level convolutional networks for multilingual geographic text classification. *Trans. GIS, 22*(2), 394–408. HTTPS://DOI.ORG/10.1111/TGIS.12317

Chen, G., Ye, D., Cambria, E., Chen, J., & Xing, Z. (2017). *Ensemble Application of Convolutional and Recurrent Neural Networks for Multi-Label Text Categorization*. Academic Press.

Conneau, A., Schwenk, H., Barrault, L., & Lecun, Y. (2017). Very Deep Convolutional Networks for Text Classification. In *Proceedings of the 15th Conference of the European Chapter of the Association for Computational Linguistics*. Association for Computational Linguistics. 10.18653/v1/E17-1104

Devlin, J., Chang, M., Lee, K., & Toutanova, K. (2019). BERT: Pre-Training of Deep Bidirectional Transformers for Language Understanding. *Proceedings of the 2019 Conference of the North American Chapter of the Association for Computational Linguistics: Human Language Technologies, 1*, 4171–4186. 10.18653/v1/N19-1423

Dieng, A. B., Wang, C., Gao, J., & Paisley, J. (2017). TopicRNN: A Recurrent Neural Network with Long-Range Semantic Dependency. *Proceedings of International Conference on Learning Representations*. arXiv:1611.01702 [cs.CL].

He, K., Zhang, X., Ren, S., & Sun, J. (2016). Identity mappings in deep residual networks. doi:10.1007/978-3-319-46493-0_38

He, K., Zhang, X., Ren, S., & Sun, J. (2016). Deep Residual Learning for Image Recognition. *Proceedings of The IEEE Computer Society Conference on Computer Vision and Pattern Recognition (CVPR)*. 10.1109/CVPR.2016.90

Hochreiter, S., & Schmidhuber, J. (1997). Long Short-term Memory. *Neural Computation, 9*(8), 1735–1780. doi:10.1162/neco.1997.9.8.1735 PMID:9377276

Hsu, B. (2020). Comparison of Supervised Classification Models on Textual Data. *Mathematics, 8*(5), 851. Advance online publication. doi:10.3390/math8050851

Irsoy, O., & Cardie, C. (2014). Dcep Recursive Neural Networks for Compositionality in Language. *Advances in Neural Information Processing Systems, 27*, 2096–2104.

Jain, S., Jain, A. K., & Singh, S. P. (2020). A Multilayer Deep Learning Framework for Auto-content Tagging. *Advanced in Intelligent Systems and Computing, 1141*, 609–619. doi:10.1007/978-981-15-3383-9_55

Kalchbrenner, N., Grefenstette, E., & Blunsom, P. (2014). A Convolutional Neural Network for Modelling Sentences. In *Proceedings of 52nd Annual Meeting of The Association for Computational Linguistics.* Association for Computational Linguistics. 10.3115/v1/P14-1062

Khanna, S., Tiwari, B., Das, P., & Das, A. (2020). A Comparative Study on Various Text Classification Methods. *Computational Intelligence in Pattern Recognition*, 539-549.

Kilimci, Z. H., & Akyokus, S. (2018). Deep Learning- And Word Embedding-Based Heterogeneous Classifier Ensembles for Text Classification. *Complexity, 2018*, 1–10. Advance online publication. doi:10.1155/2018/7130146

Kim, Y. (2014). Convolutional Neural Networks for sentence classification. In *Proceedings of the 2014 Conference on Empirical Methods in Natural Language Processing (EMNLP)*. Association for Computational Linguistics. 10.3115/v1/D14-1181

Kim, Y., Jernite, Y., Sontag, D., & Rush, A. M. (2016). Character-Aware Neural Language Models. *Proceedings of Thirtieth AAAI Conference on Artificial Intelligence.*

Kowsari, K., Brown, D. E., Heidarysafa, M., Meimandi, K. J., Gerber, M. S., & Barnes, L. E. (2007). HDLTex: Hierarchical Deep Learning for Text Classification. In *Proceedings of 2017 16th Ieee International Conference on Machine Learning and Applications (ICMLA)*. IEEE.

Kowsari, K., Meimandi, K. J., Heidarysafa, M., Mendu, S., Barnes, L., & Brown, D. (2019). Text Classification Algorithms: A Survey. *Information (Basel), 10*(4), 150. doi:10.3390/info10040150

Lan, Z., Chen, M., Goodman, S., Gimpel, K., Sharma, P., & Soricut, R. (2020). ALBERT: A Lite Bert for Self-Supervised Learning of Language Representations. *Proceedings of ICLR.*

Larochelle, H., Bengio, Y., Louradour, J., & Lamblin, P. (2009). Exploring Strategies for Training Deep Neural Networks. *Journal of Machine Learning Research, 10*(1).

Le, Q., & Mikolov, T. (2014). Distributed Representations of Sentences and Documents. *Proceedings of the 31st International Conference on Machine Learning, 32*(2), 1188–1196.

Liu, Y., Ott, M., Goyal, N., Du, J., Joshi, M., Chen, D., Levy, O., Lewis, M., Zettlemoyer, L., & Stoyanov, V. (2019). RoBERT: A Robustly Optimized Bert Pretraining Approach. arXiv:1907.11692v1.

Melnyk, R., Snyder, M. M., & Verner, A. (2020). Towards the Development of A Classification Model for Technical Documents in Knowledge Discovery System. *Issues in Information Systems, 21*, 67–72.

Mikolov, T., Chen, K., Corrado, G., & Dean, J. (2013). Efficient Estimation of Word Representations in Vector Space. arxiv preprint arxiv:1301.3781.

Minaee, S. Kalchbrenner, Cambria, E., Nikzad, N., Chenaghlu, M., & Gao, J. (2020). Deep learning based text classification: A comprehensive review. arxiv:2004.03705 [cs.cl], 1.

Oussous, A., Benjelloun, F. Z., Lahcen, A. A., & Belfkih, S. (2018). Big Data technologies: A survey. *Journal of King Saud University – Computer and Information Sciences, 30*, 431–448.

Pelkmann, D., Tharwat, A., & Schenck, W. (2020). How to Label? Combining Experts' Knowledge for German Text Classification. *7th Swiss Conference on Data Science (Sds)*, 61-62. 10.1109/SDS49233.2020.00023

Pennington, J., Socher, R., & Manning, C. (2014). GloVe: global vectors for word representation. In *Proceedings of the 2014 Conference on Empirical Methods in Natural Language Processing (EMNLP)*. Association for Computational Linguistics. 10.3115/v1/D14-1162

Peters, M., Neumann, M., Iyyer, M., Gardner, M., Clark, C., Lee, K., & Zettlemoyer, L. (2018). Deep Contextualized Word Representations. *Proceedings of the 2018 Conference of the North American Chapter of the Association for Computational Linguistics: Human Language Technologies, 1*, 2227–2237. 10.18653/v1/N18-1202

Redondo, T., & Sandoval, A. M. (2016). Text Analytics: The Convergence of Big Data and Artificial Intelligence. *International Journal of Interactive Multimedia and Artificial Intelligence, 3*(6), 57–64. doi:10.9781/ijimai.2016.369

Salminena, J., Yoganathan, V., Corporand, J., Jansena, B. J., & Junga, S. (2019). Machine learning approach to auto-tagging online content for content marketing efficiency: A comparative analysis between methods and content type. *Journal of Business Research, 101*, 203–217. doi:10.1016/j.jbusres.2019.04.018

Schlegel, D. (2015). *Deep Machine Learning on Gpu*. University of Heidelber-Ziti.

Semberecki, P., & Maciejewski, H. (n.d.). Deep learning methods for subject text classifification of articles. *Proceedings of the Federated Conference on Computer Science and Information Systems, 11*, 357-360. doi:10.15439/2017F414

Simonyan, K., & Zisserman, A. (2015). Very Deep Convolutional Networks for Large-Scale Image Recognition. *Proceedings of 3rd International Conference on Learning Representations, ICLR- Conference Track Proceeding,* 1409-1556.

Tai, S., Socher, R., & Manning, C. D. (2015). Improved Semantic Representations from Tree-Structured Long Short-Term Memory Networks. *Proceedings of the 53rd Annual Meeting of the Association for Computational Linguistics and the 7th International Joint Conference on Natural Language Processing, 1*, 1556–1566. 10.3115/v1/P15-1150

Tharwat. A. (2020). Classification Assessment Methods. *Applied Computing and Informatics, 17*(1).

Xiao, Y., & Cho, K. (2016). Efficient Character-Level Document Classification by Combining Convolution and Recurrent Layers. arxiv:1602.00367.

Xue, W., Zhou, W., Li, T., & Wang, Q. (2017). MTNA: A Neural Multi-Task Model for Aspect Category classification and Aspect Term Extraction on Restaurant Reviews. In *Proceedings of the Eighth International Joint Conference on Natural Language Processing*. Asian Federation of Natural Language Processing.

Zhang, X., Zhao, J., & LeCun, Y. (2015). Character-Level Convolutional Networks for Text Classification. In *Proceedings of the 28th International Conference on Neural Information Processing Systems (NIPS'15)*. Advances in Neural Information Processing Systems.

Zhou, C., Sun, C., Liu, Z., & Lau, F. C. M. (2015). A C-LSTM Neural Network for Text Classification. arxiv preprint arxiv:1511.08630.

Zhou, P., Qi, Z., Zheng, S., Xu, J., Bao, H., & Xu, B. (2016).Text Classification Improved by Integrating Bidirectional Lstm with Two-Dimensional Max Pooling. *Proceedings of COLING 2016, the 26th International Conference on Computational Linguistics: Technical Papers, The COLING 2016 Organizing Committee*, 3485–3495.

Zhu, X., Sobihani, P., & Guo, H. (2015). Long Short-Term Memory Over Recursive Structures. *Proceedings of the 32nd International Conference on Machine Learning*, 37, 1604–1612.

Chapter 3
Information Retrieval in the Hidden Web

Shakeel Ahmed
https://orcid.org/0000-0003-1155-0991
King Faisal University, Saudi Arabia

Shubham Sharma
Tata Consultancy Services, India

Saneh Lata Yadav
K. R. Mangalam University, India

ABSTRACT

Information retrieval is finding material of unstructured nature within large collections stored on computers. Surface web consists of indexed content accessible by traditional browsers whereas deep or hidden web content cannot be found with traditional search engines and requires a password or network permissions. In deep web, dark web is also growing as new tools make it easier to navigate hidden content and accessible with special software like Tor. According to a study by Nature, Google indexes no more than 16% of the surface web and misses all of the deep web. Any given search turns up just 0.03% of information that exists online. So, the key part of the hidden web remains inaccessible to the users. This chapter deals with positing some questions about this research. Detailed definitions, analogies are explained, and the chapter discusses related work and puts forward all the advantages and limitations of the existing work proposed by researchers. The chapter identifies the need for a system that will process the surface and hidden web data and return integrated results to the users.

1. INTRODUCTION

Enormous amount of text, sound, video, and different reports are available and accessible on the Web, on various subjects. Users ought to have the choice to ascertain relevant data to justify their precise data requirements. The data can be sought out in two different ways: to utilize an inquiry motors or to

DOI: 10.4018/978-1-7998-8061-5.ch003

peruse indexes coordinated by classifications (like Yahoo Directories). There is still a huge portion of the Internet data that isn't accessible (for example intranets and the private information bases). Data recovery (IR) is the errand of addressing, tapping away, coordinating, and accessing the data things. IR is not quite the same as information recovery, which is tied in with finding exact information in data sets with a given construction. In IR frameworks, the data isn't organized, it is contained in free structure in text (site pages or different records) or in sight and sound substance. The first IR frameworks carried out in 1970's were intended to work with little assortments of text (for model authoritative reports). A portion of these strategies are presently utilized in web search tools. The WWW is a software protocol that runs on the internet and allows the end-users to access the files stored in the computers which are interconnected by the internet. The WWW is the largest source of digital information. It has a diverse range of information about studies, fashion, politics, tourism, social networking, mail systems, vehicles, business, sports, cooking, countries, history, illegal activities, and drugs, and so on. The WWW has become a very essential part of everyone's life. People from all walks use WWW to extract the desired information. According to the latest statistics as of January 2021 as shown in Fig.1, there were 4.66 billion active internet users worldwide - 59.5 percent of the global population. Of this total, 92.6 percent (4.32 billion) accessed the internet via mobile devices (Johnson, 2021).

Figure 1. Global Digital Population users in Billions (Johnson, 2021)

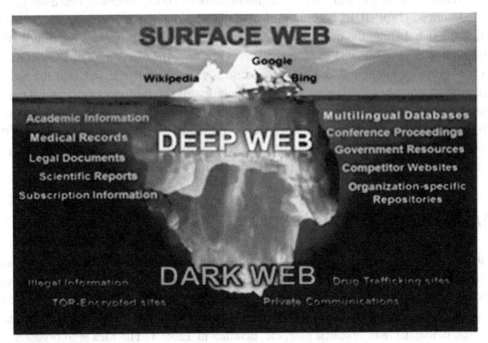

According to Internet Live Stats (Raghavan & Garcia-Molina, 2001), Real-Time international Statistics Project website every single second, roughly 7986 tweets are tweeted; beyond 66418 Google queries are searched, and beyond 2 million emails are sent. Which indicates the pace of growth of WWW. As the WWW is growing, therefore, the problem of managing and searching the information is important. To help the end-users to find desired information from this bulk information, various search engines have been developed. For e.g. Google, Bing, yahoo, Ask.com, AOL.com, etc. The information about a topic is scattered on the different types of web pages such as surface web unstructured web pages, hidden web structured web pages, file formats, etc. These search engines extract the data from all these parts of the WWW and present that data to the end-users.

So, it has become very difficult for the end-users to filter the desired data from different sections of WWW because of factors such as the size of results fetched, redundancy of data, data is hidden behind query interfaces and it is very arduous. End-user is required to endure every page, process it, and then only the desired data is extracted. The most promising solution is an information integrator, where the user can enter his/her query and he/she will get all the processed data available in different parts of WWW. It saves a lot of time for the user.

Conventionally, in most of search engines when the user enters the query, the results are shown to the users. The results contain the surface web information, some files, and some query interfaces. The user has to excerpt the desired info from the result webpages. In order to extract the data behind the query interfaces, the user need to fill and submit the query forms. The proposed system will not only process the data from the unstructured web but will also excerpt the data from the hidden web. Although there are many hidden web data extractors, however to the best of our knowledge and understanding, none of them have tried to use the artificial intelligence approach and have processed and integrated the hidden web and surface web. Thus, there is a need for a system that will process the surface web and hidden web data and returns the integrated results to the users. Hence "Dynamic Query Processing for Hidden Web Data Extraction" (DQPHDE) is being projected that exploits the artificial intelligence technique for extracting the data behind the query interfaces and integrates and processes the information from different types of WWW (Anuradha & Juneja, 2015). Therefore, the motivation of DQPHDE is to find a solution that provides integrated and processed results from the surface web and the hidden web. We present current strategies used to assess the presentation of the Information Retrieval part. Useful contemplations incorporate data about existing IR frameworks and a nitty gritty illustration of a huge scope web index (Google); we present strategies for positioning pages by their significance (the Hubs an Specialists calculation and Google's PageRank calculation). In another segment, we talk about the Imperceptible Web, the section of the Web that is not recorded thru web search tools.

2. DIGITAL ACADEMIC SERACH ENGINES

A lot of hidden web data extraction tools have been developed for different domains such as people information extraction, government federal information, geological surveys, medications, government documents, academic research documents (Ferrara et al., 2010). In this research, the academic research documents have been taken. A lot of tools have been developed to extract hidden academic research data such as DOAJ, BASE, CORE, research gate, etc. detailed in Table 1. The idea is to organize and ease the information retrieval process for the researcher.

3. Literature Review

Table 1. Comparison of Academic Digital Libraries

	Integration of Hidden Web and Surface Web	Social Networking	Clustering	Summarization
DOAJ	No	No	Yes	No
CORE	No	No	Yes	No
BASE	No	No	Yes	No
Google Scholar	No	No	Yes	No
Microsoft Academic Research	No	No	Yes	Yes
Research Gate	No	Allow Messaging	Yes	No
Academia	No	No	No	No
DQPHDE	Yes	Yes	Yes	Yes

3.1 History of Web

Initially, internet was created to connect the isolated computers in the whole network, so that machines could communicate with each other. To access the information stored on different machines, uniform data structure was required, so HTML was designed to function almost identically on all computers. HTML displays the data identically on all machines regardless of the hardware and the software. The documents in HTML were linked to each other with the help of the links called hypertext documents. Users can click on the links and can browse the web documents. To extract the information from WWW browsing and searching were the two main methods. Browsing is following the links created by the web developers. In order to browse user just has to click on the links. So browsing was easy and spontaneous. Searching on the other hand was not easy. Searching requires special software to match user keywords and extract the documents needed by the user. When the WWW was new and small, browsing was an efficient method to extract the information. But when WWW starts growing the browsing became difficult, as the user has to manually navigate from one page to another by clicking. So search tools were developed to help the users to find the desired information easily and quickly. Two search tools were created to pull information from the web. The first method was the web directory and the second one was the search engine. A web directory is a context-based framework for structured browsing while search engines help in searching for a particular keyword or a phrase.

Web directories work like the table of contents of a book while the search engines work like the index of a book. Web Directories uses the Hierarchical Graph for storing data while search engines uses Inverted Index data structures for storing the data. For example the hierarchical directory structure for storing information about the computer domain is shown in Fig. 2. The example of Inverted Index data structure for search engines is shown in Fig. 3. In Web Directories the top level of hierarchical graph contains the generic topic and the user has to go down the level to get to the specific topic. The web directories are created and maintained by the humans instead of the software. At the bottom of the hierarchical graph, the user is presented with the list of documents prepared by human intervention. In the

Figure 2. Hierarchical Graph Structure for Web Directories

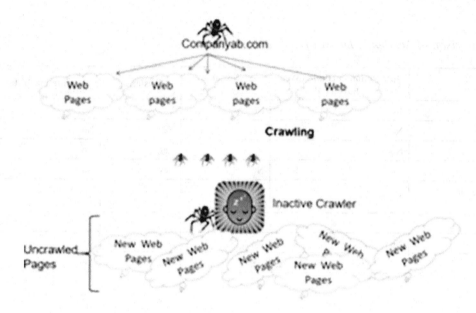

case of the search engines the millions of documents are indexed in the inverted index structure. When the end user issue the query, by the help of various algorithms the user keywords and the keywords in the inverted index are matched. The documents which are matched and are found to be most relevant are then displayed to the users.

Figure 3. Inverted Index Data Structure for Search Engine

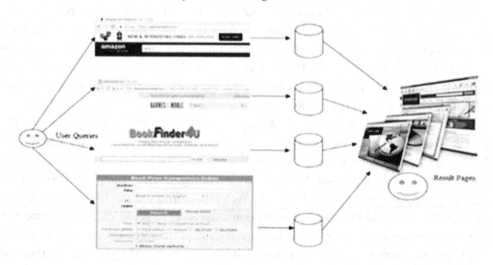

Examples of web directories are Gopher, Archie, etc. while Google, and Yahoo, etc. are examples of search engines. The difference between Web Directories and Search Engines is as shown in the below Table 2.

Table 2. Variance between Web Directories and Search Engines

Web Directories	Search Engines
The web pages in web directories are organized into subject categories.	The web pages are not organized on subject categories. The special algorithm are there which rank the web pages and organize them.
Web Directories are smaller in size.	Search Engines are very much larger than the Search Engines.
Web Directories are compiled by the humans and no software intervention is there.	Search Engines are compiled by the software and no human intervention is there.
The user query keywords are matched with the category name, site name and website annotation. The keywords are not matched thru that of the web page.	Query keywords by the user are matched with the content or text of the web pages.
The hierarchical graph based structure is used in the web directories.	The inverted index data structures for indexing in search engines

3.2 Functioning of Search Engines

Search engine is a software program which is available through the internet that helps to search documents and file found in WWW. The search engines have a database containing the full-text index of web

Figure 4. Cyclic Architecture of Search Engine (Castillo, 2005)

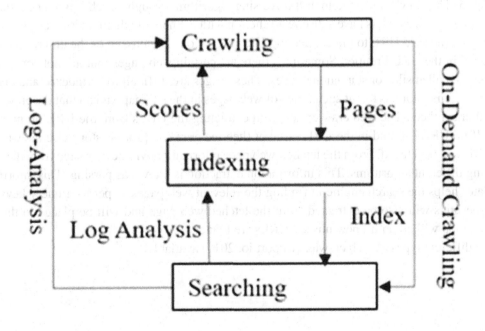

documents. Therefore, based on information required the user issues the query on the search engines, and user query keywords are searched from this database and the outcomes are exhibited to the user. The search engines consist of three components crawler, indexer, and the searching module (Yang & Gerasoulis, 2014). The cyclic architecture of search engines proposed by Carlos is shown in Fig. 4.

The first component Crawlers, also called spiders or web robots, search bot or bots, they help in finding and fetching the web pages. The second component Indexer which indexes each and every word found available on the web pages and store the indexed list of words in the database. The third module searching, also called a query processor, compares user query keywords with the index database and displays the relevant and matched documents to the end-users.

3.3 Web Crawler

Web Crawler (Akilandeswari & Gopalan, 2008; Sharma & Sharma, 2010; Sharma & Sharma, 2011) is software that traverses the WWW in a methodical, automated manner but in an orderly fashion. Web crawler finds and collects the web documents present in the WWW and then hands over those pages to the indexing module of the search engine. The web crawler starts from a set of web pages and follows the hyperlinks found on these web pages. The search engines may run multiple instances of web crawler simultaneously on multiple servers. When the crawler visits a page, then it stores the information of the web page into the search engine database. Web crawler before starting traversing a website looks for a file called "robot.txt". This file is created by the website administrator, which contains instructions for the crawler. These instructions tell the compiler which part of the website is indexable and which parts are non-indexable and should be ignored for indexing by the crawler. All the crawlers of the search engines follow these instructions and then they start crawling the website.

Before the crawler starts the crawling process, a list of URLs is prepared which is known as seed URL. The web crawler starts its journey from these URLs and will keep on extracting the web pages which are connected to the seed URL. These seed URLs are kept in a queue known as URL Frontier as shown in Fig. 5. The crawlers use the inbuilt traversing algorithm through which it will crawl the connected set of pages. The crawlers have a discover function with the help of which it discovers a new URL by jumping from the seed URL to the connecting URL and so on. The unseen or the un-crawled URLs are then placed in the URL Frontier. Sometimes there are certain web pages that are not connected to other web pages, called silos or standalone pages. These pages are difficult to be indexed and crawled. The website administrator has to put such kinds of web pages in the sitemap.xml so that the crawler can discover and crawl them. The web crawler keeps on extracting the URLs from the URL Frontier until it is empty. If no URL is found in the URL Frontier then the crawling process stops else the web page from that URL will be fetched. From the fetched web page information will be extracted from the text of the page using different algorithms. This information extraction is known as parsing. This information extraction later helps the search engine in finding the relevant web pages as per user query keywords. The new hyperlinks will also be extracted from the fetched web page and will be placed in the URL Frontier. This loop will go on till new unseen URLs are found.

There are different types of web crawler (Import.io, 2019) available.

Figure 5. Steps of Traditional Web Crawler

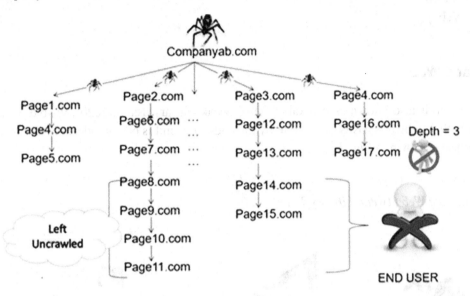

3.4 Types of Crawlers

World Wide Web which is a collection of web-pages created using HTML are accessed using the HTTP protocol. The World Wide Web developed by Tim Berners-Lee in the year1991. The World Wide Web is also known as the "Web". The WWW is of three types as shown in Fig. 6.

● Surface Web

Figure 6. Components of WWW (Import.io, 2019)

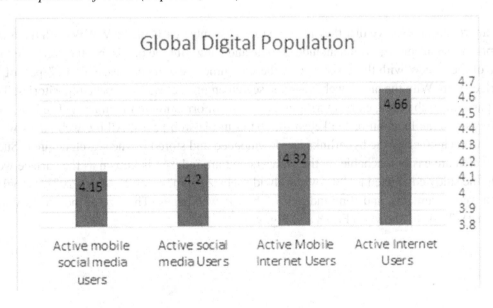

- Hidden Web
- Dark Web

3.5 Surface Web

The surface web is also known as indexable web (Tweak Library Team, 2020), visible web. It is that part of the WWW which is easily accessible by the end-users and is easily indexable and stored by the search engines as shown in Fig. 7.

Figure 7. Surface Web (Tweak Library Team, 2020)

Userid and Passwords to unlock

Most internet users believe that they are able to access most parts of the WWW with the assistance of widespread search engines which include Google and Bing. But the fact is that they are able to access only 10% of the WWW with the assistance of these common search engines. This 10% part of WWW is the surface web. With the aid of web crawlers, search engines create web page repositories. The web crawlers parse the web pages, extract terms and pass this information to the indexer. The indexer stores the keywords and the location of the keywords found in the web pages. All the web pages which are connected to each other by the hyperlinks are downloaded and stored by the search engines. Such kind of pages which are easily reachable by the crawlers and are indexed is known as the surface web. According to the study conducted by "www.worldwidewebsize.com" as of 27 March 2021, Google index 54 million web documents, and Bing indexes 7.5 billion web pages (The size of the World Wide Web (The Internet), 2021) as shown in Fig. 8 and Fig. 9.

3.6 Hidden Web

Hidden web is also well-known as invisible web, deep web/non-indexable web. It is part of WWW that

Figure 8. The extent of the WWWW: Projected size of Google's index (The size of the World Wide Web (The Internet), 2021)

Figure 9. The extent of the WWW: Projected size Bing's index (The size of the World Wide Web (The Internet), 2021)

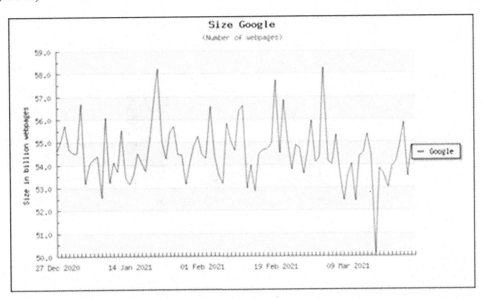

is not been crawled and indexed by the well-known search engines as shown in Fig. 10. The deep web is comprised of the web database and also dynamically generated web pages.

Figure 10. Deep Web

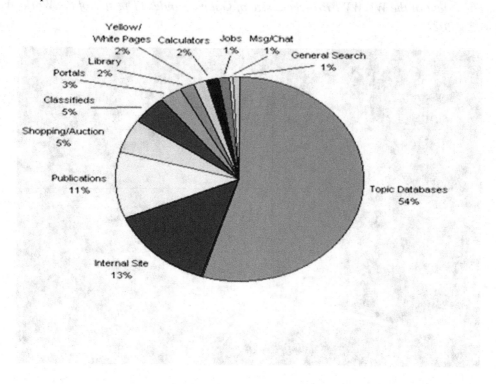

Figure 11. Distribution of Deep Web by its Content Type (Bergman, 2001)

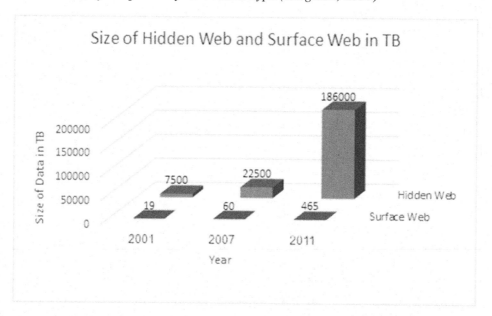

Such kinds of pages are not indexed by Google or Bing. The deep web mentions to the content which is available through the query interfaces or web forms (Khelghati et al., 2013). The end-user has to fill the web forms, submit the query, and only then they are able to access this data. This data is not hidden from the end-users but is hidden from the search engines. The deep web forms 90% of the WWW (Boughammoura & Omri, 2017). The deep web is high in both quantity and quality. Deep web comprises the structured data from web databases. According to the study conducted by Bergman, the content in the deep web and its share in the deep web is shown in Fig. 11 (Bergman, 2001). According to this study, a major part of the deep web resides in the databases, which are accessible with the help of the web forms.

3.7 Dark Web

It is that part of the WWW not indexed by the traditional search engines (Lewandowski, 2005). Data of the dark web is not intended to be seen by the end-users. The data of the dark web is encrypted, sometimes because of some legitimate reasons and certain times to hide the illegal activities (Finklea, 2015) as shown in Fig. 12.

Figure 12. Dark Web

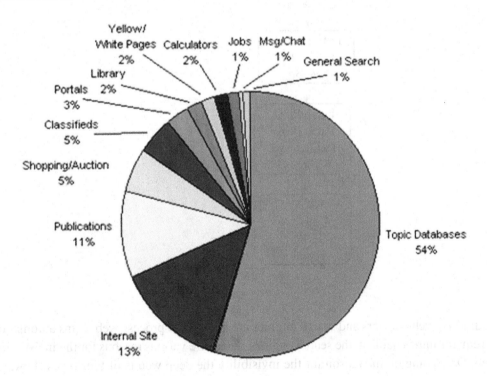

The normal web browser is not enough to access this part of WWW. Special web browsers such as TOR etc. are designed to access the dark web. The TOR web browser hides the activities of the users and makes the user's identity untraceable (Tor vs. VPN: What They Do and which is Better, n.d.).

Hidden Web Invisibility Types

Hidden web is the web that is hidden from the search engines. The web forms/query interfaces act as a doorway to admittance the hidden web. To excerpt the data from the hidden web databases the end-users fill the web forms and submit the forms as shown in Fig. 13.

Figure 13. User Interaction with Web Forms

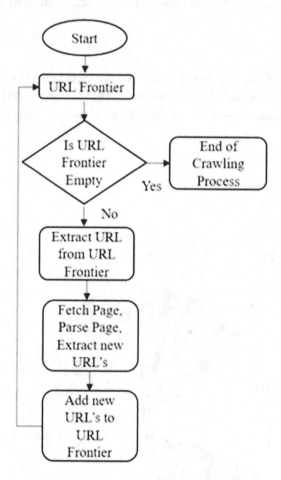

The traditional web crawlers and search engines are not-able to process web forms automatically, so deep web remains unreachable to the search engines. There are various reasons for the invisibility of the hidden web. Depending on the reason for the invisibility the deep web is of four types (Lewandowski & Mayr, 2006).

1. Opaque Web
2. Secret Web
3. Proper Invisible Web
4. Proprietary Web

3.8 Opaque Web

These kinds of web pages are invisible to the search engines because of some technical issues. If these technical issues can be resolved, then these web pages can be indexed by search engines. The main technical issue is the depth of the crawl. The web crawling process is a very resource-consuming process. So the web crawlers don't crawl each and every web page of a website. They fix their depth of the crawling in order to optimize the crawling process resource utilization as shown in Fig. 14. Because of that certain web pages remain hidden as they are not indexed.

Figure 14. Opaque Web: Depth of Crawl

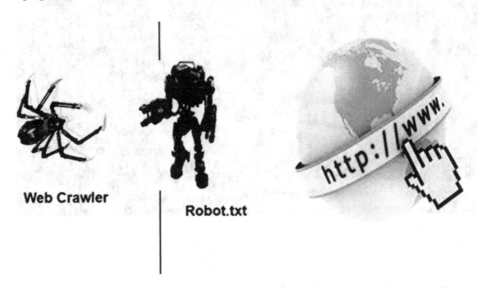

Web Crawler

Robot.txt

   The second technical reason because of which web-pages are not indexed by search engines are the disconnected URLs. Certain times few web pages of a website are not linked to other web pages of that website, neither are they linked to web pages of the other web sites. So they remain undiscovered by the web crawlers and hence are not indexed by the search engines as shown in Fig. 15.
   The third technical reason behind the invisibility in the opaque web is the frequency of crawling. The web crawlers crawl the WWW after a certain time interval. Meanwhile, thousands of web pages are deleted, updated and many more new web pages are added into the WWW as shown in Fig. 16. So the newly added web pages remain hidden from the search engine until its web crawler, crawls again.

3.9 Secret Web

There is no technical reason because of which these web pages are hidden. These web pages are hidden because the website administrator doesn't wish these web pages to be seen by the crawler and indexed by the search engine. There are several techniques with the help of which the website administrator can prohibit the web crawlers to crawl the web pages. The first technique is the robot exclusion protocol. The Website administrator makes a list of web pages that should not be crawled and places that list in

Figure 15. Opaque Web: Disconnected URL's

Figure 16. Opaque Web: Frequency of Crawling

Figure 17. Secret Web: Robot Exclusion Protocol

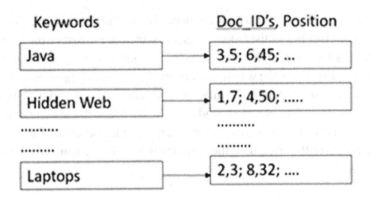

the robot.txt file. The web crawler obeys the rules and before starting crawling a particular website, the crawler reads the robot.txt file and simply ignores the web pages listed there as shown in Fig. 17.

The second technique used is the no-index protocol. The webpage developer places the no-index Meta tag in the web pages which should not be indexed. The no-index Meta tag is the page level policy while robot.txt is the website level policy.

The third technique is making the web pages accessible to only the authorized web users. Certain web pages are hidden behind the web pages which need a user id and password. Search engines don't provide the user is and password in the login form, so the web pages behind the login forms remain hidden to the web crawlers. Not every user is allowed to view those pages, only the authorized users are allowed to access them as shown in Fig. 18.

Figure 18. Secret Web: Password Protected

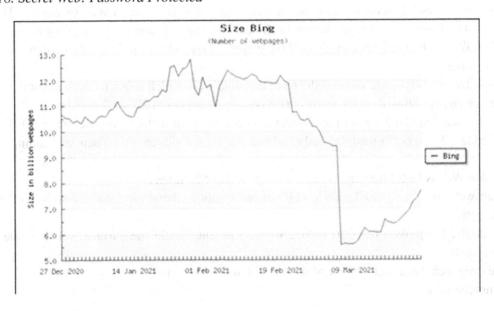

3.9 Proper Invisible Web

There are technical reasons because of which the pages in the Proper Invisible Web are hidden. There are two reasons for the invisibility of the Query Interfaces and the Format of the Files. There are certain web pages that are accessible through the query interfaces (Bhatia et al., 2020). Unlike the end-users, the web crawlers are not able to process the web forms and extract the web pages behind the query interfaces. The second reason for invisibility here is the different formats of files found in WWW. The file formats such as pdf, doc, ppt, audio, video, etc. are found on WWW. The web crawlers don't process these file formats sometimes because of technical reasons and certain times because of the spider trap problems. When the web crawlers parse the files, then there are traps because of which the crawlers keep going in a loop and lose their performance.

3.10 Proprietary Invisible Web

There are web pages in the deep web which are only visible to those set of people who agrees on certain conditions before viewing the web pages. The registration procedure is required where the users enter their personal details and register themselves. As the web crawlers are not able to complete the registration procedure, so they fail to crawl those set of pages.

HOW DIGITAL LIBRARIES WORK

3.11 Hidden Web History

At the beginning of internet development, there were few websites and web pages, so that the web pages were easily crawl able by the search engines. At the beginning of 1996 three technologies came to the surface such as database technologies, e-commerce, and dynamic web pages (Bergman, 2001). With the help of these, database-based large websites started developing. These websites no longer have static web pages. So, the e-commerce companies started creating an entirely new class of websites. This class of websites has dynamic web pages which fetch data from the database servers (Bhatia, 2020; He et al., 2007; Król, 2019). The search engines of those times were not able to index the content of this new class of websites.

In 1994, Dr. Jill Ellsworth, devised the term invisible web, which refers to the content not indexed by the search engines. Based on the study carried out by Bergman in 2004 (Bergman, 2001), hidden or invisible web was found to be 500 times greater than compared to surface web (Bergman, 2001). Bright Planet (Finklea, 2015) performed the study and analysis on the hidden web. Their key findings include

1. Hidden Web is larger than the surface web by 400 to 550 times.
2. Deep web contains 7500 Terabyte (TB) of information, though the surface web has 19 TB of information.
3. Generally, Deep Web has 550 billion web documents while the surface web has one billion documents.
4. The deep web has a high quality of data and is more relevant.
5. comprehensive

4. SIZE OF HIDDEN WEB AND THE RATE OF GROWTH OF HIDDEN WEB

Hidden web comprises a vast quantity of information. The scope of the hidden web increased at a rapid speed and it is still expanding. In year 2000, the surface web contained nearly 2.5 billion documents and had a size of 19TB. At that time Google was able to index 1.35 billion web documents out of which the total size of the surface web was estimated to be 54% of the total the surface web. The size of the deep web was measured to have roughly 550 billion documents, which is 220 times the size of the surface web and had a size of 7500TB. The quality of the Deep Web content was said to be 1000–2000 folds superior to that of the counterpart surface Web. As part of the Bergman's research (Finklea, 2015) the quality analysis was performed which lead to the conclusion that 17 years earlier deep Web indexing was in its infancy, most of the Web was not reachable proficiently. Table 3 contains instantaneous of the data described in relate to the size of the hidden web and the surface web compared with the year 2000 and 2005

Table 3. Comparison of Size of Hidden and Surface Web

	In Year 2000		In Year 2005	
	Surface Web	**Hidden Web**	**Surface Web**	**Hidden Web**
Documents	2.5 billion	550 billion	11.5 billion	1650-3850 billion
Size	19TB	7500TB	60TB – 100TB	22500 -52500TB

Compared with that of the five years the approximation of the deep Web scale increased during the year 2005 in deep web content with a total of 307,000 deep Web sites that were estimated to exist as well as 450,000 Web databases that were accessible by 1,258,000 query interfaces. The rapid increase in the deep Web has been observed with a grown rate of 3–7 times bigger compared with the year form 2000-2005 (Bhatia et al., 2020; Bhatia, 2020), as presented in Table 3 above.

Accordingly the surface Web was estimated from the year 2011 it was at least 14 billion data, with the 25k/HTML being the average size of the document and the surface Web would amount to 465 TB. If the deep web still is 400–500 times larger than the surface Web, then we would get a result of 8000–10000 billion documents in hidden web making the size of the hidden web around 186 000 TB–232500 TB, as illustrated in Table 4. The growth of hidden web and surface web from 2000 to 2011 is shown in Fig. 19.

Table 4. Size of Hidden Web and Surface Web in 2011

	Surface Web	**Hidden Web**
Documents	14 billion	8000 -10000 billion
Size	465 TB	186000- 232500TB

Figure 19. Growth of Hidden Web and Surface Web

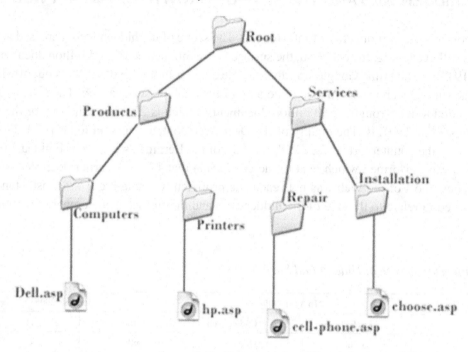

4.1 Inaccessible Deep web in the Traditional Search Engines

One of the major chunk of the hidden web are the hidden web forms where, most of the content is not indexed by traditional search engines. A study issued by Nature, Google indexes no more than 16 percent of the surface Web and misses all of the Deep Web. Generally it takes 0.03 percent of the information that exists online (one in 3,000 pages) at any given search (Bergman, 2001). It's like fly-fishing in the top two feet of the ocean. Therefore, a main portion of the hidden web remains concealed and unreachable to the users. A foremost part of the hidden web is behindhand the query interfaces, which abstract the data from the databases. The hidden web has different types of content such as online shopping data, chats, publications, databases, etc. Bergman (Bergman, 2001) calculated the percentage of the different types of content found in the hidden web as shown in Fig. 20.

4.2 Lack of Integrated Data From Surface Web and Deep Web

The details of a particular web entity can be found in the surface and the hidden web. To excerpt the complete details the users have to browse both the surface web and hidden web. There is no single source for such integrated information.

4.3 Lack of Integrated and Linked Data from Hidden Web

The details of an entity can be scattered on more than one hidden web source. Most of the hidden data extractors extract the information and place them in a single database. The information extracted is not

Figure 20. Distribution of Deep Web Site by Content (Bergman, 2001)

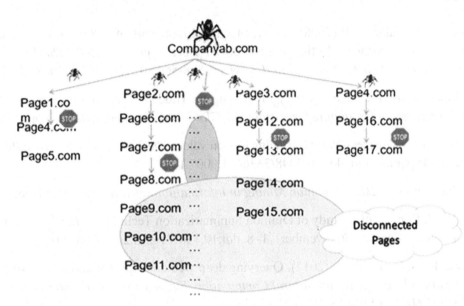

processed it is just aggregated. It results in the duplication of information. There is no integrator that links the information from multiple sources and removes the redundant information.

5. CONCLUSION AND FUTURE SCOPE

On the basis of literature grilled during the initial phase of the research work, the following objectives had been identified in the light of challenges stated in the above section such as the development of an algorithm to cluster the web documents based on the type of content present in the web pages. The designing of an algorithm to integrate the unstructured data from multiple web sources and summarize it. An intelligent approach can be designed to automatically extract the web forms from the web pages and rank the query interfaces, can be developed. An approach to intelligently extract the result section from the web pages and create an integrated and linked database. Web Information Retrieval is a relevant subject of exploration for the current day. As the web endures to fill in size, the subject of beholding through the web turns out to be just more mystifying. A number of creative procedures and policies have been anticipated which finalize guarantee. Nevertheless, it stays not yet clear which methodology at last cracks into the standard, and how much the web is actually exploited by clients. The consideration of WebIR innovation that constructs over the future would resolve if the web is guaranteed to be a huge storing capacity of to a great amount of unstructured information, or is certainly a huge information network that bids information to persons.

REFERENCES

Akilandeswari, J., & Gopalan, N. P. (2008). An Architectural Framework of a Crawler for Locating Deep Web Repositories Using Learning Multi-Agent Systems. *Proceedings of the 2008 Third International Conference on Internet & Web Applications and Services,* 558-562. 10.1109/ICIW.2008.94

Anuradha & Juneja. (2015). Dynamic Query Processing for Hidden Web Data Extraction. *2015 2nd International Conference on Computing for Sustainable Global Development (INDIACom),* 1352-1356.

Bergman, M. K. (2001). The Deep Web: Surfacing hidden value. *The Journal of Electronic Publishing, 7*(1). Advance online publication. doi:10.3998/3336451.0007.104

Bhatia, Chaudhary, & Dey. (2020). *Opinion Mining in Information Retrieval.* Springer Brief.

Bhatia, S. (2020). A Comparative Study of Opinion Summarization Techniques. *IEEE Transactions on Social Computational Systems, 18*(November), 1–8. doi:10.1109/TCSS.2020.3033810

Boughammoura, R., & Omri, M. N. (2017). Querying deep web data bases without accessing to data. *2017 13th International Conference on Natural Computation, Fuzzy Systems and Knowledge Discovery (ICNC-FSKD),* 597-603. 10.1109/FSKD.2017.8393338

Castillo, C. (2005). Effective web crawling. *ACM SIGIR Forum, 39*(1), 55-56. 10.1145/1067268.1067287

Ferrara, Fiumara, & Baumgartner. (2010). *Web Data Extraction, Applications and Techniques: A Survey.* Tech. Report.

Finklea, K. (2015). *Dark Web.* Accessed March 28, 2021. https://www.fas.org/sgp/crs/misc/R44101.pdf

He, B., Patel, M., Zhang, Z., & Chang, K. C. C. (2007). Accessing the deep web: A survey. *Communications of the ACM, 50*(5), 94–101. doi:10.1145/1230819.1241670

Import.io. (2019). *Web Data Extraction Basics – The Difference Between Surface Web, Deep Web and Dark Web.* https://www.import.io/post/the-difference-between-surface-web-deep-web-and-dark-web/

Johnson, J. (2021). *Worldwide digital population as of January 2021.* Statista. www.statista.com/statistics/617136/digital-population-worldwide/

Khelghati, M., Hiemstra, D., & Keulen, M. V. (2013). Deep web entity monitoring. *Proc. 22nd Int. Conf. World Wide Web Companion,* 377–382.

Król, K. (2019). Geoinformation in the Invisible Resources of the Internet. *Geomatics, Landmanagement and Landscape, 3,* 53–66. doi:10.15576/GLL/2019.3.53

Lewandowski, D. (2005). Web searching, search engines, and information retrieval. *Information Services & Use, 25*(3-4), 137–147. doi:10.3233/ISU-2005-253-402

Lewandowski, D., & Mayr, P. (2006). Exploring the academic invisible web. *Library Hi Tech, 24*(4), 529–539. doi:10.1108/07378830610715392

Raghavan, S., & Garcia-Molina, H. (2001). Crawling the Hidden Web. *Proceedings of the 27th International Conference on Very Large Data Bases,* 129–138.

Sharma & Sharma. (2010). Deep Web Information Retrieval Process: A Technical Survey. *International Journal of Information Technology & Web Engineering, 5*(1), 1-22.

Sharma & Sharma. (2011). Search Engine: A Backbone for Information Extraction in ICT Scenario. *International Journal of ICTHD, 3*(2), 38-51.

The size of the World Wide Web (The Internet). (2021). https://www.worldwidewebsize.com/

Tor vs. VPN: What They Do and which is Better. (n.d.). Accessed March 28, 2021. https://www.pandasecurity.com/en/mediacenter/privacy/tor-vs-vpn/

Tweak Library Team. (2020). *What Is The Difference Between Dark Web, Deep Web and Surface Web?* https://tweaklibrary.com/what-is-the-difference-between-dark-web-deep-web-and-surface-web/

Yang, T., & Gerasoulis, A. (2014). Web Search Engines: Practice and Experience. In Computing Handbook (3rd ed.). Chapman & Hall/CRC Press.

Chapter 4
Social Media Induced Transformations in Healthcare:
A Data Perspective

Puneet Misra
https://orcid.org/0000-0003-2297-9072
University of Lucknow, India

Arun Singh Yadav
https://orcid.org/0000-0002-5783-8344
University of Lucknow, India

Siddharth Chaurasia
https://orcid.org/0000-0002-6348-8600
University of Lucknow, India

ABSTRACT

Technological advancements and their adaptation have made social media one of the most used platforms for sharing ideas and expressing views and experiences. Fields like finance and retail have mined and used information on social platforms to a good effect. The healthcare domain too can leverage social forums in various ways, and it has just started its journey by taking baby steps. Events like the COVID-19 pandemic have accelerated the adaptation to increase the pace and breadth of information outreach. The chapter discusses social media usage in healthcare. The chapter highlights challenges, opportunities, and issues encountered so far and the way forward.

DOI: 10.4018/978-1-7998-8061-5.ch004

INTRODUCTION

Social media adaptation has grown leaps and bounds in the last few years. Its usage for healthcare is comparatively slow when compared with fields like finance, sports, or even its adoption for generic sharing of thoughts and opinions. The reason for slow adoption in the field of health can be attributed to privacy and an inherent reluctance to share one's experiences which are very personal to individuals.

Different entities that can be involved in exchanges related to healthcare can be - Individual to Individual, Individual to Expert, Individual to Public. All three communication channels are possible with different degrees of involvement. Individual to public exchanges can happen in generic social platforms like Twitter, Facebook, or any similar platform. While others have a pretty limited scope and are more proctored.

The growth of acceptance of social media as a platform to share views, experiences, and feelings is enabling its outreach to the healthcare domain. Currently, there is a lot of information getting poured (*Figure* 1) in, and unless it gets processed to extract insights it will be just like a pile of raw data hardly providing any value. This is where the contribution from new technology is leveraged. Technologies like Artificial Intelligence (AI), Machine Learning (ML), Data Mining (DM), Data Science (DS), and Analytics are utilized to get value from the data.

Like all the domains that attempt at applying Natural Language Processing (NLP) to decipher the text written to express one's views, the healthcare field too comes with its own challenges. (Padmavathy & Pakkir Mohideen, 2020) have studied the best Sentiment Analysis (SA) technique to examine people's opinions by analyzing the language used on different medical forums. Their findings were not that unique and clearly signified that like all other fields, application of NLP is not going to be straightforward, they expressed it verbatim 'Despite the fact that most reviews of doctors/ medical practitioners and medicines/drugs are written by non-professional users, reviews of physicians are distinguished by the use of informal language, while reviews of drugs are characterized by a mixture of informal language and technical medical terms with greater lexical diversity, making SA difficult'. Thus again signifying the potential and challenges that exist together.

Chapter first reviews the existing usage of social media in the field of healthcare and how modern-day technology innovations are finding new ways to pace up the cycle of inception to delivery in various fields. It discusses the potential aspects that can be extended in each field. We conclude with innovative usage of this immensely powerful technological concept in one of the most important domains for humans.

BACKGROUND

The field of healthcare can have multiple subfields – medical, pharmaceutical, psychological, epidemical, and many more. In essence, all these domains are interrelated and are concerned with human well-being. Few of these subfields have leveraged the power of social media, while few are laggards. This section provides a comprehensive review of the adoption of social media in various subfields of healthcare.

Pharmaceutical

In the healthcare domain, drug discovery and drug analysis is a fascinating area that falls under the pharmaceutical subfield. The drug development and clinical trial is a time taking process. Data-driven

Figure 1. Various social media data sources used by NLP for sentiment analysis

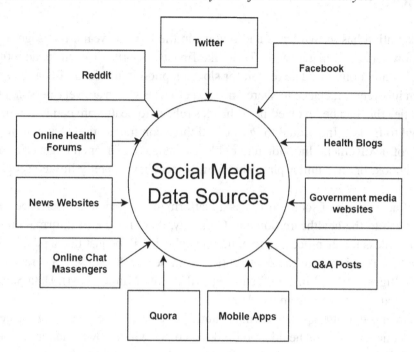

technology is playing a major role in drug discovery and drug analysis and advancement in technology. SA or opinion mining is carried by analyzing the textual information by using NLP as the tool to unearth the essence of the expressed views. Social media is becoming the common platform to express one's feelings, so is with the patients(Jiménez-Zafra, Martín-Valdivia, Molina-González, & Ureña-López, 2019). They share their views on the treatment and drug usage on social media platforms. This unstructured textual data can further be used for an important application like finding the Adverse Drug Reactions(ADRs). This is assisting in diagnosis, treatment of choices, recommending the personalized therapy options, and finding quick relief drug usage(Ru, Li, Hu, & Yao, 2019).

Pharmaceutical industry has a big cycle time from inception to drug approval. Even when marketed, there is a continuous endeavor to monitor the efficacy of the drug. SA is getting popular to monitor the effects and side-effects of each drug on the masses. The reported side effects are taken from the documented reports of several years of research and clinical trials, the process is known as pharmacovigilance. Adverse Drug Event(ADE) is a common term used in Pharmacovigilance. In a recent study(Davazdahemami & Delen, 2019) researchers were able to establish the correlation between diabetic medications increasing or decreasing the chances of retinal failure. The experimental result showed that some drugs positive confounding impact on retinal failure and some show a negative impact. Findings like these can further aid to this very human-centric field.

Drug review analysis can also be carried with the help of masses sharing their experiences. A sentiment classifier that can interpret the category of emotions being shared can bucket the reviews based on the polarity of the message. The categorization of reviews can then be used to analyze the feedbacks, trends, establish co-relations, and even in types of effects and side-effects. (Padmavathy & Pakkir Mohideen, 2020) focused on predicting the level of satisfaction by understanding the sentiments among other patient who already experienced the effect of a drug. Positive when a patient has a positive experience with the drug taken and vice-versa. To analyze the drug satisfaction, researchers utilized two types of the dataset which were collected from www.askapatient.com. The first dataset consists of reviews of popular mental disorder treating drug and second dataset consists of reviews of popular drug related of progesterone, a female hormone that prevents ovulation their approach was to leverage Machine learning to do the processing of the reviews.

Another similar work (Hiremath & Patil, 2020) was done to analyze the personal therapy sessions to build the clinical decision system based on the patient's review of drugs given to them. This review data then processed by NLP technique to determine the patient experience (positive, negative, or neutral) about the used drugs, medical products, treatment strategy during treatment. The polarities obtained after the NLP Process are then compared for further analysis for a better clinical decision system.

Micro-blogging platforms too are becoming a popular platform for the patients to write their feelings in fewer words hence gaining the attention of the researchers, medical practitioners, and Pharma companies. A comparative analysis of two pipelined approaches for adverse drug event extractions from the Twitter micro-blogging platform was presented in (Moh, Moh, Peng, & Wu, 2017). The first pipeline consists of five steps in capturing the real-time tweets, preprocessing, identifying related-drug, user experience tweets SA, and extracting adverse drug effects. The second pipeline has used the same tools but has done classification-based (Drug-related classification & Polarity) SA. The first pipeline achieves better results with all three classifications, yet pipeline 2 performs better with a single classifier.

A similar review was carried in (Jiménez-Zafra et al., 2019) where review comments were given for both physician and the drug. The way humans expressed themselves in both cases was different. It was all about the good or poor patient experience for physicians. Patients reviewing a medication, on the other hand, are most likely to write about various topics such as effectiveness, adverse effects, diseases, and symptoms, resulting in a larger vocabulary. Thus, again signifying the inherent challenge in any such endeavor. When applying data-based methods – this simply means in its current form, there may be a need to have different models for different scenarios and it will be difficult to have 'one size fits all' kind of system.

Table 1 presents a few more work done in the pharmaceutical area. It only presents very prominent and recent ones. Similar attempts are being made for quite some time now with still miles to be covered before it can be adopted in real life.

Public Health - Epidemic/Pandemic

In the context of public health, systems aim at early detection and diagnosis to provide treatment of diseases that can result in prevention from infectious diseases, prolong life and promote health care. The requirement of more accurate predictions of the disease outbreak, early detection, diagnosis, and forecasting of infectious diseases can lead to minimization of the mortality, morbidity rate in public health. Data is the fuel for the modern computational intelligence technologies, adding people sentiments and opinions from social media may significantly improve the system performance.

The decade of 1970 marks the beginning of a formal setup to send warning signals on any Disease Outbreak or spread of any high-impact infectious disease worldwide. The World Health Organization (WHO) and Ministry of Health Canada founded Global Public Health Intelligence Network (GPHIN). Later in the year 2000, WHO provided the framework to other developing countries to establish the early warning system (EWS) for infectious diseases and discovered the possibilities, difficulties, and problems in the development and implementation of EWS.

Table 1. Recent publications in pharmaceutical area on adverse drug reactions using data driven technologies

Authors	Proposed approach	Publication Year	AI based Approaches	Algorithms used (see appendix *Table 5*)
Basiri, Abdar, Cifci, Nemati, & Acharya	Two pass deep fusion 3-way decision theory	2020	Classical Machine Learning & Deep Learning based	Classical model: NB, DT, RF, kNN, Deep learning model: GRU, CNN hybrids
Hiremath & Patil	Aspect based Sentiment Analysis	2020	Classical Machine Learning based	SVM, RFC, NB
Davazdahemami & Delen	Association rule mining using SAS Rapid minor tool	2019	Rule Based	Apriori algorithm and support threshold calculation
Jiménez-Zafra et al.	Supervised-lexicon based opinion polarity classifier	2019	Classical Machine Learning based	SVM and iSOL
Liu & Lee	Position encoding based feature extraction	2019	Classical Machine Learning based	NB, SVM, RF, RBF
Gopalakrishnan & Ramaswamy	Probabilistic Neural Network approach	2017	Classical Machine Learning based	SVM, PNN, RBF
Moh et al.	Pipelined Polarity classification-based Sentiment Analysis approach	2017	Classical Machine Learning and Rule based	Association rule mining, SVM, NB
Casillas, Pérez, Oronoz, Gojenola, & Santiso	Morpho-syntactic and semantic analyser	2016	Classical Machine Learning and Rule based	SVM, RF, Hybrid Rule Based+SVM, Rule Based+RF
Korkontzelos et al.	Supervised-sequence labelling based conditional random field classifier	2016	Classical Machine Learning based	ADRMine, Conditional Random Field, and other baseline methods of ADRMine
Alvaro et al.	Comparative Approach	2015	Classical Machine Learning based	SVM, DT, GLM, MLP, BGLM, NB
Padmavathy & Pakkir Mohideen	Hybrid two-pass classifier	2020	Classical Machine Learning based	SVM, ANN, BPNN

In a similar study with respect to Middle East Respiratory Syndrome(MERS) (Choi et al., 2017) was conducted with the objectives to understand Disease-Media-Emotion Interaction(to understand the underplay between the disease, media and emotion variables), Disease-Media Interaction(mass media reaction to the MERS epidemic), and Media-Emotion Interaction(anger, sorrow, fear, and hate). Their experiment has used news articles and short-text comments from Korean news media and Korean corpora, NRC emotion lexicon and generated the three types of dictionaries that translated and expanded emotion lexicon (TEEL), Internet slang-emotion dictionary (ISED), and emoticon-emotion dictionary (EED) for capturing the explicit and implicit emotions. The results in the study showed that the applied methodology that required quite a bit of preliminary work in the aspect of language is effective to achieve the objectives. (Jain & Kumar, 2018) proposed a social media-based outbreak management system using temporal and spatial information. The study shows that geo-tagged data significantly impacts the prevention and tracking of mosquito-borne diseases. It is more effective than traditional surveillance techniques.(John, Baulch, & Wickramasinghe, 2020) has proposed a study on the ebola virus and presented the unique way by integrating geo-analytics and sentiments from the social media and microblogging platform to analyze which countries have more negative sentiments than positive. This analysis helps the governments to create early countermeasures to stop the spread.

Another comprehensive review (Edo-Osagie, De La Iglesia, Lake, & Edeghere, 2020), covered six different healthcare domains. Study shows that support vector machine & lexicon-based approaches are most used techniques while Event detection and Surveillance are the most used application areas. Before any data-based technique is applied, the usage of feature extraction methods plays a vital role in sentiment analysis. Early detection of dengue or flu diseases can control the spreading of diseases or becoming the outbreak was also studied by using Twitter data by (Amin et al., 2020). SA has also been implemented to detect epidemics from non-English tweets. The study was conducted by analyzing Arabic tweets for detecting the influenza cases(Baker, Shatnawi, Rawashdeh, Al-Smadi, & Jararweh, 2020).

Studying and analyzing the public awareness towards the study(Xue, Chen, Hu, et al., 2020) collected 4 million tweets and applied Latent Dirichlet Allocation(LDA) algorithm which categorized the discussions into four groups. In this order, SA of people sentiments are analyzed(Samuel, Ali, Rahman, Esawi, & Samuel, 2020)using NLP, and psychological reactions about the disease are also be analyzed from 1.9 million tweets(Xue, Chen, Chen, et al., 2020)using ML. A ML method to characterize disease symptoms, testing experiences, and recovery theories have been proposed by(Mackey et al., 2020).

Recently covid-19 pandemic triggered the publication of a plethora of papers in various facets related to epidemics and public health. The study(Tayarani-N., 2020) shows that AI and NLP-based approaches playing a key role in battling the covid-19 in the area of studying the nature and pattern of the virus, and the clinical experiments of it. Once covid-19 was declared as pandemic people started expressing their views on various health forums and several specialized healthcare-oriented forums have been formed where users start writing not only about the symptoms but their fear, depression, and other mental issues due to lockdown and spread-rate of this virus. But the biggest problem is that one cannot draw any conclusion because every user wrote the view or symptoms by writing their own subject, so here the best approach is to identify the common topics and then organizing the posts accordingly will be helpful to apply any NLP method to draw any conclusion.

With formal setups from the health field in place, today's need is to augment it by current advances in technology to increase the outreach and decrease the response time. In the event of Covid-19 pandemic, the importance of such systems gets reinforced. Multiple studies have been conducted in the light of the greatest disruption the whole world faced in the year 2020. (Tayarani-N., 2020) focused on the contribution of AI in the fight towards covid-19 while (Edo-Osagie et al., 2020) researched on the different ways in which public platforms like Twitter can be used in public health research. Another similar review (Alamoodi et al., 2020) focused on the applications of sentiment analysis in the fight against infectious diseases was done.

Another recent research (Jelodar, Wang, Orji, & Huang, 2020) has used a similar approach by first doing the topic modeling to fetch covid-19 related comments of Reddit and has found a total of 93 topics with their ranking 11 to 25. Some of the topics are found that had similar concepts and while ranking on the top rank topics were further used for NLP-based SentiStrength algorithm to check sentiments and polarity results. For each of the polar comments, negative, positive, and neutral scores have been assigned. The author then used the deep learning method to automatically classify the sentiments.

Buzzing topics lead to the generation of fake news too. These epidemic rumors spread at a rapid pace due to internet and public forums(Rodrigues & Xu, 2020)(Al-Zaman, 2020). This affects one`s judgments about the pandemic and creates a situation of panic, which hampers the government's plans to reduce the spread and provide everyone`s proper food, shelter, and medical facilities. Hence identifying these rumors or outliers from the social media posts is again a challenging task while applying NLP. (Xia, An, Li, & Zhang, 2020) presented a novel approach to tackle this issue and proposed an outlier knowledge management framework which again depends on the dataset and has limitations on the granularity of the study where is insufficient like the weight of each topic, keyword strength under the given topic, exclusion of news sites and timeliness of it.

Although the above-discussed studies prove a great help in fighting the covid-19 but the proposed approaches cannot be generalized due to limitations in the number of tweets and geographical coverage. Large-scale datasets are desirable to achieve the generalization(Lamsal, 2020). The volume of English tweets in multilingual datasets has a limit to fetch 450 requests/15 minutes per app(Lamsal, 2020) (Qazi, Imran, & Ofli, 2020). Various research groups, government agencies, and other sources are releasing the data and publication at an unparalleled rate in real-time to understand the disease dynamics but this real-time data have some serious concerns about data validation and preprocessing (Banda et al., 2020).

The lockdown situation has created various challenges for the world and the removal of lockdown, reopening the country in the new normal scenario has created mixed feelings in public. People have different opinions and feelings on early reopening and delayed opening which further needs to be analyzed. Only a few studies have reported on these issues(Ahmed, Rabin, & Chowdhury, 2020; Samuel, Rahman, et al., 2020). However, these studies have limitations in the context of data quality and tools used for SA. But this area has still been relatively unexplored and has a lot more potential to fetch meaningful insights from it. (Iqbal et al., 2021) have presented a comprehensive review on COVID-19 which summarizes how the AI & NLP is helping the tracking, tackling, and finding the effective drug for the treatment of this disease. The technology used in these studies can serve as a support mechanism in decision making but other factors (economy, shortage of livelihood, etc.) should also be included because users can write inaccurate and fake information. NLP-based studies are not limited to analyze the past scenarios only but can help to predict future happenings. People have mixed feelings about the vaccination against covid-19 and keeping in mind that the public uses social media as a primary means of learning and communicating about covid-19 vaccination. Anti-vaccine activities on social media are a big concern for government agencies and need to be analyzed to make further distribution plans.

Table 2 presents recently published research work in the public area, which includes infectious diseases, epidemics, and pandemics. It only presents very prominent and recent ones that leveraged data-driven methods to improve the study outcomes.

Mental Health

Mental disorders are highly prevalent, but only a small proportion of individuals in need receive treatment. But the advent of the internet and its easy availability for consumers have seemed to one of the solutions to the challenges faced in the field of mental health care. Internet-based involvements can be made at a nominal cost among large populations where these can be easily used with flexibility. Internet-based treatments in the field of mood disorders, anxiety syndromes, and other conditions have found promising outcomes (Andrews, Cuijpers, Craske, Mcevoy, & Titov, 2010)(Carlbring, Andersson, Cuijpers, & Riper, 2018). During the last two decades, Internet-delivered Cognitive Behavior Therapy (ICBT) has been tested in hundreds of randomized controlled trials, often with promising results (Mata et al., 2018). Since most of the attempts have been proctored, the relative efficacy of ICBT as compared to face-to-face cognitive behavior therapy (CBT) needs to be studied. Even though within the healthcare

Table 2. Recent publications in the area of public health augmented by data-driven algorithms

Authors	Proposed approach	Publication Year	AI based Approaches	Algorithms used (see appendix *Table 5*)
Alamoodi et al.	A systematic review	2020	Classical Machine Learning & Deep Learning based	Review Paper
Choi et al.	Topic modelling on disease-media interactions	2017	Classical Machine Learning based	LDA
Jain & Kumar	Latent Dirichlet allocation (LDA) based topic modelling techniques	2018	Classical Machine Learning based	LDA, NB and SVM
Edo-Osagie et al.	Review Paper	2020	Classical Machine Learning & Deep Learning based	Review Paper
Amin et al.	Deep Learning and word embedding based automated approach	2020	Classical Machine Learning & Deep Learning based	LR, NB, SVM, ANN, DNN, LSTM
Baker et al.	A novel ML approach to detect influenza from arebic tweets	2020	Classical Machine Learning based	NB, SVM, DT, and k-NN
Tayarani-N.	A Literature Review	2020	Classical Machine Learning & Deep Learning based	Review Paper
Xue, Chen, Hu, et al.	An unsupervised approach to sentiments in covid-19 pandemics	2020	Classical Machine Learning based	LDA
Samuel, Ali, et al.	Effectiveness of baseline methods in varying length covid-19 tweet classification	2020	Classical Machine Learning based	NB, LR
Xue, Chen, Chen, et al.	Topic modelling	2020	Classical Machine Learning based	LDA
Mackey et al.	An unsupervised approach for topic modelling	2020	Classical Machine Learning based	BTM
Jelodar et al.	SA using Deep learning approach	2020	Deep Learning based	LSTM
Xia et al.	BERT + LDA hybrid approach	2020	Classical Machine Learning & Deep Learning based	BERT-NN, LDA
Samuel, Rahman, et al.	Sentiment polarity based public sentiment scenarios (PSS) framework	2020	Rule Based & Classical Machine Learning based	Syuzhet and Sentiment pakage of R
Lamsal	Deep Learning based large scale spatio-temporal SA	2020	Classical Machine Learning & Deep Learning based	LSTM
Al-Zaman	Quantitative content analysis of social media data	2020	Quantitative content analysis, deductive coding	Traditional methods
Qazi et al.	A gazetteer-based approach to infer the geolocation of tweets	2020	Classical Machine Learning & Deep Learning based	CNN
Banda et al.	Large scale Covid-19 dataset creation by aggregating multiple datasets used in researches	2020	Classical Machine Learning & Deep Learning based	Social Media Mining Toolkit
Ahmed et al.,	Sentiment and emotion analysis using IBM tone analyzer service	2020	Classical Machine Learning	NB, SVM

domain, psychological cases have seen early adoption of data-driven technology, several studies that are conducted at scale are lacking.

Another instance of controlled setup is by the analysis of email communication that happens between a domain expert which can be a doctor, a specialist, psychologist with the patient – one who receives the treatment. (Hoogendoorn, Berger, Schulz, Stolz, & Szolovits, 2017) proposed a model for analyzing and predicting the outcome of social media anxiety treatment from a doctor-patient email conversation.

In the mental health domain, predicting the therapeutic outcome is critical for clinicians to deliver the most appropriate care to a patient. Another research as in (Mata et al., 2018) was done for social anxiety disorder patients. Analysis was done on the words used, the topics in the underlying conversation, the sentiment conveyed in the messages, and the writing style. Additionally, trends over time with respect to those measures were also analyzed. The data set size was small that may limit the generalization of the results but applications of ML algorithms were able to predict the therapy outcomes with decent accuracy.

Table 3. Recent publications in the area of mental health augmented by data-driven algorithms

Authors	Proposed approach	Publication Year	AI based Approaches	Algorithms used (see appendix *Table 5*)
Lin et al.	A novel hybrid model-afactor graph model combined with CNN	2017	Classical Machine Learning based	RF, SVM, LR, GBDT, DNN, CNN hybrids
Hoogendoorn et al.	Predictive modelling using writings of patients under treatment for social anxiety disorder	2017	Classical Machine Learning based	CART, LR,RF, LDA
Wang, Brede, Ianni, & Mentzakis	ML based eating disorder SA	2017	Classical Machine Learning based	NB, SVM, RBF, k-NN
Cheng, Li, Kwok, Zhu, & Yip	Classifier based suicide probability and emotional distress Analysis	2017	Classical Machine Learning based	SVM
Yadav, Ekbal, Saha, & Bhattacharyya	Classification framework for SA of medication and medical condition	2019	Classical Machine Learning based	CNN, SVM, RF, MLP
Ru et al.	Comparative Approach	2019	Deep Learning based	CNN, CNN hybrids, LSTM, LSTM hybrids
Carlbring et al.	Systematic review and meta-analysis	2018	Classical Machine Learning & Deep Learning based	Review Paper
Andrews et al.	Meta Analysis approach	2010	Traditional methods	----------

Social media interactions can be one of the avenues to take the trials from proctored to the uncontrolled and at-scale environment. Recent researches in mental health have started taking steps towards this direction with the motive to be quick at the discovery of early signs of any disorder. The user's stress level was closely linked to that of his or her social media peers, according to observations derived from knowledge posted on social networks. The research employed a large-scale dataset from real-world social platforms to systematically study the correlation of user's stress states and social interactions (Lin et al., 2017).

Nowadays patients are writing their medical conditions and feelings on medical forums. These narrations can be about a medical condition or about medication's effects. A benchmark setup has been proposed in (Yadav et al., 2019) for analyzing the sentiments of user narrations of some popular domains such as depression, anxiety, asthma, and allergy. The setup has used state-of-the-art AI-based techniques for two different types of classifications i.e. medical Problem (exist, recover, deteriorate) and medication(Effective, Ineffective, Serious adverse effects).

Table 3 presents research publication done in the mental health and wellness area. The mental health area is still unexplored by data-driven algorithms; hence it only presents very prominent and recent ones. Similar attempts are being made for quite some time now with still miles to be covered before it can be adopted in real life.

Patient Care and Tracking

Monitoring patient care and public health care deals with the detection of healthcare & patient-related problems experienced by the patients themselves. This takes the opinions into a new perspective for providing the best treatments, resource availability, and making the new policies. Due to advancements in Smartphone technologies several patient care health applications have been developed. A mobile-based health monitoring architecture has been proposed for monitoring the suggestion of obesity management using sensory and social media data(Harous, El Menshawy, Serhani, & Benharref, 2018). This architecture captures the sensory data and by analyzing this data with tweeter sentiments it generates suggestions, warnings, and recommendations.

Another cross-domain framework proposed for developing a mobile application for healthcare tracking analyses patient's sentiments from various social media platforms to generate exercise diet plans(Mata et al., 2018). These nutrition plans get re-adjusted and upgraded using an AI-based classifier which classifieds user emotions like joy, sadness, or anger from generated social media feature set. Social media interactions are used to analyze patient treatment experiences of diseases like cancer and diabetes. A SA analysis of Twitter data of chemotherapy treatment has been proposed(Zhang, Hall, & Bastola, 2018). In this study, various health apps comments on the Twitter data have been taken for SA. The study shows the positive polarity on patient's sentiments about fitness, diabetes, obesity, and medication apps(Pai & Alathur, 2018). Further, this sentiment score used by a differential equation for the study of dependent/independent variables, and a causal loop diagram (CLD) developed to measure the factors that influence Health.

Table 4. List of published work with applied algorithms in the Public Patient Care/Tracking area

Authors	Proposed Approach	Publication Year	AI based Approaches	Algorithms used (see appendix *Table 5*)
Harous et al.	MA4OCMP architecture	2018	Classical Machine Learning based	NLTK (Natural language Toolkit), MATLAB
Mata et al.	Patient-based approach through cross semantic information	2018	Classical Machine Learning based	NB
Zhang et al.	Deep learning with GloVe word embedding framework	2018	Deep Learning based	LSTM
Pai & Alathur	CLD based Technology Adoption model	2018	Classical Machine Learning based	Rstudio NLP package, CLD
Lenzi, Maranghi, Stilo, & Velardi	Generative Statistical models based SA	2019	Classical Machine Learning based	NMF, LDA, LSA, PCA, FA, fastICA
Ojo & Rizun	A novel Conceptual Framework for identifying the degree of criticality of a negative healthcare event	2019	Traditional methods	Computational methods

Lenzi (Lenzi et al., 2019) proposed automated textual analysis of diabetic patient's views written on social media. This approach has used state-of-art topic modeling methods based on improved word embedded generative statistical models. Patient feedback is the key to enhance healthcare treatments and services. The negative service experience-based SA has been presented to the deep linguistic analyzer of the patient's experiences at different stages of services(Ojo & Rizun, 2019). A statistical technique has been used for processing of negative sentiments and then applied thematic & conceptual framework techniques with free-text questionnaires responses and in last linguistic & NLP approaches used to monitor patients perceptions. *Table 4* presents few research publication work done in the area of patient care and tracking. It only presents very prominent and recent ones. Similar attempts are being made for quite some time now with still miles to be covered before it can be adopted in real life.

CHALLENGES AND OPPORTUNITIES

In the previous section, we have discussed the potential areas where social media can be pivotal at achieving better and faster results. Depending on the field in the discussion, the nature of interaction will change and this poses a big challenge. Within healthcare, a conversation or expression for adverse drug reaction, side effects will be a lot different from the expression that can signal anxiety or mental disorder. Similarly, public health messages will be different from patient tracking or any other sub-field. Even within the subfield interactions over the internet will be very different though they will tend to have more commonality too. For instance, feedback for respiratory medication will be different from muscular or diabetic medication. Thus, from the domain per se, the challenges look to be overwhelming.

These challenges only get better with the number of the way an emotion or thought that can be expressed by humans. NLP the subfield of AI dealing with human languages has matured fast. Still, domain knowledge plays an important role in improving the results. AI and NLP-driven methods can be the way forward as it will be able to deal with another very important challenge – the unprecedented pace of data generation. The sheer amount of data makes use of technology-driven solutions to be more realistic.

From technology standpoints, NLP-based approaches can be divided into three: Rule-based, Classical Machine Learning based and Deep Learning based.

Rule-based: Rule-based approaches are the oldest. Rules applied to text can reveal multiple insights. Regular expressions and context-free grammar are examples of these approaches. These approaches tend to focus on text parsing and pattern matching, and often provide low precision and high recall implying that they can give high performance on specific use cases.

Classical Machine Learning: Traditional machine learning based approaches include probabilistic modeling, likelihood maximization, and other shallow methods. These methods involve feature engineering as a separate step. The domain expert can bring in his experience in form of feature engineering and semantic rules.

Deep Learning based: These are based on deep neural networks and can be said to be the current state of the art. The recent breakthroughs in the field of NLP can be attributed to approaches based on this class. Language models get trained on very big generic corpus like Wikipedia and then these get augmented with the domain-specific vocabulary. The biggest challenge with this class of methods is that they are very resource-heavy – compute data and memory. Another challenge is to imbibe the rules that the domain person would want the models to use. Often methods from this class skip the step of feature engineering, they act more like a black box where such augmentation can be done but they are not that straightforward.

Already few researches have been done where comparisons of multiple algorithms from all the three NLP classes are made. Studies like (Wang et al., 2017) apply both classical algorithms and complex deep learning algorithms have been applied for the characterization of mental health conditions from social media. Another instance applies an informed deep neural network-based approach on Reddit posts. More often than not deep learning-based approaches stands out but their application requires fine-tuning on the data and features before they start providing good results. Often accuracies are quoted in excess of 90% on the prediction of whatever problem formulation they discuss about. These studies are not limited to the English language. AI-based methods are also getting applied to other languages like Arabic, Chinese and reported results are not very dissimilar giving an overall indication that such methods can be the answer.

SOLUTIONS AND RECOMMENDATIONS

Studies that have tried to use NLP-based methods have been presented in the table. Few notable ones with reasonable success have often worked on in more traditional ways (Lin et al., 2017) by defining a set of stress-related textual, visual, and social attributes from various aspects, and then apply data-based models to provide insights or categorization based on the problem statement. The general conclusion that can be extracted is the importance of domain adaptation when dealing with health records. It is difficult to find a study that advocates against the need for domain-specific knowledge inclusion.

In light of the above discussions and findings from the previous works, a generic framework for the marriage of healthcare and AI methods can be laid out as in *Figure* 2.

Figure 2. Generic framework for sentiment analysis on healthcare data

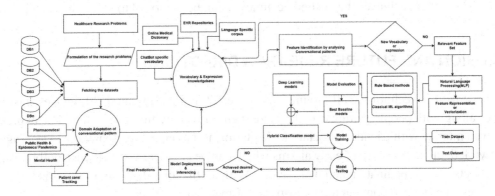

Step 1: Formulate the problem statement.

Step 2: Domain adaptation of the conversational patterns

Step 3: Creation and regular updates of domain-specific vocabulary and expressions

Step 4: Feature identification based on the conversational patterns.

Step 5: Feature reinforced NLP-based methods to decipher the emotions and underlying messages.

Step 6: Compare more than one method. Classical and rule-based methods can form as a baseline.

Step 7: Train the model and test on the generalized scenario.

Step 8: Repeat until the desired level of results are obtained.

The proposed framework has presented the complete process of approaching and applying any NLP-based solution to healthcare problem. It starts with the problem formulation which helps to build the clarity of the research problem and narrow down the research area. These steps include specifying the objective, reviewing the current research status, exploring variables and its relationship, and studying alternative approaches.

After the research formulation, the next step is to gather and fetch the relevant datasets which eventually needs to be integrated into a pipeline that can be served for downstream processing. Moreover, to tackle any NLP based problem, one need to include the conversational patterns of the applied domain. These patterns can be related with pharmaceutical, public health and epidemics, mental health, patient care, and etc. This pattern will alone not solve the problem until vocabulary and expression will be included into the knowledgebase. These can be brought directly from the existing sources like EHR repositories, online medical dictionaries, language specific corpus, etc. or can be updated manually/ programmatically.

The next and very important step of preprocessing is the identification of new features from the conversational patterns and having a feedback loop to keep the vocabulary and expression knowledgebase updated and relevant. These features reinforce the NLP based methods to decipher the emotions and underlying messages.

The next phase in the proposed framework is model building and this start with the establishment of baseline model which further can be improved by iterating and refining various steps performed earlier. Often multiple approaches are applied together viz. creating ensemble, hybrid models which function by completing each other.

Finally good generalization is what is aimed by any AI based system. Thus, training several models with different features and test on generalized scenario will be an iterative process that may require several cycles. Once the model achieves the desired accuracy it can be deployed to make the final predictions.

CONCLUSION AND FUTURE RESEARCH DIRECTIONS

With advancement in technology all around viz. powerful and cheap handheld devices, fast internet availability along with people getting used to share their daily activities, share thoughts, express opinions and even interact with friends on social media platforms, has enabled researchers to leverage online social network data for detection of early alarms which can be stress, anxiety, disease outbreaks, effects and side-effects of any medication and many more. With all the ingredients in place, this field is at the breakout level where it can come in the mainstream of medical practices.

From technical onset – work done in this area can broadly be categorized as Feature-based ML techniques and Deep Learning methods. Both approaches are being used by the researchers. Controlled group experiments have resulted in promising results which are echoed across this field. Challenge lies in moving proctored experimentation to large-scale and generic adaptation.

Breakthroughs in the field of NLP have made the generic implementation possible to almost any field once they get reinforced with the domain-specific knowledge. Thus, the current biggest challenge in any such usage stands at the crossroads of domain experts and technical experts. A more adaptable and generic framework at least for each subfield can be the first step in our way forward.

REFERENCES

Ahmed, M. E., Rabin, M. R. I., & Chowdhury, F. N. (2020). *COVID-19: Social Media Sentiment Analysis on Reopening*. ArXiv.

Al-Zaman, M. S. (2020). COVID-19-related fake news in social media. MedRxiv, 1–12. doi:10.1101/2020.07.06.20147066

Alamoodi, A. H., Zaidan, B. B., Zaidan, A. A., Albahri, O. S., Mohammed, K. I., Malik, R. Q., ... Alaa, M. (2020). Sentiment analysis and its applications in fighting COVID-19 and infectious diseases: A systematic review. *Expert Systems with Applications, 114155*. Advance online publication. doi:10.1016/j.eswa.2020.114155 PMID:33139966

Alvaro, N., Conway, M., Doan, S., Lofi, C., Overington, J., & Collier, N. (2015). Crowdsourcing Twitter annotations to identify first-hand experiences of prescription drug use. *Journal of Biomedical Informatics, 58*, 280–287. doi:10.1016/j.jbi.2015.11.004 PMID:26556646

Amin, S., Uddin, M. I., Zeb, M. A., Alarood, A. A., Mahmoud, M., & Alkinani, M. H. (2020). Detecting Dengue/Flu Infections Based on Tweets Using LSTM and Word Embedding. *IEEE Access: Practical Innovations, Open Solutions, 8*, 189054–189068. doi:10.1109/ACCESS.2020.3031174

Andrews, G., Cuijpers, P., Craske, M. G., Mcevoy, P., & Titov, N. (2010). Computer Therapy for the Anxiety and Depressive Disorders Is Effective, Acceptable and Practical Health Care : A Meta-Analysis. *PLoS One, 5*(10), e13196. Advance online publication. doi:10.1371/journal.pone.0013196 PMID:20967242

Baker, Q. B., Shatnawi, F., Rawashdeh, S., Al-Smadi, M., & Jararweh, Y. (2020). Detecting epidemic diseases using sentiment analysis of arabic tweets. *Journal of Universal Computer Science, 26*(1), 50–70.

BandaJ. M.TekumallaR.WangG.YuJ.LiuT.DingY.ChowellG. (2020). A large-scale COVID-19 twitter chatter dataset for open scientific research - An international collaboration. *ArXiv*. doi:10.5281/zenodo.3766929

Basiri, M. E., Abdar, M., Cifci, M. A., Nemati, S., & Acharya, U. R. (2020). A novel method for sentiment classification of drug reviews using fusion of deep and machine learning techniques. *Knowledge-Based Systems, 198*, 105949. doi:10.1016/j.knosys.2020.105949

Carlbring, P., Andersson, G., Cuijpers, P., Riper, H., & Hedman-Lagerlöf, E. (2018). Internet-based vs. face-to-face cognitive behavior therapy for psychiatric and somatic disorders : An updated systematic review and meta-analysis. *Cognitive Behaviour Therapy, 6073*(1), 1–21. doi:10.1080/16506073.2017.1401115 PMID:29215315

Casillas, A., Pérez, A., Oronoz, M., Gojenola, K., & Santiso, S. (2016). Learning to extract adverse drug reaction events from electronic health records in Spanish. *Expert Systems with Applications, 61*, 235–245. doi:10.1016/j.eswa.2016.05.034

Cheng, Q., Li, T. M., Kwok, C. L., Zhu, T., & Yip, P. S. (2017). Assessing suicide risk and emotional distress in Chinese social media: A text mining and machine learning study. *Journal of Medical Internet Research*, *19*(7), 1–10. doi:10.2196/jmir.7276 PMID:28694239

Choi, S., Lee, J., Kang, M. G., Min, H., Chang, Y. S., & Yoon, S. (2017). Large-scale machine learning of media outlets for understanding public reactions to nation-wide viral infection outbreaks. *Methods (San Diego, Calif.)*, *129*, 50–59. doi:10.1016/j.ymeth.2017.07.027 PMID:28813689

Davazdahemami, B., & Delen, D. (2019). The confounding role of common diabetes medications in developing acute renal failure: A data mining approach with emphasis on drug-drug interactions. *Expert Systems with Applications*, *123*, 168–177. doi:10.1016/j.eswa.2019.01.006

Edo-Osagie, O., De La Iglesia, B., Lake, I., & Edeghere, O. (2020). A scoping review of the use of Twitter for public health research. *Computers in Biology and Medicine*, *122*(May), 103770. doi:10.1016/j.compbiomed.2020.103770 PMID:32502758

Gopalakrishnan, V., & Ramaswamy, C. (2017). Patient opinion mining to analyze drugs satisfaction using supervised learning. *Journal of Applied Research and Technology*, *15*(4), 311–319. doi:10.1016/j.jart.2017.02.005

Harous, S., El Menshawy, M., Serhani, M. A., & Benharref, A. (2018). Mobile health architecture for obesity management using sensory and social data. *Informatics in Medicine Unlocked*, *10*(December), 27–44. doi:10.1016/j.imu.2017.12.005

Hiremath, B. N., & Patil, M. M. (2020). Enhancing Optimized Personalized Therapy in Clinical Decision Support System using Natural Language Processing. *Journal of King Saud University - Computer and Information Sciences*. doi:10.1016/j.jksuci.2020.03.006

Hoogendoorn, M., Berger, T., Schulz, A., Stolz, T., & Szolovits, P. (2017). Predicting Social Anxiety Treatment Outcome Based on Therapeutic Email Conversations. *IEEE Journal of Biomedical and Health Informatics*, *21*(5), 1449–1459. doi:10.1109/JBHI.2016.2601123 PMID:27542187

Iqbal, S., Ahmad, S., Bano, B., Akkour, K., Alghamdi, M. A. A., & Alothri, A. M. (2021). A Systematic Review: Role of Artificial Intelligence During the COVID-19 Pandemic in the Healthcare System. *International Journal of Intelligent Information Technologies*, 17.

Jain, V. K., & Kumar, S. (2018). Effective surveillance and predictive mapping of mosquito-borne diseases using social media. *Journal of Computational Science*, *25*, 406–415. doi:10.1016/j.jocs.2017.07.003

Jelodar, H., Wang, Y., Orji, R., & Huang, H. (2020). Deep sentiment classification and topic discovery on novel coronavirus or COVID-19 online discussions: NLP using LSTM recurrent neural network approach. *IEEE Journal of Biomedical and Health Informatics*, *24*(10), 2733–2742. doi:10.1109/JBHI.2020.3001216 PMID:32750931

Jiménez-Zafra, S. M., Martín-Valdivia, M. T., Molina-González, M. D., & Ureña-López, L. A. (2019). How do we talk about doctors and drugs? Sentiment analysis in forums expressing opinions for medical domain. *Artificial Intelligence in Medicine*, *93*, 50–57. doi:10.1016/j.artmed.2018.03.007 PMID:29685725

John, B., Baulch, B., & Wickramasinghe, N. (2020). A Sentiment Analysis of the 2014-15 Ebola Outbreak in the Media and Social Media. In Handbook of Research on Optimizing Healthcare Management Techniques (p. 11). Academic Press.

Korkontzelos, I., Nikfarjam, A., Shardlow, M., Sarker, A., Ananiadou, S., & Gonzalez, G. H. (2016). Analysis of the effect of sentiment analysis on extracting adverse drug reactions from tweets and forum posts. *Journal of Biomedical Informatics*, *62*, 148–158. doi:10.1016/j.jbi.2016.06.007 PMID:27363901

Lamsal, R. (2020). Design and analysis of a large-scale COVID-19 tweets dataset. *Applied Intelligence*, (October). Advance online publication. doi:10.100710489-020-02029-z

Lenzi, A., Maranghi, M., Stilo, G., & Velardi, P. (2019). The social phenotype: Extracting a patient-centered perspective of diabetes from health-related blogs. *Artificial Intelligence in Medicine*, *101*(September), 101727. doi:10.1016/j.artmed.2019.101727 PMID:31813490

Lin, H., Jia, J., Qiu, J., Zhang, Y., Shen, G., Xie, L., Tang, J., Feng, L., & Chua, T. S. (2017). Detecting stress based on social interactions in social networks. *IEEE Transactions on Knowledge and Data Engineering*, *29*(9), 1820–1833. doi:10.1109/TKDE.2017.2686382

Liu, S., & Lee, I. (2019). Extracting features with medical sentiment lexicon and position encoding for drug reviews. *Health Information Science and Systems*, *7*(1), 11. Advance online publication. doi:10.100713755-019-0072-6 PMID:31168364

Mackey, T., Purushothaman, V., Li, J., Shah, N., Nali, M., Bardier, C., Liang, B., Cai, M., & Cuomo, R. (2020). Machine Learning to Detect Self-Reporting of Symptoms, Testing Access, and Recovery Associated With COVID-19 on Twitter: Retrospective Big Data Infoveillance Study. *JMIR Public Health and Surveillance*, *6*(2), e19509. doi:10.2196/19509 PMID:32490846

Mata, F., Torres-Ruiz, M., Zagal, R., Guzman, G., Moreno-Ibarra, M., & Quintero, R. (2018). A cross-domain framework for designing healthcare mobile applications mining social networks to generate recommendations of training and nutrition planning. *Telematics and Informatics*, *35*(4), 837–853. doi:10.1016/j.tele.2017.04.005

Moh, M., Moh, T. S., Peng, Y., & Wu, L. (2017). On adverse drug event extractions using twitter sentiment analysis. *Network Modeling and Analysis in Health Informatics and Bioinformatics*, *6*(1), 1–12. doi:10.100713721-017-0159-4

Ojo, A., & Rizun, N. (2019). Enabling deeper linguistic-based text analytics - Construct development for the criticality of negative service experience. *IEEE Access: Practical Innovations, Open Solutions*, *7*, 169217–169256. doi:10.1109/ACCESS.2019.2947593

Padmavathy, P., & Pakkir Mohideen, S. (2020). An efficient two-pass classifier system for patient opinion mining to analyze drugs satisfaction. *Biomedical Signal Processing and Control*, *57*, 101755. doi:10.1016/j.bspc.2019.101755

Pai, R. R., & Alathur, S. (2018). Assessing mobile health applications with twitter analytics. *International Journal of Medical Informatics*, *113*, 72–84. doi:10.1016/j.ijmedinf.2018.02.016 PMID:29602436

Qazi, U., Imran, M., & Ofli, F. (2020). GeoCoV19: A Dataset of Hundreds of Millions of Multilingual COVID-19 Tweets with Location Information. *ArXiv*, 1–3.

Rodrigues, U. M., & Xu, J. (2020). Regulation of COVID-19 fake news infodemic in China and India. *Media International Australia*, *177*(1), 125–131. doi:10.1177/1329878X20948202

Ru, B., Li, D., Hu, Y., & Yao, L. (2019). Serendipity - A Machine-Learning Application for Mining Serendipitous Drug Usage from Social Media. *IEEE Transactions on Nanobioscience*, *18*(3), 324–334. doi:10.1109/TNB.2019.2909094 PMID:30951476

Samuel, J., Ali, G. G. M. N., Rahman, M. M., Esawi, E., & Samuel, Y. (2020). COVID-19 public sentiment insights and machine learning for tweets classification. *Information (Switzerland)*, *11*(6), 1–23. doi:10.3390/info11060314

Samuel, J., Rahman, M. M., Ali, G. G. M. N., Samuel, Y., Pelaez, A., Chong, P. H. J., & Yakubov, M. (2020). Feeling Positive about Reopening? New Normal Scenarios from COVID-19 US Reopen Sentiment Analytics. *IEEE Access: Practical Innovations, Open Solutions*, *8*, 142173–142190. doi:10.1109/ACCESS.2020.3013933

Tayarani-N., M.-H. (2020). Applications of Artificial Intelligence in Battling Against Covid-19: A Literature Review. *Chaos, Solitons, and Fractals*, *110338*. Advance online publication. doi:10.1016/j.chaos.2020.110338 PMID:33041533

Wang, T., Brede, M., Ianni, A., & Mentzakis, E. (2017). Detecting and characterizing eating-disorder communities on social media. *WSDM 2017 - Proceedings of the 10th ACM International Conference on Web Search and Data Mining*, 91–100. 10.1145/3018661.3018706

Xia, H., An, W., Li, J., & Zhang, Z. (2020). Outlier knowledge management for extreme public health events: Understanding public opinions about COVID-19 based on microblog data. *Socio-Economic Planning Sciences*, *100941*(July), 100941. doi:10.1016/j.seps.2020.100941 PMID:32921839

Xue, J., Chen, J., Chen, C., Zheng, C., Li, S., & Zhu, T. (2020). Public discourse and sentiment during the COVID 19 pandemic: Using latent dirichlet allocation for topic modeling on twitter. *PLoS ONE*, *15*(9), 1–23. doi:10.1371/journal.pone.0239441

Xue, J., Chen, J., Hu, R., Chen, C., Zheng, C., Liu, X., & Zhu, T. (2020). Twitter discussions and emotions about COVID-19 pandemic: a machine learning approach. *ArXivLabs*. Retrieved from http://library1.nida.ac.th/termpaper6/sd/2554/19755.pdf

Yadav, S., Ekbal, A., Saha, S., & Bhattacharyya, P. (2019). Medical sentiment analysis using social media: Towards building a patient assisted system. *LREC 2018 - 11th International Conference on Language Resources and Evaluation*, 2790–2797.

Zhang, L., Hall, M., & Bastola, D. (2018). Utilizing Twitter data for analysis of chemotherapy. *International Journal of Medical Informatics*, *120*, 92–100. doi:10.1016/j.ijmedinf.2018.10.002 PMID:30409350

APPENDIX

Table 5. List of abbreviations used in the chapter

Abbreviations	Meaning
ANN	Artificial Neural Network
MLP	Multilayer Perceptron
BPNN	Back-propagation Neural Network
RBF	Radial Basis Function
SVM	Support Vector Machine
GLM	Generalized Linear Model
NB	Naïve Bayes
DT	Decision Tree
RF	Random Forest
RFC	Random Forest Classification
GBDT	Gradient Boosted Decision Tree
CART	Classification And Regression Tree
kNN	K-Nearest Neighbour
LDA	Latent Dirichlet allocation
BTM	Biterm topic model
LR	Logistic Regression
PCA	Principal Components Analysis
LSA	Latent semantic analysis
FastICA	Fast Independent Component Analysis
CLD	Causal Loop Diagram
CNN	Convolutional Neural Network
DNN	Deep Neural Network
LSTM	Long short-term memory
FCN	Fully Convolutional Network
NFM	Non-negative matrix factorization
FA	Finite Automata algorithm
NLTK	Natural language Toolkit
BERT	Bidirectional Encoder Representations
GRU	Gated recurrent units

Chapter 5
Testing the SmartMunk's Story.ly App for the Analysis of Online Customer Reviews on Face Masks

Arabela Briciu
iD https://orcid.org/0000-0002-7506-8099
Transilvania University of Brasov, Romania

Cristian-Laurențiu Roman
Transilvania University of Brasov, Romania

Victor-Alexandru Briciu
iD https://orcid.org/0000-0003-1202-5830
Transilvania University of Brasov, Romania

ABSTRACT

This chapter aims to present the process of selecting and analyzing a number of reviews using a software solution (an online application) created specifically for text analysis and extracting user sentiment. This software measures the level of user satisfaction, analyzing product reviews and taking into account the qualitative part of the content generated by users. Analyzing online customer reviews with the help of specialized software can help both companies and other users. The software can also help us reach a conclusion regarding the analysis of reviews and customer feedback on products or services. This study can also be useful for customers or buyers who want to know the opinion of others about a product, having the opportunity to differentiate between positive and negative reviews.

DOI: 10.4018/978-1-7998-8061-5.ch005

INTRODUCTION

Analyzing online customer reviews with the help of specialized software can help both companies and other users. The software can also help us reach a conclusion regarding the analysis of reviews and customer feedback on products or services.

The biggest benefits of this study are aimed at organizations, which can adapt their products, services or promotion according to the wishes of their customers, as well as the level of customer satisfaction, because they can find out their customers' opinions of what they offer with the help of online customer reviews analysis. A software solution for the analysis of online customer reviews can provide reports very quickly after extracting information from reviews, forums or interviews. This study can also be useful for customers who want to know the opinion of others on a product, having the opportunity to differentiate between positive and negative reviews. Given that customer behaviors and reactions to product design and marketing are essential for manufacturers (Wang, Lu & Tan, 2018), such a program can help the research about how product qualities can affect consumer satisfaction (Wang et al., 2018).

The main objectives of this chapter are suggested by the online reviews, putting the focus on the importance of the reviews in the user purchase decision, which are the most important elements of a review and what users take into account when writing a review. Also, in the study provided, the interest is to reveal if there are differences between the online shops (e.g. Amazon and Walmart), in terms of reviews and the attitude towards the stores.

This paper will present the process of selecting and analyzing a number of reviews, using a software solution (an online application) created specifically for text analysis and extracting users' sentiments. This software measures the level of user satisfaction, analyzing product reviews and taking into account the qualitative part of the content generated by users. The broader concept of "User Generated Content" has the ability to identify as many customer needs as possible, unlike the use of direct interviews, being a faster research solution, with lower costs (Timoshenko & Hauser, 2018). Therefore, this type of content has spread a lot due to this great advantage, whether we are talking about online reviews, social media or blogs (Timoshenko & Hauser, 2018), and they must be carefully analyzed because they can play an important role in the purchase decision.

Under these specific conditions, companies are taking into account more and more user reviews, and a growing number of them choose customer satisfaction as the main performance indicator (Mihelis, Grigoroudis, Siskos, Politis & Malandrakis, 2001).

Story.ly is the name of the software/ application we will use in this paper and this is a solution from the German company SmartMunk, which aggregates qualitative ideas and reduces the complexity of rich data sets by automatically extracting meaning from text - in almost any language (Boje, 2018). SmartMunk GmbH was created in 2012 by Andera Gadeib and Volker Gadeib, starting from the idea of offering online software to improve customer relations, and the startup business specialized in the development of smart software as a Service solution for co-creation and text analysis (SmartMunk, 2020). The tools they provide want to show companies, first and foremost, what is in the customers' minds: "We call this 'Voice-of-the-Customer Intelligence'" (SmartMunk, 2020).

SmartMunk's story.ly program supports marketing, sales and new product development in companies (SmartMunk, 2020), promising a very enjoyable experience due to the fact that any amount of text will be semantically condensed and displayed in concise visual analysis and allows the users to easily read the "story" at a glance (smartmunk.com). In addition to the software being easy to use and the intuitive nature of the interface, the program is compatible with any platform and is available in any language around the world.

Therefore, this chapter aims to track the behavior of buyers towards companies in the online environment, given the communication between the two elements, promotion techniques and reviews, trying to reach a conclusion regarding their importance and influence on the purchase decision.

BACKGROUND. THE RELATIONSHIP BETWEEN ORGANIZATION AND CONSUMERS

Corporate communication is a concept that refers to all the actions of a company through which it communicates, both internally and externally, with employees, partners or customers. Cornelissen (2008) confirms that the future of any company "depends critically on how it is viewed by key stakeholders such as shareholders and investors, customers and consumers, employees and members of the community in which the company resides" (p.18). Thus, companies need to establish a strong connection with all of them to ensure their continuity, because partners, investors, customers and employees are the ones who keep a company alive.

In addition to the communication with customers or employees, we must also take into account the fact that "at its most comprehensive (total corporate communications) it also takes into account the communications effects of management, employee and product behaviour and of word-of mouth and media/competitor commentary (Balmer & Greyser, 2003 cited in Balmer & Greyser, 2006, p. 735). Word-of-mouth plays a very important role, because it is one of the most used ways to disseminate information, without direct involvement from companies, and the public continues to communicate their opinion, be it positive or negative.

The most used form of communication is probably the online one, online corporate communication referring to "online communication by an organization using a computer and a specific Internet resource to employ online actions to attain specific goals. Primary benefits of online communication are the immediacy and flexibility that characterize the online environment" (Plessis, Angelopulo & Plessis, 2012, p. 241). The online environment allows corporations to be highly visible, and this flexibility and ease of use that the authors talked about has made people switch to the Internet, where they can track almost anything related to any company.

A company's reputation can refer to the way it is seen and perceived by the public, whether this public is among the company's customers or not. In the article by Weiss, Anderson and MacInnis (1999) a more explicit definition appears, and we are told that the reputation of companies is "defined as 'an impression of public esteem or high regard judged by others'" (p. 75). The definition refers to the fact that any company must be visible first, so that a very large number of people can have contact with that company, then credibility intervenes, because "individual persons may have perceptions of an organization's reputation for specific things (e.g., its reputation for fairness, quality, and good hiring practices)" (Weiss et al., 1999, p. 75). The authors believe that reputation is built on these two elements: visibility and credibility.

In the article by Carmeli and Tishler (2005), there are many definitions and opinions of other authors on this concept. One of them states that "reputation and an organization's identity arguing that they include everything the organization does regarding four major areas of its activity: first, products/services — what it makes or sells; secondly, environments — where (in which physical place) it makes or sells its products/services; thirdly, information — how it describes and publicizes its activities; and fourthly, behavior — how the members of the organization behave to each other and to non-members" (Olins, 1990 cited in Carmeli & Tishler, 2005, p. 15). The four elements listed by the authors certainly have an important role in building the image of a company, because they are all related to customers' expectations and demands. Another definition in the book "suggests that corporate reputation consists of four interrelated characteristics: credibility, reliability, responsibility and trustworthiness" (Fombrun, 1996 cited in Carmeli & Tishler, 2005, p. 15).

We can also define organizational reputation as "stakeholders' perceptions about an organization's ability to create value relative to competitors" (Rindova, Williamson, Petkova & Sever, 2005, p. 3), stakeholders are parties that have an interest in the company or partners of that company, and their involvement "is a critical aspect for organizations in an environment that is sensitive to power relations, thus they need to value the interactions with diverse stakeholders" (Ji, Li, North & Liu, 2016, p. 3). In principle, they have an important role for companies because "assigning a favorable or unfavorable reputation to an organization has become even more important with the emergence of social media" (Ji et al., 2016, p. 1), so they can help the company succeed as well as they can cause failures, building its image and having the power to influence audiences.

An element that is directly related to the reputation may be the quality of services or products that the customer expects; otherwise the reputation suffers from information transmitted from one person to another, regarding the poor performance of the company. Therefore, it is confirmed that "organizations that customers perceive as having high quality are likely to be mentioned or patronized more frequently leading more customers to choose them in the future" (Rindova et al., 2005, p. 12). At the same time, there is this concept that we discussed earlier, namely word-of-mouth, which can force companies to provide quality services, because even a single customer's negative opinion can spread to many people, especially because "for many consumers, WOM is more influential than information from media, such as newspaper, magazine, and radio advertisements" (Yang & Hong, 2009, p. 383).

It is said that word-of-mouth is much more effective than all of these media channels, it even "strongly influences an individual's product judgment—more so than printed information about extensive, diagnostic attributes of the product—and that a single, favorable WOM communication can make an individual form a favorable attitude toward a company or a product" (Yang & Hong, 2009, p. 383). This concept can change opinions or attitudes, but it can also shape the public's image of a company.

Following the reputation and provided quality, there is also the price demanded by each company, and "favorable reputation can induce buyers to pay a price premium" (Rindova et al., 2005, p. 13), while there is also the idea that any premium product or service costs more, but also offers you more than cheaper ones. Along with them, we can also mention the satisfaction of customers who are happy with these services, but also a close connection between the company and the customer, because "perceived quality is likely to have a positive effect on the prices that customers are willing to pay because it increases their confidence in the quality of an organization's goods" (Rindova et al., 2005, p. 13).

Marketing communication is a concept that refers to all the ways in which a company communicates with the public, including advertisements, announcements or e-mails. Odunlami and Ofoegbu (2011) come with broader definitions, defining the concept "as the promotional tools that favourably communicate information about the organization and its products to target market" (Odunlami & Ofoegbu, 2011, p. 408) or, in another one of their definitions, they state that "marketing communication can also be defined as those promotional tools used in communicating favorably with the targeted market" (Odunlami &

Ofoegbu, 2011, p. 408). Therefore, the role of marketing communication is to keep the public informed about the latest offers, products or services.

From a content point of view, the message can vary in marketing communication, presenting details about the brand, in case of prints for example, or only promoting the brand name or a product, without much detail. Also, the message can focus on "tangible aspects (e.g. physical product attributes) or intangible aspects (e.g. user or usage imagery, brand personality, the company behind the brand, etc.)" (Keller, 2010, p. 828), and all of these can be transmitted in an "infinite number of different ways (e.g. through informational or emotional means; employing fear, music, sex, appeals, special effects, etc.)" (Keller, 2010, p. 828), all of which have a strong impact on the public.

The public's purchase behavior was also studied, and it "may be viewed from three perspectives — the decision making, the experiential and the behavioural influence" (Mowen, 1988 cited in Mihart, 2012, p. 123), the elements that influence the purchase decision being the most important, whether it is about making a decision after watching an advertisement, based on past experiences or advice from a close person, or if the quality-price ratio plays an important role for the buyer. In addition, three levels of the purchase decision were identified, referring to "extensive problem solving, limited problem solving and routinized response behaviour" (Howard, 1977 cited in Mihart, 2012, p. 123).

Pauwels, Ergunu and Yildirim (2013) also propose a model in relation to the functioning of marketing communication and customer purchase behavior. Certainly, marketing efficiency "differs in the extent to which consumers (1) become aware of marketing communication, (2) are open to change their minds and hearts and (3) change their buying patterns accordingly" (Pauwels, Ergunu & Yildirim, 2013, p. 2). Also, these elements also depend on the environment the customer comes from, the country or his attitude towards certain companies.

Odunlami and Ofoegbu (2011) compiled a list of several tools that should not be missing in order to obtain effective marketing communication. Among them, there is the creation of notoriety, because "promotional efforts may be aimed at increasing brand awareness, product features awareness, image awareness etc." (Odunlami & Ofoegbu, 2011, p. 410), and the notoriety brought to a new product or to an existing one can attract the attention of many customers, plus word-of-mouth can help this process. Driving demand is just as important, and a solution in this regard is that "promotion also stimulate primary demand – demand for a product category rather than for a specific brand of product through pioneer promotion" (Odunlami & Ofoegbu, 2011, p. 410), and other elements are encouraging customers to try the product for a certain period of time, beating the competition in terms of promotions, or customer loyalty, the latter having many advantages, especially for the fact that it "can help an organization control its costs because the costs of retaining customers are usually considerably lower than those of acquiring new ones" (Odunlami & Ofoegbu, 2011, p. 410), in this way, the company can spend less in terms of promotion.

One of the most important aspects for any company is to know the needs of its customers or even potential customers, to know exactly what it should offer. Customer relationship management (CRM) can handle these aspects. We can define this concept as "an information industry term for methodologies, software, and usually Internet capabilities that help an enterprise manage customer relationships in an organized way" (Xu, Yen, Lin & Chou, 2002, p. 442). In other words, CRM is a system that collects customer data through the Internet, helping the company to get to know them better. The main goal of this software is that it increases "companies' abilities to understand the customers' current needs, what they have done in the past, and what they plan to do in the future to meet their own objectives" (Xu et al.,

2002, p. 442). Knowing the past actions of potential customers has an important role because purchase decisions are similar, and customers can be approached in various ways for awareness or persuasion.

King and Burgess (2008) defined CRM as "an integration of technologies and business processes that are adopted to satisfy the needs of a customer during any given interaction" (Bose, 2002 cited in King & Burges, 2007). Their definition is not very different from the one we talked about in the beginning, the only difference being that one of them focuses on the needs of companies in relation to customers, and the second one focuses on customer needs and customer satisfaction.

This system appeared, first of all, due to the "globalisation of markets, technological development, the larger number of competitors, and increased customer demands" (Chalmeta, 2005, p. 1015), thus, companies had to renew their methods of communication with the customers, but also their methods of studying the market. Secondly, since the year 2000, technology has evolved a lot, and it has determined people to evolve as well. Likewise, companies "have achieved a high level of maturity in the use of computer applications to improve the efficiency of the firms everyday activities" (Chalmeta, 2005, p. 1015). This is how online stores or official company websites (Briciu, Briciu & Pilipinschi, 2017), through which they promote their products, as well as other websites or social networks were born, the public being more and more present in the online environment, regardless of their age.

Nowadays, the concept can also be found under the name of Social CRM or CRM 2.0, as a more recent version, although not much more evolved than the classic one. Social CRM is stated to be "a philosophy and a business strategy, supported by a technology platform, business rules, processes and social characteristics, designed to engage the customer in a collaborative conversation in order to provide mutually beneficial value in a trusted and transparent business environment. It is the company's programmatic response to the customer's control of the conversation" (Giannakis-Bompolis & Boutsouki, 2014, p. 69). The basic idea remains the same, the company and the client are in contact so that everyone can fulfill their interest.

Data mining is the extraction of knowledge from data and is part of the Customer relationship management sphere, and the idea behind this system is "that data from the past contains information that will be useful in the future" (Berry & Linoff, 2004, p. 6). As we stated earlier, the data collected from the customers' past helps the company to fit them into certain categories, then they will adapt their message or type of promotion depending on the buyers' history, but also according to their needs.

Another advantage of CRM is that "systems, current customer, deal, product and competitor information are all stored in the CRM central database for salesforce retrieval" (Xu et al., 2002, p. 443), which means that all actions regarding the product and its sale are automated, the data collection being done very quickly. Certainly, many elements are needed for the system to reach this information, such as "IVR (interactive voice response), e-mail, Web site messages, fax, image, etc." (Xu et al. 2002, p. 444).

Regarding customer engagement, or in other words, customer involvement, there are several definitions. One of them tells us that this term represents "the customers' behavioral manifestation toward a brand or firm, beyond purchase, resulting from motivational drivers" (Gannakis-Bompolis & Boutsouki, 2014, p. 69), being more like a behavior that is not solely based on a product or a transaction, but on a closer relationship between the company and the customer. Also, customer engagement is motivated by "an eagerness for participation in business processes and highlight the fact that engagement behaviors may be manifested by a wide range of different agents, like current and/or prospective customers, suppliers, the public, legislators, even by employees of the company and can have either positive or negative outcome for the enterprise" (Gannakis-Bompolis & Boutsouki, 2014, p. 69). Therefore, the outcome may or may not bring results to the company, depending on the actions of the employees, but also on customer involvement.

All these concepts discussed in this section of the chapter have a strong connection, depending on each other. Corporate communication and customer relationship management are the basis for a company's communication, whether it is about stakeholders, employees, customers or other publics; this helps companies to keep the stakeholders close or to get out of extreme situations. Word-of-mouth and organizational reputation have also a strong connection to the described subject because the company's actions can affect the latter, as individuals find, use and spread the information very fast.

PROMOTION AND ONLINE STORES

Today, more and more companies have diversified their promotion strategies and methods, the evolution of technology bringing more possibilities than in the past. Consumers can find information about a company or a product much more easily, but this also means that "there are more variables affecting consumers' purchasing decisions due to the amount of information on products that are made available to consumers" (Chong, Li, Ngai, Ch'ng & Lee, 2016, p. 360), and the fact that all buyers can publish their opinion on a product in the online environment through reviews or social networks can affect the image of a brand or can bring a positive contribution. Second, with this freedom on the Internet, companies have more obligations, for their own safety and the safety of their customers, they "are becoming increasingly pressured to secure sales on their products within a shorter time period" (Chong et al., 2016, p. 360).

In the case of promotion techniques, we must mention the elements of the marketing mix, because they "influence consumers' equity perceptions toward brands" (Pappu & Quester, 2008 cited in Buil, de Chernatony & Martinez, 2011, p. 116). These elements are very important because they bring a positive contribution both in terms of the company's image and sales. It is said that a positive and strong brand image is built through elements such as "high advertising spend, high price, high distribution intensity and distribution through retailers with good store image" (Buil et al., 2011, p. 16), the explanation being that the public will trust a company with financial power, that invests in its services and collaborates with serious partners. The most common and used marketing tools are advertising and sales promotion.

Sales promotion is "an action-focused marketing event whose purpose is to have a direct impact on the behavior of the firm's customer" (Blattberg & Briesch, 2012, p. 2) and should not be confused with price reduction, which can be categorized as a promotion method. Among the characteristics of sales promotion, we can enumerate that it is "always combined with some type of communication (e.g., a retailer ad) that the price is reduced and that the time period is limited (price is reduced only up to some point in time)" (Blattberg & Briesch, 2012, p. 2), which can lead to increased sales due to the fact that customers buy more and faster when there is a promotion that takes place over a limited period of time. Also, many theories demonstrate that audiences "respond more strongly to sales promotions than to a price decrease and shows the benefits to managers of understanding why sales promotions are used" (Blattberg & Briesch, 2012, p. 3). Sales promotion can be divided into two categories, namely "monetary promotions (e.g., shelf-price discounts, coupons, rebates and price packs)" (Kwok & Uncles, 2002, p. 2), where customers are rewarded financially, and "non-monetary promotions (e.g., sweepstakes, free gifts and loyalty programs)" (Kwok & Uncles, 2002, p. 2) that reward the customer from a sentimental point of view, aiming to strengthen the company-customer relationship.

Other important promotion methods, but in which companies are not directly involved, are online reviews, that can appear on "several platforms such as blogs, product reviews, wikis and Twitter" (Tirunillai & Tellis, 2012 cited in Chong et al., 2016, p. 362), including on sites that specialize in sales, regardless of the type of products they sell. We can define online reviews as "media content created by users to share information and/or opinions with other users" (Chong et al., 2016, p. 362). The number of reviews for a single product also has an important role, as it has been shown that "online review volume has a quantitatively measurable impact on product sales" (Chong et al., 2016, p. 363). A product with a large number of reviews will always attract attention, and if most of them are positive, the customer will begin to become convinced that it is the right product. Of course, the relevance of each review must be considered, because a "large proportion of reviews tend to have either extremely high numeric ratings or extremely low ones" (Chong et al., 2016, p. 365).

Trade promotions have the role of "generating a price decrease by retailers to consumers or gaining distribution for a new product" (Blattberg & Briesch, 2012, p. 7). The concept is based on the relationship between producers and traders, the former offering certain advantages to traders in order to stimulate them, then the discounts reach customers as well, through producers. The main objectives of commercial promotions are to "gain or maintain distribution, obtain temporary price discount, display product, include product in retailer's advertisements, increase sales, reduce inventory" (Blattberg & Briesch, 2012, p. 8).

Another strategy for attracting customers is to deliver the products for free, because "delivery service offerings have a positive relationship with customers' trust and loyalty" (Chong et al. 2016, p. 362), the purchase decision can even depend solely on this aspect, customers usually comparing the services offered by each company.

Most of the time, sales promotion is "associated with large increases in consumer sales" (Blattberg & Briesch, 2012, p. 17), and the most important thing is to offer quality services or products, not just lower prices than the competition, because the public will also pay attention to these issues. In other words, reviews and price reductions seem to have the biggest impact on buyers, when it comes to online shopping.

With the advent of Web 2.0 (Briciu & Briciu, 2021), all sites have developed a lot and many sites that promote brands and all the products and services they offer have appeared, and people have also adapted to this technology and began to expresses their opinions in the online environment, either through reviews or through social networks, thus using word-of-mouth so that others know as many details about the product before buying it. Very quickly after that, "retailers such as Amazon, traditional consumer magazines (e.g. Car and Driver's caranddriver.com and PC Magazine's pcmag.com and independent consumer community intermediaries (e.g. epinions and consumerreview.com)" (Chen, Fay & Wang, 2011, p. 85) have implemented online reviews and forum pages for consumers to discuss with each other or with the manufacturer.

These reviews can help, to some extent, but online shopping cannot effectively match in-store shopping or the virtual cannot overcome product experience to some extent (Briciu & Briciu, 2020a) because "consumer-purchases are mainly based on the cyberspace appearance such as pictures, images, quality information, and video clips of the product, not on the actual experience (Park & Kim, 2003, p. 16) and, often enough, the reality is different from expectations. Park and Kim (2003) say that online shopping resembles "shopping through a paper catalog because both involve mail delivery of the purchases and in both cases customers cannot touch or smell the items" (Spiller and Lohse, 1997 cited in Park & Kim, 2003, p.16).

McKechnie (1992) talks about buyers' behavior and the stages they have to go through before making a decision. They have to go through "problem recognition; information search; evaluation of alternatives;

purchase decision; and post-purchase behaviour" (McKechnie, 1992, p. 6) before buying a product, plus reviews are the only ones that can help them and there is always uncertainty.

Desires and preferences differ from person to person, as do "interests and attitudes vary with age, and the youngest consumers have the most positive attitude toward innovation" (Bigne, Ruiz & Sanz, 2005, p. 196), and teenagers and young people are more likely to shop online than adults and the elderly because they are familiar with this environment. A study shows that age is not the only factor that can influence buying methods, but also the culture the buyers come from. Under these conditions, "consumers from individualist cultures develop a more innovative profile and are more predisposed to shop via Internet than consumers from cultures which favour collectivism" (Jarvenpaa, Tractinsky, Saarinen & Vitale, 1999 cited in Bigne et al., 2005, p. 196), thus, consumers in North America or Western Europe may see the idea of online shopping differently than consumers in Asia and Eastern Europe.

Another element that is part of consumer behavior is the review, and what motivates consumers, first of all, to post, is "to gain social approval or self-approval by demonstrating their superb purchase decision and through altruistic behavior of sharing their expertise with others" (Chen et al., 2011, p. 86). So, there is a psychological reason behind it, that of confirming that they made a good choice, but also helping others, giving them information about their own experience.

Regarding Word of Mouth, in many cases, it is necessary "that individuals optimally ignore private signals and instead rely entirely on information from the aggregate behavior of others" (Chen et al., 2011), following, in the dialogue with others, the aspects that the potential buyer is interested in, only then will a broader picture of the product be offered and a decision will be formed. The main idea is that it is not always good to follow our senses and sentiments towards a product, but that it is better to be objective, weighing the quality-price ratio and our real need to buy it.

Regarding the purchase decision, it is said that "since in many product categories, women make the purchase decision" (Bigne et al., 2005, p. 197), being also about many home care appliances or other product categories in which women are theoretically more specialized in than men. Very interesting is the fact that "several authors state that women are the main users of direct shopping media" (Bigne et al., 2005, p. 197). Studies show that women buy online more than men, "who usually have mainly utilitarian purchase motivations, valuing personal contact and social relations to a lesser degree" (Bigne et al., 2005, p. 197).

To reduce the risks of future transactions, consumers tend to be active in their relationships with other users, in order to be informed at all times and to make the right choices. In time, "after a few successful transactions, a consumer starts to feel safe with the service provider or supplier" (Park & Kim, 2003, p. 18), then follows the trust gained in a certain company, which "is able to fulfill their needs and wants and eventually, they become committed to the company" (Park & Kim, 2003, p. 18).

Online stores are websites that specialize in selling products, whether we are talking about sites that specialize in certain fields, or sites that offer products from different fields (Briciu, Briciu & Găitan, 2020). Given that these sites offer customers a wide variety of products, we need to understand the public's tendency to shop online, plus that they receive the products at home without having to travel.

To define online stores, we can say that they sell goods and services for which the buyer places an order on the Internet, extranet, electronic data exchange network, e-mail or another online system (Kacen, Hess & Chiang, 2013, p. 2), and the biggest advantage of online shopping is that it takes much less time to place an order via the Internet, unlike traditional stores. Also, since online shopping has become part of our daily lives, many consumers are still afraid of negative experiences (Utz, Kerkhof & van den Bos, 2012, p. 49), and the trust that customers gain is very important for companies and their long-term business. The customers' trust in the company can be influenced by the quality of the products or services it offers, but also by online reviews or Word of Mouth.

E-commerce refers to online commerce, but also to the process by which the product is transferred from the manufacturer to the customer. First of all, customers can only see the product on the site, where they can also read information about it, and here is the big disadvantage of online shopping: the products cannot be seen live, touched or tested before being bought. Most of the time, the product cannot be delivered at all, cannot be delivered on time or a product of a lower quality reaches the destination instead (Utz et al., 2012, p. 49), therefore, there are many risks for buyers and they are forced to choose the right product, as well as a reliable online store (Utz et al., 2012, p. 50).

Trust is what underlies any business, and it represents the expectation that other companies will not take advantage of attracting customers based on a dependency (Gefen, Karahanna & Straub, 2003, p. 308). In our case, the trust of customers in companies that own online stores is very important; during transactions, errors may occur or certain companies may violate regulations, even reaching unfair prices, violations of private information, transmission of inaccurate information, unauthorized transaction tracking and unauthorized use of credit card information, to name a few (Gefen, 2000 cited in Gefen et al., 2003, p. 308), thus, the customer experience is a negative one and the connection with the company in question will be permanently broken.

These days, when everything is digitized, the companies must adapt to the times to achieve success. Web 2.0 brought big changes in the world and the companies are almost non-existent without a website or an online store, because it is easier to enter a site than to move to a physical store and maintain it. That is why it is important to invest in e-commerce and sales promotion to reach costumers more easily and to make a company be known faster.

THE STUDY

Analyzing user reviews with the help of specialized software can help both companies and other users. The results of the paper will present the impact of reviews on customers' purchase decisions, as well as the importance of good communication in organizations, both with employees and customers, to achieve the established goals. The software will also help us reach a conclusion regarding the analysis of reviews and customer feedback on products or services.

This research will present the actual selection and analysis of a number of reviews, with the help of a software that was specifically created for text analysis and the extraction of users' sentiments, namely the online solution called story.ly, developed by the SmartMunk company. Several review analysis software applications are available, such as Revuze, Aspectiva, SmartMunk story.ly, SentiGeek etc., presented comparatively in Table 1 below:

The differences between these software programs are not very big, as they all analyze customer satisfaction, in one way or another. The only significant differences are the architecture of the programs or the way in which they present the reports.

The research was conducted between May 28, 2020 and June 18, 2020, and the hypothesis we started from was: "Reviews can substantially influence the purchase decision because studies show that most users read reviews first before buying." In addition, the fact that reviews generally have ratings or responses demonstrates that users communicate and take each other's views into account. In order to investigate how reviews influence consumers' purchase decisions, we used the document analysis method (in our

Table 1. Characteristics of review analysis software

Review analysis software			
Revuze	**Aspectiva**	**SmartMunk story.ly**	**SentiGeek**
• focuses on products and their quality, with the help of differentiators • follows the attitude and language of people in relation to a certain topic/subject • looks for words like "good", "happy" or "terrible" to identify the sentiments of the audience	• follows the perception of the audience, but also the products' specifications • it looks for as many users who have actually tried a certain product as possible, their opinion being very important because the review has arguments behind it • the generated graph shows the user satisfaction, considering usability, appearance, etc.	• analyzes customer satisfaction based on the quality of the services or product offered by the company • the elements that can cause joy or disappointment among customers are taken into account • also uses material from forums	• takes into account the customer's feedback, as well as his opinion on the brand and product • extracts keywords or even phrases to define the users' sentiments and opinions, expressed in the reports, while also generating their profile

Source: (authors' own research)

case, the documents are the reports obtained from the software, which we analyzed), the purpose being to answer several research questions: What aspects do buyers emphasize in their reviews? What are the elements of a review that can influence the purchase decision? Is the evaluation of a product different depending on the country where you live?

For the analysis and testing of this online app, we chose a relatively promoted and popular product, namely protective face masks. Given the new COVID-19 (SARS-CoV-2) virus that appeared in early 2020 and spread worldwide (Briciu & Briciu, 2020b), these masks, along with protective gloves and disinfectant solutions have become the most sought-after products on the market. Taking into account other methodological decisions regarding the size of the analyzed corpus (Wang, Zhu & Li, 2013; Otto & Wagner, 2004; Raghupathi, Yannou, Farel & Poirson, 2015), we selected 30 reviews that will be analyzed using story.ly app, 15 of these were selected from Walmart and 15 from Amazon. At this stage of the study, the selection of the reviews was based on several criteria, in terms of the number of reviews, grammatically correct reviews which could be analyzed by the software. After that, every review was introduced in the software and passed through each phase for a detailed analysis. Data interpretation from software was also very important to achieve a realistic result.

In order to achieve the research objectives, the authors opted for the use of a descriptive-explanatory research, because "descriptive and explanatory researches are only extreme types of sociological research. There are intermediate forms and both descriptive and explanatory research" (Chelcea, 2004, p. 183). The broader research objectives were to identify the public's attitude towards protective masks (the degree of protection is directly proportional to the price of the masks); establishing the degree of positive and negative reviews; the degree of efficiency of the masks based on the analysis of user reviews; identifying the public's attitude towards Amazon and Walmart.

From Amazon online store, we chose the product "Face Mask (10/1, 5/1, 1/1) Cotton Mask with Elastic Strap Washable Face Mask" (see Figure 1) from *Sevello Clothing*, priced at £6.99 (Think Ink, 2020). The mask is produced in the UK by the previously mentioned company. If we refer to some specifications, it is made of 100% cotton, specifying that the material is premium, being delicate, and the mask is comfortable to wear, in addition it promises good protection against dust, polluted air and viruses. In terms of customers' opinion, the product has 24 reviews, the rating being 3.4 points (stars) out of 5 (at the time of the analysis).

The selected product from Walmart online store is "Washable Cotton Face Mask Reusable Made in the USA", with the price of $15 (reduced to $9.98) (Blended, 2020). The mask is produced in the United States of America, being made of 97% cotton and 3% spandex, with the advantage that it can be washed and used several times, in addition, it promises protection against pollution and harmful particles, but it is specified that without other protective measures, such as gloves or disinfectant, it will not offer full protection against the virus. The product collected 28 reviews (at the time of the analysis), which means 3.6 points (stars) out of 5.

Additionally, to describe the main functions of this online solution, once we enter the story.ly site, we have the opportunity to start a new project by clicking on "Start a new story.ly project", and then we must choose the name of our project, the language in which we want to develop the project and the project number. Next, we need to import the text we want the software to analyze, and in this regard, there are two possibilities: "Copy and paste text" or "Import Excel or CSV file", the first option referring to actually copying text from an internet source, and the second option refers to importing text using Excel, the software being able to analyze multiple texts at the same time.

After completing these initial steps, the program will analyze our text and display six windows, each containing information about the text. The first window is called "Dashboard" (see Appendix, Figure 1) and specifies the percentage of existing words in the text already found in other categories, so it is a framing of the text in a specific topic or subject, making links to other texts; in addition, the number of entered texts is displayed here, as well as the number of words and the number of unique words. The second window is called "Ontology Skyline" (exemplified in Appendix, Figure 2) and displays nine criteria that are taken into account in the text analysis, each keyword being framed in a criterion. The criteria are: brand, product, advertising, emotions, persona, actions, location, functionality and time, each of them being visual or graphical correspondents of the analyzed text. "Ontology Treemap" (reference in Appendix, Figure 3) is the next window, and only the prevailing criteria are presented here, plus the words that are more important. "Network Map" (please refer to Appendix, Figure 4) shows us the relationship between all the keywords of the text, "Content Cloud" (detailed in Appendix, Figure 5) shows the different words used throughout the text, and "Text Cleaning" (presented in Appendix, Figure 6) gives us the ability to categorize the words in the text, using different font sizes and colors.

All of these options help us to reach a conclusion about customer satisfaction, the program having a database that it connects to in order to analyze texts much more easily.

To exemplify the analysis procedure involved in using the story.ly application, we will present one case from Amazon and one from Walmart.

The first review we analyzed was posted on Amazon on June 7, 2020, by "Amazon Costumer", from the UK, who gave the product a rating of 2 stars out of 5, and next to the review is the "Verified Purchase" confirmation, which reinforces the idea that the review is not fake, and the title of the review is "Too thick to wear in hot weather and not made of pure cotton" (Think Ink, 2020). The user wrote the following: "I was disappointed by the product because it was described as made of cotton, which why I ordered it, however it isn't made of cotton, at least not pure cotton. This means that it is thicker than expected. On a very warm day I can't wear it. I can only wear it when the weather is cool. The other issue is that there is no way of telling which way round you are, putting it on as it is symmetrical and identical back to front. This is important because if you take it off to reuse later, you need to know which way round you took it off to avoid putting it on wrong side down (I don't want to put the side that was previously in contact with the air and presumably therefore foreign germs, over my mouth and nose). It is a decently made, well-fitting and durable product otherwise" (Think Ink, 2020). Our text was included in the subject "Amazon review" (see Figure 1), with 62 words and 51 unique words, of which 90% were included in the identified subject. As 26 words appear in this sense, the actions occupy a percentage of 45.6% of the review structure, with repetitions also being used in order to emphasize certain actions. The user repeatedly uses the words "made", "worn" and "put" to express his dissatisfaction with the fact that the mask is not made of cotton, as specified by the manufacturer, and therefore he cannot wear it when it is warm outside, and, in addition, the two sides of the mask are similar and it is difficult to wear it properly. The data on the functionality of the product occupies 28.1% of the review, and here we can refer to the fact that the user considers the product to be durable, but otherwise, he only finds disadvantages (the two similar sides, the mask does not fit because it is too big, not made from the specified material). In terms of emotions, they occupy 14% of the review, with the words "disappointed", "wrong" or "decent" being used. Then we have the product (5.3%) through the word "cotton", the location (3.5%), but also the time (3.5%) through "day" and "later". We can say that the user is not satisfied with the product, as he finds many flaws with the mask, in addition to very few advantages, so the reason why he offered only 2 stars is understandable. He focuses on actions and functionality, and less on location or time, and not at all on brand, advertising or people.

For the Walmart site, the topic in which the software will search for information will be called "Walmart review/reviews", the American site being very well known, as a result of which there were many analyzes of the reviews there, the reviews coming only from the USA. An example in this research may be the one that was posted on May 19, 2020, by "48nholdin", who wrote: "Great Mask. I find this more comfortable than the paper or molded masks. Also, it was received within a week" (Blended, 2020). The product received 5 stars from this user, and the title of the review is "A great mask", which proves, from the beginning, that we are dealing with a good opinion about the product and a positive review.

The text focuses equally on the most important categories (product, actions, emotional factor and time), each occupying 22.2%, namely the product itself, the rather fast delivery and the pleasant feelings caused by the good quality of the product, shown by the use of words like "great" and "comfortable". In regards to the material from which it is made, a comparison is made with masks of lower quality, but also with masks that are made of harder materials (FFP3 type, with valve), that can leave traces on the skin because of this. Advertising also occupies 11.1% of the text (see Figure 7). Being very satisfied with the product and the received services, the user offered a positive review, along with a maximum rating.

FINDINGS

The websites of the two companies are quite similar, and their level is forcing the two brands to offer customers the best services. Both pages highlight images with the products, along with their price, as well as details about the product. At the bottom of the page, we can find the reviews, which can be sorted in any order we want, plus they are accompanied by ratings, as well as the potential "Verified Purchase" confirmation.

To answer the first question of the research (What aspects do buyers focus on in their reviews?), We can say that both amazon.co.uk and walmart.com users place great emphasis on the functionality and features of the product, the actions related to its purchase and use, the emotions it triggered, as well as the time elapsed until its arrival. To answer the question: What are the elements of a review that can influence the purchase decision?, we can say that an important element is that anyone can choose to rate a review or not, the review being visible to everyone, so certain reviews can be affected, this aspect being as important as the general rating or the one offered by each user. Also, the fact that "Verified Purchase" is written next to the review is another important element, and the idea that the supplier has verified the user regarding the purchase removes any doubt regarding the veracity of the information. In our research, we found a review in which the following statement is made: "The mask cannot protect you from the virus", which received dislikes due to the fact that it did not bring any relevant argument in this regard. That is why this option is useful, and some reviews can be sent back in terms of relevance.

The two sites are similar, and in terms of the question: How is the evaluation of a product different depending on the country where you live? We can say that the perception of the users who bought the products is similar, and the demographic factors did not affect this aspect in any way, the users from the two continents mainly focusing on the functionality of the product, the emotions, the actions and the delivery. It seems that the face masks on the two sites are quite effective, most of the reviews being positive and many of the buyers stating that they would buy that mask again.

The first two objectives of the research are closely related, the attitude of the consumers being visible in the positive or negative reviews. In the case of www.amazon.co.uk, we identified 10 positive and 5 negative reviews, and from www.walmart.com, we analyzed 11 positive reviews and 4 negative ones. We can say that most buyers have a positive attitude towards the two products, given that the percentages for both sites are positive, namely 60% of the reviews on Amazon are positive, and for Walmart the percentage is 73%.

Regarding the degree of efficiency of the products, which is another objective of the research, we can look at the rating, the product on Amazon collected a score of 3.3 out of 5, while the product on Walmart has 3.6 out of 5, which is a negligible difference, the two products being close from this point of view, a large part of the analyzed reviews being positive, most consumers finding the products to be efficient and very useful. In this same direction, we will discuss the strengths and weaknesses found by the buyers of the two protective masks.

If we refer to the positive reviews we have analyzed, we can say that most buyers on the two sites found the masks to be comfortable, easy to wear due to the high-quality material, and the design also plays an important role, because, for some people, this type of product does not only mean a piece of material that protects you, but an article of clothing. In this same regard, we can talk about the importance of delivering the product safely and in the shortest possible time, this factor being very important.

On the other hand, negative reviews presented a small number of common problems, but many of them contradict with the testimonials of those who left positive reviews. Thus, the negative reviews mainly refer to the poor quality of the materials, due to which one cannot breathe at all while wearing the mask. The most common problem that is found among negative reviews refers to the inappropriate dimensions of the mask, which make it very frustrating for the buyers, who are not able to use the product they ordered because of this. Also, another big problem can be that people do not feel safe wearing these masks, even claiming that the mask cannot protect you from the virus.

If we refer to the last declared objective of the research, it is noteworthy that, in all off the 30 reviews, we only identified one reference to the brand (and one to advertising), which indicates that the usefulness of the product and its quality are in the foreground, regardless of the brand name or its efforts to attract customers. Therefore, we cannot get a clear idea about the consumers' attitude towards the two suppliers, but only towards the products.

CONCLUSION

Following this research, it must be stated that one of the most important element in the review ecosystem is the rating system, because a review with a high level of appreciation can generate confidence to the users. In addition, dubious reviews will not be taken into account, because will not be appreciated by others. Another important thing is the appearance of "Verified purchase" option because the user and/or the purchase were verified and the review is justified. The research also revealed that the customers refer usually to the quality of the product, not to the brand directly.

Organizational communication proves to be essential (Briciu, Mircea & Briciu, 2020) because it ensures a close connection between the company and all the factors on which it depends. Whether we are referring to employees or the other side, people who are somehow interested in its success, such as investors, suppliers, creditors and ultimately customers, communication ensures the development and continuity of any business, this process often taking place through the Internet, where the connection is made quickly and efficiently, with the visibility of brands increasing more and more in the online environment. Customer relationship management is equally important, and, in this regard, a system is used that helps to better understand customers, which gathers information on past acquisitions for better anticipation of future actions, plus that, in this way, companies get to know the needs of their customers and can thus adapt their services.

As technology has evolved a lot in recent years, strategies and methods of promotion have also diversified, but companies are forced to respect customers even more, and the wrong steps can be much more visible, given this development and freedom of the Internet. Among the important methods of promotion, we can mention sales promotion, which is the reduction of the price for a defined period of time, generally accompanied by a type of communication, even an advertisement. We can also mention commercial promotions, an agreement between producers and traders that offers customers benefits in terms of prices, or even offers free services, such as product delivery. These few techniques have a very important role because they can bring the public much closer and establish a long-lasting relationship, by offering them some advantages and high-quality services.

In the case of Word of Mouth or Electronic Word of Mouth, companies do not have a direct involvement, as it is more about the information that circulates from one person to another, in our case it is about a service or product. These concepts are of great importance because there will always be a flow of positive and negative information, depending on the satisfaction of each customer. Therefore, it is very important that the offered services be at a high level, and the criticism as little as possible, in order to prevent the company's image from being affected, along with its sales and profit.

Reviews play a very important role as well, as they are also a form of promotion, as in the case of Word of Mouth, with many companies encouraging users to leave a review of their products. Here, too, there is a risk when there are several negative reviews, which can substantially affect sales. Therefore, it is very important, as we previously stated, to offer customers the best services, but it is also important to detect, by any means possible, any false or unfounded reviews, where no relevant arguments are offered.

Following this research, we also found out that customers can be pleased and satisfied if what we offer meets the following conditions: the manufacturing materials or offered services must be of high-quality and in accordance with the product's price, the delivery should be as fast as possible in order to keep the waiting time as short as possible, customer support is also important, if they want additional information, and the images and information presented on the site have to fully correspond to reality.

The present research reinforces the idea that reviews play a crucial role in the purchase decision, exposing that, in their reviews, the users of the two websites also refer to the opinions of other customers, and another important element is that reviews get likes or dislikes, a sign that other users have read that review and also tested the product themselves, agreeing with someone else's words. Another scenario may refer to prevention, for some users, in case of a negative review, as they give up on a certain product. Therefore, reviews have become a crucial aspect of the purchase decision, with the studies presented in this chapter proving this, and the present research reinforcing these ideas.

REFERENCES

Balmer, J., & Greyser, S. (2006). Integrate corporate identity, corporate branding, corporate communications, corporate image and corporate reputation. *European Journal of Marketing, 40*(7/8), 730–741. doi:10.1108/03090560610669964

Berry, M., & Linoff, G. (2004). *Data Mining Techniques. For Marketing, Sales and Costumer Relationship Management*. Wiley Publishing.

Bigne, E., Ruiz, C., & Sanz, S. (2005). The Impact of Internet User Shopping Patterns and Demographics on Consumer Mobile Buying Behavior. *Journal of Electronic Commerce Research, 6*(3), 193–209.

Blattberg, R. C., & Briesch, R. A. (2012). Sales Promotion. In Ö. Özer & R. Phillips (Eds.), *The Oxford Handbook of Pricing Management* (pp. 585–619). Oxford University Press.

Blended. (2020). *Washable Cotton Face Mask Reusable Made in the USA*. https://www.walmart.com/ip/Washable-Cotton-Face-Mask-Reusable-Made-in-the-USA/625326064

Boje, D. (2018). *Organizational Research: Storytelling in Action*. Routledge. doi:10.4324/9781315205854

Briciu, A., & Briciu, V.-A. (2020a). Designing the Virtual Product Experience: Learnings from Shenzhen, China and the ESUN Solutions. In A. Kavoura, E. Kefallonitis, & P. Theodoridis (Eds.), *Strategic Innovative Marketing and Tourism. Springer Proceedings in Business and Economics* (pp. 435–442). Springer. doi:10.1007/978-3-030-36126-6_48

Briciu, A., Briciu, V.-A., & Pilipinschi, A.-M. (2017). A Website Brand Analysis of Romanian Companies from Automotive Industry. *Bulletin of the Transilvania University of Brasov, 10*(59), 133–142.

Briciu, V.-A., Briciu, A., & Găitan, Ş-M. (2020). Impression Management through Websites: An Analysis of the Romanian Banking Industry. In *Strategic Innovative Marketing and Tourism. Springer Proceedings in Business and Economics* (pp. 417-424). Springer.

Briciu, V.-A., & Briciu, A. (2020b). COVID-19 Influence and Future Perspectives of Artificial Intelligence on the Labour Market. *BRAIN. Broad Research in Artificial Intelligence and Neuroscience, 11*(2Sup1), 21-28.

Briciu, V.-A., & Briciu, A. (2021). Social Media and Organizational Communication. In M. Khosrow-Pour (Ed.), Encyclopedia of Organizational Knowledge, Administration, and Technology (pp. 2609-2624). IGI Global. doi:10.4018/978-1-7998-3473-1.ch180

Briciu, V.-A., Mircea, I., & Briciu, A. (2020). Communication and Entrepreneurship in Romania: Dissimulation of First Impression in 30 Seconds. In A. Masouras, G. Maris, & A. Kavoura (Eds.), *Entrepreneurial Development and Innovation in Family Businesses and SMEs* (pp. 22–38). IGI Global. doi:10.4018/978-1-7998-3648-3.ch002

Buil, I., de Chernatony, L., & Martinez, E. (2011). Examining the role of advertising and sales promotion in brand equity creation. *Journal of Business Research, 66*(1), 115–122. doi:10.1016/j.jbusres.2011.07.030

Carmeli, A., & Tishler, A. (2005). Perceived Organizational Reputation and Organizational Performance: An Empirical Investigation of Industrial Enterprises. *Corporate Reputation Review, 8*(1), 13–30. doi:10.1057/palgrave.crr.1540236

Chalmeta, R. (2005). Methodology for costumer relationship mangement. *Journal of Systems and Software, 79*(7), 1015–1024. doi:10.1016/j.jss.2005.10.018

Chelcea, S. (2004). *Metodologia cercetării sociologice. Metode cantitative şi calitative* [Sociological research methodology. Quantitative and qualitative methods] (2nd ed.). Economic Publishing House.

Chen, Y., Fay, S., & Wang, Q. (2011). The Role of Marketing in Social Media: How Online Consumers Reviews Evolve. *Journal of Interactive Marketing, 25*(2), 85–94. doi:10.1016/j.intmar.2011.01.003

Chong, A., Li, B., Ngai, E., Ch'ng, E., & Lee, F. (2016). Predicting online product sales via online reviews, sentiments, and promotion strategies. *International Journal of Operations & Production Management, 36*(4), 358–383. doi:10.1108/IJOPM-03-2015-0151

Cornelissen, J. P. (2008). *Corporate Communication. A guide to Theory and Practice.* SAGE Publications.

Gefen, D., Karahanna, E., & Straub, D. W. (2003). Inexperience and Experience with Online Stores: The Importance of TAM and Trust. *IEEE Transactions on Engineering Management, 50*(3), 307–321. doi:10.1109/TEM.2003.817277

Giannakis-Bompolis, C., & Boutsouki, C. (2014). Customer Relationship Management in the Era of Social Web and Social Customer: An Investigation of Customer Engagement in the Greek Retail Banking Sector. *Procedia: Social and Behavioral Sciences, 148*, 67–78. doi:10.1016/j.sbspro.2014.07.018

Ji, G., Li, C., North, M., & Liu, J. (2016). Staking reputation on stakeholders: How does stakeholders' Facebook engagement help or ruin a company's reputation. *Public Relations Review, 43*(1), 1–10.

Kacen, J., Hess, J., & Chiang, W. (2013). Bricks or Clicks? Consumer Attitudes toward Traditional Stores and Online Stores. *Global Economics and Management Review, 18*(1), 12–21. doi:10.1016/S2340-1540(13)70003-3

Keller, K. L. (2010). Mastering the Marketing Communication Mix: Micro and Macro Perspectives on Integrated Marketing Communication Programs. *Journal of Marketing Management, 17*(7-8), 819–847. doi:10.1362/026725701323366836

King, S. F., & Burgess, T. F. (2008). Understanding succes and failure in costumer relationship management. *Industrial Marketing Management, 37*(4), 421–431. doi:10.1016/j.indmarman.2007.02.005

Kwok, S., & Uncles, M. (2002). Sales Promotion Effectiveness: The Impact of Culture at an Ethnic-Group Level. *School of Marketing Working Paper, 2*(4), 1-37.

McKechnie, S. (1992). Consumer Buying Behaviour in Financial Services: An Overview. *International Journal of Bank Marketing, 10*(5), 4–12. doi:10.1108/02652329210016803

Mihart, C. (2012). Impact of Integrated Marketing Communication on Consumer Behavior. Effect on Consumer Decision-Making Process. *International Journal of Marketing Studies, 4*(2), 121–129. doi:10.5539/ijms.v4n2p121

Mihelis, G., Grigoroudis, E., Siskos, Y., Politis, Y., & Malandrakis, Y. (2001). Customer satisfaction measurement in the private bank sector. *European Journal of Operational Research, 130*(2), 347–360. doi:10.1016/S0377-2217(00)00036-9

Odunlami, I., & Ofoegbu, O. (2011). Effect of Marketing Communication in Promoting Organisational Sales. A Case Study of Sunshine Company. *Journal of Emerging Trends in Economics and Management Science, 2*(5), 408–412.

Otto, J., & Wagner, W. (2004). Analysis of Online Customer Review. *Journal of Business & Economics Research, 2*(10), 17–22.

Park, C.-H., & Kim, Y.-G. (2003). Identifying key factors affecting consumer purchase behavior in an online shopping context. *International Journal of Retail & Distribution Management, 31*(1), 16–29. doi:10.1108/09590550310457818

Pauwels, K., Erguncu, S., & Yildirim, G. (2013). Winning hearts, minds and sales: How marketing communication enters the purchase process in emerging and mature markets. *International Journal of Research in Marketing, 30*(1), 57–68. doi:10.1016/j.ijresmar.2012.09.006

Plessis, C., Angelopulo, G., & Plessis, D. (2012). A conceptual framework of corporate online communication: A marketing public relations (MPR) perspectives. *South African Journal of Communication Theory and Research, 32*(2), 241–263.

Raghupathi, D., Yannou, B., Farel, R., & Poirson, E. (2015). Customer sentiment appraisal from user-generated product reviews: A domain independent heuristic algorithm. *International Journal on Interactive Design and Manufacturing, 9*(3), 201–211. doi:10.100712008-015-0273-4

Rindova, V., Williamson, I., Petkova, A., & Sever, J. (2005). Being good or being known: An empirical examination of the dimensions, antecedents and consequences of organizational reputation. *Academy of Management Journal, 48*(6), 2–42. doi:10.5465/amj.2005.19573108

SmartMunk. (2020). *Text mining software.* https://www.smartmunk.com/en/text-mining-software/

Think Ink. (2020). *Think Ink Face Mask (10/1, 5/1, 1/1) Cotton Mask with Elastic Strap Washable Face Mask.* https://www.amazon.co.uk/Think-Ink-Cotton-Elastic-Washable/dp/B086QTXY9Y/ref=mp_s_a_1_1?dchild=1&keywords=think+ink+face+mask&qid=1591548206&quartzVehicle=3514-1426&replacementKeywords=ink+face+mask&sprefix=think+inc+face+&sr=8-1

Timoshenko, A., & Hauser, J. (2018). Identifying Customer Needs from User-Generated Content. *Marketing Science, 38*(1), 1–20. doi:10.1287/mksc.2018.1123

Utz, S., Kerkhof, P., & van den Bos, J. (2012). Consumers rule: How consumer reviews influence perceived trustworthiness of online stores. *Electronic Commerce Research and Applications, 11*(1), 49–58. doi:10.1016/j.elerap.2011.07.010

Wang, D., Zhu, S., & Li, T. (2013). SumView: A Web-based engine for summarizing product reviews and customer opinions. *Expert Systems with Applications, 40*(1), 27–33. doi:10.1016/j.eswa.2012.05.070

Wang, Y., Lu, X., & Tan, Y. (2018). Impact of product attributes on customer satisfaction: An analysis of online reviews for washing machines. *Electronic Commerce Research and Applications, 29*, 1–11. doi:10.1016/j.elerap.2018.03.003

Weiss, A., Anderson, E., & MacInnis, J. (1999). Reputation Management as a Motivation for Sales Structure Decisions. *Journal of Marketing, 63*(4), 74–89. doi:10.1177/002224299906300407

Xu, Y., Yen, D., Lin, B., & Chou, D. (2002). Adopting costumer relationship management technology. *Industrial Management & Data Systems, 102*(8), 442–452. doi:10.1108/02635570210445871

Yang, S., & Hong, S. (2009). Effects of Reputation, Relational Satisfaction and Costumer-Company Identification on Positive Word-of-Mouth Intenstions. *Journal of Public Relations Research, 21*(4), 381–403. doi:10.1080/10627260902966433

ADDITIONAL READING

Agesti, N., Ridwan, M. S., & Budiarti, E. (2021). The Effect of Viral Marketing, Online Customer Review, Price Perception, Trust on Purchase Decisions with Lifestyle as Intervening Variables in the Marketplace Shopee in Surabaya City. *International Journal of Multicultural and Multireligious Understanding, 8*(3), 496–507.

Eslami, S. P., Ghasemaghaei, M., & Hassanein, K. (2018). Which online reviews do consumers find most helpful? A multi-method investigation. *Decision Support Systems, 113*, 32–42. doi:10.1016/j.dss.2018.06.012

Hossin, M. A., Mu, Y., Fang, J., & Frimpong, A. N. K. (2019). Influence of picture presence in reviews on online seller product rating: Moderation role approach. *Transactions on Internet and Information Systems (Seoul), 13*(12), 6097–6120.

Jain, V. K., & Kumar, S. (2017). Improving customer experience using sentiment analysis in e-commerce. In A. Kumar, M. K. Dash, S. K. Trivedi, & T. K. Panda (Eds.), *Handbook of Research on Intelligent Techniques and Modeling Applications in Marketing Analytics* (pp. 216–224). IGI Global. doi:10.4018/978-1-5225-0997-4.ch012

Lawani, A., Reed, M. R., Mark, T., & Zheng, Y. (2019). Reviews and price on online platforms: Evidence from sentiment analysis of Airbnb reviews in Boston. *Regional Science and Urban Economics, 75*, 22–34. doi:10.1016/j.regsciurbeco.2018.11.003

Luo, J., Huang, S., & Wang, R. (2021). A fine-grained sentiment analysis of online guest reviews of economy hotels in China. *Journal of Hospitality Marketing & Management, 30*(1), 71–95. doi:10.108 0/19368623.2020.1772163

Phillips, P., Barnes, S., Zigan, K., & Schegg, R. (2017). Understanding the impact of online reviews on hotel performance: An empirical analysis. *Journal of Travel Research, 56*(2), 235–249. doi:10.1177/0047287516636481

Thinnukool, O., Charoenkwan, P., Khuwuthyakorn, P., & Tinamat, P. (2020). Word Cloud Analysis of Customer Satisfaction in Cosmetic Products in Thailand. In *Proceedings of the 2020 the 4th International Conference on Compute and Data Analysis* (pp. 179-182). Association for Computing Machinery. 10.1145/3388142.3388152

Zhang, M., Fan, B., Zhang, N., Wang, W., & Fan, W. (2021). Mining product innovation ideas from online reviews. *Information Processing & Management, 58*(1), 102389. doi:10.1016/j.ipm.2020.102389

KEY TERMS AND DEFINITIONS

Corporate: Messages sent by company with a clear purpose to important audiences: employees, mass-media, stakeholders.

Online Store: Online site that sells products or services, customers having the opportunity to receive everything at home, or it can be tested offline before.

Purchasing Decision: The decision taken by a client to buy something, after he read the reviews, studied the product and, in the end, decide to buy it.

Qualitative: A research method that considering the reviews from the point of view of relevance, clarity and transparency of the user text, numbers are not taken into account, for example the stars achieved by the product or number of reviews.

Quantitative measure: Measuring the number of reviews, stars, likes and dislikes, positive and negative experiences for positioning a product or a service.

Software: Basic application which set in motion the program through we can analyze reviews, having a powerful database.

Story.ly: High performance program which has the capacity to extract the sentiment from text and can show us important elements for the customers.

Web 2.0: The Internet after the year 2000, much more developed and available to anyone due to technological and economic advancement.

Word-of-Mouth: Information transmitted from one person to another, it has the power to spread some details that can reach to thousands of people and even influencing them.

APPENDIX

Figure 1. Dashboard example in story.ly
Source: SmartMunk, 2020

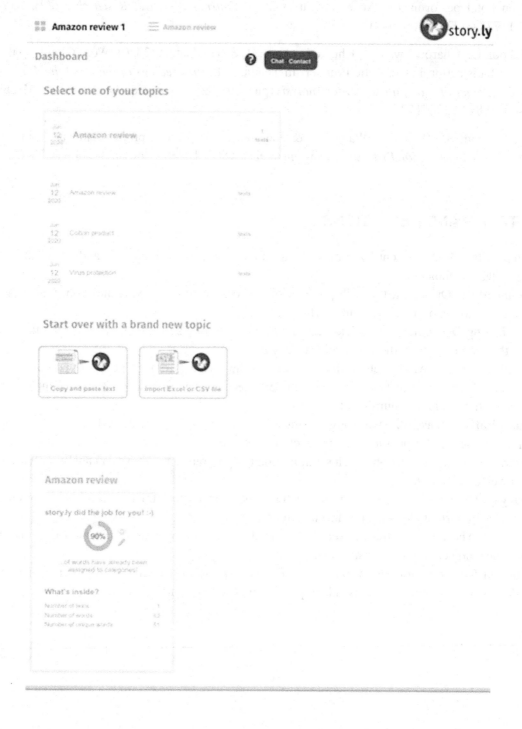

Figure 2. Ontology Skyline example in story.ly
Source: SmartMunk, 2020

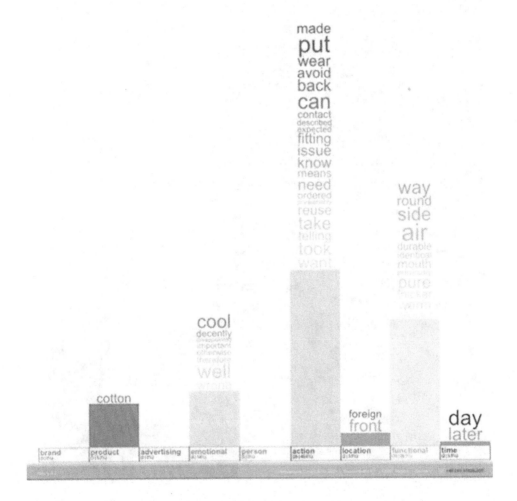

Figure 3. Ontology Treemap example in story.ly
Source: SmartMunk, 2020

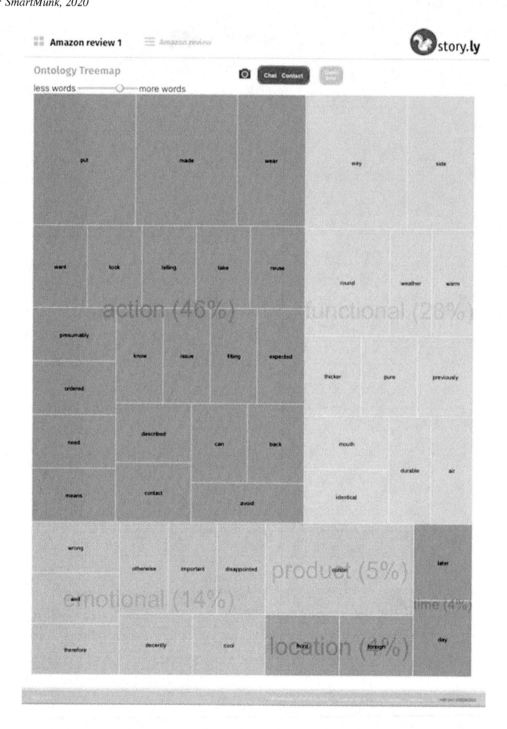

Figure 4. Network Map example in story.ly
Source: SmartMunk, 2020

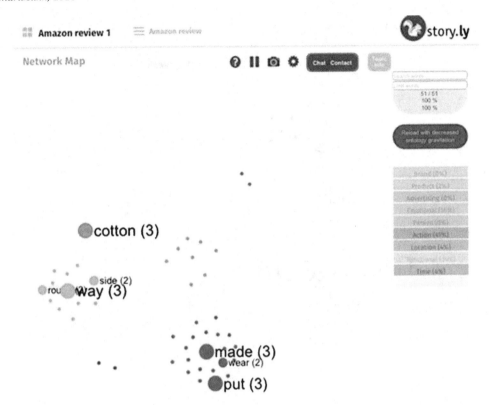

Figure 5. Content Cloud example in story.ly
Source: SmartMunk, 2020

Figure 6. Textcleaning example in story.ly
Source: SmartMunk, 2020

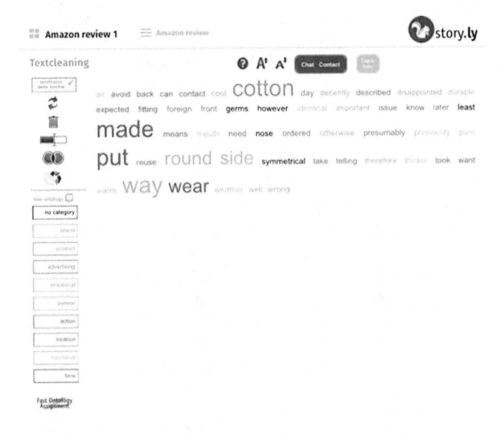

Figure 7. Ontology Skyline for Review #1 Walmart
Source: SmartMunk, 2020

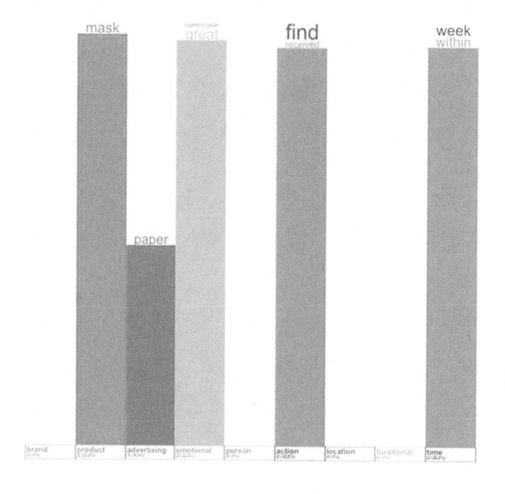

Chapter 6
Exploring Critical Success Factors Towards Adoption of M–Government Services in Tanzania:
A Web Analytics Study

Fredrick Ishengoma
The University of Dodoma, Tanzania

ABSTRACT

Recently, the Tanzanian government has started making m-government initiatives. However, little is known about the factors and conditions surrounding m-government adoption in Tanzania. Consequently, some m-government services have been successfully adopted while others are still struggling (having a low level of adoption). This study investigates critical success factors (CSFs) that led m-government services belonging to the same family to have varying degrees of adoption level. The study employs a set of web analytics tools that monitored and analyzed the traffic data of the selected three m-government services. The results show that inspecting the web analytics data from multiple viewpoints and varying levels of detail gives insights on the CSFs towards the adoption of m-government services. The findings suggest that perceived usefulness, user needs, and usability favor the adoption of one m-government service over the other.

INTRODUCTION

As the current frontier of delivery of public services, mobile government (m-Government) is revolutionizing how governments can provide services to their citizens. Governments in developing countries are gradually implementing m-Government initiatives to offer people, businesses, and public servants with more accessibility to government information and services. The potential of m-Government lies in high

DOI: 10.4018/978-1-7998-8061-5.ch006

mobile penetration, increasing low cost of mobile devices and ubiquitous feature (Ishengoma, Mselle & Mongi, 2018; Malaquias & Júnior, 2021).

In Tanzania, government services that were previously provided in a manual format are now being converted into a mobile platform, allowing people to access them from anywhere and at any time. Recent studies have revealed that, despite the growing number of m-Government initiatives, the Critical Success Factors (CSFs) that underpin its successful adoption are largely untapped (Mtingwi, 2015, Ishengoma et al., 2018). Furthermore, the CSFs that drive the adoption of m-Government vary by country and are affected by the social-cultural aspects (Almuraqab, 2017). Since the concept of m-Government is an add-on to e-Government that originates in the public administration systems of industrialized countries, how it operates outside that domain, such as in developing African countries, is mainly influenced by the context of that region (Wakhu, Fuyuan & Kakonge, 2020).

Researchers have looked into the what influence citizens' adoption of mobile government in the contexts of developed countries (Shareef, Dwivedi, Laumer& Archer, 2016; Annie, Choy, Krishna & Alex, 2017; Jinho, Jong & Timothy, 2021). However, existing research has not adequately provided a better understanding of the factors influencing citizen adoption of m-Government services in Tanzania. Currently, there is a varying degree of adoption between m-Government services that are members of the same family, i.e., serve the same category of citizens. Some of these m-Government services are successfully adopted, while others have been struggling for adoption. To guarantee the successful adoption of m-Government services in Tanzania, CSFs needs to be known.

Furthermore, the current study on the adoption of m-Government services (Ishengoma, Mselle & Mongi, 2018) has focused on the empirical perspectives of the users. Yet, there is little to no study from the web analytics perspectives. This study bridges this gap by investigating the CSFs for adopting m-Government services from the web analytics viewpoint.

Based on the above assertions, this chapter aims to investigate the CSFs for the adoption of m-Government services in Tanzania by employing a web analytics approach. The chapter examines user behaviour and the whys and wherefores that led to different levels of adoption among m-Government services belonging to the same family.

The chapter's organizational structure is as follows: The study's historical setting is discussed in Section 2. The case studies that have been used throughout this chapter are described in Section 3. Section 4 discusses the materials and methods that were employed in this study. Section 5 discusses the findings and discussion. Section 6 covers the study's shortcomings, and Section 7 concludes the chapter.

BACKGROUND

Web Analytics (WA) refers to the assessment, compilation, review, and reporting of web-based data with the aim of better understanding and improving web use (Sleeper, Consolvo, & Staddon, 2014). We can, for example, use WA to track the number of visitors, where they came from, how many times they visited, how far the visitors explored the site and where they went next. (Clifton, 2012). Web analytics' strength lies in its ability to deliver unbiased results, overcoming the shortage of experts, being low cost, and evades inconsistent results from experts (Dingli and Misfud, 2011). Moreover, WA collects data from the user's unobtrusiveness.

Using WA, Researchers can gather data from users without interfering with their responses, i.e., in a non-reactive manner. As opposed to the intrusive approach, where the participant is fully conscious that they are being observed, their viewpoints and reactions will be affected (the Hawthorne effect). Studies have shown that the Hawthorne effect (HE) affects participants' responses and behaviour in studies (Burton, 2018). WA invisibly collects data from the users behind the scenes and thus prevents the Hawthorne effect (Burton, 2018).

The study can understand user behaviour and the complexities surrounding the adoption of m-Government services by using web analytics. Web analytics may also expose potentially problematic areas or features that successfully prevent users from embracing the m-Government service. While several researchers have looked at m-Government adoption from the user's viewpoint, very little research has been done explicitly on web analytics.

In a study by (Pakkalaa et al., 2012) Google Analytics (GA) was used for monitoring visitor data on 3 food sites (Denmark, Switzerland and Finland). All of the websites had many users, which appeared to grow as the websites matured. According to the research findings, GA provided valuable and flexible knowledge that can be used to understand user behaviour better and improve the site's adoption accordingly. Brooks and Persaud (2015) used web analytics tools to perform a comparative analysis of local e-government portals throughout Canada and the United Kingdom to measure usability and accessibility. In order to evaluate local e-government web pages, local officials and web administrators were found to use on-line diagnostic tools to provide a useful and feasible solution for internal assessment.

Cai, Li, and Feng (2019) developed a methodology and an automated evaluation method for evaluating the real-time efficiency of government websites. The study's authors developed a computerized assessment framework for extracting information from government websites and generating a real-time review report. The researchers validated the proposed methodology by applying it to a list of 70 local sites in China's Shaanxi Province. The study established that automated frameworks and tools are effective methods for gaining access to government websites' efficiency.

The study by (Bhagat and Joshi, 2019) investigated the usability of online services and their test procedures using free and open-source automated audits on some of India's government websites. The study shows that the majority of the websites reviewed by e-government were not constructed as per global guidelines and accessibility standards (WCAG 2.0).

The study by (Ishengoma, Mselle & Mongi, 2019) investigated the influence of cultural dimension power distance (Hofstede, 1981) in adopting m-Government services using web analytics tools in Tanzania. The research looked at 1-year transaction data for water utilities before and after the mandatory electronic payment system. Moreover, the analysis used web analytics to evaluate the 1-year traffic of data from a government recruitment agency to understand usage patterns fully. The study found power distance to influence the adoption of m-Government services in Tanzania.

According to the analysis of the above literature, there is little research on user behaviour and understanding of the success factors for adopting m-Government services from the viewpoint of web analytics. This chapter aims to close this gap by looking at the behaviour of users and the factors that lead m-Government services from the same family to have different levels of adoption.

CASE STUDIES

For the case study, the author picked three websites with different adoption rate according to traffic rank. All of the case studies fall under the same category of carrier and education according to category rank traffic data of 2018 (Alexa, 2018b). The chosen case studies are tabulated in table 1. From table 1, the website refers to the name of the website under investigation. The two first sites (ajira.go.tz and necta.go.tz) have a higher degree of adoption compared to the third site (nacte.go.tz).

Table 1. Three case studies selected for the study according to traffic rank

SN	Website	Rank in Tanzania	Category rank
1	Ajira.go.tz	10	709
2	Necta.go.tz	34	4,473
3	Nacte.go.tz	75	12,180

www.ajira.go.tz

The website www.ajira.go.tz is run by the Public Service Recruitment Secretariat (PSRS), a government body created specifically to make hiring public servants easier. One of its primary responsibilities is to advertise open positions in the government. Moreover, the site facilitates the registration of graduates and professionals for ease of reference in the recruitment process of employees to the public service. For example, a user may visit this website (www.ajira.go.tz) searching for a new job and upload his or her cv to a database where he or she will be contacted about future job opportunities.

www.necta.go.tz

The Tanzanian National Examination Council (NECTA) was created in accordance with Act 21 of 1973 of the Parliament. The website of NECTA started in 2003. It mainly deals with administering secondary examinations and the publication of students' results in Tanzania. The website is operated by the Information Technology (IT) section, which is part of the NECTA's research, evaluation, and data processing department. NECTA delivers secondary examination results, used mainly by students, teachers, parents, and guardians. Universities, colleges, government agencies, scholars, non-governmental organizations, and other education stakeholders are among the other users.

The examination results can be accessed via the website (necta.go.tz) or via SMS. The user sends a coded message to the specific number 15311 via SMS. The results are sent to the sender in a response message. The study chose this site as one of the case studies because it is one of Tanzania's most popular m-Government sites and fits well with our research goals.

www.nacte.go.tz

In 1997, the National Council for Technical Education (NACTE) was formed by the Act of Parliament Cap. 129 to supervise and organize the provision of technical education and training in Tanzania. NACTE's jurisdiction extends to all tertiary education and training institutions, excluding universities and their affiliated colleges, that offer technician, semiprofessional, and professional courses. These websites have been chosen for this study since they bear a resemblance and are exact in the following manner.

1.   They all share similar demographic profiles of users, i.e., university, college and tertiary education graduates.
2.   They all publish information that has a similar context to the user (education and carrier). Necta. go.tz and nacte.go.tz publish examination results, and ajira.go.tz publishes available job vacancies in the government.
3.   Users on both platforms experience anxiety, with students waiting for test results to be released on necta.go.tz and nacte.go.tz, equivalent to a graduate waiting for a work vacancy announced on ajira.go.tz.
4.   They are both related to education and employment.

MATERIALS AND METHODS

The information requirements of this chapter determined the data sources and data collection techniques used. The authors needed data that assist the understanding of the level of adoption and potential issues that could clarify the level of adoption from a web analytics standpoint. In this chapter, authors evaluate various network parameters using a collection of web analytics tools (Alexa Web Analytics, Webpage Test tool, OWASP ZAP, and MAUVE tool), to see whether one m-Government service is more likely to be adopted than the others.

This chapter presents the findings of a one-year web traffic monitoring project (September 2017 to September 2018) where authors analyzed the following metrics: Users' demographic profiles, number of sessions, bounce rates, loading time, page size, number of requests, broken links, privacy, security, and accessibility.

Alexa Web Analytics

Alexa Web Analytics (AWA) is a front-runner in web traffic rankings, offering web analytics such as website traffic data, site assessments, and website user information (Alexa, 2018). There are over 25,000 browser extensions and plugins that are used by millions of people all over the world, and this is how they are measured (Redkina, 2017). Over 25,000 browser extensions and plugins are accessible, and millions of people use them all over the world. This is the basis on which it is built. Because AWA is usually recognized as the most reputable source of web analytics data, it was selected as the sole source of data for this study (Redkina, 2017).

WebPagetest

The WebPagetest tool was used to calculate the loading time, the number of requests, and page size of the selected m-Government sites in this chapter. The authors used this tool since it is the best open-source tool for measuring the three-web metrics (loading time, page size and the number of requests). Several researchers have used this method to investigate the efficiency of various web systems. The tool allows for the analysis of web traffic data for a large number of Internet users. Several researchers have used this tool to investigate the efficiency of various web systems.

Open Web Application Security Project (OWASP)

OWASP was employed to evaluate the security of our selected m-Government sites in this chapter (Makino and Klyuev, 2015). OWASP ZAP is a vulnerability identification tool for web applications. OWASP was adopted for this study because it is open source, and studies have shown that it is the most accurate vulnerability scanner from both commercial and open-source web application penetration testing tools (Makino and Klyuev, 2015; Rafique, Humayun, Hamid, Abbas, Akhtar and Iqbal, 2015).

Multiguideline Accessibility Usability Validation Environment (MAUVE)

MAUVE is a platform for evaluating the accessibility of web applications (Schiavone & Paterna, 2015; Kous & Polani, 2021). It checks the accessibility of web sites according to the Web Content Accessibility Guidelines (WCAG) standards automatically (WCAG 1.0 and WCAG 2.0). The World Wide Web Consortium (WCAG) aims to create a universally accepted standard for web content accessibility that will meet the needs of individuals, businesses, and governments all around the world. It is created and maintained by tens of thousands of web users, web specialists, and organizations from all over the world. MAUVE is utilized in this inquiry since it is the most generally used tool for measuring the accessibility of websites.

RESULTS AND DISCUSSION

The data analysis and discussion are presented in this section of the chapter. The findings are examined and explored regarding their potential form-Government service adoption along three dimensions: What, Who, and How.

Who are the Users of m-Government Services?

Understanding the audience of m-Government services and where they access the service can significantly assist in focusing and allowing to structure service content to meet the perceived needs of this audience. Figure 1 provides the geography of the users of the selected m-Government services in this study, observed for one year (September 2017 to September 2018).

From figure 1, we observe that most users (more than 85%) are from within the country Tanzania. Studies have shown that the potential benefits of m-Government can only be obtained if the initiatives are accepted and used by the intended users (Alonazi, Beloff, and White, 2020). From figure 1, the results suggest that the engaged users entirely use the selected m-Government sites.

Figure 2 depicts the gender profiles of users of the selected m-Government services in Tanzania. From figure 2, it is observed that the number of male users outnumbered female users in all m-Government sites, as shown in Figure 2. For necta.go.tz, male users are 61.02% compared to female users 38.98%. Also, for ajira.go.tz, male users are 66.91% compared to female users 33.09% and 72.81% male users versus 27.19% female users for necta.go.tz.

This is consistent with the demographic profile of Tanzanian students, where female enrollment in tertiary education has remained lower than male enrollment. According to the World Economic Forum (WEF, 2017), there were about twice as many men as women enrolled in tertiary education in 2017.

Figure 1. Audience geography of users of the selected m-Government services

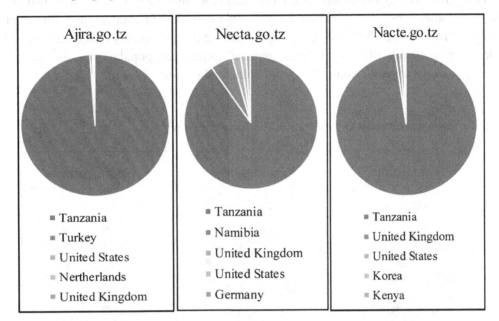

The trend is the same for the last five years in the country. This translates to our study results that more male engages more with the m-Government services compared to females.

The study then examined the age distribution of users of the selected m-Government services. Figure 3 shows that most users (more than 37%) are young people aged between 25 years and 34 years. This group is composed of young university students/graduate's tech-savvy and looking for a job (Müller, Hornung, Hamm and Wulf, 2015). The first group is the age of (25 - 34) years who are the most users.

Figure 2. The gender profile of the selected m-Government services

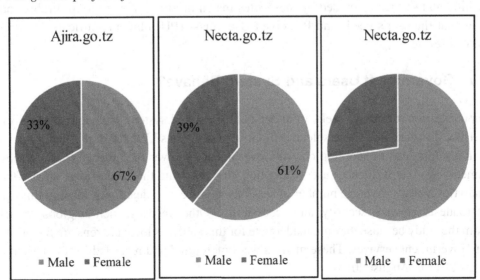

This group is followed by two groups of age (18 - 24) years and (30 - 44) years, as shown in figure 3. These groups are also tech-savvy, searching for jobs and assisting their younger ones who need service from the m-Government sites. In Tanzania, young people are the ones mainly observed to be ICT reliant in daily life. Terms such as 'BBC - born before computer' became very popular in the social commentary, which signifies elderly who are "non-tech-savvy" compared to young people.

Figure 3. User's age distribution for selected m-Government sites

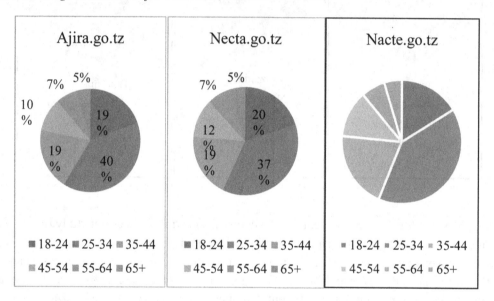

The study argues that this is the targeted population of these selected m-Government sites since the demand for employment (Ajira.go.tz) and information about education and examinations (Necta.go.tz and Nacte.go.tz) match well with the age of the most users. Hence, users' needs and the usefulness of the information and services provided by these sites match most users' age group. In this context, the study argues that the user's needs and Perceived Usefulness (PU) play a significant role in adopting m-Government services.

How Do m-Government Users and System Behave?

In this chapter section, the study seeks to understand users and system behaviour by exploring these questions: How do users find these selected m-Government sites? What are the features of their engagement that might lead to adopting one m-Government site over the other? What nuances exist in m-Government sites that influences users' adoption? In answering these questions, we use the following web analytics metrics: Average number of sessions, bounce rate, deadlinks, loading time, page size, number of requests, privacy, security, and accessibility. Other metrics, such as global "reach," were omitted from the study because they are inadequate for this study, as local citizens are the primary users of these m-Government services. These metrics were monitored and recorded for the period of 1 year (from August 2017 to August 2018).

How Do Users Find the Selected m-Government Sites?

Our study shows that most users use direct traffic followed by an organic search in attracting visitors to m-Government sites, as shown in figure 4. Nearly 58% of visits from ajira.go.tz and 40% of visits from necta.go.tz come from direct traffic. Few percentages of visits originated from referrals, email, and social media. No visit was found to arise from a paid search. Most of the users of ajira.go.tz (more than 57%) come through direct search. A higher percentage from organic search indicate more heightened awareness of the users. Most of these users are aware of the site, and they know the URL. Historically, we've ascribed these visitors to having entered the website's URL manually or clicking on a cached link. As for the necta.go.tz and nacte.go.tz, most of its users (48%) come from the organic channel. The following most users for ajira.go.tz is the organic searchers while for necta.go.tz, and nacte.go.tz are direct search. Referrals and email sources had a low influence on visits on all sites, whereby paid campaigns do not generate any visits.

Figure 4. How users find the selected m-Government sites

How Users Find the Selected m-Government Sites

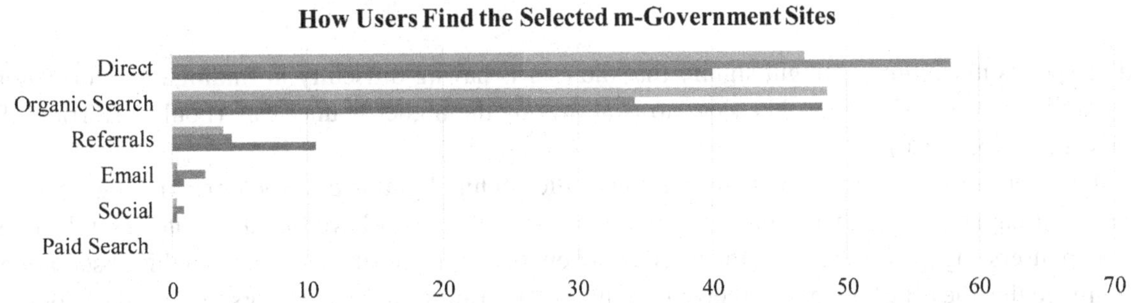

	Paid Search	Social	Email	Referrals	Organic Search	Direct
▪ nacte.go.tz (%)	0	0.31	0.39	3.79	48.58	46.89
▪ ajira.go.tz (%)	0	0.87	2.51	4.43	34.3	57.87
▪ necta.go.tz (%)	0	0.28	0.85	10.7	48.17	39.98

Usability

Average Number of Sessions

The key performance indicator that shed light on m-Government adoption from a web analytics perspective is user engagement (Alonazi, Beloff &White, 2020). Studies (Ishengoma et al., 2018; Frohlich, Nieminen & Panama, 2020) have shown that the success of technology adoption is heavily dependent on how the adopters use it. As people become more engaged with the sites, hence the likelihood of adoption is increased. The higher number of sessions indicates that there is a high level of engagement between users and the services. This section examines user engagement within the selected m-Government sites by using an average number of sessions for one year.

From figure 5, it is observed that ajira.go.tz has a higher number of sessions followed by necta.go.tz and nacte.go.tz. The high number of sessions incline that users use the site more than a lower number of sessions. This also suggests that users find the site useful. However, it can also be argued that when

Figure 5. Average number of sessions for the period of 1 year

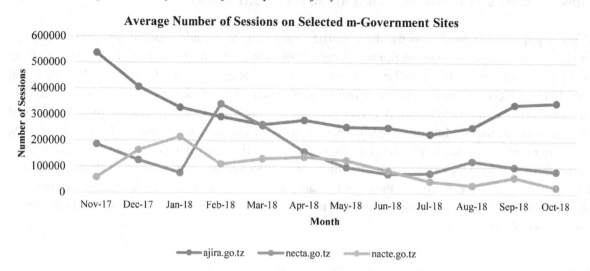

a user spends much time, it might signify that the user is having difficulty in finding the information they are looking for. However, this scenario is always by the higher bounce rate (Poulos, Korfiatis & Papavlassooulos, 2020).

Moreover, since the study has not observed any indicator highlighting the problem in finding information (in ajira.go.tz), the higher number of sessions denotes that users have found the site helpful. Also, the more users engage with the site, the more are likely to adopt that site. Hence, from this observation, it is argued that the actual use and perceived usefulness (PU) are significant factors towards the adoption of one m-Government service over the other.

Bounce Rate

The study examines the bounce rate to understand whether visitors interact with the site by viewing other pages or exit after landing on the homepage. A 50% bounce rate score is considered average, while anything above 60% is deemed to be problematic (Poulos et al., 2020). Figure 6 depicts the bounce rate comparison of the three m-Government sites. Nacte.go.tz was found to have a higher bounce rate than ajira.go.tz and necta.go.tz. The bounce rate for nacte.go.tz reaches up to 56.7, which is higher than the average bounce rate (Poulos et al., 2020).

This indicates that 56.7% of the people who enter nacte.got.tz, don't reach other pages on the site. The majority of reasons for the increased bounce rate can be attributed to poor page quality or content. One reason for poor page performance is poor site design; for instance, an unresponsive site, link error (404 or File Not Found error), and incompatible site design. Poor page content led visitors to face material which is not valuable for them. Hence, they leave the site immediately.

In trying to understand the high bounce rate in nacte.go.tz, the study examined the keywords used by users to access this site by tracing the site using the second top keyword for nacte.go.tz "Saut Mwanza" leads us to a NACTE page with no valuable content for "Saut Mwanza", as shown in figure 7. The same occurred for the fourth top keyword, "Arusha technical college." This indicates that poor content leads

Figure 6. Bounce rate comparison for the selected m-Government sites

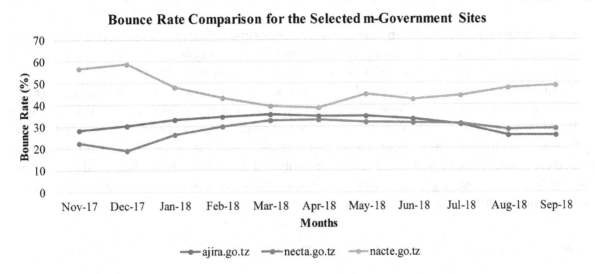

Figure 7. Screenshot of "Saut Mwanza" page on <u>necta.go.tz</u> *site*

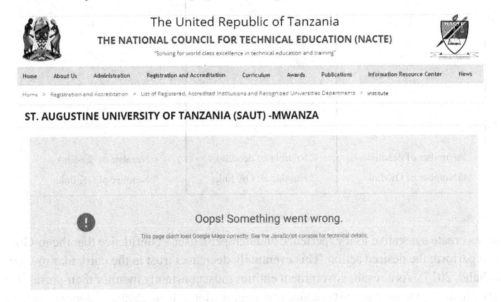

users to miss the needed information leading to a higher bounce rate in m-Government sites. From this observation, it is argued that content and usability are significant factors that favor the adoption of one m-Government service over the other.

Dead Links

The study further explores usability by measuring the number of deadlinks on the selected m-Government sites. The dead link checker tool was used to perform a full scan and analysis for the chosen m-Government sites. The scans were performed once a month for one year (November 2017 to October 2018).

The analysis found an average of 13 broken links out of 1987 links on necta.go.tz, which equals 0.65%, as shown in Figure 8. Nacte.go.tz was found to have an average of 12 deadlinks out of 287 links, which is 4%. Meanwhile, ajira.go.tz had an average number of 50 dead links out of 425 links, which equals 11%. According to the analysis above, whenever a user clicks on a link on the selected m-Government sites, there is indeed a (0.65%, 4%, and 11%) probability that the user will be directed to an unreachable page on (necta.go.tz, nacte.go.tz, and ajira.go.tz, respectively. Deadlinks annoy visitors and limit their odds of returning to the site, lowering user engagement and adoption (Khalid, 2017).

Figure 8. Number of deadlinks and OK links on necta.go.tz

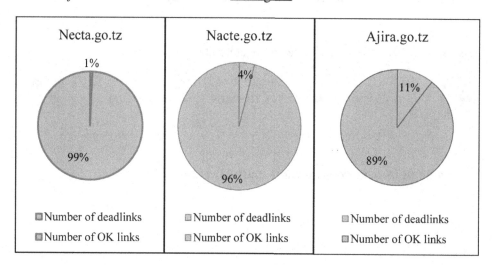

Deadlinks create a negative user experience and hamper a user's confidence that the m-Government service will perform the desired action. This eventually decreases trust in the particular m-Government service (Khalid, 2017). As a result, government entities must constantly monitor their portals for broken links and fix them as soon as possible to reduce user aggravation and encourage m-Government adoption.

Loading Time, Page Size and Number of Requests

The study then explores the influence of loading time, page size and the number of requests towards the adoption of the selected m-Government sites. The page loading time depends on several factors, such as the size of the site, the number of files, and the size of the images. Loading time is measured when the browser contacts servers to download the required files. The loading time, page size and the number of requests of the three selected sites on a network with an Internet download speed of 5 Mbps were measured. The results are shown in Table 2.

Table 2. Loading Time, Page Size and Number of Requests of selected m-Government sites

SN	Metric	Site		
		Necta.go.tz	Ajira.go.tz	Nacte.go.tz
1	Loading time	4.8 seconds	8.25 seconds	4.69 seconds
2	Page size	1.3 MB	2.3 MB	2.2 MB
3	Number of requests	44	99	33

From table 2, it is observed that the number of requests of ajira.go.tz is more than twice the number of necta.go.tz and thrice the number of nacte.go.tz. This indicates that ajira.go.tz has got a much larger number of loaded files than nacte.go.tz and necta.go.tz. The study then tries to understand what makes the number of requests and loading time on ajira.go.tz so high compared to other m-Government sites. The study explored the waterfall chart of ajira.go.tz web structure using the WebPagetest tool. The site HAR file was captured and analyzed the requests made while the site is loading, as shown in Figure 9.

Figure 9. Waterfall view structure of the loading ajira.go.tz

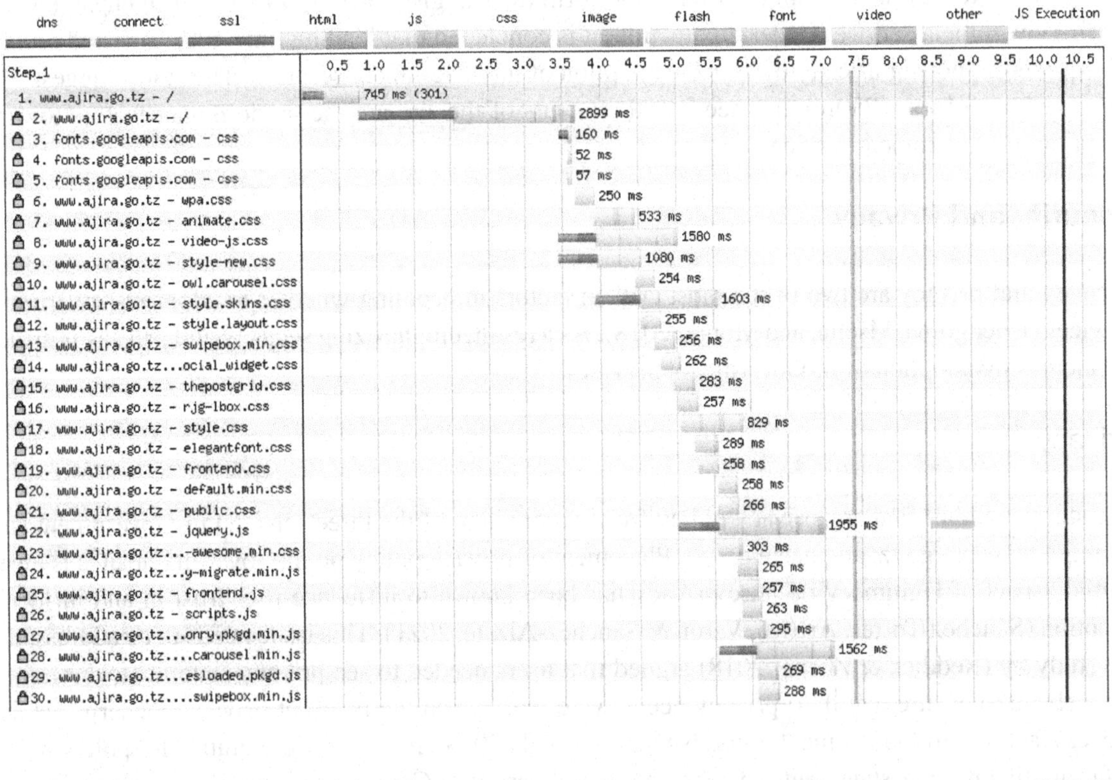

The study found that most of the requests made to the server load multiple JavaScript and CSS files (as shown in Figure 9) compared to a low number of JavaScript and CSS files on nacte.go.tz and necta. go.tz. While most of these files are mere kilobytes in size, the user can only download a few of them simultaneously; browsers limit users to a maximum number of parallel connections. The number of HTTP connections to the same domain name is limited by browsers. The majority of modern browsers support up to 6 connections per domain.

It is evidently that most older browsers sustain 2 domain connections (Narayanan, 2016). As a result, most of these request times are spent waiting for a connection to become available. This adds seconds of wasted time to the page's load. This problem can be fixed by consolidating JavaScript and CSS files or by limiting the number of files that load. Fewer files mean fewer requests and, therefore, a faster website

Despite ajira.go.tz having a higher number of sessions (Fig. 5) and a reasonable bounce rate (Fig. 6), it has a higher loading time and a number of requests. Studies have shown that when people have to wait a long time for a site to load too long, they tend to abandon what they were browsing on altogether (Hassan, Amer & Sawsan, 2021). The study by (Al-Sakran & Alsudairi, 2021) confirmed that long waiting times experienced by users to download or open websites negatively impact website users' experience. A recent report by Google argues that "As page load time goes from one second to five seconds, the probability of bounce increases by 90%" (Semerádová & Weinlich, 2020).

However, in this study, despite the higher loading time of ajira.go.tz, the site still had a lower bounce rate and an increased number of sessions. This suggests that loading time is not a predominant factor influencing the user to engage or disengage with the m-Government sites. Based on these observations, it is argued that perceived usefulness (PU) and users' needs of the site are the predominant factors that led users to wait for higher loading time. The need for the user to access the information is a vital factor. In this study context, the need for young people to get information about available job vacancies and the perceived usefulness of this information outperform the sluggish loading time factor in engaging with the m-Government service. Under this section, it is concluded that loading time, page size and number of requests are not significant towards the adoption of m-Government services. The study suggests that perceived usefulness (PU), users' needs and contents of the site are the predominant factors towards adopting m-Government services.

Security and Privacy

Security and privacy are two of the most critical factors in deciding whether to adopt m-Government services (Ishengoma, Mselle, and Mongi, 2018). As a result, emphasizing security and privacy is critical for increasing adoption of m-Government services.

Privacy

The study couldn't find any privacy policy from observation of the three selected m-Government sites (ajira.go.tz, necta.go.tz, and nacte.go.tz). Placement of privacy policy on m-Government sites is an essential aspect of legitimacy because privacy has been known to influence user trust in and influence adoption (Sánchez-Torres, Arroyo, Varon & Sánchez-Alzate, 2021). This issue needs to be addressed as the study by (Reddick & Zheng, 2018) argued that users needed to see privacy statements throughout the website to ensure that their privacy needs were met. Given the fact that privacy concerns act as a success factor to m-Government users (Ishengoma et al., 2018), it becomes imperative for policymakers to ensure that privacy statements become an integral part of m-Government sites to encourage citizens' adoption. While privacy policy can affect the adoption of m-Government sites, it is argued that it is not significant in the context of this study. This is because all of the selected m-Government services had no privacy policy. Hence, it could not affect one m-Government service being adopted more than the other.

Security

In our study context, security refers to any nuances that created security vulnerability for an m-Government service. The study used the Open Web Application Security Project's, OWASP ZAP, to assess the security of our selected m-Government sites (Makino and Klyuev, 2015). The results of OWASP ZAP analysis indicated all sites had no high-level risk vulnerabilities. The site ajira.go.tz was more vulnerable than necta.go.tz and nacte.go.tz. Ajira.go.tz was found to have 89 medium risk level compared to necta.go.tz and nacte.go.tz, which had no medium level alerts. Low-risk alerts were found to be 303 for ajira.go.tz, 175 for necta.go.tz and 4 for nacte.go.tz as shown in table 3.

Table 3. OWASP Vulnerability Assessment on Selected m-Government Sites

Name of vulnerability	Risk Level	Number of vulnerabilities		
		Ajira.go.tz	Necta.go.tz	Nacte.go.tz
Application error disclosure	Medium	1	0	0
Buffer Overflow	Medium	1	0	0
X-Frame Options Header Not Set	Medium	87	0	0
Cross-Domain JavaScript Source File Inclusion	Low	27	4	16
Incomplete or No-Cache Control and Pragma HTTP Header Set	Low	1	80	0
Secure Pages includes mixed content	Low	1	0	0
Web browser XSS Protection Not Enabled	Low	92	95	3
X-Content-Type-Options Header Missing	Low	209	0	1

In this study, we will focus on the medium-level alerts founds which are "application error disclosure," "buffer overflow", and "x-frame options header not set." We explore the medium-level risks discovered to understand the nuances that led to these security risks. For instance, if the fault causes it in designing or a technology bug has not been patched yet.

- X-Frame Options Header Not Set. This medium-level vulnerability had a high number of occurrences on ajira.go.tz. The HTTP response header can be used to specify whether a browser should be permitted to render a page in a <frame>, iframe>, or <object>. If the site is not configured properly, it may become a victim of clickjacking attacks. Proper configuration should be used to avoid embedding site content into other sites. There are three possible configurations for X-Frame-Options: "Deny", which will deny loading a page from both within and from other sites. "Same origin," which page can still be used in a frame as long as the site includes it in a frame is the same as the one serving the page. "Allow-from https://example.com/" will display the page from a specified origin. The above three options, depending on the server locations of the m-Government services, "same-origin" and "allow from https://example.com/" could be used.
- Application Error Disclosure. This vulnerability manifests itself when pages contain an error/warning message that may reveal confidential information such as the location of the file that generated the unhandled exception. This data may be used to conduct additional attacks against the

web application. The answer to this vulnerability is to enforce a mechanism that offers a unique error reference/identifier to the client (browser) while logging the information on the server-side and preventing them from being exposed to the user.

- Buffer Overflow. When a program attempts to store more information in a buffer than it can keep, or when an application tries to store data in a memory area beyond a buffer, a buffer overflow condition occurs. At the code level, buffer overflow vulnerabilities typically result from a programmer's assumptions being violated. Buffer overruns can be mitigated to some extent by ensuring that development takes place in an environment that promotes high-quality code and requires developers to participate in code review and testing. To address this vulnerability, it is necessary to review and rewrite the background program. Security concerns are critical because, along with privacy concerns, they serve as the foundation for trust in e-government systems (Alzahrani et al., 2016; Karkin & Janssen, 2014).

A user's perception of the website's security is critical in convincing them to use it. This is critical because the majority of m-Government services require users to provide personal information. Security efforts, on the other hand, are an ongoing process, as new security threats emerge as new technologies evolve. According to the literature, privacy and security must be protected in order to increase user trust when interacting with e-government services (Liu and Carter, 2018; Ishengoma et al., 2018). As technologies advance, the number of complex attacks increases, and cyber-criminals develop new attack methods on a daily basis. As a result, security and privacy of systems and users are critical for increasing adoption of m-Government services.

Accessibility

All citizens' access to m-Government services is a key element of m-Government adoption. In this study, multiple channels, accessibility for disabled individuals, and accessibility in a foreign language were all considered when evaluating the accessibility of selected m-Government services. The World Wide Web Consortium's (W3C) Web Accessibility Initiative (WAI) has established accessibility standards for web developers. The Web Content Accessibility Guidelines are the name given to these guidelines (WCAG). The MAUVE tool is used in this study to assess the degree to which the selected guidelines are being applied satisfactorily to the m-government-selected sites. WCAG is currently available in two versions (WCAG version 1 and WCAG version 2). The most recent version, WCAG 2.0, is examined in this study. The WCAG 2.0 specification is divided into three priority levels of guidelines (A-AA-AAA).

Table 4. WCAG Guidelines Priority on Web Accessibility

Priority	Description	Conformance Level
Priority 1	To make sure that the information is accessible to all users, including those with disabilities, the developer is required to follow the guidelines outlined in this document.	A
Priority 2	In order to remove important barriers to accessing information on a website, the developer should follow these guidelines.	AA
Priority 3	The developer may follow these guidelines because they are not critical but do make the website more accessible to disabled users.	AAA

Level A focuses on the fundamental characteristics of web accessibility. As shown in Table 4, level AA addresses advanced barriers to web accessibility for disabled users, whereas level AAA addresses the highest level of web accessibility.

For ajira.go.tz, the analysis found 32 errors under level A-WCAG 2.0 and 135 errors under level AA-WCAG 2.0. Total warnings were 19. For necta.go.tz, the analysis found 49 errors under level A-WCAG and 24 errors under level AA-WCAG 2.0. Necta.go.tz and nacte.go.tz proved to have higher accessibility than ajira.go.tz (Figure 10). However, both sites fell short of the required level of accessibility conformance, which is zero errors for level A. Since the results show that all sites do not pass the A or AA compliance level, the AAA compliance test was not performed. Resolving the existing errors in ajira.go.tz could increase accessibility hence the number of users, influencing more adoption.

Figure 10. Web accessibility compliance on selected m-Government sites

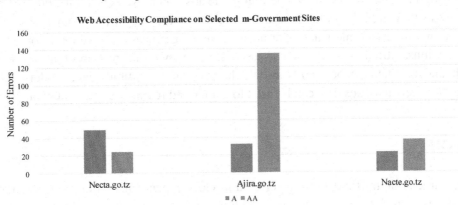

Cost and Infrastructure

The factors of cost and infrastructure were ignored in this study since the cost of accessing the information on all three selected m-Government sites is the same. In this case, the cost will not be a factor for one site to be adopted more than the other. Similarly, to infrastructure, all the m-Government sites operate under the same infrastructure. Hence, infrastructure cannot favor one m-Government service over the other.

IMPLICATIONS AND LIMITATIONS

Practical Implications

It is critical for practitioners, such as government agencies and other stakeholders responsible for delivering m-Government services, to be informed that affect m-Government service adoption from a web analytics viewpoint. Moreover, the findings will also assist government agencies and stakeholders in understanding the key issues that underpin the adoption of m-Government services from web analytics perspectives, enabling them to improve and accelerate its adoption. Developers, regulators, and politicians must emphasize concerns like usability, accessibility, privacy, and security to encourage Tanzanians to use mobile government services.

Limitations

As with any methodology, web analytics methodology has some limitations. The study points out some limitations associated with this study. In web analytics, an IP address symbolizes a user. Since more than one person can use the same computer for m-Government services, an IP address seems limited as a representation of the user. Another constraint is that WATs are unable to provide answers to why questions. For example, why did users behave as they did? Why did users abandon the task they began? Web analytics cannot provide any insight into the users' motivations or decision-making processes. To elicit information about the users' motivations, attitudinal data, such as surveys, interviews, or direct observations, is required. However, web analytics data can be used to initiate the collection of attitude data. Undefined behavior discovered through web analytics data can be used to gather and research attitudinal data.

Another constraint is that WATs are unable to provide answers to why questions. For example, why did users behave as they did? Why did users abandon the task they began? Web analytics cannot provide any insight into the users' motivations or decision-making processes. To elicit information about the users' motivations, attitudinal data, such as surveys, interviews, or direct observations, is required. However, web analytics data can be used to initiate the collection of attitude data. Undefined behavior discovered through web analytics data can be used to gather and research attitudinal data.

CONCLUSION

In this chapter, large-scale traffic data from selected m-Government sites (ajira.go.tz, necta.go.tz, and nacte.go.tz) were examined to understand the underlying factors favoring the successful adoption of one site compared to the other. Usability issues (bounce rate, page size, loading time, number of requests and deadlinks) were found to influence users to adopt one m-Government service over the other. Users also consider the security and privacy of the m-Government services. Poor security and privacy issues (such as buffer overflow and application error disclosure) are likely to have a negative effect on the adoption. However, the cost and infrastructure did not affect the adoption preference.

The findings prove that web analytics methodology is suitable for exploring the system and the user's behaviour of m-Government sites. The study found that both sites have similar demographic profiles of main males between the ages of 25 and 34. The majority of these are in college and those who have just finished colleges and universities. They visit the sites mainly from direct search and organic search.

Additionally, the study noted that users' keywords include the primary information's name and the date, for example, "necta results 2018". All of the websites examined demonstrated a low level of accessibility, usability, and security. The study enlightens developers and designers about the critical nature of adhering to international accessibility and usability standards for websites. The chapter's findings should be contextualized by drawing on additional qualitative and quantitative research. For instance, the study indicates which pages are accessed and how frequently and how long they arc visited, but not why visitors behave in certain ways.

ACKNOWLEDGMENT

The University of Dodoma in Tanzania provided financial support for this study.

REFERENCES

Akamai (2017). *The state of online retail performance.* https://www.soasta.com/wp-content/uploads/2017/04/Stateof-Online-Retail-Performance-Spring-2017.pdf

Al-Sakran, H., & Almutairi, M. (2021). Usability and accessibility assessment of Saudi Arabia mobile e-Government websites. *IEEE Access: Practical Innovations, Open Solutions, 9,* 48254–48275. doi:10.1109/ACCESS.2021.3068917

Alexa. (2018a). *Alexa: Keyword research, competitive analysis, & website ranking.* http://www.alexa.com

Alexa. (2018b). *Top Sites in Tanzania.* https://www.alexa.com/topsites/countries/TZ

Alonazi, M., Beloff, N., & White, M. (2020). Perceptions towards the adoption and utilization of m-government services: A study from the citizens' perspective in Saudi Arabia. In E. Ziemba (Ed.), *Information Technology for Management: Current Research and Future Directions* (pp. 3–26). Springer. doi:10.1007/978-3-030-43353-6_1

Alshahwan, N., & Harman, M. (2012). State aware test case regeneration for improving web application test suite coverage and fault detection. *Proceedings of the 2012 International Symposium on Software Testing and Analysis,* 45-55. 10.1145/2338965.2336759

Annie, C.S., Choy, J.Y, Krishna, M., & Alex, L. (2017). Intention to use m-Government services: Does age, gender and education matter? *International Journal of e-business and e-Government Studies, 9*(2).

Aubert, B. A., & Hamel, G. (2001). Adoption of smart cards in the medical sector: The Canadian experience. *Social Science & Medicine, 53*(7), 879–894. doi:10.1016/S0277-9536(00)00388-9 PMID:11522135

Axelsson, K., & Melin, U. (2012). Citizens' Attitudes towards Electronic Identification in a Public E-Service Context – An Essential Perspective in the eID Development Process. In *Pro JavaScript Performance: Monitoring and Visualization.* Apress. doi:10.1007/978-3-642-33489-4_22

Bhagat, S., & Joshi, P. (2019). Evaluation of accessibility and accessibility audit methods for e-Governance Portals. *ICEGOV2019: Proceedings of the 12th International Conference on Theory and Practice of Electronic Governance,* 220–226. 10.1145/3326365.3326394

Brooks, L., & Persaud, A. (2015). Comparing local e-government websites in Canada and the UK. In Lecture Notes in Computer Science: Vol. 9248. *Electronic Government. EGOV 2015.* Springer. doi:10.1007/978-3-319-22479-4_22

Burton, R. M. (2018). Hawthorne effect, the. In M. Augier & D. J. Teece (Eds.), *The Palgrave Encyclopedia of Strategic Management.* Palgrave Macmillan. doi:10.1057/978-1-137-00772-8_316

Cai X., Li S., Feng G. (2020). Evaluating the performance of government websites: An automatic assessment system based on the TFN-AHP methodology. *Journal of Information Science, 46*(6), 760-775.

CDT, & infoDev. (2007). *E-Government Handbook: Accessibility*. Retrieved June 19, 2007, from https://www.cdt.org/egov/handbook/accessibility.shtml

Chamorro, Miranda, Rodrigo, & González. (2001). A new web assessment Index: Spanish universities analysis. *Internet Research, 11*(3), 226-234.

Dingli, A., & Mifsud, J. (2011). USEFul: A framework to mainstream web site usability through automated evaluation. *International Journal of Human-Computer Interaction, 2*(1).

Doupé, A., Cui, W., Jakubowski, M., Peinado, M., Kruegel, C., & Vigna, D. (2013). deDacota: Toward preventing server-side XSS via automatic code and data separation. *Proceedings of the 2013 ACM SIGSAC Conference on Computer & Communications Security.*

Fong, E. M., & Chung, W. Y. (2013). Mobile cloud-computing-based healthcare service by noncontact ECG monitoring. *Sensors (Basel), 12*(12), 16451–16473. doi:10.3390131216451 PMID:24316562

Frohlich, K., Nieminen, M., & Pinomaa, A. (2020). Factors influencing the adoption of m-Government: Perspectives from a Namibian marginalised community. In R. Zitouni, M. Agueh, P. Houngue, & H. Soude (Eds.), *e-Infrastructure and e-Services for Developing Countries. AFRICOMM 2019. Lecture Notes of the Institute for Computer Sciences, Social Informatics and Telecommunications Engineering* (Vol. 311). Springer. doi:10.1007/978-3-030-41593-8_17

Hasan, L. (2009). *Usability Evaluation Framework for E-commerce Websites in Developing Countries* (Doctoral Thesis). Loughborough University.

Hassan, N., Amer, A., & Sawsan, A. (2021). A review of website evaluation using web diagnostic tools and data envelopment analysis. *Bulletin of Electrical Engineering and Informatics.*

HESLB. (2006). *Annual report, 2005 – 2006*. Higher Education Students' Loans Board.

Hofstede, G. (1981). *Culture and organisations*. McGraw-Hill.

Ishengoma, F., Mselle, L., & Mongi, H. (2018). Critical success factors towards the adoption of m-Government services in Tanzania. A conceptual framework. *The Electronic Journal on Information Systems in Developing Countries, 85*(1), e12064. doi:10.1002/isd2.12064

Ishengoma, F., Mselle, L., & Mongi, H. (2019). Power distance and user's behavior towards the adoption of m-Government services in Tanzania: A web analytics study. *International Journal of Open Information Technologies, 7*(9).

Janssen, M., Wimmer, M. A., Moe, C. E., & Flak, L. S. (Eds.). Electronic Government. Lecture Notes in Computer Science, 7443.

Karkin, N., & Janssen, M. (2014). Evaluating websites from a public value perspective: A review of Turkish local government websites. *International Journal of Information Management, 34*(3), 351–363. doi:10.1016/j.ijinfomgt.2013.11.004

Khalid, A. (2017). Automated usability evaluation of e-learning websites in Saudi Arabia. *5th International Conference of Advanced Computer Science & Information Technology*, 1-10. 10.5121/csit.2017.70801

Kous, K., & Polančič, G. (2021). An empirical investigation of the accessibility of official European tourism websites. In C. Eusébio, L. Teixeira, & M. Carneiro (Eds.), *ICT Tools and Applications for Accessible Tourism* (pp. 169–195). IGI Global. doi:10.4018/978-1-7998-6428-8.ch008

Liwen, V., & Rongbin, Y. (2013). Web traffic and organisation performance measures: Relationships and data sources examined. *Journal of Informetrics*, *7*(3), 699–711. doi:10.1016/j.joi.2013.04.005

Makino, Y., & Klyuev, V. (2015). Evaluation of web vulnerability scanners. *The 8th IEEE International Conference on Intelligent Data Acquisition and Advanced Computing Systems: Technology and Applications.*

Malaquias, F. & Júnior, R. (2021). The use of m-government applications: Empirical evidence from the smartest cities of Brazil. *Information Technology & People.* ahead-of-print. doi:10.1108/ITP-05-2020-0346

Mateos, J. Jong, & Timothy. (2021). The impact of mobile ICT on national productivity in developed and developing countries. *Information & Management, 58*(3). doi:10.1016/j.im.2021.103442

Morgan, C., Liu, D., & Carter, L. (2018). Impact of citizens' privacy concerns on e-Government adoption. In *Proceedings of the 19th Annual International Conference on Digital Government Research: Governance in the Data Age*. ACM.

Mtingwi, J. E. (2015). Mobile Government in African Least Developed Countries (LDCs): Proposed Implementing Framework. *Proceedings of IST-Africa*, 1-14.

Müller, C., Hornung, D., Hamm, T., & Wulf, V. (2015). Measures and tools for supporting ICT appropriation by elderly and non-tech-savvy persons in a long-term perspective. In *ECSCW 2015: Proceedings of the 14th European Conference on Computer Supported Cooperative Work*. Springer. 10.1007/978-3-319-20499-4_14

Narayanan, S. P. (2016). A holistic approach to lowering latency in geo-distributed web applications. *Open Access Dissertations*, 834.

Nejati, J., & Balasubramanian, A. (2016). An in-depth study of mobile browser performance. *Proceedings of the 25th International Conference on World Wide Web (WWW '16)*, 1305-1315. 10.1145/2872427.2883014

Pakkala, H., Presser, K., & Christensenc, T. (2012). Using Google analytics to measure visitor statistics: The case of food composition websites. *International Journal of Information Management, 32*(6), 504–512. doi:10.1016/j.ijinfomgt.2012.04.008

Poulos, M., Korfiatis, N., & Papavlassooulos, S. (2020). Assessing stationarity in web analytics: A study of bounce rates. *Expert Systems, 37*(3).

Rafique, S., Humayun, M., Hamid, B., Abbas, A., Akhtar, M., & Iqbal, K. (2015). Web application security vulnerabilities detection approaches: A systematic mapping study. *IEEE/ACIS 16th International Conference on Software Engineering, Artificial Intelligence, Networking and Parallel/Distributed Computing (SNPD)*, 1-6. 10.1109/SNPD.2015.7176244

Reddick, C. G., & Zheng, Y. (2018). Online privacy protection in Chinese city Governments: An analysis of privacy statements. In L. Alcaide Muñoz & M. Rodríguez Bolívar (Eds.), *International E-Government Development*. Palgrave Macmillan. doi:10.1007/978-3-319-63284-1_5

Sánchez-Torres, J., Arroyo, X., Varon, S., & Sánchez-Alzate, J. (2021). Adoption of e-government in Colombia: The importance of government policy in citizens' use of e-government. *An International Journal of Electronic Government*, *17*(2), 220–236. doi:10.1504/EG.2021.114577

Schiavone, A. & Paternò, F. (2015). An extensible environment for guideline-based accessibility evaluation of dynamic web applications. In *Universal Access in the Information Society* (vol. 14, pp. 111-132). . doi:10.100710209-014-0399-3

Semerádová, T., & Weinlich, P. (2020). Using Google Analytics to Examine the Website Traffic. In *Website Quality and Shopping Behavior*. Springer. doi:10.1007/978-3-030-44440-2_5

Shareef, M., Dwivedi, Y., Laumer, S., & Archer, N. (2016). Citizens' adoption behavior of mobile government (mGov): A cross-cultural study. *Information Systems Management*, *33*(3), 268–283. doi:10.1080/10580530.2016.1188573

Sleeper, M., Consolvo, S., & Staddon, J. (2014). Exploring the benefits and uses of web analytics tools for non-transactional websites. In *Proceedings of the Conference on Designing Interactive Systems: Processes, Practices, Methods, and Techniques*. Springer. 10.1145/2598510.2598555

The United Republic of Tanzania. (2004). *Higher Education Students Loans Board (HELBS) Act, 2004*. URT.

Venkatesh, V., & David, F. R. (2000). A Theoretical Extension of the Technology Acceptance Model: Four Longitudinal Field Studies. *Management Science*, *46*(2), 186–204. doi:10.1287/mnsc.46.2.186.11926

Wakhu, S. M., Fuyuan, X., & Kakonge, J. O. (2020). Enhancing e/m-Government synergy in Kenya: citizens' perspectives on the driving factors for m-government diffusion. In G. Salvendy & J. Wei (Eds.), Lecture Notes in Computer Science: Vol. 12216. *Design, Operation and Evaluation of Mobile Communications. HCII 2020*. Springer. doi:10.1007/978-3-030-50350-5_11

World Economic Forum (WEF). (2017). Global Gender Gap Report. WEF.

ADDITIONAL READING

Balusamy, B., Venkata Krishna, P., & Sridhar, J. (2016). Web Analytics: Assessing the Quality of Websites Using Web Analytics Metrics. In G. Sreedhar (Ed.), *Design Solutions for Improving Website Quality and Effectiveness* (pp. 253–275). IGI Global. doi:10.4018/978-1-4666-9764-5.ch010

Burns, M., & Colbert, M. (2013). Web Analytics: The New Purpose towards Predictive Mobile Games. In D. Reidsma, H. Katayose, & A. Nijholt (Eds.), Lecture Notes in Computer Science: Vol. 8253. *Advances in Computer Entertainment. ACE 2013*. Springer. doi:10.1007/978-3-319-03161-3_1

Kaur, S., Kaur, K., Singh, H., & Kaur, P. (2016). An Empirical Study of Usability Metric for Websites. In G. Sreedhar (Ed.), *Design Solutions for Improving Website Quality and Effectiveness* (pp. 162–186). IGI Global. doi:10.4018/978-1-4666-9764-5.ch007

Rao, A. P. (2016). Quality Measures for Semantic Web Application. In G. Sreedhar (Ed.), *Design Solutions for Improving Website Quality and Effectiveness* (pp. 130–139). IGI Global. doi:10.4018/978-1-4666-9764-5.ch005

Redkina, N. S. (2017). The development tendencies of web analytics tools. *Automatic Documentation and Mathematical Linguistics, 51*(3), 112–116. doi:10.3103/S0005105517030050

Rohloff, T., Oldag, S., Renz, J., & Meinel, C. (2019). Utilising Web Analytics in the Context of Learning Analytics for Large-Scale Online Learning. *IEEE Global Engineering Education Conference (EDUCON)*, Dubai, United Arab Emirates, 2019, pp. 296-305, DOI: 10.1109/EDUCON.2019.8725118

Salini, I. Malavolta and F. Rossi. (2016). Leveraging Web Analytics for Automatically Generating Mobile Navigation Models. *IEEE International Conference on Mobile Services* (MS), San Francisco, CA, USA, 2016, pp. 103-110, DOI: 10.1109/MobServ.2016.25

Sreedhar, G. (2016). Identifying and Evaluating Web Metrics for Assuring the Quality of Web Designing. In G. Sreedhar (Ed.), *Design Solutions for Improving Website Quality and Effectiveness* (pp. 1–23). IGI Global. doi:10.4018/978-1-4666-9764-5.ch001

Xun, J. (2015). Return on website visit duration: Applying web analytics data. *Journal of Direct, Data and Digital Marketing Practice, 17*(1), 54–70. doi:10.1057/dddmp.2015.33

Zheng, G., & Peltsverger, S. (2015). Web Analytics Overview. In Khosrow-Pour, D.B.A., M. (Ed.), Encyclopedia of Information Science and Technology, Third Edition (pp. 7674-7683). IGI Global. http://doi:10.4018/978-1-4666-5888-2.ch756

KEY TERMS AND DEFINITIONS

Accessibility: The ease with which an e-government medium may provide information and services.

Bounce Rate: Measures the website's effectiveness in keeping visitors engaged and is often used as an indicator of a site's relevance and ability to generate interest.

Direct Traffic: Traffic generated from users familiar with the site name, and they go directly to the website by typing the site URL.

Loading Time: The amount of time needed by the browser to load and display the web page.

Number of Requests: The total number of requests needed to be executed to retrieve a complete web page.

Organic Search Results: The size (in bytes) of the web page that is rendered by the browser when it is requested.

Page Size: The size (in bytes) of the web page that is rendered by the browser when it is requested.

Chapter 7
Biomedical Text Summarization Based on the Itemset Mining Approach

Supriya Gupta
National Institute of Technology, Raipur, India

Aakanksha Sharaff
National Institute of Technology, Raipur, India

Naresh Kumar Nagwani
National Institute of Technology, Raipur, India

ABSTRACT

The expanding amount of text-based biomedical information has prompted mining valuable or intriguing frequent patterns (words/terms) from extremely massive content, which is still a very challenging task. In the chapter, the authors have conceived a practical methodology for text mining dependent on the frequent item sets. This chapter presents a strategy utilizing item set mining graph-based summarization for summing up biomedical literature. They address the difficulties of recognizing important subjects or concepts in the given biomedical document text and display the relations between the strings by choosing the high pertinent lines from biomedical literature using apriori itemset mining algorithm. This method utilizes essential criteria to distinguish the significant concepts, events, for example, the fundamental subjects of the input record. These sentences are determined as exceptionally educational, applicable, and chosen to create the final summary.

DOI: 10.4018/978-1-7998-8061-5.ch007

1. INTRODUCTION

In this present era, the vast data of biomedical literature is accessible in digital form, which keeps on developing at a stunning rate. The utilization of frequent patterns for the biomedical area is critical since the mined item sets diminish the dimensionality of the biomedical reports radically. The biomedical field's clinical researchers and medical practitioners consistently face overseeing, extricating valuable data from the vast amount of biomedical repositories (Fleuren & Alkema, 2015). People use automatic text summarization to acquire data that they search to save their time required for pursuing long content archives (Moradi & Ghadiri, 2017). A few methodologies from linguistics, computer application, and arithmetic addresses various issues in generic text summarization (Gambhir & Gupta, 2017; Yao et al., 2017). The biomedical researchers have focused on graph-based methods for summarizing the domain-independent and biomedical corpus (Gambhir & Gupta, 2017; Mishra et al., 2014). In any case, a few difficulties are there that actually should be tended to by implementing unique methodologies. A graph-based summarizer can resolve the principal challenge of distinguishing significant actions inside the given document and finding the method of identifying this critical event by making a practical summary. This recent research is focused on solving these challenges to make the event-based summary.

This graph-based summarization technique starts with data harvesting with preprocessing methods, mapping the biomedical corpus to the essential biomedical concepts. Then, the summarizer finds regular itemsets that address the content's fundamental subjects by utilizing the item-set mining technique, a prestigious technique called Apriori calculation, and is used for mining the frequent patterns. The proposed biomedical summarizer uses an item-set mining technique for finding the themes from ideas chosen from the information archive. The proposed summarizer applies the necessary and apt calculation to distinguish the item sets in the biomedical document. The extracted item-sets are considered essential concepts for building the word network, which passes on the relations and connections between sentences of the article. Summarizer utilizes the degree of measurement that evaluates the relatedness of sentences inside the diagram. The most elevated scored sentences are chosen for incorporation in the last summary. Theories of essential subjects are utilized to build a word network that describes the relationship among the strings inside the content. Several experiments were performed to evaluate the different parameters, including Recall for the biomedical text with the biomedical graph summarizer. The outcome depicted that the item-set mining-based graph summarizer can beat other techniques regarding ROUGE measurements (Lin, 2004).

The description of the chapter is coordinated as follows. A concise audit of the past work is presented in segment 2. In segment 3 Methods, a bit by bit clarification of our summary generation approach is shown. Segment 4 provides the details of investigations and assessments with results and discussion. In the end, we bring up some closing comments in segment 5 as the conclusion.

2. BACKGROUND

Various methodologies with machine intelligence, linguistics, and statistics are projected to create biomedical document summarization frameworks (Gambhir & Gupta, 2017; Yao et al., 2017). Numerous summarization systems evaluate significance with strings dependent on the top of conventional estimates, for example, sentence length, term position, sentence location, cue phrase, etc. (Gupta & Lehal, 2010). In this biomedical text summarization, various performances have revealed that such general features can perform better for the domain-specific methods (Moradi, 2018b; Moradi & Ghadiri, 2018; Plaza et al., 2011). The biomedical corpus has its uniqueness (Erhardt et al., 2014; Plaza et al., 2011) which can cause some trouble using area-independent summarization techniques. This acted as the main impetus to create domain-specific summarizers which can counter the distinctive biomedical document. In this research, biomedical text summarization utilizes a preprocessing step where input text is designed, including the UMLS metathesarus (Nelson et al., 2017). Many different techniques are uses for comparative study on opinion summarization in extractive and abstractive way with the help of dimensionality reduction (Bhatia S, 2020).

In the proposed methodology, ideas structure the primary building block of information content. It can prompt a structure that presents the thoughts and concepts of the content more precisely than considering direct concepts (Moradi & Ghadiri, 2017). As per the experiment revealed in the methods section, the summaries are created by the event. The concept-based strategy contains added instructive substance than made by concept-based contenders. The deep learning based classifiers are also perform the good results for the text data and medical text data (Basheer et al., 2021; Chakraborty et al., 2020) The summarizer is partitioned into four classifications with AI, NLP, statically, and fusion techniques to deal with biomedical literature (Mishra et al., 2014). The methods deal with various difficulties of text summarization which are identified with multiple sorts of reports like clinical records, scientific articles, legal corpus, clinical notes, medical transcripts, etc. (Moradi & Ghadiri, 2018). Frequent patterns mining is the method of information investigation used for summarizing the transactional data (Altemeier, 1997), clinical data (Mallick et al., n.d.), and text-based information (Baralis et al., 2013; Cagliero et al., 2019).

The item-set-based graph summarizer is focused on summarizing biomedical articles. It employs item-set mining to find principal thoughts inside the given input biomedical text. This method ranks the sentences depending on their closeness to the astounding number of significant points (Moradi, 2018a). The strategy introduced in this chapter additionally presents item-set mining to recognize the crucial concepts from the corpus. These themes, identified as the most significant concepts, are utilized to make the word graph that shows how the sentences are connected. The proposed trial results illustrate that the item-set graph-based procedure knows how to upgrade the critical and valuable concepts that make summaries designed for biomedical documents.

Graph-based summarizers think about various content units, like words, events, concepts, strings, etc. Nodes characterize edges dependent on proximity measures or connection capacities (Gambhir & Gupta, 2017). This last graph passes on the closeness of nodes; the ranking method finds the most informative and valuable sentences within-corpus to produce a precise length extract. (Balinsky et al. 2011) did research specific to experiments with petite word arrangements in document summarization. Even though, in previous work, authors didn't assess their methodology by summing up a corpus of archives with a correlation of different strategies. In the proposed approach, the helpfulness of the graph-based single extractive text summarization is evaluated for the biomedical libraries via comparison through the state of art methods.

3. METHODS

The biomedical extractive text summarization uses the frequent items to make an informative summary with all the information about the corpus. These are the building blocks in the generation of biomedical summaries. The graph-based summarizer performs these primary strides to create the ultimate output summary from the input biomedical archive. These are the fundamental steps involved (1) preprocessing of text, (2) frequent item-set mining for finding concepts, (3) finding significant concepts, (4) deconstructing graph, and (5) generation of summary.

a. Pre-Processing

First and foremost, the XML and JSON parser needs to extract the biomedical text in usable form. After that, the summarizer separates the primary body of the content for designing and consistent construction of given input text. The input text is picked from biomedical scientific literature, and then the primary body is separated by disposing of the trivial and repetitive parts. These sections might be the author's details, book headings, book index segment, bibliography, etc. The NLP methods are utilized to harvest the data for further processing.

Figure 1. Preprocessing steps of biomedical text

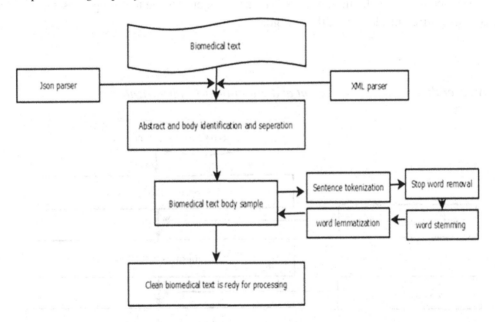

It recognizes multiple concept mappings (Larose et al., 2014) for each noun expression and collects the concept with the most noteworthy rank scores. Alongside every concept, semantic meaning is restored that indicates a semantic order of the biomedical keywords. Figure 1 depicts an illustration of planning biomedical text preparation for itemset mining and generating a graph-based summary.

i. Tokenization and Stop Word Removal

Tokenization is additionally called Feature Extraction in text mining. The extraction of features from an input text into a vector space is called Feature Extraction. In this period of preprocessing, non-informative words like "the," "is," "was," "were" are eliminated. The non-informative words in the text collection don't have any colossal importance (Tutkan et al., 2016). For the maximum time, a stop list is referred to containing stop phrases that need to be eliminated during the preprocessing stage.

ii. Stemming and Noise Removal

Stemming may be a procedure of emitting the standard person morphological endings from words in English. When stopping, the stemming preprocessing method is carried out over the textual content collection (Moradi, 2018a). As an example, the words "improve," "improved," "improving" are going to be modified over to the word "improve" to its root significance to confirm that the terms are thought-about systematically as one-of-a-kind word for textual analysis. The elimination of obscure text, symbols, or words from features for e.g., signs like, etc., is known as noise removal.

There are nine semantic sorts whose ideas are non-exclusive; and can be ignored in messages identified with the biomedical area (Plaza et al., 2011). Here, the conventional semantic analysis types are qualitative model, temporal conception, quantitative concept, mental process, thought, spatial idea, useful idea, intellectual artifact, and language. Towards the end of the text preprocessing venture, each sentence contains different ideas with the end goal.

Figure 2. An overall framework for concept and graph-based summarization

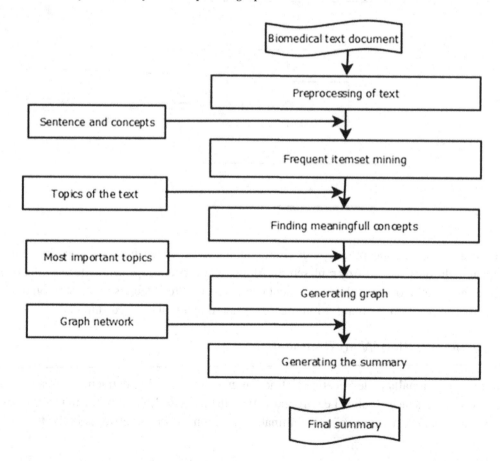

b. Frequent Item-Set Mining

After preprocessing, the clean biomedical data goes for further processing. With this progression, the system considers the key item-sets regularly repeating inside the input biomedical text to discover fundamentally connected ideas, as shown in Figure 2. The proposed approach utilizes the apriori algorithm (DIng et al., 2020), a generally utilized technique for information mining. This algorithm is capable of discovering things that are present in the dataset. Summarizer thinks about each string as a transaction and every concept like an item. The supported property is evaluated for each item or item-set present in the document. The frequency of that item set is separated across the size of the original text article. The item-set mining algorithm digs out the frequent patterns by the corpus with the most frequent concept, which has their support value equivalent or greater than the threshold of min-sup. In this approach, we know how to find several frequent item-sets from the biomedical corpus where some concepts are recurrently appearing together. The summarizer can take this item-set as the essential concept for generating the summary.

This section describes the item-set mining process to extract the pre-processed biomedical document's frequent word terms and concepts. For each biomedical document d_i the top frequent words p selected for making an efficient summary can be defined by Equation 1:

$$K_w = \{ d_i \mid P(d_i): \forall d_i \subseteq D \} \tag{1}$$

Where, $p(d_i) = T_{wj} : 1 \leq j \leq p$

From the transactional database B_T of biomedical data, as depicted in Equation 2, the T transaction contains the unique words u1, u2, uq, and q attributes calculated for biomedical document d_i.

$$B_T = \begin{cases} 0 \; if \; u_j \notin d_i \\ 1 \; if \; u_j \in d_i \end{cases} : 1 \leq j \leq q, 1 \leq I \leq n \tag{2}$$

Then this data can be used for the apriori algorithm, where we can find the most informative words and concepts for the summary generation.

c. Apriori Algorithm

Apriori is a conventional algorithm first presented in (Gashaw & Liu, 2018) for association mining rules. The stages which are utilized for mining association rules are as per the following. (1) Identifying the frequent patterns (2) Creating association rules. The patterns occurring frequently are mined in two stages. Firstly, the candidate itemset is generated, and then it can unearth the frequent patterns. Frequent patterns are only the item sets whose support is more noteworthy than the minimum sup given by the user. In the proposed approach, we have utilized frequent patterns for further summarization; we went through just the initial step of the apriori calculation. The pseudocode relating to the apriori calculation (Chee et al., 2019) is,

Pseudocode
C_k : Item-set candidate having k size
I_k : Frequent item-set having k size
1: I = { large, 1-item-set};
2: for (k =2; I_k ≠0; k + +) do begin
3: C_k = Apriori – gen (I_{k-1}); // new candidate
4: for all transaction T ∈ D do
5: C_T = subset (C_T , T); // candidates presents in T
6: for all candidates c ∈ C_T do
7: c.count + +;
8: end
9: end
10: I_k = { c ∈ C_T I c.count ≥ min sup}
5: end
6: Final concepts = $\cup_k I_k$

4. EVALUATION AND RESULTS

a. Assessment Corpus

In assessing automatic biomedical text summarization strategies, the biomedical document corpus is provided for this framework. A summary is created against the state-of-the-art summarization methods. Greater closeness among framework and model summary regarding shared content of frequent items alludes to elevated summarization execution. The proposed assessment corpus consists of biomedical full-text literature retrieved by the BioMed text archives (Raju et al., 2018). The system generates a biomedical extract of the single biomedical document, and the abstract of that literature is utilized as a golden summary. In the proposed research, specific literature is selected, and then the record is retrieved from the BioMed central corpus. If we choose 0.3 as the compression rate, and if the input document is 100 lines, then the summary is 30% of the original document.

b. Dataset Description

The MEDLINE database consists of 22 million and above references from NLM based in the USA, which is rapidly swelling dramatically (Hunter and Cohen, 2006). The examination of the absolute size and continued improvement of the combination of biomedical data collection is depicted in Table 1.

Similarly, finding the appropriate control in the consolidation of models for outline age possibly causes an information over-trouble (Hunter and Cohen, 2006; Lu, 2011).

Table 1. The Biomedical corpus Biomed literature single document contains the min, max, average sentences, and words present in full text and abstract

	Sentence Count			Terms Count		
	Minimum	**Maximum**	**Average**	**Minimum**	**Maximum**	**Average**
Full text	52	396	166	1032	9897	3976
Abstract	8	20	14	107	386	254

c. Assessment Measurements

The ROUGE scores are evaluated by the golden summary and proposed method summary. It assesses the common substance among system summary and submitted model summary dependent on various matrices and generates scores which are defined as shown in Equation 3:

$$ROUGE - N = \frac{\sum_{s \in s_H} \sum_{g_n \in s} C_m(g_n)}{\sum_{s \in s_H} \sum_{g_n \in s} C(g_n)} \qquad (3)$$

s_H is the group of human-made summary (abstract)

s is the individual human-made summary

g_n is an N-Gram

$C(g_n)$ is the number of co-occurrences of g_n in the human-made summary and proposed generated summary. In this chapter, the ROUGE measurements are done for calculating average Recall scores. Assessment of ROUGE-2 is performed regarding bigrams to evaluate system-generated summary and proposed model developed outline which shares some content. ROUGE-SU4 is dependent on common bigrams present in summaries, even as it permits skip distance up to the four terms.

d. Comparison Methods

The obtained ROUGE values are weighed among the item-set dependent summarization system (Moradi & Ghadiri, 2017), SUMMA (Saggion et al. 2002), MEAD (Radev et al., 2004), and TextRank. The solution based on the item-set graph mining strategy is used for summarizing biomedical articles. It finds frequent item-sets in the form of events and concepts present in the input biomedical text. Summarizer allocates ranks to the sentences concerning the item-sets that give the actual informative content of the article. This method, at last, chooses the sentences from the text that accomplish the most elevated values and delivers the ultimate summary. The SUMMA summarizer is an openly accessible system that utilizes several non-exclusive highlights, for example, sentence position and length and the frequent words, to score the sentences of the article. In this process, the sentences which get the most elevated scores are chosen, and then the final summary is produced. MEAD is a famous strategy that uses various conventional highlights from different methods, for example, term likeness, term length, centroid, and term position. The TextRank is a programmed system dependent on token extraction and an assortment of cue phrases. The correlation strategies are evaluated with the best-tuned settings utilizing improved corpus in the proposed assessments.

e. Evaluation Results

In this section, the results for the item-set mining-based summarization technique are provided. In this method, the key parameter is the primary measure of design for building the graph from the input biomedical article. In this manner, the parameters can influence the quality of the summary and the summarizer evaluation by the ROUGE score (Alami et al., 2019; Alguliyev et al., 2019). The main parameter is the item set to be viewed as continuous. For upper estimations of minimum-support, less incessant item sets are extricated; consequently, the graph developed regarding fewer subjects (Alguliyev et al., 2019; Dutta et al., 2019; Mallick et al.,2019). The rank of the sentence is the parameter that is decided according to the informative concepts. By this concept, the rank-based summarization calculates the graph matrix (Rahman & Borah, 2020), and the node and edges belong to the essential keywords linked or related to each other. At last higher-ranked sentences are picked for drafting the summary. In this way, the proposed model generates a summary and compares it with the golden summary, which is an abstract of the input biomedical literature with the help of the ROUGE evaluation.

The evaluation shown in Table 2 presents the consequences of conclusive assessment that demonstrates the item-set graph-based summarizer next to different techniques. The average Recall values for ROUGE 1, ROUGE 2, and ROUGE SU4 are evaluated by allowing for the abstract of the biomedical articles as golden summaries. As indicated, the ROUGE-1 score of 0.7642 of average Recall is best using the recommended approach among all the other methods. The outcome revealed that the proposed item-set mining-based graph summarization method is superior to the existing methods.

Table 2. ROUGE performance comparison of item-set based graph summarizer and the state of art techniques.

Techniques	ROUGE 1	ROUGE 2	ROUGE SU4
SweSum	.6983	.3014	.3462
TextRank	.6891	.2956	.3420
SUMMA	**.7164**	**.3178**	**.3548**
GraphSum	**.7460**	**.3359**	**.3795**
AutoSummarize	.6281	.2436	.3125
Baseline summarizer	.6322	.2529	.3196
Item-set based graph summarizer	**.7642**	**.3367**	**.3798**

For example, in contrast with area-free contenders, SUMMA, MEAD, TextRank, and item-set mining-based graph summarizers generate a summary that gives a more informative and precise length summary with meaningful substance. It shows that the recommended approach performed well in rendering the concepts from the biomedical text compared to the existing methods. In this research, the biomedical text summarizer takes the itemset mining approach for finding the very informative concepts and events by the biomedical literature that shows the uniqueness (Jiang et al., 2020) of text. Still, the existing methods did not explain it effectively. Moreover, the item-set-based graph summarizer uses successive item sets to discover the bond among the strings and concentrate on the majority correlated sentences. As per the outcome, the technique prompts a better correlation instead of only thinking about word frequency, string position, or string length.

Figure 3. ROUGE values distribution over different summarization methods

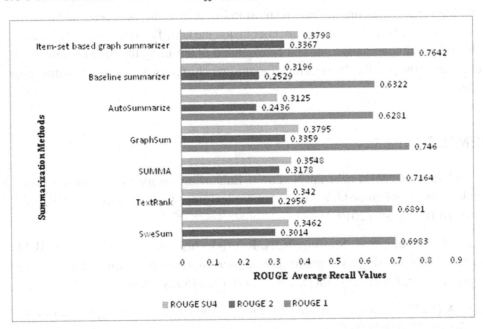

The ROUGE scores produced by the proposed item-set mining graph-based strategy are marginally improved than the existing summarizers as demonstrated in Figure 3. The proposed method depicts that the unwanted frequent item-sets should be omitted from the given input biomedical text. Each concept is not related and does not provide meaningful insights. The content goes astray due to irregularity for filtering, the weightiness measure to distinguish the item-sets. The different system that is capable of prompt elevated execution is a graph that causes the summarizer for creating associations among sentences dependent on the important topic with their relations. The recommended summarization system utilizes and enhances the sharing of essential data and procedures.

5. CONCLUSION

The proposed work presents an extractive document summarization system that is based upon graph and item-set mining methodology. This system uses mining of specific item-sets for finding primary themes inside the biomedical articles. An important measure causes the summarizer to distinguish the item-sets which would be able to measure as the majority significant ones. After concept retrieval, the significant item-sets demonstrate biomedical input articles like word network, which addresses the strings, which are mutually connected on the main points. Then the significance of every line inside the graph is evaluated utilizing the ranking score. The strings that give the topmost qualities are extricated in the form of an ultimate summary. The outcome of experiments demonstrates that the hybrid method can upgrade the summary created for biomedical literature. As observed from the outcome, the item-set graph-based summarizer may successfully deal with the difficulties present in the existing methods. The future work will incorporate contemplating different kinds of the graph to display the input biomedical text, researching various measures to find the most informative topics, concepts and assessing different capacities to recognize the most critical sentences inside the text. The research work is currently limited to single-document summarization and can be extended to outlining multiple documents. Researchers can further enhance the pipeline by selecting appropriate clustering and item-set mining approaches for better results.

REFERENCES

Alami, N., Meknassi, M., & En-nahnahi, N. (2019). Enhancing unsupervised neural networks based text summarization with word embedding and ensemble learning. *Expert Systems with Applications, 123,* 195–211. doi:10.1016/j.eswa.2019.01.037

Alguliyev, R. M., Aliguliyev, R. M., Isazade, N. R., Abdi, A., & Idris, N. (2019). COSUM: Text summarization based on clustering and optimization. *Expert Systems: International Journal of Knowledge Engineering and Neural Networks, 36*(1), 1–17. doi:10.1111/exsy.12340

Altemeier, W. A. (1997). Just tell me what I need to know. *Pediatric Annals, 26*(2), 74–76. doi:10.3928/0090-4481-19970201-03 PMID:9121844

Baralis, E., Cagliero, L., Mahoto, N., & Fiori, A. (2013). GraphSum: Discovering correlations among multiple terms for graph-based summarization. *Information Sciences, 249,* 96–109. doi:10.1016/j.ins.2013.06.046

Basheer, S., Bhatia, S., & Sakri, S. B. (2021). Computational Modeling of Dementia Prediction Using Deep Neural Network: Analysis on OASIS Dataset. *IEEE Access: Practical Innovations, Open Solutions, 9,* 42449–42462. doi:10.1109/ACCESS.2021.3066213

Cagliero, L., Garza, P., & Baralis, E. (2019). ELSA: A multilingual document summarization algorithm based on frequent itemsets and latent semantic analysis. *ACM Transactions on Information Systems, 37*(2), 1–33. doi:10.1145/3298987

Chakraborty, K., Bhatia, S., Bhattacharyya, S., Platos, J., Bag, R., & Hassanien, A. E. (2020). Sentiment Analysis of COVID-19 tweets by Deep Learning Classifiers—A study to show how popularity is affecting accuracy in social media. *Applied Soft Computing*, *97*, 106754. doi:10.1016/j.asoc.2020.106754 PMID:33013254

Chee, C. H., Jaafar, J., Aziz, I. A., Hasan, M. H., & Yeoh, W. (2019). Algorithms for frequent itemset mining: A literature review. *Artificial Intelligence Review*, *52*(4), 2603–2621. doi:10.100710462-018-9629-z

Ding, J., Li, Y., Ni, H., & Yang, Z. (2020). Generative Text Summary Based on Enhanced Semantic Attention and Gain-Benefit Gate. *IEEE Access: Practical Innovations, Open Solutions*, *8*, 92659–92668. doi:10.1109/ACCESS.2020.2994092

Dutta, S., Das, A. K., Bhattacharya, A., Dutta, G., Parikh, K. K., Das, A., & Ganguly, D. (2019). Community detection based tweet summarization. *Advances in Intelligent Systems and Computing*, *813*(September), 797–808. doi:10.1007/978-981-13-1498-8_70

Fleuren, W. W. M., & Alkema, W. (2015). Application of text mining in the biomedical domain. *Methods (San Diego, Calif.)*, *74*, 97–106. doi:10.1016/j.ymeth.2015.01.015 PMID:25641519

Gambhir, M., & Gupta, V. (2017). Recent automatic text summarization techniques: A survey. *Artificial Intelligence Review*, *47*(1), 1–66. doi:10.100710462-016-9475-9

Gashaw, Y., & Liu, F. (2018). Performance evaluation of frequent pattern mining algorithms using web log data for web usage mining. *Proceedings - 2017 10th International Congress on Image and Signal Processing, BioMedical Engineering and Informatics, CISP-BMEI 2017*, 1–5. 10.1109/CISP-BMEI.2017.8302317

Gupta, V., & Lehal, G. S. (2010). A Survey of Text Summarization Extractive techniques. *Journal of Emerging Technologies in Web Intelligence*, *2*(3), 258–268. doi:10.4304/jetwi.2.3.258-268

Jiang, S., Wu, W., Tomita, N., Ganoe, C., & Hassanpour, S. (2020). Multi-ontology refined embeddings (MORE): A hybrid multi-ontology and corpus-based semantic representation for biomedical concepts. *ArXiv*, 1–25.

Lin, C.-Y. (2004). ROUGE: A Package for Automatic Evaluation of Summaries. *Association for Computational Linguistics Anthology*, *34*(12), 1213–1220. doi:10.1253/jcj.34.1213

Mallick, C., Das, A. K., Dutta, M., Das, A. K., & Sarkar, A. (n.d.). *Graph-BasedTextSummarizationUsing ModifiedTextRank.pdf*. Springer Singapore. doi:10.1007/978-981-13-0514-6

Mishra, R., Bian, J., Fiszman, M., Weir, C. R., Jonnalagadda, S., Mostafa, J., & Del, G. (2014). Text summarization in the biomedical domain : A systematic review of recent research. *Journal of Biomedical Informatics*, *52*, 457–467. doi:10.1016/j.jbi.2014.06.009 PMID:25016293

Moradi, M. (2018a). CIBS: A biomedical text summarizer using topic-based sentence clustering. *Journal of Biomedical Informatics*, *88*(November), 53–61. doi:10.1016/j.jbi.2018.11.006 PMID:30445218

Moradi, M. (2018b). *Concept-based single- and multi-document biomedical text summarization Concept-based single- and multi-document biomedical text summarization*. Milad Moradi Department of Electrical and Computer Engineering Language : Farsi Abstract.

Moradi, M., & Ghadiri, N. (2017). Quantifying the informativeness for biomedical literature summarization: An itemset mining method. In *Computer Methods and Programs in Biomedicine* (Vol. 146). doi:10.1016/j.cmpb.2017.05.011

Moradi, M., & Ghadiri, N. (2018). Different approaches for identifying important concepts in probabilistic biomedical text summarization. *Artificial Intelligence in Medicine, 84,* 101–116. doi:10.1016/j.artmed.2017.11.004 PMID:29208328

Plaza, L., Díaz, A., & Gervás, P. (2011). A semantic graph-based approach to biomedical summarisation. *Artificial Intelligence in Medicine, 53*(1), 1–14. doi:10.1016/j.artmed.2011.06.005 PMID:21752612

Radev, D. R., Jing, H., Styś, M., & Tam, D. (2004). Centroid-based summarization of multiple documents. *Information Processing & Management, 40*(6), 919–938. doi:10.1016/j.ipm.2003.10.006

Rahman, N., & Borah, B. (2020). Improvement of query-based text summarization using word sense disambiguation. *Complex & Intelligent Systems, 6*(1), 75–85. doi:10.100740747-019-0115-2

Raju, C., Philipsy, E., Chacko, S., & Suresh, L. P. (2018). *Mining Techniques.* Academic Press.

Tutkan, M., Ganiz, M. C., & Akyokuş, S. (2016). Helmholtz principle based supervised and unsupervised feature selection methods for text mining. *Information Processing & Management, 52*(5), 885–910. doi:10.1016/j.ipm.2016.03.007

Yao, J., Wan, X., & Xiao, J. (2017). Recent advances in document summarization. *Knowledge and Information Systems, 53*(2), 297–336. doi:10.100710115-017-1042-4

Chapter 8
Answer Selection in Community Question Answering Using LSTM

Saman Qureshi

Maulana Azad National Institute of Technology, India

Sri Khetwat Saritha

Maulana Azad National Institute of Technology, India

D. Kishan

Maulana Azad National Institute of Technology, India

ABSTRACT

Websites like Quora, Yahoo! Answers, and Reddit are examples of community question answering (CQA) systems that enable users to ask questions as well as to answer questions. Answer selection is the most challenging task in CQA systems to get the good and relevant answer for the user questions. The short-comings in the current approaches are lexical gap between text pairs, dependency on external sources, and manual features which lead to lack of generalization ability. These shortcomings are resolved by already proposed work, but they lack generalization, and their performance is not satisfying. Whereas to focus on rich quality answers, attention mechanism can be integrates with neural network. This chapter proposes two models BLSTM and BLSTM with attention mechanism. Attention mechanism aligns question to the answer with the answer's more informative part. So, when it is applied in the model, BLSTM with attention mechanism model surpasses the top approaches.

DOI: 10.4018/978-1-7998-8061-5.ch008

INTRODUCTION

Community question-answering (CQA) systems belong to well established and a major group of Web applications, such as Stack Overflow or Reddit. Billions of users are using these applications every day to get an answer for their questions. Community Question Answering (CQA) in web forums, which provides large number of high-quality useful answers as a classic forum for user communication, in comparison with traditional question answering. The increasing popularity of CQA websites has caused number of questions and new forum members to surge without restriction. Unfortunately, much effort must be exerted to select one that is the most accurate for a specific question and to assess all answers possible.

Answer Selection is one of the Answer Processing in the final stage of question answering system where answer extraction is done. It is the most challenging task in CQA systems. When a user post any question in a community site the answer to the question is given by other users. There can be more than one answer to a question all these answers in an all is called as candidate answers. The main task in answer processing is to select the right and related one answers to a question from these bunch of answers called as candidate answer.

The main problem in a community site is that when a question is posted a bunch of answers is given by users and in these answers, many are not so related to question asked and, in some answers, even shift in the topic, to the context to different subject. An example of this problem is shown in Fig 1.

Many researchers has studied the Answer Selection task in Community Question Answering system and proposes the different models based on features like non-textual, syntactic, textual entailment. As all the proposed methods are works on independent dataset and also independent evaluation metrics, which leads to difficulty in comparison of these methods results. Therefore, the common framework is provided by the Task 3 of Semantic Evaluation(SemEval) (SemEval-2015 Task 3,) to compare different methods in multiple languages. The task 3 in SemEval -2015 is related to answer selection in CQA. The feature of the task is semantic similarity, natural language inference and textual entailment. This task is initiated to automate the process of identifying the correct answer from the answer thread by classifying the answers as good, bad and potential.

The existing frameworks is quite time intensive and it involves manual featurization requiring domain expertise and some external resources. This paper aims to use BLSTM with Attention Mechanism

Figure 1. Example from Qatar Living community forum

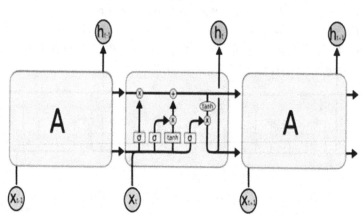

for answer selection task in Community Question Answering System to improve the Macro-F1 score, remove feature engineering and external resources.

BACKGROUND

Semantic Evaluation is an ongoing series of evaluations to evaluate semantic analysis system, where semantic analysis means analysis of meaning that is the nature of meaning in language is explored. Before SemEval Task 3, the proposed methods are on different independent datasets and to compare these methods results is a complex task. Therefore the common framework is provided by the Task 3 of SemEval to compare different methods in multiple languages.The task 3 in SemEval -2015 is related to answer selection in CQA. The feature of the task is semantic similarity, natural language inference and textual entailment. This task is initiated to automate the process of identifying the correct answer from the answer thread by classifying the answers as good, bad and potential

To identify answer quality, JAIST (Tran et al., 2015) works on only Task for English by extracting 16 features which belongs to 5 groups (word-matching features, topic- modelling-based features, translation based features, special component features and non-textual features). The system although achieves high results and holds rank one but due to heavily dependency on the bag-of- word the potential class is not handled properly.

A hierarchical classification method and a multi- classifier method is proposed by HITSZ-ICRC (Hou et al., 2015) team for English subtask A and Arabic task. Two-level hierarchical classification and ensemble learning are proposed to classify answers for tasks. Fatwa dataset is used for Arabic task. Three submission (primary, contrastive1, contrastive 2) were submitted for all three tasks. The method holds the second rank.

QCRI (Nicosia et al., 2015), this team also works on the three task as HITSZ-ICRC works. In the Arabic task this team holds first rank and in the English subtasks third rank. A supervised Machine learning approach is used considering numerous features i.e. text similarity, context of a comment, sentiment analysis, Word n - grams, and the presence of specific words. For Arabic task logistic regression is used and linear SVM is used for English subtask. The team has also conducted a Post Experiment without and only a feature to understand the different features performance.

ICRC-HIT (Xiaoqiang et al., 2015) proposed a deep learning strategy and present a comment labelling system. To recognize a good comment, recurrent convolution neural network is used.

Hongjie Fan. (Fan et al., 2019) the answer selection is done using multi-dimensional feature combination method. From every question and comment in the dataset the information is extracted. The total twenty features were extracted based on similarity between texts, the content description and also the attribute description. Using the SVM. Gradient Boosting Decision Tree (GBDT) and random forest, a model is build from the extracted features to classify dimensions obtained. Then an experiment is conducted which shows that the proposed approaches performs better than baseline models, and as compared to other proposed methods, relatively its ranking is on an all high. The selection of super -parameter of the model is randomly done which are not fine-grained and only 20 features were selected. But despite these limitations the model's ranking is high as compared to others.

The performances of the previous methods depend on the external resources qualities, feature engineering and some rules. In most of the cases, they lack the generalization. These shortcomings can be overcome by deep learning framework. The more accurate semantic matching between the question and its comments can get by deep learning framework which also remove the dependency of external resources and featurization.

MAIN FOCUS OF THE CHAPTER[1]

The work proposes two models based on deep learning which uses similarity calculation method to evaluate semantically matching of question and its comments and then classify the comments as good, potential and bad. The Figure(Krizhevsky et al., n.d.) shows the architecture of the proposed method and further paragraphs explain the architecture.

The answer selection task stated as follows: given a question q and its comments set $\{a_1, a_2, ..., a_n\}$, classify the comments as good, potential and bad. The method is based on similarity calculation which is done through vector representations to calculate the similarity between the question and its comments. While training, the update of the parameters of the models are done according to a threshold. knowing the threshold value and which similarity evaluation method to be used are the key factors. The proposed method uses the cosine similarity and as in Tan (Tan et al., 2015) got the best result at 0.2 threshold so in this method also threshold value is set 0.2.

Pre-Processing

It is the first and essential step which is performed while building a model and the model results also depends on how well data is been processed. The various steps which are performed for this are explained below with the input examples taken as:

Input: "Yes Formatted Soul, you were ignoring me the day you start having an opinion. Sad".

-Tokenization will split the sentence into words called as tokens.

Output: ['Yes', 'Formatted', 'Soul', 'you', 'were','ignoring', 'me', 'the', 'day', 'you', 'start', 'having', 'an', 'opinion', 'Sad'].

-Stopword Removal, the words like (a, an, the, etc) are removed as they are least significant one and does not help in differentiate two documents.

Output: ['Yes', 'Formatted', 'Soul', 'you', 'were','ignoring', 'me', 'day', 'you', 'start', 'having', 'opinion', 'Sad'].

-Lower Casing converts the all the words into lower case as 'Soul' and 'soul' both means the same but two will be represented as different in the vector.

Output: ['yes', 'formatted', 'soul', 'you', 'were', 'ignoring','me', 'day', 'you', 'start', 'having', 'opinion', 'sad'].

-Stemming will transform the words into root form of that word.

Output: ['yes', 'format', 'soul', 'you', 'were', 'ignor', 'me','day', 'you', 'start', 'hav', 'opinion', 'sad'].

With the help of these steps the preprocessing of the questions and answers is done. All of the steps can be done by using a Natural Language Processing Toolkit (Manning et al., 2014).

The text is represented in multi-dimensional space in the form of vector and all these steps are used for reduction of dimensionality. The number of dimensions means the number of unique words.

Word Embedding

Also, there are methods for vectorizing words based on relationships between words, on large volumes of texts, to create high-dimensional (50 to 300 dimensional) representations. Word embedding is define as the collective name for the set of language models. It is a techniques to learn features in natural language processing where the mapping of words are done to vectors of real number from the vocabulary.

For example: Let the **sentence**=" Answer Selection Task in Community Question Answering System" In this **sentence a** *word* **can be** "Community" or "System" etc.

A *dictionary* is the list of all the words in **sentence** which are unique. For the above sentence a dictionary will be

– ['Answer', 'Selection', 'Task', 'in', 'Community', 'Question', 'Answering', 'System'].

The representation of words are encoded in one-hot form where if the word exists then in its position 1 is encoded and 0 in all other position. So, in this format on the basis of the above dictionary the "Answer" representation will be [1,0,0,0,0,0,0,0] and for "Question" is [0,0,0,0,0,1,0,0]. [https://en.wikipedia.org/wiki/ Word_embedding]. Word embedding algorithms divided on two main ideas Continuous Bag-of-Words model (CBOW), and a Continuous Skip-gram model. The most famous implementation of the algorithm is word2vec, developed by Google in 2013. In the Internet you can download already trained word2vec models.

The idea of sliding window is used in the algorithm, where the central word is put in focus with the other 4 words precede it and the other 4 words follow it. A Word2Vec is a fully connected neural network with one hidden layer and all neurons are linear in the hidden layer. In continuous bag-of-words model, the context words encoded in one-hot form and sent to the input layer. The objective of training while observing the focused output word with reference to the input context words, is to get maximum conditional probability.

Whereas the skip-gram model methodology is opposite to that of CBOW model. Instead of focusing in the central word it focuses at the single input vector. And at the output layer there will be target context words.

Cosine Similarity

This method is very popular in text analysis. Irrespective of document size it determines how similar documents are from one another. Each of the words in the document has its own axis then cosine similarity determines how similar are the documents.

The Question and its sequence of comments are input to the model, the question is combined with each of the comments to generate a QA pair. The pre-trained word embedding is used to encode the QA pair in the two input metrices for the question and the comments respectively.

The **CQA-BLSTM and CQA-Attention Mechanism** are the two proposed model based on semantic similarity.

LSTM and BLSTM

Recurrent networks described in many sources(Learning, n.d.)[12],In 1997 (Krizhevsky et al., n.d.) build an approach called **LSTM (Long Short-Term Memory)**. Recurrent Neural Network based on this approach have an improved (and more complex) method calculate the state of the hidden layer h(t). This method, in addition to input values, and the previous state of the network uses filters (gates), defining how information is used to calculate the output values for a current layer $y^{(t)}$. And the values of the hidden layer in the next step $h^{(t+1)}$. Calculation $h^{(t)}$ is called LSTM layer(LSTM unit) Fig. 2.

Figure 2.. LSTM model with four interacting layers.

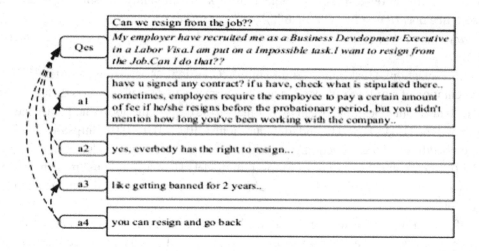

Along with the network state h, at each step calculated storage unit (memory cell) using the current input value $x^{(t)}$ and the value of the block in the previous step $c^{((t-1))}$.

Input filter (input gate) $i^{(t)}$ determines whether the value of the memory block in the current step should influence the result. Filter values range from 0 (completely ignore the input values) to 1, that provided by a sigmoidal function in equation (1).

$$i^{(t)} = \sigma(W^i x^{(t)} + U^i h(t-1)) \tag{1}$$

For each hidden layer, it shares a unique weight W and weight U. "Filter forgetting» (forget gate) allows to exclude when calculating the value of the previous step memory as shown in (2)

$$f^{(t)} = \sigma(W^f x^{(t)} + U^f h^{(t-1)}) \tag{2}$$

$$\tilde{c}^{(t)} = tanh(W^c x^{(t)} + U^z h^{(t-1)}) \tag{3}$$

$$c^{(t)} = f^{(t)} \circ c^{(t-1)} + i^{(t)} \tilde{c}^{(t)} \tag{4}$$

Output filter (output gate) shown in (5) is similar to the previous two and looks like:

$$o^{(t)} = \sigma(W^o x^{(t)} + U^o h^{(t-1)}) \tag{5}$$

The total value LSTM-layer is determined by the output filter and non-linear transformation on the state of the memory block (6).

$$h^{(t)} = o^{(t)} \circ tanh(c^{(t)}) \qquad (6)$$

Bidirectional LSTM overcome the limitation of Single direction LSTM as the it suffer from the weakness of ignoring the contextual information from the future context and only uses the prior context information. Hence BLSTM works in two direction one in the forward and one in reverse to process the previous as well as future context and it generates the two LSTM output vector both of which are independent sequences. Then at each time step the 2 output vectors from forward and reverse direction are concatenated ht= h→t ‖ h←t.

Answer Selection Through BiLSTM

The Fig. 3 show the proposed BLSTM model. In order to deeply match question and answer semantic information the model uses two layers of BLSTM neural networks. Each BLSTM layer forms a distributed representation for the question as well as its comments independently, and then their distance is measured by cosine similarity.

The ranking loss define in (Mikolov et al., 2013) is used in this model:

$$L = max \{0, M - cosine(q, a^+) + cosine(q, a^-)\} \qquad (7)$$

where a$^+$ is a ground truth comment, a$^-$ is an incorrect comment and M is constant margin.

Figure 3. CQA-BLSTM

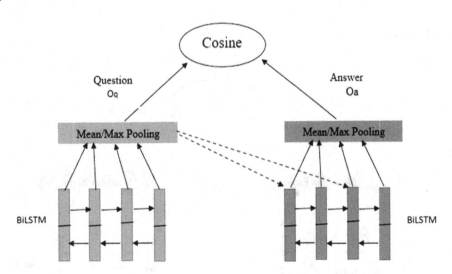

Maxpooling is used to represent questions and comments based on world-level BLSTM output. At the last, a layer called as Softmax layer which gives two- dimensional output vector Is added to the model. Finally, the similarity score is used for the prediction of good and bad. Before calculating cosine similarity on the representations of QA Dropout is performed.

Answer Selection through Attention Mechanism

The earlier model provides a composite embedding for question and its comments. This model is the extension of CQA-BLSTM model. The previous model works on a fixed width of hidden vectors and this constraint becomes bottleneck when the long dependencies between the question and comments needs to be propagate in BLSTM model. Therefore, a simple attention model inspired by (Hermann et al., 2015) can be build for the vector representation of answer based on questions. The Attention Mechanism improves the long distance dependency of the text. In our model the attention mechanism helps to dynamically align the more of the informative parts of comments related to the question.

In the basic BLSTM model, an efficient word-level attention is developed. Firstly BLSTM represents the question and comments separately. Then before the max pooling, the attention mechanism is applied to update the representation of answer according to the BLSTM output on the question side. Hence, at time t, output vector of BLSTM on the comment side is $h^{(t)}$ and the output vector on the question side is oq. The updating of $h^{(t)}$ for each of comment token is done as shown:

$$m_{a,q}(t) = tanh\ (W_{am}h_a(t) + W_{qm}o_q) \tag{8}$$

$$s_{a,q}(t) \propto exp\left(w_{ms}^T m_{a,q}(t)\right). \tag{9}$$

Figure 4. CQA-Attention Mechanism

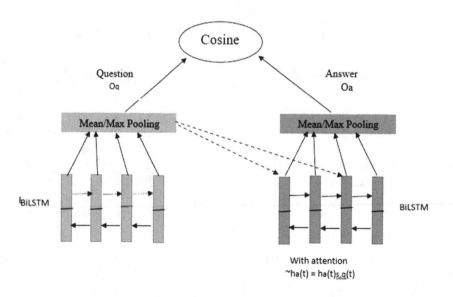

$$\tilde{h}_a(t) = h_a(t) s_{a,q}(t) \tag{10}$$

$\tilde{h}_a(t)$ is the updated comment representation. Then this output vector is combines into next BLSTM, and through softmax layer the semantic similarity calculated. This model shown in Fig. 4 use directly the representations based on attention to get the distance between question and comments.

Experiment Evaluation

To compute the performance of the proposed work, the test results are taken and compared with the other models. The proposed model evaluate the answer selection task on SemEval2015 Task 3. The task 3 of SemEval-2015 is about answer selection in Community Question Answering data. It covers the negative side of community system, that is if a question is having hundreds of answers then it will take more time for the user to validate the answer and select the best or right one. The task 3 of Semantic Evaluation is to automate this process by classifying the comments/answers of a question into three category good, bad and potential.

Dataset Description

The task provide a CQA-QL corpus from a forum named Qatar Living. There are 3229 questions in the dataset and 21,062 answers. The data are split into three files: training, test and development. Also the answers/comments falls into three classes: with 51% good, 39% bad, and 10% potential. In the Table 1 the dataset is summarized.

Table 1. CQA-QL Corpus Description

Data	Question	Answer	Average
Training	2600	16,541	6.36
Development	300	1645	5.48
Test	329	1976	6.00
Overall	3229	21,062	6.00

Experimental Setup

The implementation of the model is done with help Theano(Bastien et al., 2012). A GPU is used to process the experiment. Word2vec (Mikolov et al., 2013) is used to train the word embedding with the word vector size as 200 and length of sentence is limit to 100

the sentence length is limited to maximum 100 words. As word embedding is a parameters which is to be provided to BLSMT unit it should also be optimize while in the training part. Hence stochastic gradient descent (SGD) is used for optimization. L2 regularization is applied in training objective and the margin value is fixed at 0.05. For one direction of LSTM the dimension of the output vector is 141, and hence BLSTM has 200 dimension with a number of comparable parameters with its single direction LSTM. The batch size is of 20 as mini-batches to train the proposed model. Whereas to reduce the effects of overfitting dropout(Krizhevsky et al., n.d.) is used at the time of training. As Rectifier linear unit (ReLU) activation function has the advantages as compare to other activation function so the model uses ReLU for the hidden layers.

Results and Discussion

The key evaluation criteria for the task is Macro-F1. On the basis of the Macro-F1 the proposed is evaluated and compared with the other models. The F1 score is used to calculate the score per class. So to get an overall F1 score for classifier's the per class F1 score is combined through Macro F1.

Table 2. F1 Score of the proposed model

Model	Good	Bad	Potential
Proposed model (BiLSTM)	77.91	75.03	11.33
Proposed model (BiLSTM with attention mechanism	78.81	79.95	16.24

$$F1 = \frac{2 * Precision * recall}{Precision + recall} . \qquad (11)$$

$$Macro\ F1 = \frac{\sum_n F1\ score}{Total\ number\ of\ classes} . \qquad (12)$$

The F1 score of Good, Bad and Potential for both of the proposed model is shown in Table 2. The classical methods i.e. SVM and Random Forest give Macro-F1 43.35% and 46.74% respectively which is less as compared to the other model. The CQA-QL corpus is a noisy data, SVM and Random Forest performs a feature engineering by generating a large amount of features to detect good and bad answers and hence this featurization suffers from the noisy data. It also faces sparse problem of features for short text pairs in the dataset.

The model proposed by JAIST (Tran et al., 2015) is very encouraging one, it uses a supervised feature-rich approach to cover different types of features. The Macro-F1 achieves by this model is 57.19% and our BLSTM model achieves 54.33%. As our model just uses QA pair as a input, so it cannot overcome the JAIST and HITSZ_ICRI results. But at the same time, when an Attention Mechanism aligns question to the answer with answer's more informative part. So, when it is applied in the model then our model surpass the HITSZ_ICRI by 1.92% and JAIST by 1.14% that is the Macro-F1 score achieves by BLSTM-Attention Mechanism is 59.00%. The Table 3 compare all the proposed model and Fig. 5 show the comparison graph.

Table 3. Macro F1 score of the proposed model and the other competitive model

Model	Macro F1 (%)
JAIST (Tran et al., 2015)	57.19
HITSZ_ICRI (Hou et al., 2015)	56.41
QCRI (Nicosia et al., 2015)	53.74
ECNU (Xiaoqiang et al., 2015)	53.47
GBDT (Fan et al., 2019)	46.90
Random Forest (Fan et al., 2019)	46.74
SVM (Fan et al., 2019)	43.35
Proposed model (BiLSTM)	54.33
Proposed model (BiLSTM with attention mechanism)	59.00

CONCLUSION

Based on Semantic Similarity calculation method our work of answer selection task in CQA system is done by constructing two models BLSTM and BLSTM with attention mechanism. Our model removes the dependency of manual features and external resources with the help of deep learning methods as compared to other methods which based on machine learning and also on grammatical analysis. The experiment is conducted on CQA-QL corpus. The model out performs the other competitor models by

Figure 5. Comparison Graph

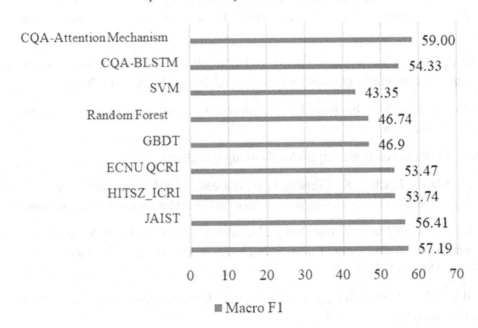

achieving 59.00% of Macro-F1 score. Results shows that our model improves the performance of community question answering system and can effectively classify the answers/comments in the three classes.

FUTURE SCOPE

Still there are improving space for the task and the results can be improved. As the other kind of deep learning methods like can be combines to further improve the results as to more deeply mine the semantic matching between questions and its comments. The future work include, to mine more deeply the question and its comments by combining different kind of deep learning frameworks. And also to work on matching of answer-answer of a question by learning the associate patterns between answers.

REFERENCES

Bastien, F., Lamblin, P., Pascanu, R., Bergstra, J., Goodfellow, I. J., Bergeron, A., Bouchard, N., & Bengio, Y. (2012). Theano: new features and speed improvements. Deep Learning and Unsupervised Feature Learning NIPS 2012 Workshop.

Fan, H., Ma, Z., Li, H., Wang, D., & Liu, J. (2019). Enhanced answer selection in CQA using multi-dimensional features combination. Tsinghua Science and Technology, 24(3), 346–359. doi:10.26599/TST.2018.9010050

Feng, M., Xiang, B., Glass, M., Wang, L., & Zhou, B. (2015). Applying deep learning to answer selection: A study and an open task. IEEE Automatic Speech Recognition and Understanding Workshop (ASRU). 10.1109/ASRU.2015.7404872

Hermann, K. M., Kocisky, T., Grefenstette, E., Espeholt, L., Kay, W., Suley-man, M., & Blunsom, P. (2015). Teaching machines to read and comprehend. In Advances in Neural Information Processing System. NIPS.

Hou, Tan, Wang, Zhang, Xu, & Chen. (2015). HITSZ-ICRC: Exploiting Classification Approach for Answer Selection in Community Question Answering. . doi:10.18653/v1/S15-2035

Krizhevsky, Sutskever, & Salakhutdinov. (n.d.). Dropout: A simple way to prevent neural networks from overfitting. Academic Press.

LearningD. (n.d.). Retrieved from: https://deeplearning4j.org/lstm

Mikolov, T., Sutskever, I., Chen, K., Corrado, G. S., & Dean, J. (2013). Distributed rep- resentations of words and phrases and their compositionality. Advances in Neural Information Processing Systems. NIPS.

Nicosia, Filice, No, Saleh, Mubarak, Gao, Nakov, Martino, Moschitti, Darwish, Màrquez, Joty, & Magdy. (2015). QCRI: Answer Selection for Community Question Answering – Experiments for Arabic and English. . doi:10.18653/v1/S15-2036

SemEval-2015 Task 3: Answer Selection in Community Question Answering. (n.d.). Retrieved from: https://alt.qcri.org/semeval2015/task3

Tan, M., Santos, C. D., Xiang, B., & Zhou, B. W. (2015). LSTM-based deep learning models for non-factoid answer selection. arXiv preprint arXiv:1511.04108.

Tran, Tran, Vu, Nguyen, & Pham. (2015). *JAIST: Combining multiple features for Answer Selection in Community Question Answering.* . doi:10.18653/v1/S15-2038

Xiaoqiang, Hu, Lin, Xiang, & Wang. (2015). *ICRC-HIT: A Deep Learning based Comment Sequence Labeling System for Answer Selection Challenge.* . doi:10.18653/v1/S15-2037

YaunE. (n.d.). Retrieved from: https://eric-yuan.me/rnn1/

Chapter 9
An Analysis on E–Learning and Its Recommendations

Lalitha T. B.
Hindustan Institute of Technology and Science, Chennai, India

Sreeja P. S.
https://orcid.org/0000-0002-2995-3580
Hindustan Institute of Technology and Science, Chennai, India

ABSTRACT

Education provides a predominant source of worldly knowledge around us and changes the perspective of the living society as a global village. However, education has revealed fragmentary remains in the professional competence and personal growth of the learners without the involvement of online learning. E-learning brings out a broader vision of sources to the learners available over the web with the holistic approach to learning from anywhere without cost and minimal effort. The proposed theoretical framework analyses the long-term evolution of e-learning and its effect on mankind. The various methods, technologies, and approaches of e-learning that exist in various forms were discussed exponentially according to the range of necessities among the learners. The recommendation system plays a pivotal role in referring contents and enhancing the learning environment. The education promoted to the learners through the recommendations system over their personal preferences were explored here in detail.

INTRODUCTION

In the modern era, each person is obliged to learn but just the learning differs from one to one. Based on few factors the education can be categorized into three types, mainly, Formal education: which is the basic and traditional type of learning acquired in the school premises. Informal education: which is a natural type of learning from worldly knowledge through parent-child teaching or by self-learning through experience or personal interest. Non-Formal Education: which involves open-ended adult education, a very long process of learning with the flexibility of age, time, and syllabus without interrupting the learner's workflow. Learning defines the sense of abstracting the meaning with the transformative

DOI: 10.4018/978-1-7998-8061-5.ch009

process of behaviour and knowledge in the person permanently based on the long- or short-term experiences or changes. The process of learning involves two categories like traditional learning and online learning. Traditional learning is also known as face-to-face learning or classroom learning where the learning is teacher-centric. Whereas, online learning or web-based learning also known as E-Learning is learner-centric (Swan, 2003) where the student can take part in learning using technology by virtually connecting with or without teachers. The main differentiating aspects are given in Figure 1 below.

Figure 1. Traditional vs online learning

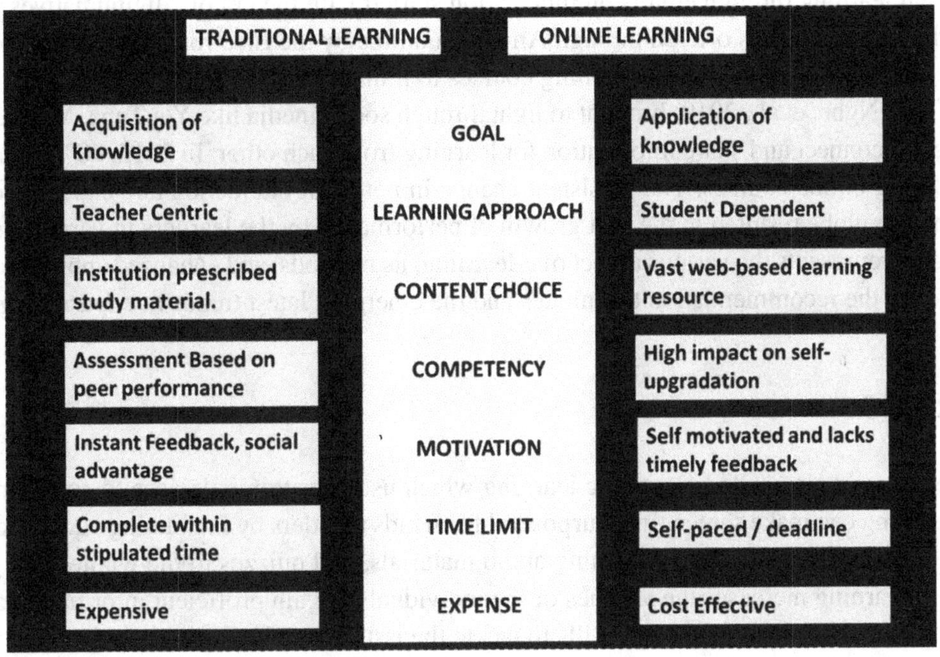

TRADITIONAL LEARNING		ONLINE LEARNING
Acquisition of knowledge	GOAL	Application of knowledge
Teacher Centric	LEARNING APPROACH	Student Dependent
Institution prescribed study material.	CONTENT CHOICE	Vast web-based learning resource
Assessment Based on peer performance	COMPETENCY	High impact on self-upgradation
Instant Feedback, social advantage	MOTIVATION	Self motivated and lacks timely feedback
Complete within stipulated time	TIME LIMIT	Self-paced / deadline
Expensive	EXPENSE	Cost Effective

BACKGROUND

The history of new technologies and pioneers in online learning tells, in 1728 the world's first and foremost distance learning course was started through the post in Boston to the learner. In 1840, Great Britain offered a correspondence course for shorthand. In 1922, the courses were offered through the radio in Penn state. In 1924, Ohio University professor Sidney Pressey invented the first e-learning device "testing machine" called "automatic teacher" which was a failed project. In 1927 - Thomas Edison quoted "The motion picture will replace textbooks in schools". In the 1930s during World War II, the first e-learning took place using film to train the soldiers (Chen, 2008). Then in 1945, the "teaching machines" (Skinner, 1961) were developed by B.F. Skinner for school use. In the 1960s the teaching gradually flourished were PLATO- Programmed Logic for Automated Teaching Operations a computer-based-training program was developed and made machines/computers inevitably skilled, more reliable, and easier to access. In1965, the University of Wisconsin offered the first state-wide telephone-based education program. In 1966, Stanford University professors Petrick Suppes and Richard C. Atkinson offered reading and teaching math to young elementary school students using computer-aided instructions (CAI). In 1968,

Stanford University accessed television networks for part-time instructions. In 1969, the US department of defence authorized ARPANET Heralds in establishing the internet for communication and training soldiers. In 1970, modern computing was defined through the invention of the Computer mouse and the GUI which enhanced computer-based training. In 1976, adult online education was offered by the University of Phoenix. In the 1980s the personal computer came into existence with Macintosh where information sharing within online communities raised the path for e-Learning, thereby leveraging the initiatives to expand e-learning to schools, organizations, and self-development (Harasim, 2006). In 1981, the learning leaped into new trends through audio recordings, radio, and television broadcasting [64] as taped classes. In 1982, a computer-based learning center (CALC) was found for adult learning. In the 1990s virtual learning through email communication started with the era of "digital natives". In 1992, the first Ph.D. program was offered through American online by the Electronic University Network. In the 2000s business began to adopt e-learning courses to train employees. In the 2010s a new way of e-learning (Thai-Nghe, et al., 2010) brought to light through social media like YouTube, MOOC, Twitter, Skype, etc., to connect and share information for learning from each other. In 2012, 90% of universities started offering online courses. The persistent change in potential interaction and experience with the web around the globe resulted in the vast growth of performance by the learners in various aspects.

This paper represents the various aspect of e-learning, its methods, and enhanced approaches prevailing along with the recommendation techniques and the emerging latest trends in e-learning globally.

E-LEARNING

Online Learning is also called electronic learning which uses electronic devices to communicate and learn. E-learning can make screen time purposeful from kids to elders by facilitating various knowledge providers who offer books, videos, learning audio materials, and quizzes to the wholesome growth of everyone. E-learning increases the abilities of the individuals to gain proficient information and frame the mind to attain essential innovative skills to tackle the issues and the capacity to do inventiveness.

E-learning can be classified into fundamental two categories: Synchronous e-learning and Asynchronous e-learning (Hrastinski, 2008). The synchronous e-learning can be called virtual classroom or distance online education where the conventional method of learning happens at the same time or in real-time with the virtual presence of tutor and learner at a stipulated time. Whereas, asynchronous e-learning is an unconventional method of learning that occurs through the online platform without the virtual presence and real-time interaction. The six various types of e-learning were classified based on students with/without presence and e-communications (Negash & Wilcox, 2008) which involves face-to-face, synchronous, asynchronous, self-learning, hybrid synchronous, and hybrid asynchronous. Below figure 2 shows the main difference in learning styles (Shahabadi & Uplane, 2015) between the synchronous and asynchronous in varied aspects.

The pros and cons of learning exist in both synchronous and asynchronous e-learning. The advantages of e-learning are effective and performance yielding than traditional classroom learning (Peat & Helland, 2004).

Some of the main perspectives of e-learning include:

- Convenience: e-learning gives immense flexibility and convenience to learn regardless of time and place.

Figure 2. Synchronous vs. Asynchronous E-Learning

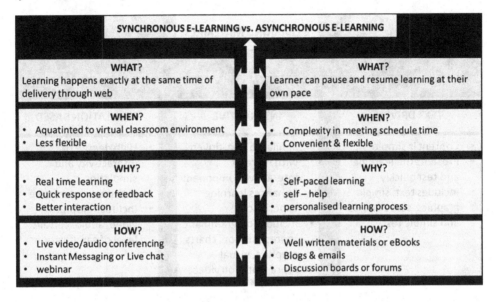

- Cost-effective: It is cheaper when compared to traditional learning.
- Provides continuous up-gradation of skills and knowledge.
- Higher opportunity to access the contents from worldwide.
- Updating the contents to access is easy and materials are permanently available.

In the same way, e-learning possesses certain challenges:

- Interaction: It lacks face-to-face or peer-to-peer communication.
- Self-Dependent: The learning will be taken on the individual's exertion and preferences.
- Self-Motivation: The learners should take up and complete this learning with their strength without encouragement from others.
- Misconception: Learners may misunderstand the content and conclude the context in the wrong way.
- Periodical Growth: The learner must determine which concepts to know and necessary to learn further.
- Evaluating the process growth of the individual and getting feedback will be harder or even negligible.

E-Learning materials and courses over the web are categorized into three types (see Figure 3).

The perspectives of eLearning materials are, the learner acquires a greater degree of flexibility, convenience, cost-effective, immersive, and amusing learning experiences (Littlejohn, et al., 2008). Whereas the challenges of eLearning materials are more relevantly based on a qualitative check of the content such as the poor instructional design of course materials, the relevancy of subject, placing the textbook content and lectures notes over online in the same format, repetitive or similarity of content and lacking new course design or learning contents in-depth with new technologies or contents.

Figure 3. Types of eLearning materials

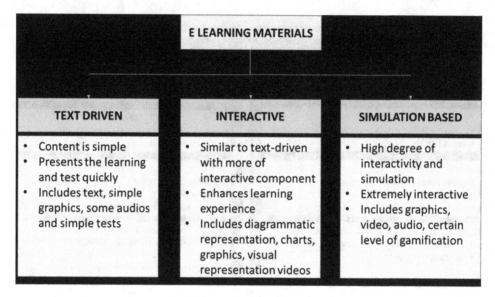

The current and future trend in the enhanced e-learning involves different types of methods and technologies that promote and leverage the user's needs which facilitates active participation in learning activities. Now will see various learning methods that are making the head away with technological growth.

Hybrid Learning

Recently the usage of eLearning concepts emphasized in the Hybrid learning technique that clubs online learning and traditional learning together (Wang, et al., 2010). In the current scenario, incorporating the teacher-centric and online resources in the learning styles for the enhanced academic performance of the students, explicitly getting acknowledged throughout the world. Hybrid learning is a recent deployment in the epidemic trend with different strategies such as Blended Learning and Flipped learning.

Blended Learning

Blended Learning is the merging of e-learning and classroom learning. It provides learners with tremendous potential and the most logical way of learning (Poon, 2013). Thus, the approach overcomes the challenges of one-to-one contact of instructors by integrating with the technological benefits of online learning. This learning strategy has placed a strong step in the broader context of educational institutes and business organization developments. Hence made a huge change in the learning process (Brookfield, 2009) and unfolded efficient opportunities for every individual who desires to learn something new in an appropriate field. But it has a negative impact on learners who are trying to sync up to the pace of the course and peers, creating cognitive load by over-delivering of materials and learning activities from the instructor.

Advantages of blended learning:

- Flexibility

- Increases interaction
- Technical skills improvement
- Asynchronous Interactions

Disadvantages of Blended learning:

- Time Constraints
- Technical Support
- Student and faculty perception over learning technics and relationship between them

Flipped Learning

In the field of education, we are witnessing a major transformation in the style of teaching and learning environments. Here comes the emerging theory of Flipped learning which was developed in the late '90s as a "peer instruction model" by Harvard Professor Eric Mazur in the name of "just in time teaching" (Crouch & Mazur, 2001) and then in 2012, it got popularized by the chemistry teachers Jon Bergman and Aaron Sams of Woodland park high school, Colorado. Flipped learning is also known as Reverse learning. This uses the typical concept of combining online and offline learning (O'Flaherty & Philips, 2015). The students learn through the eLearning materials before attending the class and after that, the instructor guides the students to implement the concepts via assignments and engaging them actively in the subject matters practically (Jordan, et al, 2020).

Advantages of Flipped learning:

- Helps in developing prior knowledge
- Enhanced applications of learning
- Adequate time for learning and implementing

Disadvantages of Flipped learning:

- Motivation
- Timing to cope with peers

Adaptive Learning

The eLearning concept indulges also in adaptive learning. Depending on the upraising tendencies of growth in the industrial or business organization, explicitly opting for individualized adaptive learning by replacing traditional web-based learning that is delivered to the employees for the competitive advancement of their organizations. In this adaptive learning, the information producers customize the presentation of eLearning materials according to the learner's performance level in real-time. Adaptive learning methodology carries the data-driven approach to provide customized learning paths (Paramythis, & Loidl-Reisinger, 2004). This learning strategy determines the e-learning activities dynamically, which can be delivered to a learner based on their data that are gathered before and an ongoing e-learning process using some sort of data mining technique (Yarandi, et al., 2013). The learner experiences the shifting of presentation or course flow to accommodate the performance level and by not repeating the materials they've known already thus, by completing the course at their own pace and path. The adaptive learning path will be approached non-linearly and helps in an enormous procreative learning environment for the learners. The learning objective involves creating, evaluating, analyzing, applying the skillsets that offer a personalised content learning experience for the learners. The main issue relies on the material developer who faces few challenges on how to analyse course content, generate the adaptive learning data, and pattern recognition of the learner.

Advantages of Adaptive learning:

- Flexible and adjustable for learners
- Individualised and effective content learning path
- great time and competence for completion

Disadvantages of Adaptive learning:

- Numerous Tests and assessments to find the path
- The path could lead to over jumping of important materials and contents that need to be learned
- Accuracy problem arises with the complexity of adaptive content creation

Self-Directed Learning (SDL)

Self-Directed Learning is subjectively called adult learning (Knowles, 1975; Knowles, et al., 1998) or life-long learning which has a specific capacity for critical self-reflection with continuous modelling of new knowledge for increasing access to information for necessary skill acquisitions to change their learning experiences positively (Merriam, 2001). Learning in a solitary state can be a strenuous job even for impelled learners as this method is an instruction based on design, conceptualization, performance, and assessment over the learning materials handled by the learners themselves (Brookfield, 2009). Learners can prefer any one of the strategies to get resourced learning.

- Deep mode – includes the transformation of learners by understanding, implementing knowledge and ideas to new circumstances which are more than what is required
- Surface mode – includes reproduction, where learners go for what is required to accomplish a task with a good understanding
- Strategic mode – includes organization, where learners prefer what is required to get the highest grades with minimal effort.

This creates a cooperative learning environment and the utmost flexibility where the learners self-motivate by engaging in self-evaluation and accepting constructive feedback from their past experiences to achieve their goals productively with no age barriers (Lalitha & Sreeja, 2020).

Advantages of SDL:

- Learning at one's own pace
- Access to feedbacks
- Continuous Surplus materials and sites
- Increases the involvement by owing the learning process

- Appropriate for Employees without disturbing the workforce

Disadvantages of SDL:

- Self-motivation
- Sometimes misleading in learning things will occur due to learning on their own.

Mobile Learning

Based on the upcoming new Learning methods in the field of eLearning are prominently focusing on the growth of digital technologies and devices like cell phones (Sarrab, et al., 2012). This Mobile learning is applied in many distinct scenarios with the help of a Personal digital assistant (PDA), where the happenings of live lectures or conference talk presenting by the instructor are broadcasted directly to the learners over their mobile devices (Ozdamil & Cavus, 2011) and simultaneously can generate the digital video library through the procured video clips that are accessed by the learners or created by their own to view subsequently either by web-based or by mobile devices.

Advantages of Mobile Learning:

- Accessing contents easily
- The Flexibility of involving time and place for the learning process
- Engaging and provides feedbacks instantly.

Disadvantages of Mobile Learning:

- Resolution size and accessing with a small device
- Distractions during the learning process
- Speed and connectivity issues
- Doesn't seems appropriate for children's usage for long hours.

The various approaches incorporated in using e-learning which facilitates the learners and instructors in transferring of knowledge and skills mainly focus on

- Paragogy (Peergogy) (Corneli & Danoff, 2011) – involves instructor-led learning where learners dependent on peers.
- Andragogy (Merriam, 2001) – involves self-directed learning where learners are independent.
- Heutagogy (Hase & Kenyon 2013)– involves self-determined learning where learners are problem-finders
- Cybergogy (Wang & Kang, 2006)– involves engaged online learning where learners are influenced by emotional, behavioural, and intellectual in learning tasks.

E-LEARNING RECOMMENDATION SYSTEM AND RELATED WORKS

The recommendation System (RS) is a distinct model of intelligent systems that plays a critical role in the personalisation of user's requests and needs. This information filtering system first and foremost used in online commercial applications. Recently recommendation systems were substantially used in various domains to customize applications through prediction and recommendations according to the user's needs. Similarly, the recommendation system has put its Bigfoot in the e-learning domain and becoming a significant part in recommending the items to the users based on their interests and requirements. The recommendation system can be categorized as constraint-based recommenders (Felfernig, et al., 2015), knowledge-based recommender (Tarus, et al., 2018), and context-aware recommendation systems (Verbert, et al., 2012). It helps the learners to find out the most relevant topics and materials by scrutinizing the large data available over the web. E-learning recommendation system gathers information on the preferences and interest of the learners based on the list of user-items like basic profile (age, qualification, occupation, etc.), prior knowledge, learner's performance (Nguyen, et al., 2010), user's behaviour, user's ratings, weblogs, nearest neighbour navigation list (Salehi & Kamalabadi, 2012), opinion mining from social platforms (Ortigosa, et al., 2014), demographic data (Goga, et al., 2015), etc., were used in generating a personalised recommendation that assists the learners in collecting the appropriate learning materials, learning patterns and paths (Zhang, et al., 2020; Nabizadeh, et al., 2020) for their career growth. The system uses Machine learning techniques like social filtering (Madani, et al., 2019), user-based & memory-based collaborative filtering (Rabahallah, et al., 2018), content-based filtering (Jordan, et al., 2020), hybrid filtering, K-means algorithm (Salehi & Kamalabadi, 2013), web mining techniques (Herath & Jayaratne, 2017), ontologies (Agbonifo & Akinsete, 2020; Rabahallah, et al., 2018), fuzzy logic techniques (Nilashi, et al., 2014), association rule (Wu & Gu, 2015), ensemble classifiers techniques (Kausar, et al., 2020), etc., to generate the e-learning recommendation model for extract the preference and valued learning objects. Some detailed views of methods and datasets usage in a certain paper on e-learning recommendation systems are given in the table.1 below.

Some latest works presented in the field of e-learning recommendation systems were discussed below.

Jordan, et al., (2020) proposed a hybrid learning recommending model using the content-based filtering techniques to extract and recommend the learning videos for both students and instructors from the central repository of the university. Daher, et al., (2018) proposed a new data mining algorithm to search complex multi-data items called multi-source data mining algorithm for a Metal project that includes primary and secondary school students in the e-learning domain. Goga, et al., (2015) proposed a framework of intelligent recommender based on students' academic performance and their family background using techniques like decision tree, and multilayer perceptron to take corrective measures and improve the students' performance. Rabahallah, et al., (2018) proposed a recommendation engine that focuses on the prediction of top online courses to the learners using ontologies and memory-based collaborative filtering techniques. Demertzi, et al., (2020) proposed a hybrid personalised eLearning system using ontology, machine learning classification techniques, collaborative and content-based filtering based on data extracting from learning material repositories and curriculum courses to generate recommendations that match learner's needs and skills. Wu, et al., (2015) proposed a novel framework for filtering and predicting educational metadata using the cloud model to generate the personalised recommendation model for online learning. Chen, et al., (2020) proposed a new learning style model to generate personalised recommendation feature sets for online learners by clustering them based on online behaviour styles and extracting preferences and patterns using association rule and collaborative filtering resulting

Table 1. ML Methods with Datasets

YEAR	ML METHODS	DATASET	REF.
2010	collaborative filtering, Matrix Factorization, linear regression, logistic regression	log files of interactions between students and computer-aided-tutoring systems	Nguyen, et al., 2010
2012	content-based and collaborative based filtering tools	frequently visited materials, most similarly visited materials to target learners	Salehi & Kmalabadi, 2012
2013	K-means algorithm, association rules, collaborative filtering, content-based filtering	rating of learners, multidimensional attributes of the material, sequential patterns of learner's accessed material	Salehi & kamalabadi, 2013
2014	Adaptive Neuro-Fuzzy Interference systems (ANFIS) and self-organizing map (SOM) clustering, fuzzy-based algorithms	Real-world datasets to improve the accuracy	Nilashi, et al., 2014
2017	Web-mining techniques, Collaborative Filtering, content filtering tool	navigation behaviours, web contents, performances, profiles	Herath & Jayaratne, 2017
2018	Collaborative Filtering, Matrix Factorization	Similar user's preference, contents of the document	Lai, et al., 2018
2019	social filtering, collaborative filtering, K-nearest neighbours' algorithm	social network profiles (Facebook, Twitter)	Madani, et al., 2019
2020	Naïve Bayes classifier, fuzzy c-means clustering algorithm, Semantic Ontologies technique, Collaborative filtering	Educative content repositories: ADRIADNE & MERLOT, student's info & grades	Demertzi & Demertzis, 2020

in an adaptive recommendation of online learning styles model. Rivero-Albarrán, et al., (2018) proposed a framework for a teaching agent system to obtain appropriate teaching and learning content as per the needs of the student using a multi-agent system design to provide an intelligent classroom environment to each student. Apoki, et al., (2020) proposed an adaptive eLearning model to provide specialized courses that merges the text, video, audio learning resources for common curriculum generation correlating with learners' preferences and needs. Azzi, et al., (2020) proposed the architecture for personalised course design based on artificial neural networks using learner's historic data and prior knowledge to produce the appropriate learning materials for the learners. Mondal, et al., (2020) proposed a framework to study in a personalised environment using machine learning techniques like collaborative filtering and k-mean clustering algorithm based on learner's historic data and prior performance to form clusters that can be utilized for recommending suitable courses. Shi, et al., (2020) proposed a model for learning path recommendation using a multidimensional knowledge graph framework to fulfill the learning needs by targeting learner's interests that help in generating the personalised learning path recommendation model. Krauss (2018) proposed a new time-weighted knowledge-based filtering algorithm to analyze the accuracy of top N item recommendations at different time instances when the users access it and by using multi contextual activity data to provide explicit recommendations to the learners. Ali Ahmed, et al., (2020) proposed the architecture for e-tutoring to design and update course contents based on learner's abilities and to resolve certain problems by using an isolated database. Monsalve-Pulido, et al., (2020) proposed an architecture of a hybrid recommendation model using content-based, collaborative, and knowledge filtering based on the demographic data, online content, students learning style, student's historic data, etc., to produce the precise academic course for the students. Rani, et al., (2015) proposed an ontology-driven adaptive personalised e-learning system using cloud storage, ontologies for query creation, and the Felder-Silverman model for determining learning style which assists in semantic web education learning. Ismail, et al., (2019) proposed a framework for personalised content recommendation and evaluation model for generating appropriate adaptive recommendations with the changes in learner's interest and then analyze the impact of learning objects recommendation from wikis. Klasnja Milicevic, et al., (2018) proposed an online tutoring system to utilize collaborative tagging and using social tagging, sequential pattern mining to generate a hybrid recommendation model by comparing the most popular tags to give out suitable learning objects to the learners.

LATEST TRENDS AND FUTURE SCOPE OF E-LEARNING

Education is the road to advancement and brings betterment to one's life through natural and everlasting positive behavioural changes to achieve their goals. The emerging generation centralizes over goal-oriented learning. The current pandemic involuntarily made us take a remarkable transformation in education and further changed everyone's day-to-day lives including toddlers by fast-tracking digitalization worldwide (Livari, et al., 2020). Charles Darwin quotes "It is not the strongest of the species survives, nor the most intelligent that survives, it is the most adaptable to change". The unleashing technological transformation with the impact of the COVID-19 pandemic has reshaped the education sector adversely creating unprecedented challenges in the learning system (Dwivedi, et al., 2020) as more goal-oriented. It forced us to experience a new digital revolution by changing the conventional teaching and learning practices globally by pushing it to switch to eLearning. With the high growth and demand of eLearning system, the recent study on the e-learning market has estimated $144 billion in 2019 and forecasted $374.3 billion gain by 2026, thus even the government has initiated R&D projects and funding the prevailing works to become mainstream with an expected growth of USD 14.6% compound annual growth rate (CAGR) from 2019 to 2026. The persistent change in potential interaction and experience with the web around the globe resulted in the vast growth of performance by the learners in various aspects, 90% of universities started offering online courses.

This COVID-19 pandemic put us in a challenging position by forcing us to move towards digitalization from the physical world by migrating students learning to undergo 100% online learning programs. India is gearing up to pedagogical evolution and digital revolution with rapid speed and the e-learning industry is dominating the overall education system by permanently incorporating computerized technology by infusing online classes and courses for the learners. The future of India's education system drastically changed by introducing e-learning in every step of the learner's life making them convenient, interesting, and engaging while learning. This pandemic situation with more than 1.2 billion children's needs for education, has tweaked the e-learning adoption rates in many countries to reach the desired success in teaching and learning for the students. In the recent study done by BINUS University, the statistical growth of major countries with the highest growth in e-learning adoption rate is given in below figure 4.

In this 'New Normal' condition, the whole education system has been obligatory in offering solutions to the study-from-home state and social distancing issues by incorporating necessary online tools into the academic environment. Prior to the Covid-19 situation, technology-supported education was not mandatory for students, where the medium of instruction is mainly concentrated on physical teaching and learning environment and students get additional blended learning benefits from online technology

Figure 4. Countries with the high e-learning adoption rate
Source: BINUS University, 2019

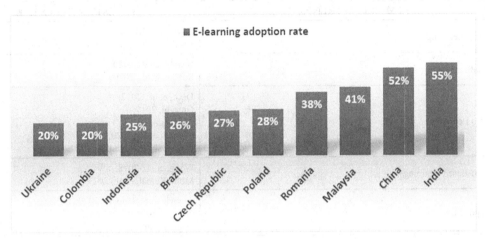

(Aggarwal, 2009). But now due to the lockdown situation, the compulsory implementation of new online medium is widely spreading not only to the urban landscape but even reaching the rural sectors in India (Anusudha, et al., 2021) by offering ample variety of learning facilities ranging to more than 500 million internet users regardless of their age, location and status. The digital transformation is providing online courses through MOOC (Pant, et al., 2021; Bordoloi, et al., 2020) platform some of them like Udemy, Coursera, edX, Udacity, Swayam (initiated by the Govt. Of India), etc., allowing unlimited learning to students and employees. In recent times in India, several ed-tech companies like Byju's, Edukart, Vedantu, Toppscholars, Cuemath are some of the learning apps actively encouraging eLearning ranging from elementary school students to high school students, in that Byju's attained a 150% surge in this business. Thus, E-Learning has been an accelerated transformation in learning strategies with varied trends (Zain, 2020) and recommendation system at all the levels in the best way possible for the learners to focus and carry on with their learning activities virtually and more spontaneously without major hindrance. Adult education is highly engrossed with the technological evolution in eLearning recommendations that paved the way to the individual-centered and personalized learning experiences for the learners to enhance their strategic abilities and goals without disrupting the workforce (Bariso, 2010). Corporate e-learning (Arnquist, 2020) entails learning and training over the web by engaging the employees to learn efficiently, enhancing their skills, increasing benefits to the organization, and maximizing the results with 40% to 60% less time duration to complete the course contrast to conventional learning. According to current market statistics (Source: Businesswire, 2020), the corporate e-learning market has predicted a growth of 11% compound annual growth rate (CAGR) between 2020 to 2024.

The most innovative e-learning trends (Lara, et al., 2020) emerging across the globe in the crisis of covid-19 pandemic which is helpful to initiate learning activities most effectively were listed in table 2. below.

Thus, speculating the current trends and changing enhancements in the area of e-learning were dealt with rapid digital transformation in this pandemic situation significantly broadening the growth of e-learning practice to the international market in order to improve the learner's performance by winding up the barriers to growth and adoption. In this grapple time of the pandemic, the usage of the latest technolo-

Table 2. Emerging Trends in E-Learning

	EMERGING TRENDS	LATEST ARTICLES REF.
1	Mobile Learning	Sattarov & Khaitova, 2019; Banane & Belangour, 2020
2	Social Learning	Souabi, et al., 2020; Souabi, et al., 2020
3	Micro Learning	Dixit, et al., 2012; Giurgiu, 2017; Alqurashi, 2017; Corbell, et al., 2020; Dolasinski & Reynolds, 2020;
4	Video-Based Learning	Wong, et al., 2018; Mohd Kamal, et al., 2019
5	Adaptive Learning	Arsovic & Stefanovic, 2020; Nabizadeh, et al., 2020; Morze, et al., 2021
6	Big Data in e-learning	Sheshasaayee & Malathi, 2017; Banane & Belangour, 2020; Mentsiev, et al., 2020; Moharm & Eltahan, 2020; Khan & Alqahtani, 2020; Chweya, et al., 2020
7	Internet of Things (IoT) in e-learning	Razzaque & Hamdan, 2020; Amasha, et al., 2020; Rukmana & Mulyanti, 2020; Doychev, et al., 2020; Chweya, et al., 2020
8	Beacon Learning	Rajesh, et al., 2018; Griffiths, et al., 2019; Lingwood, et al., 2020
9	Cloud-based e-learning	Rahman, 2016; Siddiqui, et al., 2019; Herdradi, et al., 2020
10	Blockchain-based e-learning	Li, 2019; Humayun, 2020; Lam & Dongol, 2020;
11	Artificial Intelligence in e-learning	Herdradi, et al., 2020; Muniasamy & Alasiry, 2020; Ray, et al., 2020; Tang, et al., 2021; Ouyang & Jiao, 2021
12	Game-based e-learning and Gamification	Yi, et al., 2020; Boytchev & Boytcheva, 2020; Bennani, et al., 2020
13	Virtual-reality, Augmented-reality & Mixed-reality in e-learning	Calin, 2018; Martin, et al., 2018; Jung, et al., 2020
14	Content Curator in e-learning	Kukharenko & Syrotenko, 2014; Wang, et al., 2020; Dede & Forster, 2021
15	User-Generated Content for e-learning	Reimers, 2015; Ganapathi, 2019; Ray, et al., 2020

gies and recommendation systems are extending a huge amount of support to the learners systematically causing an up-gradation in digital skillsets and modifying basic eLearning philosophy in every industry.

CONCLUSION

Online learning has entirely modified how efficient teaching and revolutionised learning is imparted to the learners in contrast to traditional learning. E-learning technology provides a window to the world's information and growing up facilities that can be accessed universally by users. The eLearning tasks can be segmented as creativity, technologies, learning, and business where both learning and knowledge management involved that empowers learners effectively and contentedly. This field is becoming the mainstream for research in recent days with a lot of investments put forth in web-based learning delivery. This paper represents the various aspect of e-learning, its methods, and enhanced recommendation approaches prevailing in e-learning. The importance of information and communication technology (ICT) in the education system for the competitive society to yield higher productivity, performance, satisfaction, and commitment by the community were clinically measured with the growth of technologies in the learning environment and the actions carried out to boost the usage were scrutinized with the help of recommendation systems. The integral part depicts a greater view of trends in the e-learning recommendation system which will pave a positive path for society's growth. The key purpose of this paper revolves over non-formal education which majorly involves e-learning for the development of professional and organizational growth focusing on the application and implementation of artificial intelligence, machine learning methodologies for the future benefits of human race. By exploring around 121 published research papers, journals, and newspaper articles, the notion of eLearning and its technological growth were identified with high definitions and learning strategies which formulates the learning goals more significant for the learners. The aim of the paper concentrates majorly on the latest trends evolving in the e-learning domain globally and the increased usage in our country during the pandemic and its raising statistics were explained clearly and to come up with the current scenarios in the field of technology ensuring the dependability on the broad domain of e-learning, creating a pathway for the employability and opportunities for evolving edupreneurs. Every latest segment of techniques incorporated with eLearning recommendation systems brings out leading incredible opportunities to see the rapid change unfolding to learn and grow the skilled solutions across the world. I would like to conclude with the quote by John Dewey "If we teach today's students as we taught yesterday's, we rob them of tomorrow".

REFERENCES

Agbonifo, O. C., & Akinsete, M. (2020). Development of an Ontology-Based Personalised E-Learning Recommender System *International Journal of Computer, 38*(1), 102–112.

Aggarwal, D. (2009). Role of e-Learning in a developing country like India. *Proceedings of the 3rd national conference; INDIACom-2009 computing for nation development.*

Ali Ahmed, G. H., & Kovacs, L. (2020). Ontology Domain Model for E-Tutoring System. *Journal of Software Engineering & Intelligent Systems, 5*(1).

Alqurashi, E. (2017). Micro Learning: A Pedogogical Approach for technology integration. *The Turkish Online Journal of Educational Technology*, 942–947.

Amasha, M. A., Areed, M. F., Alkhalaf, S., Abougalala, R. A., Elatawy, S. M., & Khairy, D. (2020). The future of Internet of Things (IoTs) and Context-Aware Technology in E-Learning. *ICEIT 2020: Proceedings of the 2020 9th International Conference on Educational and Information Technology*, 114-123.

Anusudha, R. S., Krishnendu, R., & Krishnan, P. (2021). Education at the crossroads: Digitalization of Education in India During an Age of Pandemic. *Psychology and Education Journal, 58*(3). Doi:10.17762/pae.v58i3.3878

Apoki, U. C. (2020). A Model of a weighed Agent System for Personalised E-Learning Curriculum. In Communications in Computer and Information Science (Vol. 1126). Springer.

Arnquist, M. D. (2020). *The Role of the Technical Communicator in the Corporate eLearning Industry*. Retrieved from the University of Minnesota Digital Conservancy, https://hdl.handle.net/11299/213219

Arsovic, B., & Stefanovic, N. (2020). E-learning based on the adaptive learning model: Case study in Serbia. *Sadhana, 45*, 266. https://doi.org/10.1007/s12046-020-01499-8

Azzi, I. (2020). Approach Based on Artificial Neural Network to Improve Personalisation in Adaptive E-Learning System. In Advances in Intelligent Systems and Computing (Vol. 1076). Springer.

Banane, M., & Belangour, A. (2020). Towards a New Scalable Big Data System Semantic Web Applied on Mobile Learning. *International Journal of Interactive Mobile Technologies., 14*(1), 126–140. https://doi.org/10.3991/ijim.v14i01.10922

Bariso, E. U. (2010). Personalised elearning in further education. *Technology-Supported Environments for Personalised Learning: Methods and Case Studies*, 109-127.

Bennani, S., Maalel, A., & Ghezala, H. B. (2020). AGE-Learn: Ontology-Based Representation of personalized Gamification in E-Learning. *Procedia Computer Science, 176*, 1005–1014.

Bordoloi, R., Das, P., & Das, K. (2020). Lifelong learning opportunities through MOOCs in India. *Asian Association of Open Universities Journal, 15*(1), 83-95. doi:10.1108/aaouj-09-2019-0042

Boytchev, P., & Boytcheva, S. (2020). Gamified Evaluation in Game-Based Learning. In A. Lopata, R. Butkienė, D. Gudonienė, & V. Sukackė (Eds.), Information and Software Technologies. ICIST 2020. Communications in Computer and Information Science (Vol. 1283). Springer. https://doi.org/10.1007/978-3-030-59506-7_24.

Brookfield, S. D. (2009). Self-Directed Learning. In R. Maclean & D. Wilson (Eds.), *International Handbook of Education for the Changing World of Work*. Springer.

Calin, R. A. (2018). Virtual Reality, Augmented Reality and mixed Reality- trends in pedagogy. *Social Sciences and Education Research Review., 5*(1), 169–179.

Chen, E. T. (2008). Successful E-Learning in Corporations. Communications of the IIMA, 8(2).

Chen, H., Yin, C., Li, R., Rong, W., Xiong, Z., & David, B. (2020). Enhanced learning resource recommendation based on online learning style model. *Tsinghua Science and Technology, 25*(3), 348–356.

Chweya, R., Ajibade, S. S. M., Buba, A. K., & Samuel, M. (2020). IoT and Big Data Technologies: Oppurtunities and Challenges for Higher Learning. *International Journal of Recent Technology and Engineering, 9*(2).

Corbell, J. R., Kahn, B. H., & Corbell, M. E. (Eds.). (2020). *Microlearning in the digital age: The design and delivery of learning snippets.* Routledge.

Corneli, J., & Danoff, C. J. (2011). Paragogy: Synergizing individual and organizational learning. *1st International Conference on Learning Analytics and Knowledge.*

Crouch, C. H., & Mazur, E. (2001). Peer instruction: Ten years of experience and results. *American Journal of Physics, 69*(9), 970–977.

Daher, J. B., Brun, A., & Boyer, A. (2018). Multi-source data mining for e-learning. *7th International Symposium "From Data to Models and Back (DataMod)" 2018.* arXiv:2009.08791 [cs.DB]

Dede, J., & Forster, A. (2021). Automatic Content Curation for Online Learning Materials. *Conference: SIGCSE '21: The 52nd ACM Technical Symposium on Computer Science Education.* DOI: 10.1145/3408877.3439601

Demertzi, V., & Demertzis, K. (2020). *A Hybrid Adaptive Educational eLearning project based on Ontologies Matching and Recommendation System.* arXiv:2007.14771

Demertzi, V., & Demertzis, K. (2020). *An Adaptive Educational eLearning System based on Semantics, Ontologies Matching and Recommendation system.* Available: https://arvix.org/abs/2007.14771

Dixit, R. K., Yalagi, P. S., & Nirgude, M. A. (2012). Breaking the walls of classroom through Micro learning: Short burst of learning. *Journal of Physics: Conference Series, 1854*(1), 012018.

Dolasinski, M. J., & Reynolds, J. (2020). Microlearning: A new learning model. *Journal of Hospitality & Tourism Research (Washington, D.C.), 44*(3). doi:10.1177/1096348020901579

Doychev, E., Stoyanova-Doycheva, A., Stoyanov, S., Glushkova, T., & Ivanova, V. (2020). An IoT Virtual eLearning Space. *Transactions on Computational Collective Intelligence, XXXV,* 148–169.

Dwivedi, Y. K. (2020). Impact of COVID-19 pandemic on information management research and practice: Transforming education, work and life. *International Journal of Information Management, 55,* 102211.

Felfernig, A., Friedrich, G., Jannach, D., & Zanker, M. (2015). Constraint-Based Recommender Systems. In F. Ricci, L. Rokach, & B. Shapira (Eds.), *Recommender Systems Handbook.* Springer.

Ganapathi, J. (2019). User-Generated Content's Impact on the Sustainability of Open Educational Resources. *Open Praxis, 11*(2), 211-225.

Giurgiu, L. (2017). Microlearning an evolving elearning trend. Scientific Bulletin – Nicolae Balcescu Land Forces Academy, 22(1), 18-23.

Goga, M. (2015). A Recommender for Improving the Student Academic Performance. *Procedia: Social and Behavioral Sciences, 180,* 1481–1488.

Griffiths, S., Wong, M. S., Kwok, C. Y. T., Kam, R., Lam, S. C., Yang, L., Yip, T. L., Heo, J., Chan, B. S. B., Xiong, G., & Lu, K. (2019). Exploring Bluetooth Beacon Use Cases in Teaching and Learning: Increasing the Sustainability of Physical Learning Spaces. *Sustainability*, *11*, 4005. https://doi.org/10.3390/su11154005

Harasim, L. (2006). A History of E-learning: Shift Happened. In J. Weiss, J. Nolan, J. Hunsinger, & P. Trifonas (Eds.), *The International Handbook of Virtual Learning Environments*. Springer.

Hase, S., & Kenyon, C. (Eds.). (2013). *Self-determined learning: Heutagogy in action*. Bloomsbury Academic.

Hendradi, P. (2020). Artificial Intelligence Influence in Education 4.0 to Architecture Cloud based E-Learning System. *International Journal of Artificial Intelligence Research, 4*(1). doi:10.29099/ijair.v4i1.109

Herath, D., & Jayaratne, L. (2017). A personalized web content recommendation system for E-learners in E-learning environment. In *2017 National Information Technology Conference (NITC)*. IEEE.

Hoic-Bozic, N., Mornar, V., & Boticki, I. (2009). A Blended Learning Approach to Course Design and Implementation. *IEEE Transactions on Education, 52*(1), 19–30.

Hrastinski, S. (2008). Asynchronous and synchronous e-learning. *EDUCAUSE Quarterly, 31*(4), 51–55.

Humayun, M. (2020). Blockchain-Based secure framework for e-learning during COVID-19. *Indian Journal of Science and Technology, 13*(12), 1328–1341. https://doi.org/10.17485/IJST/v13i12.152

Ismail, H. M., Belkhouche, B., & Harous, S. (2019). Framework for Personalized Content Recommendations to Support Informal Learning in Massively Diverse Information Wikis. *IEEE Access: Practical Innovations, Open Solutions, 7*, 172752–172773.

Jordan, J. (2020). Recommending Learning Videos for MOOCS and flipped classrooms. Advances In Practical Applications of Agents, Multi-Agent Systems, and Trustworthiness. The PAAMS Collection. PAAMS 2020. Lecture Notes in Computer Science, Vol.12092. Springer.

Jung, T., Tom Dieck, M. C., Lee, H., & Chung, N. (2020). Moderating role of long-term orientation on augmented reality adoption. *International Journal of Human-Computer Interaction, 36*(3), 239–250.

Kausar, S. (2020). Paper-Mining Smart Learning Analytics Data Using Ensemble Analytics Data Using Ensemble Classifiers. *International Journal of Emerging Technologies in Learning., 15*, 81–102.

Khan, S., & Alqahtani, S. (2020). Big Data Application and its Impact on Education. *International Journal of Emerging Technologies in Learning, 15*(17), 36–46.

Klasnja Milicevic, A., Vesin, B., & Ivanovic, M. (2018). Social tagging strategy for enhancing e-learning experience. *Computers & Education, 118*, 166–181.

Knowles, M. S. (1975). *Self-directed learning: a guide for learners and teachers*. Cambridge Books.

Knowles, M. S., Holton, E. F., & Swanson, R. A. (1998). *The adult learner*. Gulf Publishing.

Krauss, C. (2018). *Time-dependent recommender systems for the prediction of appropriate learning objects* (Doctoral thesis). Technische Universitat Berlin.

Kukharenko, V., & Syrotenko, N. (2014). Open On-line Course "Content Curator". *Education and Information Technologies*. Advance online publication. doi:10.14308/ite000511

Lai, C. H., Liu, D. R., & Lin, S. R. (2018). Document recommendation with implicit feedback based on matrix factorization and topic model. *2018 IEEE International Conference on Applied System Invention (ICASI)*, 62-65. doi: 10.1109/ICASI.2018.8394337

Lalitha, T. B., & Sreeja, P. S. (2020). Personalised Self-Directed Learning Recommendation System. *Procedia Computer Science*, *171*, 583–592.

Lam, T. Y., & Dongol, B. (2020). A Blockchain enabled e-learning platform. *Interactive Learning Environments*, 1–23. doi:10.1080/10494820.2020.1716022

Lara, J. A., Aljawarneh, S., & Pamplona, S. (2020). Special issue on the current trends in E-learning system. *Journal of Computing in Higher Education*, *32*, 1–8. https://doi.org/10.1007/s12528-019-09235-w

Li, C. (2019). A Blockchain System for E-Learning Assessment and Certification. *IEEE International Conference on Smart Internet of Things (SmartIoT)*. doi:10.1109/SmartIoT.2019.00040

Lingwood, J., Farran, E. K., Courbois, Y., & Blades, M. (2020). Investigating route learning, metacognition, and beacon-based strategies using virtual environments. *European Review of Applied Psychology*, *70*(4), 100570.

Littlejohn, A., Falconer, I., & Mcgill, L. (2008). Characterising effective eLearning resources. *Computer Education*, *50*(3), 757–771.

Livari, N., Sharma, S., & Venta-Olkkonen, L. (2020). Digital transformation of everyday life- How COVID-19 pandemic transformed the basic education of the young generation and why information management research should care? *International Journal of Information Management*, *55*, 102183.

Madani, Y., Erritali, M., Bengourram, J., & Sailhan, F. (2019). Social Collaborative Filtering Approach for Recommending Courses in an E-learning Platform. *Procedia Computer Science*, *151*, 1164–1169.

Martin, J., Bohuslava, J., & Igor, H. (2018). Augmented Reality in Education 4.0. *2018 IEEE 13th International Scientific and Technical Conference on Computer Sciences and Information Technologies (CSIT), 2018*, 231-236. doi: 10.1109/STC-CSIT.2018.8526676

Mentsiev, A. U., Magomaev, T. R., & Dauletukaeva, K. D. (2020). The impact of big data on the development of education. *Journal of Physics: Conference Series*, *1691*(1), 012181.

Merriam, S. B. (2001). Andragogy and Self-Directed Learning: Pillars of Adult Learning Theory. In S. B. Merriam (Ed.), *The new update on adult learning theory. New Directions for Adult and Continuing Education, No. 89*. Jossey-Bass. Springer.

Moharm, K., & Eltahan, M. (2020). The role of big data in improving e-learning transition. *IOP Conference Series. Materials Science and Engineering*, *885*(1), 012003.

Mohd Kamal, M. A., Adnan, A. H. M., Azamri, N. M., Idris, K. B., Zuraimi, N. A., & Yusof, M. N. (2019). Video-based learing as an Education 4.0 technique for blended learning in flipped classrooms. Proc. of the International Invention, Innovative & Creative (InIIC) Conference (series 2/2019), 17-27.

Mondal, B., Patra, O., Mishra, S., & Patra, P. (2020). A course recommendation system based on grades. *2020 International Conference on Computer Science, Engineering and Applications (ICCSEA)*, 1-5.

Monsalve-Pulido, J. (2020). Autonomous recommender system architecture for virtual learning environments. In Applied Computing and Informatics. Elsevier.

Morze, N., Varchenko-Trotsenko, L., Terletska, T., & Smyrnova-Trybulska, E. (2021). Implementation of adaptive learning at higher education institutions by means of Moodle LMS. *Journal of Physics: Conference Series, 1840*(1), 012062.

Muniasamy, A., & Alasiry, A. (2020). Deep learning: The impact on future eLearning. *International Journal of Emerging Technologies in Learning, 15*(1), 188–199. https://doi.org/10.3991/ijet.v15i01.11435

Nabizadeh, A. H. (2020). Learning Path Personalization and Recommendation Methods: A Survey of the State-Of-The-Art. *Expert Systems with Applications, 159*, 113596.

Nabizadeh, A. H., Goncalves, D., Gama, S., Jorge, J., & Rafsanjani, H. N. (2020). Adaptive learning path recommender approach using auxiliary learning objects. *Computers & Education, 147*, 103777.

Negash, S., & Wilcox, M. V. (2008). E-Learning Classifications: Differences and Similarities. Handbook of Distance Learning for Real-Time and Asynchronous Information Technology Education.

Nilashi, M., & Ibrahim, O., & Ithnin, N. (2014). Hybrid recommendation approaches for multi-criteria collaborative filtering. *Expert Systems with Applications, 41*(8), 3879–3900.

O'Flaherty, J., & Philips, C. (2015). The Use of Flipped Classrooms in Higher Education: A Scoping Review. *Internet and Higher Education, 25*, 85–95.

Ortigosa, A., Martín, J. M., & Carro, R. M. (2014). Sentiment analysis in Facebook and its application to e-learning. *Computers in Human Behavior, 31*, 527–541.

Ouyang, F., & Jiao, P. (2021). Artificial intelligence in education: The three Paradigms. *Computers and Education: Artificial Intelligence, 2*. doi:10.1016/j.caeai.2021.100020

Ozdamil, F., & Cavus, N. (2011). Basic elements and Characteristics of mobile learning. *Procedia: Social and Behavioral Sciences, 28*, 937–942.

Pant, H. V., Lohani, M. C., & Pande, J. (2021). *MOOCs in Higher Education: Current Trends in India and Developed Countries*. Ubiquitous Technologies for Human Development and Knowledge Management. doi:10.4018/978-1-7998-7844-5.ch004

Paramythis, A., & Loidl-Reisinger, S. (2004). Adaptive Learning Environments and e-Learning Standards. *Electronic Journal of e-Learning, 2*(1), 181–194.

Peat, J., & Helland, K. (2004). *The competitive advantage of online versus traditional education*. University of Tennessee. ERIC Document Reproduction Service No. ED492477.

Poon, J. (2013). Blended learning: An institutional approach for enhancing students' learning experiences. *Journal of Online Learning and Teaching, 9*(2), 271–288.

Rabahallah, K., Mahdaoui, L., & Azouaou, F. (2018). MOOCs Recommender System Using Ontology and Memory-based Collaborative Filtering. *20th International Conference on Enterprise Information Systems.*

Rahman, A. (2016). Cloud based E-Learning, security threats and security measures. *Indian Journal of Science and Technology, 9*(48), 1–8.

Rajesh, M., Illayaraja, K., & Kalaiselvi, R. (2018). Emerging Trends of E-Learning in India. *Shanlax International Journal of Commerce, 6*(S1), 52-29. zenodo.1438190 doi:10.5281/

Rani, M., Nayak, R., & Vyas, O. P. (2015). An Ontology-based Adaptive Personalized E-learning System, Assisted by Software Agents on Cloud Storage. *Knowledge-Based Systems, 90*, 33–48.

Ray, A., Bala, P. K., & Dwivedi, Y. K. (2020). Exploring barriers affecting usage intentions: an NLP-based multi-method approach. *Behaviour & Information Technology.* doi:10.1080/0144929X.2020.1849403

Ray, A., Bala, P. K., & Dwivedi, Y. K. (2020). Exploring Values affecting e-Learning adoption from the user-generated-content: A Consumption-value-theory perspective. *Journal of Strategic Marketing.* doi :10.1080/0965254X.2020.1749875

Razzaque, A., & Hamdan, A. (2020). Internet of Things for Learning Styles and Learning Outcomes Improve e-Learning: A Review of Literature. *Joint European-US Workshop on Applications of Invariance in Computer Vision*, 783-791.

Reimers, G. (2015). Learner Generated Content - Fostering and Valuing User Generated Content in eLearning using Social Feedback. Doctoral Consortium - DCCSEDU, 3-7.

Rivero-Albarran, D. (2018). Design of a Recommender System for Intelligent Classrooms Based on Multiagent Systems. In Advances in Intelligent Systems and Computing (Vol. 721). Springer.

Rukmana, A. A., & Mulyanti, B. (2020). Internet of Things (IoT): Web learning for smart school system. *IOP Conference Series. Materials Science and Engineering, 830*(3), 032042.

Salehi, M., & Kamalabadi, I. N. (2013). Hybrid recommendation approach for learning material based on sequential pattern of the accessed material and the learner's preference tree. *Knowledge-Based Systems, 48*, 57–69.

Salehi, M., & Kmalabadi, I. N. (2012). A hybrid attribute-based recommender system for e-learning material recommendation. *IERI Procedia, 2*, 565–570.

Sarrab, M., Elgamel, L., & Aldabbas, H. (2012). Mobile Learning (m-learning) and educational environments. *International Journal of Distributed and Parallel Systems, 3*(4).

Sattarov, A. R., & Khaitova, N. F. (2019). Mobile learning as new forms and methods of increasing the effectiveness of education. *European Journal of Research and Reflection in Educational Sciences, 7*(12), 1169–1175.

Shahabadi, M. M., & Uplane, M. (2015). Synchronous and asynchronous learning styles and academic performance of e-learners. *Procedia: Social and Behavioral Sciences, 176*(20), 129–138.

Sheshasaayee, A., & Malathi, S. (2017). Impact and consequences of BIG DATA in e-learning. *2017 International Conference on Innovative Mechanisms for Industry Applications (ICIMIA)*, 726-729. doi: 10.1109/ICIMIA.2017.7975560

Shi, D. (2020). A learning path recommendation model based on a multidimensional knowledge graph framework for e-learning. *Knowledge-Based Systems, 193*, 105618.

Siddiqui, S. T., Alam, S., Khan, Z. A., & Gupta, A. (2019). Cloud-Based E-Learning: Using Cloud Computing Platform for an Effective E-Learning. In S. Tiwari, M. Trivedi, K. Mishra, A. Misra, & K. Kumar (Eds.), Smart Innovations in Communication and Computational Sciences. Advances in Intelligent Systems and Computing (Vol. 851). Springer., https://doi.org/10.1007/978-981-13-2414-7_31.

Skinner, B. F. (1961). Teaching machines. *Scientific American, 205*(3), 90–112.

Souabi, S., Retbi, A., Idrissi, M. K., & Bennani, S. (2020). A Recommendation Approach in Social Learning Based on K-Means Clustering. *2020 International Conference on Intelligent Systems and Computer Vision (ISVC)*, 1-5. doi: 10.1109/ISCV49265.2020.9204203

Souabi, S., Retbi, A., Idrissi, M. K., & Bennani, S. (2020). Toward a Recommendation-Oriented Approach Based on Community Detection Within Social Learning Network. In M. Ezziyyani (Ed.), Advanced Intelligent Systems for Sustainable Development (AI2SD'2019). AI2SD 2019. Advances in Intelligent Systems and Computing (Vol. 1102). Springer. https://doi.org/10.1007/978-3-030-36653-7_22.

Southworth, J. H., Flanigan, J. M., & Knezek, G. (1981). *Computers in education: international multimode electronic conferencing*. The Printout.

Swan, K. (2003). Learning effectiveness Online: what the research tells us. In J. Bourne & J. C. Moore (Eds.), *Elements of Quality Online Education, Practice and Direction*. Needham, MA: Sloan Center for Online Education.

Tang, K. Y., Chang, C. Y., & Hwang, G. J. (2021). Trends in artificial intelligence-supported e-learning: A systematic review and co-citation network analysis (1998-2019). *Interactive Learning Environments*. Advance online publication. doi:10.1080/10494820.2021.1875001

Tarus, J. K., Niu, Z., & Mustafa, G. (2018). Knowledge-based Recommendation: A review of ontology-based recommender systems for e-learning. *Artificial Intelligence Review, 50*, 21–48.

Thai-Nghe, N., Drumond, L., Krohn-Grimberghe, A., & Schmidt-Thieme, L. (2010). Recommender system for predicting student performance. *Procedia Computer Science, 1*, 2811–2819.

Verbert, K. (2012). Context-Aware Recommender Systems for Learning: A Survey and Future Challenges. *IEEE Transactions on Learning Technologies, 5*(4), 318–335.

Wang, F., Fong, J., & Kwan, R. (Eds.). (2010). *Research on hybrid learning models: Advanced tools, technologies, and applications*. Information Science Reference.

Wang, J., Zhu, Z., & Caverlee, J. (2020). User Recommendation in Content Curation Platforms. *Conference: WSDM'20: The Thirteenth ACM International Conference on Web Search and Data Mining.* DOI: 10.1145/3336191.3371822

Wang, M., & Kang, M. (2006). Cybergogy for Engaged Learning: A Framework for Creating Learner Engagement through Information and Communication Technology. In *Engaged Learning with Emerging Technologies*. Academic Press.

Wong, J. K., Oladinrin, O. T., Ho, C. M., Guilbert, E., & Kam, R. (2018). Assessment of video-based e-learning in a construction measurement course. *International Journal of Construction Management*, 1-7. doi:10.1080/15623599.2018.1435152

Wu, T., & Gu, C. (2015). Metadata-based method for online learning resources recommendation. *ICIC Express Letters. An International Journal of Research and Surveys.*, 6(11), 2929–2935.

Yarandi, M., Jahankhani, H., & Tawil, A. (2013). A Personalized Adaptive e-learning approach based on semantic web technology. *Webology, 10*(2).

Yi, L., Zhou, Q., Xiao, T., Qing, G., & Mayer, I. (2020). Conscientiousness in Game-Based Learning. *Simulation & Gaming, 51*(5), 712–734. doi:10.1177/1046878120927061

Zain, S. (2020). *Digital transformation trends in education*. Future Directions in Digital Information.

Zhang, Z., Brun, A., & Boyer, A. (2020). New Measures for Offline Evaluation of Learning path Recommenders. In Addressing Global Challenges and Quality Education. Springer International Publishing.

Chapter 10
A Proposed Solution for Identifying Online Fake Reviews in the Research Process

Victor-Alexandru Briciu

https://orcid.org/0000-0002-7506-8099

Transilvania University of Brasov, Romania

Cristian-Laurențiu Roman

Transilvania University of Brasov, Romania

Arabela Briciu

https://orcid.org/0000-0003-1202-5830

Transilvania University of Brasov, Romania

ABSTRACT

This chapter aims to present the issue of manipulation of online reviews, behind which there is always an interest, whether it is about increasing sales, promoting a product, degrading the image of a competing brand or product. Such reviews can influence the purchase decision or the sales of a company. Combining users' text with their behavior has yielded the best results in identifying fake reviews, and this remains probably the most effective method to date. The chapter proposes, as a novelty factor, a methodological solution before analyzing reviews through specialized software (e.g., SmartMunk, Revuze, Aspectiva, SentiGeek, etc.), a filter for identifying fake reviews by introducing them into a fake review application called Fakespot. Moreover, the idea that these false reviews can influence the purchase decision of customers in any field is emphasized, so it is very important that large companies develop programs or systems that detect them.

DOI: 10.4018/978-1-7998-8061-5.ch010

INTRODUCTION

Web 2.0 is the platform that underlies the concepts we will discuss in this chapter and represents the second version of the Internet, the one that appeared after the 2000s, the one in which the possibilities to browse online have become much more diverse, websites and applications have grown a lot, and people have started to keep in touch more and more in the online environment. At the same time, companies have also started to concentrate a large part of their resources for promotion in the online environment, and marketing strategies have also developed greatly.

Web 2.0 consists of all "online tools, applications and approaches, such as blogs, social networking sites, online communities and customer review sites" (Constantinides & Holleschovsky, 2016, p. 271); in addition, the Internet has started "facilitating the 'social' customer electronic word of mouth (eWOM) and a major source of customer information and empowerment" (Constantinides & Holleschovsky, 2016, p. 271), which has made reviews become an important source of information.

Another definition states that Web 2.0 is "a collection of open-source, interactive and user controlled online applications expanding the experiences, knowledge and market power of the users as participants in business and social processes" (Constantinides & Fountain, 2008, p. 232). The authors also discuss the importance of Web 2.0 for marketing and business in general. For brands, there are many possibilities to stay closer to people, learning "about the needs and opinions of their customers as well as interacting with them in a direct and personalised way" (Constantinides & Fountain, 2008, p. 233).

There are many differences between Web 1.0 and 2.0 (Briciu & Briciu, 2019), but it is said that one of the most important ones is that "content creators were few in Web 1.0 with the vast majority of users simply acting as consumers of content, while any participant can be a content creator in Web 2.0 and numerous technological aids have been created to maximize the potential for content creation" (Cormode & Krishnamurthy, 2008, p. 2). With the advent of Web 2.0 (Briciu & Briciu, 2021), many users have learned to create content, and this is how vlogging appeared, a phenomenon that has grown today, as well as Internet advertising, online stores, but also social networks (Briciu & Briciu, 2020), on which people have become dependent. Also, the Internet "is present in all areas of human life and activity" (Czerwinska, 2020, p. 77) and takes up more and more people's time, the most important effect being that "is displacing traditional media such as television, radio and newspapers" (Czerwinska, 2020, p. 77).

Another big difference is that Web 2.0 addresses users differently, most sites "encourage users to spend as much time as possible on their site" (Cormode & Krishnamurthy, 2008, p. 7). The interest of the sites is to have as much traffic as possible, as they post quite a few ads from which they earn significant amounts of money. Instead, Web 1.0 was much more limited, and fewer users visited the sites, their main disadvantage being that they used to "tend to cover a single topic and do not require users to log in to access them" (Cormode & Krishnamurthy, 2008, p.7).

Six dimensions seem to underlie the concept, referring to "Individual production and User Generated Content, Harness the power of the crowd, Data on an epic sale, Architecture of Participation, Network Effects, Openness" (Anderson, 2007, p. 14). In short, even before the advent of Web 2.0, thoughts were directed towards user-created content and sales through the Internet, and the goals were met, these two dimensions being of great importance today.

From the point of view of participation in the online environment, Moria Levy presents the three types of users. Passive users are those for whom "the history of their activity is what is collected, giving an added value" (Levy, 2009, p. 122), meaning that they do not generate a lot of content for other users, their actions being rather directed to themselves. The second type of users are those who use the Internet minimally, "adding content to other people's content (i.e. Tagging) or write content themselves, but as individuals" (Levy, 2009, p. 122), and the third category includes users who collaborate more, "users that work together over the net, adding collaborative content. For examples: Wiki, Google's spreadsheet, etc." (Levy, 2009, p. 122), this being the most active category of users, being present on many sites (Briciu, Rezeanu & Briciu, 2020).

Customers' purchasing decisions began to be influenced by the online environment with the advent of this concept, which became "increasingly popular due to the advantages they offer to users (transparency, referrals, contacts with other users, etc.) and their effect on customer power" (Constantinides & Fountain, 2008, p. 239), and in addition to this power offered to customers, they also started to trust buying through online stores, companies taking greater care of their customers, and user reviews charging any mistake they made. Following the presentation of the broader context defined by Web 2.0, the next part expresses the opinions of the authors in relation to other concepts that will ultimately lead to the topic of online fake reviews, namely Word of Mouth, Electronic Word of Mouth, Customer Generated Content or User Generated Content.

Fake reviews are the most dangerous element that can affect the purchase decision, having the power to create a false image of a product or service by spreading false information through reviews, whether positive or negative. Besides this, numerous threatening elements affects companies and customers, like "consumer scams, piracy, counterfeit products, malware, viruses, and spam" (He, Proserpio & Hollenbeck, 2021, p. 1). Ordinary people often resort to these for various reasons, but "in some cases, firms are using dubious and illegal means for promoting products, including through the creation of fake consumer identities and the payment of people to write fake reviews using those fake identities" (Malbon, 2012, p. 9). Due to the fact that publishing false information in the online environment is illegal, Malbon (2012) states that "governments and regulators should take the problem of fake reviews and reviewers seriously" (p. 5), so sanctioning people who publish such reviews is very important.

The main objective of this chapter regards answering to the following questions: "Is the purchase decision influenced by users' reviews?", "Why do fake reviews appear and who posts them?", "How we or companies can detect fake reviews and users who post them?" and "How companies find out the level of customer satisfaction?"

LITERATURE REVIEW

Word of Mouth, or WOM for short, can be interpreted as information that is transmitted from mouth to mouth. It is a common concept in areas such as marketing or advertising, but it is also present in our daily lives, because it represents information that circulates through oral communication from person to person, usually in an informal manner. This concept can be important for a business (Briciu, Mircea & Briciu, 2020), being one of the easiest and cheapest ways to promote a product or service.

According to the author Eugene W. Anderson (1998), word-of-mouth represents "informal communications between private parties concerning evaluations of goods and services rather than formal complaints to firms and/or personnel" (Anderson, 1998, p. 6). Certainly, the opinion of customers is the most important, and it is influenced by the quality of the product or service, so "the valence of word of mouth may be positive, neutral or negative" (Anderson, 1998, p. 6). A similar definition specifies that WOM is "a form of interpersonal communication among consumers concerning their personal experiences with a firm or a product, has undoubtedly always been a powerful marketing force" (Sundaram, Mitra, & Webster, 1998, p. 527).

In addition, it is considered that word-of-mouth "can have an enormous impact on purchasing decisions: consumer WOM has been touted as the single most powerful factor in predicting the long-term success of experience goods" (Robson, Bredican, Farshid & Humphrey, 2013, p. 523). It is also said that "WOM can make or break a consumer's decision to buy" (Robson et al., 2013, p. 523), which seems to be very logical, because no one would want to buy a product that has a very bad reputation.

People tend to trust their acquaintances or friends more, and generally take their opinion into account, so a brand should please everyone, because even one dissatisfied customer can express his or her opinion and a decline can occur due to the fact that people will start losing trust, and the company's image may suffer. To build and maintain a good relationship with the costumers, it is suggested that "each educational institution strives to always hear and understand what customers want, solve problems faced by customers, pay attention to customers, and always help customers so that customer loyalty is one of the keys to successful existence companies" (Astono, 2021, p. 91). A study shows that "57% of people visiting a new Web site did so based on a personal recommendation; this is higher than any other source of influence" (Godes & Mayzlin, 2004, p. 545). We can say that this percentage is very high, and the chances of a person hearing about a certain brand from a friend are also high.

One problem with this concept is that it is very difficult to manage and measure, primarily due to the fact that "the information is exchanged in private conversations, direct observation has traditionally been difficult" (Godes & Mayzlin, 2004, p. 545). The fact that WOM is based on people's personal conversations makes it almost impossible to analyze customer opinions. One solution is to observe conversations in online communities, using a simple method: "The most common approach is to use simple counts. This approach is similar to news-clipping services that monitor how many times a firm's products are mentioned" (Godes & Mayzlin, 2004, p. 546). With this method, you can find out what customers think about the company and its products, based on how often the product name is mentioned and how it is described.

Anderson (1998) also mentions these measurements, which are based on satisfaction levels: the first one informs us that "satisfied customers engage in more word of mouth than dissatisfied customers. Greater word of mouth is also found to occur as a result of greater satisfaction with complaint handling" (Anderson, 1998, p. 6), and the second hypothesis states that "low-satisfaction customers should engage in greater word of mouth than high-satisfaction customers" (Anderson, 1998, p. 7).

Regarding consumer behavior, sociologists and psychologists say that this need to buy products and then express our opinion about them comes from a human motivation, as well as the fact that we sometimes feel the need to buy products, even if we don't necessarily need them. Therefore, this motivation determines the nature of post-consumption behavior such as WOM communication, complaints and repurchases intentions (Sundaram et al., 1998).

Word of mouth is very important in terms of promoting a brand, but it is also the only method of promotion - along with Electronic Word of Mouth - in which the brand does not have a direct involvement, being only about customers who have tried the product and who will express their opinion about it, be it positive or negative. With the development of the Internet, eWOM appeared, which is much more developed than WOM, being about the opinions of thousands or even millions of users, that are very easy to access, but we will discuss this concept further.

Unlike WOM, which is the transmission of information through oral communication, Electronic Word of Mouth (eWOM) offers more communication possibilities because it takes place in the online environment, where we can find out certain details about a product even from an unknown person. With the development of the Internet, this concept also developed, having a very important role in the purchase decision, because "prospective customers visit Web sites and read reviews from other customers (eWOM) to learn more about a product before making a purchase" (Doh & Hwang, 2009, p. 193).

According to Wolfgang Weitzl (2017), eWOM represents "peer-generated, text-based product evaluations and recommendations made by potential, actual, and former customers about a product or company, which are made available to a multitude of consumers via postings on the Internet" (Weitzl, 2017, p. 2). The author sees "eWOM reviews or recommendations as positive, neutral or negative information about a product released on the Internet by a consumer" (Weitzl, 2017, p. 2), which it is also true for Word of Mouth, as they have the power to persuade a potential customer to buy or give up a particular product.

eWOM brings more advantages than classic, face-to-face communication, and Cui & Lui (2012) present two of them. First, we are told that it is more efficient because "of its speed, convenience, wide reach, and the absence of face-to-face human pressure" (Cui & Lui, 2012, p. 41), and the fact that there is a large volume of information can help us, so we can find out the opinion of hundreds or thousands of people, "from a vast, geographically dispersed group of people, who have experience with relevant products or services" (Jalilvand, Esfahani & Samiei, 2011, p. 44). Second, the measurement problem with Word of Mouth is diminished due to the fact that "e-commerce operators today can archive WOM interactions from online forums in databases, which lends opportunities to estimate their effects directly and perhaps more accurately" (Cui & Lui, 2012, p. 41). It is very clear that data can be collected and analyzed much more easily in the online environment, so the measurements are much more accurate and brands can be aware of consumer preferences. On the other hand, "in traditional WOM communication, the information is exchanged in private conversations, so direct observation has been difficult" (Jalilvand et al., 2011, p. 43).

We can say that there is also a problem with getting informed about products on the Internet, because "customers cannot always experience the true features of a product purchased via the Internet, there are difficulties in making the correct purchasing decision" (Jalilvand et al., 2011, p. 43). The advantage is that we can find out people's opinion about a product used for a certain period of time, but the biggest disadvantage is that most of the time we will not be able to test the product before buying it and we can convince ourselves of certain features only after we buy it.

In a study conducted in Asia, the members of a community were asked how often they use eWOM. The results show that "the majority of participants find eWOM to be important and that 83% of them do read eWOM" (Almana & Mirza, 2013, p. 24). This figure represents community members, people who spend more time online, so the percentage is quite high. Another interesting aspect is emphasized by the authors, in most cases "a positive shopping experience will lead to participation in the writing of eWOM more than a negative experience" (Almana & Mirza, 2013, p. 24).

Another study, which was based on "the causal relationship between the ratio of eWOM messages (positive–negative) and eWOM effects with the moderating roles of involvement and prior knowledge" (Doh & Hwang, 2009, p. 193), and collected over a thousand people from South Korean universities, shows us that "96.5% had made online purchases of one or more items and did so, on average, nine times per year. Specifically, 97.9% of them usually referred to customer reviews (eWOM) prior to making online purchases. They read an average of 13.9 reviews per purchase" (Doh & Hwang, 2009, p. 195). The results of the study give us very high figures, even if we are talking about young people, most of them place great value on online shopping and on reviews written by other users.

eWOM has the power to change opinions, but a great deal of attention must also be paid to erroneous information that appears related to certain products, most likely to denigrate certain brands. Thus, "a significant number of studies have been published which all strive to investigate the effectiveness or persuasiveness of eWOM messages. They all more or less agree that customer reviews can be a very powerful marketing force" (Weitzl, 2017, p. 5). This can have a very big impact on a company, and if there is a "wave" of criticism in the online environment, its image may suffer or an image crisis may even occur.

Electronic Word of Mouth is one of the most widespread phenomena on the Internet, since there is always a lot of information circulating on the internet, from one person to another. eWOM is the basis of online reviews, as well as of any recommendation of a product between acquaintances or friends, so it is very important in terms of promotion.

Customer Generated Content (CGC) or User Generated Content (UGC) can be understood as material or content that is generated by users or customers, whether it is text, video, audio or photos, users publish them on the Internet in order to express certain opinions or feelings to other people. Regarding the previous concept, Customer Generated Content is closely related to eWOM, and "since the online discussions were essentially about the product and the company, a considerable proportion of CGC was in the form of eWOM throughout the entire advertising campaign" (Wang & Rodgers, 2011, p. 214). The idea is that Customer Generated Content refers to users who create a material about your company or product, and eWOM refers to potential or current customers who will express their opinion about your brand, be it positive or negative. Thus, "eWOM is a specific type of CGC about products or companies" (Wang & Rodgers, 2011, p. 213).

As a broader definition, we can say that CGC is "online content that is publicly available and created by end-users in a creative effort - and its manifestation in social media applications has recently attracted much research interest" (Dennhardt, 2014, p. 4). It is obvious that this concept can be a very good promotion method, with no direct involvement of the company and without very high expenses.

Customer Generated Content helps people share "opinions and experiences on companies, brands, products or services and create large-scale word of mouth networks" (Constantinides & Holleschovsky, 2016, p. 271), thus creating information that circulates "from mouth to mouth", and "consumers can make their personal opinions easily accessible to global communities or individual peers who use the information as an extra factor supporting their purchasing decisions" (Constantinides & Holleschovsky, 2016, p. 271). Online shopping is easier to do because we can use the opinions of users to know if the products we want to buy live up to our expectations.

This concept is also defined as "media content created or produced by the general public rather than by paid professionals and primarily distributed on the Internet" (Daugherty, Eastin & Bright, 2008, p. 16). It is also noted that YouTube, Facebook, Wikipedia, Flickr, Blogger or personal web pages are some of the applications and sites that host this type of content, so influencers, artists or public figures are some the users who generate content.

A major advantage of CGC is the fact that "online information resources provided not by typical Internet users themselves but rather by traditionally recognized 'expert' sources" (Flanagin & Metzger, 2013, p. 1627), often a famous person or expert in the field can increase credibility, and potential customers will buy that product with confidence. The situation is different when a product or service is promoted by an unknown user; people will not trust it as much or will overlook its content more easily.

With the development of User Generated Content, a new concept emerged, called user generated brands (UGB), representing "brands that originated from single users or a group of users through user-generated content, rather than companies" (Dennhardt, 2014, p. 4). Users took advantage of the possibilities offered by the Internet and created their own smaller brands, the idea being based on "their professional routines in social media environments, where their products are publicly available and show a creative effort" (Dennhardt, 2014, p. 5). Many of these users get to run a business unexpectedly, and all actions take place online.

Daughtery, Eastin and Bright (2008) suggest certain reasons why users create content. These reasons "represent functional sources designed to meet specific consumer needs and serve as the foundation for attitude formation, ultimately influencing behavior" (Daughtery et al., 2008, p. 17). So, it is about the attitude of users towards the consumption and the creation of UGC, hence the behavior. In addition, another reason why users use UGC is explained. It is about their personal experience gained through this concept, but also about the satisfaction they feel because they can contribute to the success of a brand. In other words, the creators of "of UGC therefore would produce UGC because it helps them understand their environment, the topic at hand, and/or ultimately themselves, because they feel a sense of intrinsic wisdom" (Daughtery et al., 2008, p.17).

UGC has proven to be very successful, as proven by the fact that some companies have even allowed users to actively participate in promoting services or products, such as VWs, which "give users the opportunity to create and capture the value of their efforts, VWs provide ideal premises for the creation of UGBs" (Dennhardt, 2014, p.5). Also, the fact that users have been rewarded is very important, as they are motivated to create other materials. As a result of the theoretical clarifications operated on the concepts of Word of Mouth, Electronic Word of Mouth and Customer Generated Content (CGC) or User Generated Content (UGC) in this subchapter, we can see the ideas and theoretical perspectives related to searching for product information and recommendations that will highlight the concepts of Online Consumer Reviews, Online Product Reviews in the next section.

SEARCHING FOR PRODUCT INFORMATION AND RECOMMENDATIONS

Influence of Online Reviews on Consumer Purchase Decision

Online Consumer Reviews are based on another concept we discussed, namely electronic Word of Mouth, as it is related to the opinion of people on certain products, exposed in the online environment. We can define Online Consumer Reviews as "one type of electronic word-of-mouth, provide product information and recommendations from the customer perspective" (Yayli & Bayram, 2012, p. 3) or as "a form of eWOM in a decision-making process to purchase products online and offline" (Park & Nicolau, 2015, p.5). The definitions are similar, and the basic function of these reviews is to help buyers make the right purchase decision.

Studies show that people tend to trust their close ones more when they recommend a particular product, compared to a random customer who has written a review, and this is due to their fear of being manipulated. Also, "empirical studies show that buyers seriously consider online feedback when making purchasing decisions" (Yayli & Bayram, 2012, p. 4). It is clear that people want to talk to someone before making an important purchase, in order to find out certain details or pleasant/unpleasant experiences related to a product or service, hence the idea that a person who is close to us is better suited to recommend a product or not.

Regarding the customers' motivation to write and post these reviews, we observe, first of all, their need to share a positive experience with others. According to the literature, sharing these experiences with others may come from a desire to feel satisfied, not necessarily from a desire to help others with information about a product. Thus, spreading "positive word-of-mouth is to gain social approval or self-approval by demonstrating their superb purchase decision, and trough altruistic behavior of sharing their expertise with others" (Chen, Fay & Wang, 2011, p. 86).

This motivation to post can also be influenced by the quality and price of a product, an important element being whether or not the product meets the customer's expectations or if he is disappointed, because for a given price, very low quality generates a high level of costumer dissatisfaction and a very high quality generates a high level of customer satisfaction (Chen et al., 2011).

Reviews have come to play a very important role in purchase decisions, with a report from eMarketer showing that "92 percent of online consumers read product reviews before they make a purchase decision" (Li, Huang, Tan & Wei, 2013, p. 4). This is normal, if we also consider the development of the Internet and how easy to access are various sites where people's opinions appear.

Companies also play an important part in posting reviews, because they create an advantage for themselves and it is a form of promotion, as they "encourage consumers to write reviews to express their opinions on various aspects of the products" (Yu, Zha, Wang & Chua, 2011, p. 1496). There are also advantages on the other side, because consumers commonly seek quality information from online consumer reviews prior to purchasing a product (Yu et al., 2011), this being the main reason why so many people read several reviews before buying something.

In the article by Park and Nicolau (2015) we find the opinions of other authors on the effect of online reviews. First, positive reviews are believed to help increase sales, while negative reviews affect them. On the other hand, it is shown that there is no link between sales and user reviews, the two hypotheses being in opposition. The authors of the article conclude that the number of positive or negative reviews a product has is not very important, and that the volume is more important, i.e. their total number, because "products reviewed by consumers have a greater chance of staying in consumers' consideration sets than products that have not been reviewed" (Park & Nicolau, 2015, p. 6).

Chen et al. (2011) also discuss the value and volume of reviews. According to the authors, the best decision is to monitor the products with a low price, but with a constant quality, and in terms of the volume of posts, the number of postings will be negatively correlated with product price in the early online consumer review stage (Chen et al., 2011). This applies to users who have been using reviews for a very short time. As far as regular users are concerned, the emphasis is on customer satisfaction. In theory, a good quality product with a low price will also have a very high rating; in opposition, when high-priced products can signal high quality, which increase product ratings, high price also leads to higher dissatisfaction, which decreases ratings (Chen et al., 2011).

Regarding Online Products Reviews, it can be said that the concept is very similar to Online Customer Reviews. It is also based on Word of Mouth and can be defined as "peer-generated product evaluations posted on the company's or a third party's websites" (Alzate, Arce-Urriza & Cebollada, 2021, p.638). Next, it will be discussed the types of reviews that can appear in the online environment, the credibility and language used in their writing, but also certain models created by specialists in the field.

As previously stated, reviews are very important to both customers and companies, and as a definition, it can be stated that they represent "a potentially valuable tool for firms, who can use them to monitor consumer attitudes toward their products in real time, and adapt their manufacturing, distribution, and marketing strategies accordingly" (Dellarocas, Zhang & Awad, 2007, p. 24). According to this definition, companies can improve the manufacture, materials, distribution or promotion of their products by taking into account the opinions of their customers, but the fact that they can find out people's preferences so easily and without investment, as in the case of some studies, is the biggest advantage.

Thus, reviews are "third-party evaluations by consumers of the product or services advertised on a website, and are displayed next to the product description in order to enhance customer perception and improve the perceived communication characteristics of the medium" (Korfiatis, Barriocanal-Garcia & Sanchez, 2012, p. 3). Next, the link between reviews and sales is mentioned, because the number of reviews a product has can make a difference, the product being more likely to sell well, because "they must rely on previous experiences which provide an indicator of whether this product or service is worthy of purchase or not" (Korfiatis et al., 2012, p. 3).

It is said that there are two main types of reviews in the online environment, those written by people who specialize in writing them, and those written by customers. The difference between the two is the following: customers write a review after using a product for a certain amount of time, and these review experts write them referring to "those posted by prior buyers who have used or experienced a focal product" (Li et al., 2013, p. 6). Both types have their advantages, with a plus for those written by specialists, since they usually contain more information than the others, being better structured and summarizing the opinion of multiple customers. The only problem that can arise is that of credibility and manipulation, because ordinary customers will always express their honest opinion of a product, but in the case of specialists, the interests of companies may arise and thus, their reviews may only place products in a good light.

When it comes to credibility, it is quite complicated to identify which of the reviews can be taken into account and which are not relevant, because we do not know exactly who wrote that review. Nowadays, more and more sites use a rating, which all users must have next to their name, in order to know if they are to be trusted or not. It is very easy for anyone to access certain sites, create an account and write a review, so the rating is important. Sites like Epinions have been using comments and ratings for reviews for a long time, using "a 1-to-5-star rating, as do reviewers of products, review readers assign a different type of ordinal- scale rating: 'very helpful', 'helpful', 'somewhat helpful', 'not helpful', or 'off topic'" (Mackiewicz, 2010, p. 405), so those who write good reviews will be recognized by the community.

This rating is also valid for products, and it appears on most e-commerce sites, accompanying reviews and representing an average of the customers' opinions of the product, the higher the product is rated, the higher are its chances to sell. Therefore, "we argue that ratings may have a large indirect effect on sales while sentiments have a more direct effect on sales" (Hu, Koh & Reddy, 2014, p. 8). The feelings exposed in the reviews also play an important role, being often stronger than the rating, and the elements expressed "in the text provide more tacit, context-specific explanations of the reviewer's feelings, experiences, and emotions about the product or service" (Hu et al., 2014, p. 4). Customers are more likely to be touched by these stories and experiences that other people have had with a product, rather than by other formal review that is not very detailed.

Following some studies, it has been concluded that there are certain barriers that render certain reviews useless, the biggest problem that often arises being the style of writing. Such a text should be easy to read and understand, and readability is operationalized on how easy it is to read and comprehend a piece of text containing judgments related to the product being evaluated (Li et al., 2013). If someone writes a review, he or she must structure the text well, use clear words and expressions, not to leave room for interpretations, but most importantly, for that opinion to be well understood and taken into account.

The importance and help that Online Products Reviews offer cannot be questioned, and with their help we can figure out if certain products live up to our expectations or if we truly need that product. The most important aspect is to learn which are the relevant reviews, which are the ones that want to manipulate us and to study the rating of each product, because it can often be the key element that exposes the product to us.

Methodology for Identifying Online Fake Reviews in the Research Process

One point of view is that reviews have the role of manipulating as "vendors, publishers, writers, or any third-party consistently monitoring the online reviews and posting non-authentic online reviews on behalf of customers when needed, with the goal of boosting the sales of their products" (Hu, Bose, Koh & Liu, 2012, p. 674), so any text that does not come from a regular user who has used a particular product or service, because there are also users who write fake reviews, for various reasons, for example "reviewers with a material interest in consumers' purchase decisions may post reviews that are designed to influence consumers and to resemble the reviews of disinterested consumers" (Mayzlin, Dover & Chevalier, 2012, p. 1).

These fake reviews can influence the purchase decision of customers in any field, so it is very important that large companies develop programs or systems for detecting them. In 2019, even Amazon had several complaints from the Federal Trade Commission, because they found that "for the first time, a company that advertised products to lose weight on Amazon for writing false reviews on this platform" (Reyes-Menedez, Saura & Filipe, 2019, p. 2). These actions have led Amazon to invest heavily in the platform and staff, in order "to ensure that the reviews of the products presented on their platform are true and up-to-date" (Shu, 2019 cited in Reyes-Menedez, Saura & Filipe, 2019, p. 2).

Over time, systems that generate reviews, comments, and fake news have emerged and developed, which "can then be used to attack online systems or fool human readers" (Adelani, Mai, Fang, Nguyen, Yamagishi & Echizen, 2020, p. 2), and these are threatening to companies and customers, their main quality being that they "produce a large number of fake reviews with the same sentiment" (Adelani et al., 2020, p. 2), intervening in this case, because it is even harder to detect such a review without a specialized program. Thus, generated reviews "that have the same sentiment as the original review are selected to a fake review pool. Since the fake reviews are generated on the basis of an original review, the context of the original review (e.g., an Italian restaurant) should be implicitly embedded in them" (Adelani et al., 2020, p. 2).

It is a real challenge to identify fake reviews, but another method for this problem is to study the behavior of those who write reviews, for this we must consider "the average number of comments posted by reviewers every day, the time interval between the first and the last comment from a reviewer, the proportion of the first review of products in all the comments posted by a reviewer, the number of votes obtained, and the provision of video information" (Mukherjee et al., 2013 cited in Chen, Li, Chen & Geng, 2019, p. 2). Combining users' text with their behavior has yielded the best results in identifying fake reviews, and this remains probably the most effective method to date.

Even with the efforts "of review platforms to combat fraud, the percentage of fake reviews is estimated to be around 15-30%" (Sussin & Thompson, 2012 cited in Lappas, Sabnis & Valkanas, 2016, p. 4), which is a lot. Even Amazon stated that "while small in number, these reviews threaten to undermine the trust that customers, and the vast majority of sellers and manufacturers, place in Amazon, thereby tarnishing Amazon's brand" (Stempel, 2015 cited in Lappas et al., 2016, p. 4).

Another study shows that 80% of consumers have doubts about the relevance of reviews, because it is very difficult to identify the fake ones, it is possible to be wrong about the ones that are written without any specific interest, in addition, it has been proven that "language in fake reviews were similar to that used in authentic reviews" (Chen et al., 2019, p. 2). Therefore, it must be studied very well the activity of the users, their rating if necessary and the details they provide about the product. At the same time, the fact that "Verified Purchase" is written next to the review is another important element, and the idea that the supplier has verified the user regarding the purchase eliminates any doubt regarding the veracity of the information.

This chapter proposes a methodological solution before analyzing reviews through specialized software (e.g., SmartMunk, Revuze, Aspectiva, SentiGeek, etc.), a filter for identifying fake reviews by introducing them into a fake review application called *Fakespot*.

Fakespot was founded by Saoud Khalifah in 2016 and offers the possibility to analyze reviews on sites such as www.amazon.co.uk, www.bestbuy.com, www.sephora.com, www.steam.com, www.walmart.com etc. The idea behind the site's founder is that eCommerce can be an easy and secure shopping experience (Fakespot, 2020), and together with "Amazon and Walmart, which rely so much on third-party sellers, there are too many bad products from dubious sellers that use fake reviews" (Fakespot, 2020).

As a proposed methodological procedure, regarding the analysis of reviews, the first step is to import, from the site, the link of the webpage where the product is described, then enter it in *Fakespot Analyzer* and the process will start once the "Analyze Reviews" button is pressed. The program will complete the next step on its own, which consists in delivering the results to researchers, after a thorough analysis. After the filtering of reviews, one will be able to move on to the next step in the review analysis. Following this discussion, the authors propose two situations for applying the *Fakespot Analyzer* test.

For the analysis, it was chosen a trending product, namely protective masks, given the new virus that appeared in early 2020, worldwide; these masks, along with protective gloves and disinfectant have become the most sought-after products on the market. At the end of 2019, the new coronavirus called Covid-19 appears in Wuhan, China, which has been classified as pneumonia of unknown etiology (Cascella, Rajnik, Cuomo, Dulebohn & Di Napoli, 2021), because no one knows exactly which is the source of this virus. Since March 2020, the number of COVID-19 cases outside China has increased 13 times and the number of infections has tripled, with more than 118,000 cases in 114 countries and over 4,000 deaths, so the WHO declared COVID-19 a pandemic (Cascella et al., 2021). Because of this, millions of people began to stock up, buying a lot of protective masks. That is why the purpose of this chapter is to analyze the reviews of such products, but the masks that promise full safety are targeted, according to the standards imposed by international bodies, and the recommendation was to "wear a medical mask if we have respiratory symptoms and perform hand hygiene after removing the mask." (World Health Organization, 2020, p. 1), and now wearing a face mask is mandatory indoors and sales of these products have exploded.

From Amazon (Think Ink, 2020), it was selected the product "Face Mask (10/1, 5/1, 1/1) Cotton Mask with Elastic Strap Washable Face Mask" from *Sevello Clothing*, priced at £6.99 (Think Ink, 2020). The mask is made in the UK by the previously mentioned company. Referring to the specifications, it is made of 100% cotton, specifying that the material is premium, being delicate and the mask is comfortable to wear, in addition it promises good protection against dust, polluted air and viruses.

In terms of customer reviews, the product has 24 reviews (on the date of this analysis, 24th of June 2020), the rating is 3.4 points out of 5. First, for the purpose of this research, these reviews will be tested through the *Fakespot* program to identify the degree of false reviews.

Continuing the analysis, the same procedure will be applied with another product on Walmart (Blended, 2020), "Washable Cotton Face Mask Reusable Made in the USA", with the price of $9.98 (reduced from $15) (Blended, 2020). The mask is produced in the United States of America, being made of 97% cotton and 3% spandex, with the advantage that it can be washed and used several times; in addition, it promises protection against pollution and harmful particles, but it is specified that without other protective measures, such as gloves or disinfectant, it will not offer full protection against viruses. The product received 28 reviews (on the date of this analysis, 24th of June 2020), which means 3.6 points out of 5.

For the product on Amazon, the report received from Fakespot is positive, being classified in category A, which means that most reviews are correct and there are no suspicions about their validity (Fakespot, 2020a). The program offers 90% certainty about the reviews, as certain measurement errors may occur, but, in principle, no wording has been found to raise questions. The keywords by which customers described the product are: "quality", "thin" or "good".

For the other product used as a case study from Walmart, the Fakespot report is similar (Fakespot, 2020b). The safety of the reviews is 90%, being also included in category A, and the words by which the product is described are: "delicate", "comfortable" or "appropriate".

FINDINGS AND RECOMMENDATIONS

Referring to the selected products, the research followed a criterial methodology or algorithm, as the corpus was defined by products with a higher number of reviews for the relevance of the study; also, before selecting the products, the authors checked for veracity some useful elements such as: users profile, the vocabulary used in reviews, appreciations received from other users and the appearance of the graphical tick attesting the purchase of the product ("Verified Purchase"). After these steps, the selected products were analyzed using the Fakespot application solution. The last step was to observe and analyze the received results, before drawing conclusions.

An important issue that can arise in the case of online reviews is manipulation, behind which there is always an interest. Whether it is about increasing sales, promoting a product, degrading the image of a competing brand or a product, it is clear that such reviews can influence the purchase decision or sales of a company.

Even if it is not morally correct, many companies create an advantage because they "manipulate online reviews to increase sales by anonymously posting favorable reviews and/or deleting negative reviews" (Zhuang, Cui & Peng, 2018, p. 24), and the company's sales and notoriety can increase dramatically. For these reasons, it is understandable that up to one-third of all 'consumer' reviews on the Internet are fake (Zhuang et al., 2018), which means about 33%, a fairly high percentage considering the fact that many products have hundreds or thousands of reviews on different sites, and among them can be reviews that have the role of manipulating.

There are two possible solutions to this problem, the first refers to the fact that false reviews must be found and eliminated, through a fairly simple system, where many correct reviews have been posted, but even where large amounts of reviews exist, the platform has to ensure that most of these reviews are true (Gossling, Hall, Martin-Rios, Ram & Grotte, 2018), and the second solution, referring only to services, because the service quality of an accommodation business can change over time, for instance when owners change, after renovations, or because of new service offers. Reviews must thus be up-to-date (Gossling et al., 2018).

As it was mentioned before, the companies have a great power to influence the public through fake reviews or posts, without any consequence because they are almost impossible to detect. Another big problem for the users that want to buy a product is fake reviews from other users with bad intentions. We can verify some elements on the site to verify the authenticity of reviews: user profile, the confirmation "verified purchase" and for companies, software like Fakespot, and analysis of consumer satisfaction is possible through software like story.ly from SmartMunk, Aspectiva or Revuze. Another important thing is to buy things from well-known and reliable online stores, who can't afford to ruin their image because of bad products and they can verify the platform and delete any fake review detected.

Most research limitations refer to Fakespot, this soft works just with a limited number of sites and automatically our study was restricted to these online platforms. Another limitation refers to some dubious reviews that could have passed the software.

CONCLUSION

Therefore, it is very important that the websites that offer products or services constantly update the databases and follow the frequency of the posts, as well as their relevance. One of the safest methods is to verify the purchase, if a product has been purchased, or to verify that those customers have benefited from a service. Thus, along with the review of these customers, a green dot or a symbol will appear that will certify that the user is trustworthy. More and more sites are using this method, which leaves no room for interpretation.

All in all, it can be said that there is also a balance of manipulation through reviews as "firms may engage in optimal levels of review manipulation to avoid being caught, both consumers and firms benefit more if firms manipulate less" (Zhuang et al., 2018), customers having the opportunity to make the right purchase decision, and companies avoiding a serious image crisis following a possible discovery.

REFERENCES

Adelani, D. I., Mai, H., Fang, F., Nguyen, H. H., Yamagishi, J., & Echizen, I. (2020). Generating Sentiment-Preserving Fake Online Reviews Using Neural Language Models and Their Human- and Machine-Based Detection. In L. Barolli, F. Amato, F. Moscato, T. Enokido, & M. Takizawa (Eds.), *Advanced Information Networking and Applications. AINA 2020. Advances in Intelligent Systems and Computing* (Vol. 1151, pp. 1341–1354). Springer. doi:10.1007/978-3-030-44041-1_114

Almana, A., & Mirza, A. A. (2013). The Impact of Electronic Word of Mouth on Consumers' Purchasing Decisions. *International Journal of Computers and Applications*, 82(9), 23–31. doi:10.5120/14145-2286

Alzate, M., Arce-Uriza, M., & Cebollada, J. (2021). Online Reviews and Product Sales: The Role of Review Visibility. *Journal of Theoretical and Applied Electronic Commerce Research*, 16(4), 638–669. doi:10.3390/jtaer16040038

Anderson, P. (2007). What is Web 2.0? Ideas, technologies and implications for education. *Technology & Standards Watch*, 2-56.

Anderson, W. E. (1998). Customer Satisfaction and Word of Mouth. *Journal of Service Research*, *1*(1), 5–17. doi:10.1177/109467059800100102

Astono, A. D. (2021). The Effect of Reputation and Competence on Costumer Loyalty Through Costumer Trust. *International Journal of Global Accounting, Management, Education, and Entrepreneurship*, *1*(2), 90–99.

Blended. (2020). *Washable Cotton Face Mask Reusable Made in the USA*. https://www.walmart.com/ip/Washable-Cotton-Face-Mask-Reusable-Made-in-the-USA/625326064

Briciu, A., & Briciu, V.-A. (2020). Participatory Culture and Tourist Experience: Promoting Destinations through YouTube. In A. Kavoura, E. Kefallonitis, & P. Theodoridis (Eds.), *Strategic Innovative Marketing and Tourism. Springer Proceedings in Business and Economics* (pp. 425–433). Springer. doi:10.1007/978-3-030-36126-6_47

Briciu, V.-A., & Briciu, A. (2019). Web 1.0 and Web 2.0 Variations of Identity Characteristics of Official Place Brands Websites. In A.-D. Bibiri, C. Grădinaru, E. Grosu, A. Mironescu, R. Patraş (Eds.), Exploring the Digital Turn (pp. 307-324). "Alexandru Ioan Cuza" University of Iaşi Publishing House.

Briciu, V.-A., & Briciu, A. (2021). Social Media and Organizational Communication. In M. Khosrow-Pour (Ed.), Encyclopedia of Organizational Knowledge, Administration, and Technology (pp. 2609-2624). IGI Global. doi:10.4018/978-1-7998-3473-1.ch180

Briciu, V.-A., Mircea, I., & Briciu, A. (2020). Communication and Entrepreneurship in Romania: Dissimulation of First Impression in 30 Seconds. In A. Masouras, G. Maris, & A. Kavoura (Eds.), *Entrepreneurial Development and Innovation in Family Businesses and SMEs* (pp. 22–38). IGI Global. doi:10.4018/978-1-7998-3648-3.ch002

Briciu, V.-A., Rezeanu, C.-I., & Briciu, A. (2020). Online Place Branding: Is Geography 'Destiny' in a 'Space of Flows' World? *Sustainability*, *12*(10), 4073. doi:10.3390u12104073

Cascella, M., Rajnik, M., Cuomo, A., Dulebohn, S. C., & Di Napoli, R. (2021). Features, Evaluation, and Treatment of Coronavirus (COVID-19). StatPearls Publishing.

Chen, L., Li, W., Chen, H., & Geng, S. (2019). Detection of Fake Reviews: Analysis of Sellers Manipulation Behavior. *Sustainability*, *11*(4802), 1–13. doi:10.3390u11174802

Chen, Y., Fay, S., & Wang, Q. (2011). The Role of Marketing in Social Media: How Online Consumers Reviews Evolve. *Journal of Interactive Marketing*, *25*(2), 85–94. doi:10.1016/j.intmar.2011.01.003

Constantinides, E., & Fountain, S. (2008). Web 2.0: Conceptual foundations and marketing issues. *Special Issues Papers*, *9*(3), 231–244. doi:10.1057/palgrave.dddmp.4350098

Constantinides, E., & Holleschovsky, N. I. (2016). Impact of Online Products on Purchasing Decisions. In *Proceedings of the 12th International Conference on Web Information Systems and Technologies* (*vol. 1*, pp. 271-278). Scitepress – Science and Technology Publications, Lda. 10.5220/0005861002710278

Cormode, G., & Krishnamurthy, B. (2008). Key differences between Web 1.0 and Web 2.0. *First Monday*, *13*(6), 1–21. doi:10.5210/fm.v13i6.2125

Cui, G., Lui, H. K., & Guo, X. (2012). The Effect of Online Consumer Reviews on New Product Sales. *International Journal of Electronic Commerce, 17*(1), 39–57. doi:10.2753/JEC1086-4415170102

Czerwinska, M. (2020). Use of Web 2.0 Tools by Polish Health Portals. *Informatyka Automatyka Pomiary w Gospodarce i Ochronie Srodowiska, 10*(4), 77–82. doi:10.35784/iapgos.2398

Daughtery, T., Eastin, S., & Bright, L. (2008). Exploring Consumer Motivations for Creating User-Generated Content. *Journal of Interactive Advertising, 8*(2), 16–25. doi:10.1080/15252019.2008.10722139

Dellarocas, C., Zhang, X., & Awad, F. (2007). Exploring the value of online product reviews in forecasting sales: The case of motion pictures. *Journal of Interactive Marketing, 21*(4), 23–45. doi:10.1002/dir.20087

Dennhardt, S. (2014). *User Generated Content and its Impact on Branding. How Users and Communities Create and Manage Brands in Social Media.* Springer Gabler. doi:10.1007/978-3-658-02350-8

Doh, S. J., & Hwang, J. S. (2009). How Consumers Evaluate eWOM Messages. *Cyberpsychology & Behavior, 12*(2), 193–197. doi:10.1089/cpb.2008.0109 PMID:19072076

Fakespot. (2020). https://www.fakespot.com/about-us

Fakespot. (2020a). https://www.fakespot.com/product/think-ink-face-mask-10-1-5-1-1-1-cotton-mask-with-elastic-strap-washable-face-mask

Fakespot. (2020b). https://www.fakespot.com/walmart/4pcs-set-unisex-face-mask-paris-letters-print-protect-reusable-comfy-washable-made-in-usa

Flanagin, A. J., & Metzger, M. J. (2013). Trusting expert-versus user generated ratings online: The role of information volume, valence, and consumer characteristics. *Computers in Human Behavior, 29*(4), 1626–1634. doi:10.1016/j.chb.2013.02.001

Godes, D., & Mayzlin, D. (2004). Using Online Conversations to Study Word-of-Mouth Communication. *Marketing Science, 23*(4), 545–560. doi:10.1287/mksc.1040.0071

Gossling, Z. H., Hall, M., Martin-Rios, C., Ram, Y., & Grotte, P. (2018). A cross country comparison of accommodation manager perspectives on online review manipulation. *Current Issues in Tourism, 22*(14), 1744–1763. doi:10.1080/13683500.2018.1455171

He, S., Hollenbeck, B., & Proserpio, D. (2021). The Market for Fake Reviews. *Munich Personal RePEc Archive, 105507*, 1–47.

Hu, N., Bose, I., Koh, N., & Liu, L. (2012). Manipulation of online reviews: An analysis of ratings, readability, and sentiments. *Decision Support Systems, 52*(3), 674–684. doi:10.1016/j.dss.2011.11.002

Hu, N., Koh, N. S., & Reddy, S. K. (2014). Ratings Lead you to the Product Reviews Help You Clinch it? The Dynamics and Impact of Online Review Sentiments on Product Sales. *Decision Support Systems, 57*, 42–53. doi:10.1016/j.dss.2013.07.009

Jalilvand, M. R., Esfahani, S., & Samiei, N. (2011). Electronic word-of-mouth challenges and opportunities. *Procedia Computer Science, 3*, 42–46. doi:10.1016/j.procs.2010.12.008

Korfiatis, N., Barriocanal-Garcia, E., & Sanchez, S. (2012). Evaluating content quality and helpfulness of online products reviews: The interplay of review helpfulness vs. review content. *Electronic Commerce Research and Applications*, *11*(3), 205–217. doi:10.1016/j.elerap.2011.10.003

Lappas, T., Sabnis, G., & Valkanas, G. (2016). The Impact of Fake Reviews on Online Visibility: A Vulnerability Assessment of the Hotel Industry. *Information Systems Research*, *27*(4), 940–961. doi:10.1287/isre.2016.0674

Levy, M. (2009). Web 2.0 implications on Knowledge management. *Journal of Knowledge Management*, *13*(1), 120–134. doi:10.1108/13673270910931215

Li, M., Huang, L., Tan, H. C., & Wei, K. (2013). Helpfulness of online product reviews as seen by costumers: Sources and context features. *International Journal of Electronic Commerce*, *17*(4), 101–136. doi:10.2753/JEC1086-4415170404

Mackiewicz, J. (2010). The Co-Construction of Credibility in Online Product Reviews. *Technical Communication Quarterly*, *19*(4), 403–426. doi:10.1080/10572252.2010.502091

Malbon, J. (2012). Taking Fake Online Consumer Reviews Seriously. *Journal of Consumer Policy*, *36*(2), 139–157. doi:10.100710603-012-9216-7

Mayzlin, D., Dover, Y., & Chevalier, J. (2012). Promotional Reviews. An Empirical Investigation of Online Review Manipulation. *NBER Working Paper Series*, *104*(8), 1-49.

Park, S., & Nicolau, J. L. (2015). Asymmetric effects of online consumer reviews. *Annals of Tourism Research*, *50*, 67–83. doi:10.1016/j.annals.2014.10.007

Reyes-Menedez, A., Saura, J., & Filipe, F. (2019). The importance of behavioral data to identify online fake reviews for tourism businesses: A systematic review. *PeerJ. Computer Science*, *5*, e219. doi:10.7717/peerj-cs.219 PMID:33816872

Robson, K., Bredican, J., Farshid, M., & Humphrey, S. (2013). Making Sense of Online Consumer Reviews: A Methodology. *International Journal of Market Research*, *55*(4), 521–537. doi:10.2501/IJMR-2013-046

Sundaram, D. S., Mitra, K., & Webster, C. (1998). Word-of-Mouth Communication: A Motivational Analysis. *Advances in Consumer Research. Association for Consumer Research (U. S.)*, *25*, 527–531.

Think Ink. (2020). *Think Ink Face Mask (10/1, 5/1, 1/1) Cotton Mask with Elastic Strap Washable Face Mask.* https://www.amazon.co.uk/Think-Ink-Cotton-Elastic-Washable/dp/B086QTXY9Y/ref=mp_s_a_1_1?dchild=1&keywords=think+ink+face+mask&qid=1591548206&quartzVehicle=3514-1426&replacementKeywords=ink+face+mask&sprefix=think+inc+face+&sr=8-1

Wang, Y., & Rodgers, S. (2011). Electronic Word of Mouth and Consumer Generated Content: From Concept to Application. In M. S. Eastin, T. Daugherty, & N. M. Burns (Eds.), *Handbook of Research on Digital Media and Advertising: User Generated Content Consumption* (pp. 212–231). Information Science Reference.

Weitzl, W. (2017). *Measuring Electronic Word-of-Mouth Effectiveness.* Springer Gabler. doi:10.1007/978-3-658-15889-7

World Health Organization. (2020). *Advice on the use of masks in the context of COVID-19: interim guidance*. WHO.

Yayli, A., & Bayram, M. (2012). E-WOM: The effects of online consumer reviews on purchasing decisions. *International Journal of Internet Marketing and Advertising*, 7(1), 1–13.

Yu, J., Zha, Z. J., Wang, M., & Chua, T. S. (2011). Aspect Ranking: Identifying Important Product Aspects from Online Consumer Reviews. In *Proceedings of the 49th Annual Meeting of the Association for Competitional Linguistic* (pp. 1496-1505). Association for Computational Linguistics.

Zhuang, M., Cui, G., & Peng, L. (2018). Manufactured opinions: The effect of manipulating online product reviews. *Journal of Business Research*, 87, 24–35. doi:10.1016/j.jbusres.2018.02.016

ADDITIONAL READING

Cheng, L.-C., Tseng, J. C. R., & Chung, T.-Y. (2017). Case Study of Fake Web Reviews. In *Proceedings of the 2017 IEEE/ACM International Conference on Advances in Social Networks Analysis and Mining 2017 (ASONAM '17)* (pp. 706–709). Association for Computing Machinery. 10.1145/3110025.3110119

de Gregorio, F., Fox, A. K., & Yoon, H. J. (2021). Pseudo-reviews: Conceptualization and consumer effects of a new online phenomenon. *Computers in Human Behavior*, 114, 106545. doi:10.1016/j.chb.2020.106545

Dongre, S., & Pal, M. (2021). Prediction of Fake Reviews and Review Sentiments using Sentiment Analysis. *E-Commerce for Future & Trends*, 7(3), 10–14.

Hu, X., & Yang, Y. (2021). What makes online reviews helpful in tourism and hospitality? a bare-bones meta-analysis. *Journal of Hospitality Marketing & Management*, 30(2), 139–158. doi:10.1080/19368623.2020.1780178

Jadhav, Y., & Parasar, D. (2021). Fake Review Detection System through Analytics of Sales Data. In *Proceeding of First Doctoral Symposium on Natural Computing Research: DSNCR 2020* (vol. 169, p. 3). Springer Nature. 10.1007/978-981-33-4073-2_1

Lappas, T. (2012). Fake Reviews: The Malicious Perspective. In G. Bouma, A. Ittoo, E. Métais, & H. Wortmann (Eds.), *Natural Language Processing and Information Systems. NLDB 2012* (pp. 23–34). Lecture Notes in Computer Science. Springer.

Mohawesh, R., Tran, S., Ollington, R., & Xu, S. (2021). Analysis of concept drift in fake reviews detection. *Expert Systems with Applications*, 169, 114318. doi:10.1016/j.eswa.2020.114318

Raja, B., Malathy, V., Shilpa, N., & Anand, M. (2020). Eliminating products' fake reviews using network parameters and geo location. *IOP Conference Series. Materials Science and Engineering*, 981(3), 032002. doi:10.1088/1757-899X/981/3/032002

KEY TERMS AND DEFINITIONS

Credibility: The way a review is written, the feelings transmitted are very important as well as detection the intention to influence decision.

Fakespot: Software that analyze the reviews from some important sites from the world, it can detect fake reviews by analyzing the words used, the user profile and another important element: the appearance of the check mark "Verified Purchase".

Generator: An advanced tool who can post hundreds of credible reviews, very difficult to detect even with special programs.

Manipulate: Editing the reviews by the companies to create an advantage and to convince potential customers that their product is the best.

Non-Authentic: The reviews that are posted to influence the users, those who post hide usually behind fake profiles.

Rating: Users who write good reviews can be appreciated with 4 or 5 stars and others can be charged with fewer stars, in time the users with a bad rating will not be taken into account.

Self-Approval: The need to confirm a good purchase by sharing an experience with other users, this for feel at peace with the decision made.

Sentiments: Stories or experiences exposed by users on the Internet, usually in connection with a product.

Chapter 11
Sentiment, Stance, and Intent Detection in Turkish Tweets

Dilek Küçük

TÜBİTAK Marmara Research Center, Turkey

ABSTRACT

Sentiment analysis, stance detection, and intent detection on social media texts are all significant research problems with several application opportunities. In this chapter, the authors explore the possible contribution of sentiment and intent information to machine learning-based stance detection on tweets. They first annotate a Turkish tweet dataset with sentiment and proprietary intent labels, where the dataset was already annotated with stance labels. Next, they perform stance detection experiments on the dataset using sentiment and intent labels as additional features. The experiments with SVM classifiers show that using sentiment and intent labels as additional features improves stance detection performance considerably. The final form of the dataset is made publicly available for research purposes. The findings reveal the contribution of sentiment and intent information to the solution of stance detection task on the Turkish tweet dataset employed. Yet, further studies on other datasets are needed to confirm that our findings are generalizable to other languages and on other topics.

INTRODUCTION

Social media analysis has emerged as one of the most popular research areas, especially due the vast amount of social media posts produced each and every day. Significant subproblems of social media analysis include sentiment analysis, stance detection, and intent detection on social media posts, and these three research topics constitute the main focus of our chapter.

In this book chapter, we investigate the possible contribution of sentiment and intent information to stance detection in Turkish tweets. To achieve this objective, first, we extend an existing tweet corpus annotated with stance information, by annotating it further with sentiment and convenient intent labels. Next, we conduct our stance detection experiments on the ultimate dataset by using a machine learning algorithm (SVM) together with sentiment and intent information as features. By conducting these ex-

DOI: 10.4018/978-1-7998-8061-5.ch011

periments, we aim to unravel the possible effects (improving or impeding effects) of sentiment analysis and intent detection to stance detection.

Turkish is a morphologically-rich language however it is also a low-resource language with respect to different natural language processing (NLP) tasks. Although there exists previous work on sentiment analysis in Turkish such as (Balahur et al., 2014; Çoban et al., 2021), to the best of our knowledge, there is limited work on stance detection in Turkish (Küçük, 2017; Küçük & Can, 2019), and no study on intent detection in Turkish social media content.

This book chapter includes descriptive information about the tweet dataset which has sentiment, stance, and intent annotations, all at once. The dataset which is further annotated within the context of the current book chapter is made publicly available for research purposes at https://github.com/dkucuk/ Turkish-Tweet-Dataset-Stance-Sentiment-Intent. We describe the settings and results of the related experiments and discuss the corresponding findings.

We anticipate that these findings will not be limited to Turkish content only, and instead will be generalizable to other languages as well. Our book chapter is concluded together with further research tasks based on the experiments described, regarding these three significant research topics of social media analysis.

The contributions of our book chapter can be summarized as follows:

- To the best of our knowledge, we present the first tweet dataset jointly annotated with sentiment, stance, and intent information. We present the details of the annotation process and the annotation classes employed for each task. This annotated dataset is also made publicly available for research purposes.
- We also present the settings and results of our SVM-based stance detection experiments, where sentiment and intent annotations are used as the features for SVMs in addition to other features based on unigrams, hashtags, and named entities. Thereby, we reveal the effects of sentiment and intent information to the task of stance detection.

Sentiment analysis, stance detection, and intent detection have a variety of significant application areas. These areas include recommender systems, personalized advertising, market analysis, information retrieval, and predictions for elections, among others. Hence, the findings of our study which aims to determine the effects of the sentiment analysis and intent detection on stance detection, can be used practically in the aforementioned application areas. Therefore, our study will make both theoretical and practical contributions to the related literature. The findings of the current study can readily be used by future work on determining the interrelationships between these three significant subproblems of social media analysis and NLP.

LITERATURE REVIEW

Sentiment analysis (a.k.a. *opinion mining*) is defined as the automatic detection of opinions of people, by analyzing the texts that they produce (Liu 2010; Feldman, 2013; Yadav & Vishwakarma, 2020). In several related studies, sentiment analysis is limited to polarity detection which is a classification task in which an output from this set expected: *{positive, negative, neither}*. Various different methods have been employed for sentiment analysis so far. These approaches range from lexicon-based and rule-based methods to machine learning (Agarwal et al., 2011; Arslan et al., 2018) and deep learning based ones (Zhang et al., 2018; Yadav & Vishwakarma, 2020). More recently, other research problems closely related to sentiment analysis have also been studied, such as *sentiment quantification* which aims to determine (quantify) the prevalence of sentiment classes in a corpus, instead of determining the sentiment classes for each individual pieces of text in the corpus (Esuli et al., 2020).

Stance detection is considered similar to sentiment analysis in different studies, however, stance detection is usually defined as the automatic identification of the position of a person towards a target based on a piece of text produced by that person (Küçük & Can, 2020; Küçük & Can, 2021). Hence possible classification outputs of the stance detection task usually include *{favor, against, neither}* (Küçük & Can, 2020). Being a more recent research area, most of the stance detection studies date back to the past decade only (Mohammad et al., 2016a; Mohammad et al., 2016b; Sobhani et al., 2016; Xu et al., 2016; Taulé et al., 2017; Mohammad et al. 2017; Dey et al., 2018; Küçük & Can, 2020). Stance detection is also considered as a significant subproblem of other research problems such as *rumour detection and detection* (Zubiaga et al., 2018) and fake news detection (Shu et al., 2017). In several related studies, the contribution of sentiment analysis to stance detection is investigated on English tweets (Sobhani et al. 2016; Mohammad et al. 2017). Yet, it is commonly emphasized in the stance detection literature that using sentiment features does not guarantee improved stance detection performance (Küçük & Can, 2020).

Intent detection is a popular topic particularly within the context of natural language understanding and hence in dialog systems (Liu and Lane, 2016; Kim et al., 2016, Losey et al., 2018; Xia et al., 2018; Balodis and Deksne, 2019; Yolchuyeva et al., 2020; Weld et al., 2021). Intent detection is similarly important in information retrieval domain, where the problem usually turns into query intent detection (Brenes et al., 2009; Hashemi et al., 2016). Detecting intent in social media is also critical for different application settings including helping people during the course of natural disasters (Purohit et al., 2015). For instance, possible intent classes given in the related work (Purohit et al., 2015) include *{seeking (help), offering (help), none}*.

ANNOTATING THE DATASET

In this study, we work on the Turkish tweet corpus of 1,065 tweets, previously annotated with stance classes (*favor* and *against*) with respect to two sports teams (*Galatasaray (target-1)* and *Fenerbahçe (target-2)*) as targets (Küçük & Can, 2018). This dataset can be considered as balanced since the number of tweets for the first target is 537 (269 annotated with *favor* class and 268 annotated with *against* class) and the number of tweets for the second target is 528 (269 annotated as *favor* and 259 annotated as *against*).

Stance annotations for this dataset have previously been made available (Küçük & Can, 2018) at https://github.com/dkucuk/Stance-Detection-Turkish-V3. Named entity annotations (together with stance annotations) on the same dataset are also shared publicly (Küçük & Can, 2018) at https://github.com/dkucuk/Tweet-Dataset-NER-SD.

As described below, within the course of the current study, the same dataset is further annotated with sentiment and intent information, so that we have ultimately compiled a tweet dataset that is annotated with stance, sentiment, and intent information, where the dataset can readily be utilized for these three research areas.

In Figure 1, the annotations on the ultimate form of the dataset are depicted, that is, the dataset already had stance and named entity annotations (shown in italic form), within the course of the current study it now also includes sentiment and intent annotations (shown in boldface), as described in the rest of this section.

The final form of this dataset, which includes stance, sentiment, and intent annotations, is made publicly available at https://github.com/dkucuk/Turkish-Tweet-Dataset-Stance-Sentiment-Intent for research purposes. The dataset is provided at this link as a CSV (comma-separated-values) file and each tweet annotation is provided at a separate line in this file. Hence each line corresponding to a single tweet in our shared dataset file includes the tweet id and stance target, followed by stance, sentiment, and intent annotations.

Figure 1. Types of Annotated Information in the Dataset.

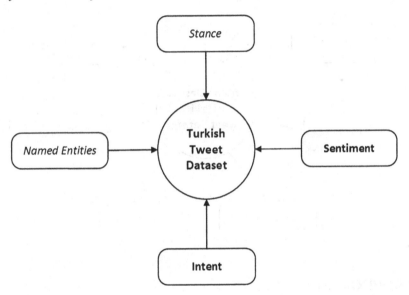

Sentiment Annotations

During the sentiment annotation process, we have followed the related annotation procedure (questionnaire) given in the work on stance and sentiment in tweets presented in (Mohammad et al., 2017) to guide our process. The annotation of the dataset is carried out by a single annotator who is a native speaker of Turkish.

Three polarity classes of *positive*, *negative*, and *neither* are used to annotate the dataset of 1,065 tweets, showing only the tweet content to the annotator during the annotation stage. After this annotation process, 472 tweets are annotated as *positive*, 535 as *negative*, and 58 as *neither*.

Intent Annotations

After the sentiment annotation process; the same annotator has also annotated the tweets in the dataset with the possible intents of the owners of the tweets, based on tweet contents only. The seven intent classes in Figure 2 are determined for this sports-related dataset.

At the end of the intent annotation procedure; the number of tweets annotated with the *cheer* intent class is 61, the number of tweets classified as *good-wishes* is 49, the number of tweets classified as *dislike* is 28, the number of tweets classified as *criticism* is 173, the number of tweets classified as *insult* is 74, the number of tweets classified as *ridicule* is 255, and finally the resulting 425 tweets are annotated as *support*.

Figure 2. Intent Classes Annotated in the Tweet Dataset.

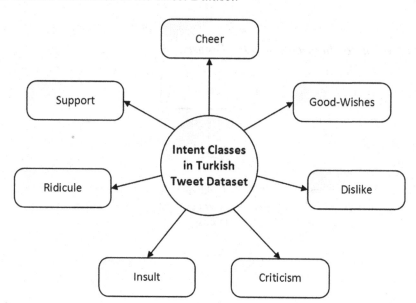

PROPOSED APPROACH

Within the course of the current study, we conduct stance detection experiments using SVM classifiers in the final annotated dataset, using sentiment and intent annotations as additional features. The initial set of features include features based on unigrams, hashtags, and named entities which are used in (Küçük & Can, 2018) and it is reported that SVMs using these initial features achieve the best results on the previous form of the Turkish tweet dataset (Küçük & Can, 2018). Hence in the current study, we have used features based on unigrams, hashtags, named entities, sentiment, and intent information.

The experiments in the current study are performed using the SVM implementation in the Weka machine learning environment (Hall et al., 2009) which uses the Sequential Minimal Optimization (SMO) algorithm (Platt, 1998) for training. The SVM classifiers employed utilize polynomial kernel functions. The value used for the regularization parameter (lambda) is 1.0. The performance metrics employed are precision (P), recall (R), and F-Measure (F) which is the harmonic mean of precision and recall. A schematic representation of the proposed approach is depicted in Figure 3.

Figure 3. Proposed Approach.

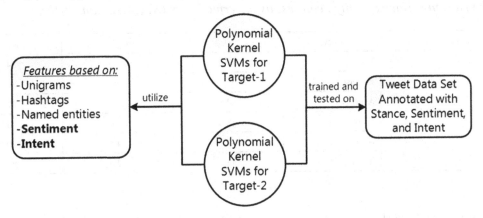

Utilized Features

Overall, five different features are utilized within the proposed approach. These are features based *unigrams*, *hashtags*, *named entities* in addition to *sentiment* and *intent* annotations (as depicted in Figure 3). The latter two features have already been described in the previous section.

Unigrams are among the commonly-employed features for stance detection (Küçük & Can, 2020). Hence, they are previously used by SVM-based stance detection experiments successfully (Küçük & Can, 2018). Similarly, feature based on the existence of hashtags is reported to boost stance detection procedure on tweets (Küçük & Can, 2018).

Lastly, using named entities as features can also improve stance detection procedure as related work shows (Küçük & Can, 2018). *Named entity recognition* is a significant NLP problem where it is usually defined as the extraction and classification of person, location, and organization names (along with other significant named entity types) within natural language texts (Goyal et al., 2018). A survey on named entity recognition in Turkish texts is presented in (Küçük et al., 2017). In this study, automatic named entity recognition on the Turkish tweet dataset is performed using the related tool presented in (Küçük & Steinberger, 2014).

Therefore, considering the feature set used by the SVM-based approach on the final form of the dataset, first unigrams and the existence of hashtags are automatically determined, next, the named entities are automatically extracted by the aforementioned tool, and finally the sentiment and intent annotations described in the previous section are readily extracted and utilized.

EXPERIMENTAL RESULTS

Stance detection experiments using SVM classifiers for each of the two targets (two sports clubs) have previously been performed on this dataset (Küçük & Can, 2018). It has been reported that joint use of unigrams, hashtags, and named entities as features has led to the best performance results for stance detection (Küçük & Can, 2018). The corresponding results are provided in Table 1 where named entities are extracted using the named entity recognition tool described in (Küçük & Steinberger, 2014).

Table 1. Stance Detection Performance Results with SVMs Using the Initial Feature Set (Unigram+Hashtag+Named Entity Features) as Excerpted from (Küçük & Can, 2018).

Target	Class	P (%)	R (%)	F (%)
Target-1	Favor	77.5	93.3	84.7
	Against	91.5	72.8	81.1
	Average	**84.5**	**83.1**	**82.9**
Target-2	Favor	78.6	90.0	83.9
	Against	87.7	74.5	80.6
	Average	**83.1**	**82.4**	**82.3**

In the current study, we have performed the following three stance detection experiments by training a separate SVM for each target, based on the initial best performing feature set (unigram+hashtag+named entity features):

- In addition to the initial set of features, *sentiment annotations* in the dataset are also used as the features for SVMs
- In addition to the initial set of features, *intent annotations* in the dataset are also used as the features for SVMs
- In addition to the initial set of features, *both sentiment and intent annotations* in the dataset are also used as the features for SVMs.

10-fold cross validation results of the above-mentioned three experimental settings are demonstrated in Table 2, Table 3, and Table 4, respectively.

Table 2. Stance Detection Performance Results with SVMs Using Sentiment Information as an Additional Feature.

Target	Class	Initial+Sentiment Features		
		P (%)	R (%)	F (%)
Target-1	Favor	94.0	93.7	93.9
	Against	93.7	94.0	93.9
	Average	**93.9**	**93.9**	**93.9**
Target-2	Favor	96.9	94.4	95.7
	Against	94.4	96.9	95.6
	Average	**95.7**	**95.6**	**95.6**

As compared to the previous results given in Table 1, the performance evaluation results in Table 2, 3, and 4 clearly demonstrate that:

Table 3. Stance Detection Performance Results with SVMs Using Intent Information as an Additional Feature.

Target	Class	Initial+Intent Features		
		P (%)	*R (%)*	*F (%)*
Target-1	Favor	96.6	95.5	96.1
	Against	95.6	96.6	96.1
	Average	**96.1**	**96.1**	**96.1**
Target-2	Favor	95.9	95.9	95.9
	Against	95.8	95.8	95.8
	Average	**95.8**	**95.8**	**95.8**

Table 4. Stance Detection Performance Results with SVMs Using Sentiment and Intent Information as Additional Features.

Target	Class	Initial + Sentiment + Intent Features		
		P (%)	*R (%)*	*F (%)*
Target-1	Favor	97.0	95.9	96.4
	Against	95.9	97.0	96.5
	Average	**96.5**	**96.5**	**96.5**
Target-2	Favor	97.0	95.5	96.3
	Against	95.4	96.9	96.2
	Average	**96.2**	**96.2**	**96.2**

1. Using sentiment as an additional feature improves stance detection performance on this dataset. The average F-Measure obtained in this settings is 93.9% for the first target and 95.6% for the second target where the corresponding rates without using sentiment information are 84.5% and 83.1%, respectively.

2. Similarly, using intent information as an additional feature also improves stance detection performance dramatically on our tweet dataset. The average F-Measure rates reach up to 96.1% and 95.8% in this settings, for target-1 and target-2, respectively.

3. Using both sentiment and intent information as additional features for SVMs also consistently increases stance detection performance on our dataset, however this increase is limited when compared to the results obtained using only intent information as an additional feature. For instance, the average F-Measure obtained in this settings is 96.5% for the target-1 and 96.2% for target-2.

To sum up, based on the results of our experiments, we can conclude that both sentiment and intent information improve stance detection performance considerably on our tweet dataset. Jointly using these two features improves the performance further, although the improvement in this case is limited.

Future work includes performing sentiment analysis and intent detection experiments on this annotated dataset, using different feature set combinations and different machine learning algorithms. Future studies also include performing similar experiments on tweets on other topics and in other languages, to determine whether these results are generalizable to tweets on other topics and in different languages.

CONCLUSION

Sentiment analysis, stance detection, and intent detection on social media are fruitful research topics. In this study, we have investigated the possible contribution of sentiment and intent annotations to the solution of the stance detection problem on tweets. We have started with a stance-annotated tweet dataset in Turkish and annotated it further with sentiment and intent information. Thereby, we have created a sports-related tweet dataset annotated with stance, sentiment, and intent labels which can readily be utilized within the context of these three research problems. We have also made this final form of the dataset publicly available for research purposes. On this dataset, we have performed stance detection experiments using sentiment and intent information as additional features. The results show that sentiment and intent features clearly improve stance detection performance on this tweet dataset. Further studies based on this study include extended experiments, with different features and different classifiers, and on different datasets, to reason about the generalizability of our results and to determine other interrelationships between these three research problems on social media texts.

REFERENCES

Agarwal, A., Xie, B., Vovsha, I., Rambow, O., & Passonneau, R. J. (2011). Sentiment analysis of Twitter data. In *Proceedings of the Workshop on Language in Social Media (LSM 2011)* (pp. 30-38). Academic Press.

Arslan, Y., Küçük, D., & Birtürk, A. (2018). Twitter sentiment analysis experiments using word embeddings on datasets of various scales. In *International Conference on Applications of Natural Language to Information Systems* (pp. 40-47). 10.1007/978-3-319-91947-8_4

Balahur, A., Turchi, M., Steinberger, R., Ortega, J. M. P., Jacquet, G., Küçük, D., Zavarella, V., & El Ghali, A. (2014). Resource creation and evaluation for multilingual sentiment analysis in social media texts. In *Proceedings of the Language Resources and Evaluation Conference (LREC)* (pp. 4265-4269). Academic Press.

Balodis, K., & Deksne, D. (2019). FastText-based intent detection for inflected languages. *Information (Basel)*, *10*(5), 161. doi:10.3390/info10050161

Brenes, D. J., Gayo-Avello, D., & Pérez-González, K. (2009). Survey and evaluation of query intent detection methods. In *Proceedings of the 2009 Workshop on Web Search Click Data* (pp. 1-7). 10.1145/1507509.1507510

Çoban, Ö., Özel, S. A., & İnan, A. (2021). Deep learning-based sentiment analysis of Facebook data: The case of Turkish users. *The Computer Journal*, *64*(3), 473–499. doi:10.1093/comjnl/bxaa172

Dey, K., Shrivastava, R., & Kaushik, S. (2018). Topical stance detection for Twitter: A two-phase LSTM model using attention. In *European Conference on Information Retrieval* (pp. 529-536). Springer. 10.1007/978-3-319-76941-7_40

Esuli, A., Moreo, A., Sebastiani, F., & Cambria, E. (2020). Cross-lingual sentiment quantification. *IEEE Intelligent Systems*, *35*(3), 106–114. doi:10.1109/MIS.2020.2979203

Feldman, R. (2013). Techniques and applications for sentiment analysis. *Communications of the ACM*, *56*(4), 82–89. doi:10.1145/2436256.2436274

Goyal, A., Gupta, V., & Kumar, M. (2018). Recent named entity recognition and classification techniques: A systematic review. *Computer Science Review*, *29*, 21–43. doi:10.1016/j.cosrev.2018.06.001

Hall, M., Frank, E., Holmes, G., Pfahringer, B., Reutemann, P., & Witten, I. H. (2009). The WEKA data mining software: An update. *SIGKDD Explorations*, *11*(1), 10–18. doi:10.1145/1656274.1656278

Hashemi, H. B., Asiaee, A., & Kraft, R. (2016). Query intent detection using convolutional neural networks. In *International Conference on Web Search and Data Mining, Workshop on Query Understanding*. Academic Press.

Kim, J. K., Tur, G., Celikyilmaz, A., Cao, B., & Wang, Y. Y. (2016). Intent detection using semantically enriched word embeddings. In *IEEE Spoken Language Technology Workshop (SLT)* (pp. 414-419). 10.1109/SLT.2016.7846297

Küçük, D. (2017). Stance detection in Turkish tweets. In *Proceedings of the International Workshop on Social Media World Sensors (SIDEWAYS) of ACM Hypertext Conference*. Prague, Czech Republic: ACM.

Küçük, D., Arıcı, N., & Küçük, D. (2017). Named entity recognition in Turkish: Approaches and issues. In *International Conference on Applications of Natural Language to Information Systems* (pp. 176-181). Springer.

Küçük, D., & Can, F. (2018). *Stance detection on tweets: An SVM-based approach*. arXiv preprint arXiv:1803.08910.

Küçük, D., & Can, F. (2019). *A tweet dataset annotated for named entity recognition and stance detection*. arXiv preprint arXiv:1901.04787.

Küçük, D., & Can, F. (2020). Stance detection: A survey. *ACM Computing Surveys*, *53*(1), 1–37. doi:10.1145/3369026

Küçük, D., & Can, F. (2021). Stance detection: Concepts, approaches, resources, and outstanding issues. *Proceedings of the 44th International ACM SIGIR Conference on Research and Development in Information Retrieval*.

Küçük, D., & Steinberger, R. (2014). Experiments to improve named entity recognition on Turkish tweets. arXiv preprint arXiv:1410.8668. doi:10.3115/v1/W14-1309

Liu, B. (2010). Sentiment analysis and subjectivity. Handbook of natural language processing, 2(2010), 627-666.

Liu, B., & Lane, I. (2016). Attention-based recurrent neural network models for joint intent detection and slot filling. arXiv preprint arXiv:1609.01454. doi:10.21437/Interspeech.2016-1352

Losey, D. P., McDonald, C. G., Battaglia, E., & O'Malley, M. K. (2018). A review of intent detection, arbitration, and communication aspects of shared control for physical human–robot interaction. *Applied Mechanics Reviews*, *70*(1), 010804. doi:10.1115/1.4039145

Mohammad, S., Kiritchenko, S., Sobhani, P., Zhu, X., & Cherry, C. (2016a). A dataset for detecting stance in tweets. In *Proceedings of the Tenth International Conference on Language Resources and Evaluation (LREC'16)* (pp. 3945-3952). Academic Press.

Mohammad, S., Kiritchenko, S., Sobhani, P., Zhu, X., & Cherry, C. (2016b). Semeval-2016 task 6: Detecting stance in tweets. In *Proceedings of the 10th International Workshop on Semantic Evaluation (SemEval-2016)* (pp. 31-41). 10.18653/v1/S16-1003

Mohammad, S. M., Sobhani, P., & Kiritchenko, S. (2017). Stance and sentiment in tweets. *ACM Transactions on Internet Technology*, *17*(3), 1–23. doi:10.1145/3003433

Platt, J. (1998). Fast training of support vector machines using sequential minimal optimization. In B. Schoelkopf, C. Burges, & A. Smola (Eds.), Advances in Kernel Methods - Support Vector Learning. Academic Press.

Purohit, H., Dong, G., Shalin, V., Thirunarayan, K., & Sheth, A. (2015). Intent classification of short-text on social media. In *Proceedings of IEEE International Conference on Smart City/SocialCom/SustainCom* (pp. 222-228). 10.1109/SmartCity.2015.75

Shu, K., Sliva, A., Wang, S., Tang, J., & Liu, H. (2017). Fake news detection on social media: A data mining perspective. *SIGKDD Explorations*, *19*(1), 22–36. doi:10.1145/3137597.3137600

Sobhani, P., Mohammad, S., & Kiritchenko, S. (2016). Detecting stance in tweets and analyzing its interaction with sentiment. In *Proceedings of the Fifth Joint Conference on Lexical and Computational Semantics* (pp. 159-169). 10.18653/v1/S16-2021

Taulé, M., Martí, M. A., Rangel, F. M., Rosso, P., Bosco, C., & Patti, V. (2017). Overview of the task on stance and gender detection in tweets on Catalan independence at IberEval 2017. In *2nd Workshop on Evaluation of Human Language Technologies for Iberian Languages, IberEval 2017* (*Vol. 1881*, pp. 157-177). CEUR-WS.

Weld, H., Huang, X., Long, S., Poon, J., & Han, S. (2021). *A survey of joint intent detection and slot-filling models in natural language understanding.* arXiv preprint arXiv:2101.08091.

Xia, C., Zhang, C., Yan, X., Chang, Y., & Yu, P. S. (2018). Zero-shot user intent detection via capsule neural networks. arXiv preprint arXiv:1809.00385. doi:10.18653/v1/D18-1348

Xu, R., Zhou, Y., Wu, D., Gui, L., Du, J., & Xue, Y. (2016). Overview of nlpcc shared task 4: Stance detection in Chinese microblogs. In *Natural Language Understanding and Intelligent Applications* (pp. 907–916). Springer. doi:10.1007/978-3-319-50496-4_85

Yadav, A., & Vishwakarma, D. K. (2020). Sentiment analysis using deep learning architectures: A review. *Artificial Intelligence Review*, *53*(6), 4335–4385. doi:10.100710462-019-09794-5

Yolchuyeva, S., Németh, G., & Gyires-Tóth, B. (2020). *Self-attention networks for intent detection.* arXiv preprint arXiv:2006.15585.

Zhang, L., Wang, S., & Liu, B. (2018). Deep learning for sentiment analysis: A survey. *Wiley Interdisciplinary Reviews. Data Mining and Knowledge Discovery, 8*(4), e1253. doi:10.1002/widm.1253

Zubiaga, A., Aker, A., Bontcheva, K., Liakata, M., & Procter, R. (2018). Detection and resolution of rumours in social media: A survey. *ACM Computing Surveys, 51*(2), 1–36. doi:10.1145/3161603

Chapter 12
FNDNLSTM:
Fake News Detection on Social Media Using Deep Learning (DL) Techniques

Steni Mol T. S.

https://orcid.org/0000-0003-1648-6415

Hindustan Institute of Technology and Science, India

P. S. Sreeja

https://orcid.org/0000-0002-2995-3580

Hindustan Institute of Technology and Science, India

ABSTRACT

In the present scenario, social media platforms have become more accessible sources for news. Social media posts need not always be truthful information. These posts are widely disseminated with little regard for the truth. It is necessary to realize the evolution and origins of false news patterns in order to improve the progression of quality news and combat fake news on social media. This chapter discusses the most frequently used social media (Facebook) and the type of information exchanged to solve this issue. This chapter proposes a novel framework based on the "Fake News Detection Network – Long Short-Term Memory" (FNDN-LSTM) model to discriminate between fake news and real news. The social media news dataset is to be taken and preprocessed using the TF BERT model (technique). The preprocessed data will be passed through a feature selection model, which will select the significant features for classification. The selected features will be passed through the FNDN-LSTM classification model for identifying fake news.

INTRODUCTION

Most messages circulated in social media these days mimic the original message and are forwarded. It isn't easy to find out the origin and genuinity of the message. Due to the forwards of fake news, a large number of social problems arise and disrupt harmony. Our research enables us to find the originality of the message. Most of the imitated messages are in text form and this research focuses on text mining to

DOI: 10.4018/978-1-7998-8061-5.ch012

identify mimicked messages. Social media users communicate with different categories of people with different moral and social values. As per our recent survey conducted on different categories of people, we have identified that many Facebook users share unverified text messages from others. Facebook is a well-known online media floor for connecting with both known and unknown people in society. We can share information like current status, photos, videos, locations, emotions, activities, text, etc. This medium of communication is very dynamic.

The appearance of the information server and the quick execution of web-based media stages prepared it to disperse data that has never been found in humankind's set of experiences. Aside from that additional applications, data sources take advantage of the broad use of web-based media stages by modernising data to their endorsers (Ahmad, et al., 2020). The media for news progressed from papers and articles to the advanced construction like online news channels, websites, web-based media channels and other automated media designs (Ahlers, 2006). It got less difficult for customers to secure the most recent news at their hands. The referrals from Facebook represent traffic of 70% to news sites (Wong, 2016). In the present status, these stages are convincing and significant because of their capacity to accept clients to talk about as well as distribute musings and conversations concerning problems like schooling, popular government, wellbeing, and so forth.

Nonetheless, these platforms also utilized an opposing viewpoint by specific entities for financial gain (Lazer, et al., 2018), (Garcia, et al., 2020) and various parodies of ludicrousness for forming skewed opinions, influencing mindsets, and disseminating misinformation. The occurrence is usually called fake news. As a solution to this problem, a novel DL framework dependent on the FNDN-LSTM model is proposed to identify the fake news in the social media platform.

LITERATURE REVIEW

This literature overview expects to accumulate different related works done in counterfeit data recognition on the online media stages like Instagram, Twitter, Facebook, and so on. In that manner, I continue with the investigation from various zones like Instagram, Twitter, Facebook, WhatsApp, and so on, planning to identify the conceivable dependability of common information.

The identification of the honesty of news on microblogs and images is a significant substance. The essential part of visual content in an automatic fake information check on microblogs was investigated (Jin, et al., 2016). The HAC algorithm and Random Forest algorithm were used. The model concentrated on images to improve authentication of the performance and discovered that apart from their popularity and great impact on news diffusion, images also have distinctive dissemination patterns for accurate and fake news statistically and visually. The accuracy might improve if both features of image and non-image are considered. The problems coherent to fake news tweets about the US election for president in 2016 were examined (Jang, et al., 2018). The Text phylogeny and analysis of the evolution tree are employed for expressing the process of a chunk of tweet texts. It was found that the fake news tweets were generally produced from accounts of general users. However, they regularly incorporated a connection to websites of non-credible news. This methodology can be only effective if plentiful sources are connected to the inception of most fake data.

A compressive investigation of classification strategies based on content to detect fake reviews (Cardoso, et al., 2018). Experiments were acted in various settings, utilizing various sorts of learning and datasets. The operation was performed in both offline and online learning tasks for non-ordered chronology and sorted posting time. A proper investigation of the outcomes gave adequate evidence to react correctly to the open inquiries, which can be utilized to guide future surveys. The detection of a suspect who's an experienced user was challenging. A detection system developed utilizing statistical methods to detect hidden Web cheating attempts in Online Social Networks (OSN) (Pendyala, et al., 2018). A dataset comprised of tweets from a genuine user and also fake tweets were used. Precision and Recall assessed the performance of this proposed framework. The algorithms accomplished fit for 99.9% accuracy in some possibilities and 80% for the other scenarios. The misinformation containment was found to be NP-hard and the proposed technique cannot solve it. Hence accuracy needs to be improved using correlation analysis.

A system dependent on Mutual Clustering Coefficient (Mcc) and users' profile data for detecting malicious or negative links in the users' communities was presented (Wani, et al., 2018). Three different classifiers like Decision Tree, SVM and Naïve Bayes are used. Different measures of similarities have been applied for computing profile similarity scores (PSS). The experimental outcomes demonstrate that the features like work, education, home town and current city and Mcc show the main part in plotting an outstanding categorization framework. Wang, et al., (2021) proposed the novel graph based neural network model name SemSeq4FD to distinguish the incorrect data. Research directed four real-world datasets in English and Chinese, including cross source and cross domain datasets.

A novel methodology to filter or delete unnecessary and irrelevant information also it is offers more insight into spam users' behavior on Twitter (Inuwa-Dutse, et al., 2018). The ML classifiers were utilized for the selection of significant features and recursive feature rejection was also used. The methodology proposes optimized feature sets not dependent on historical tweets, which are accessible for a short time on Twitter. As opposed to earlier research, it was observed that a computerized spam account posts minimum of 12 tweets each day.

A framework with the veracity data examination of various platforms of social media presence as images. A framework consisting of entity and text extractor, web scraping and processing unit was proposed for recognizing incorrect messages on online media. The text extraction algorithm should be tested for images with a large amount of text, directly affecting the Google search results. The 85% accuracy was achieved when the value of the reality parameter was 40%. The better outcomes were achieved for limited content. It was challenging to achieve high content results with more words, which is a significant drawback Vishwakarma, et al., 2019). Text analytics drive an approach to detect and diminish the hazards imposed by the consumption of fake news. The gathered genuine and fake news was changed from a processed dataset to a given topic and action interpretation. The detection was performed utilizing a two-layered methodology that involves fake subjects and events. The efficiency of this approach was demonstrated by implementing it through FEND. It achieves an accuracy of 92.49% and recall of 94.16%, dependent on the declared origin worth of 0.6. Tagging diversity is a problem associated with this approach (Zhang, et al., 2019).

The consistency of news information on investors' buying behaviour, utilizing supervised sentiment investigation, was examined. This study was conducted in Indian future markets with data from the year 2009. The Naive Bayes and SVM were being used for classification. This analysis demonstrated the better performance of sentiment classifiers with a 5-minute alignment lag. The foremost limitation faced was chaotic market behavior (Yadav, et al., 2019).

The issue of rumors was addressed for the detection of Arabic tweets. The system was developed utilizing two sorts of learning schemes with Expectation– Maximization (E–M), like unsupervised and semi-supervised learning. As a point of reference, the semi-supervised E– M classifier performs admirably the Gaussian Naive Bayes classifier., achieving an F1 score of 78.6% (Alzanin, et al., 2019). It was discovered that the authors of non-rumor tweets would have more followers.

A novel model for detecting fake news that mines the Linguistic Correlations between the words and pictures affixed. (FND-SCTI) (Zeng, et al., 2020). The experimental results from fake news data show that this significantly achieves other contending strategies but can collect the causal features between multidimensional substances. Software development for graphic designing, such as Photoshop, and deep generative networks, such as GANs and generation, makes it more difficult to distinguish between real and fake images. An answer to the detection and classification of fake news using substance properties will produce language-driven features (Choudhary, et al., 2020). The model extracts the grammatical, readability, syntactic and sentimental of specific news features. The blended model can accomplish an accuracy of 86%. A system to detect fake information on social media platforms was developed (Huang, et al., 2020). The model ensemble learning is blended with four various models like depth LSTM embedding LSTM, N-gram CNN and LIWC CNN and is developed to recognize fake information. Also, to accomplish higher detection accuracy of fake news, the enhanced ensemble learning model weights are estimated utilizing the SAHS, which accomplished the accuracy of 99.4%.

The FNDNet model learns the inequitable features for fake news classification by various hidden layers built-in deep neural networks. The CNN was developed for extricating the features at every layer. The methodology used is pre-trained word embedding, GloVe and FNDNet. The outcomes proved that this model could accomplish 98.36% for predicting fake news (Kaliyar, et al., 2020).

The ML ensemble strategy for automatic news classification was recommended. A mix of ML algorithms trained to utilize different ensemble strategies and assess its performance on four datasets. The extracted distinctive textual features of articles utilizing an LIWC tool utilized a highlight set as an information, a high authority. To achieve the best accuracy, learning simulations were performed and their parameters were fine-tuned. The experimental assessment affirms this ensemble learner's prevalent performance approach of individual learners (Ahmad, et al., 2020). The Author introduced the fake news detection model and reduced the feature using the techniques Chi-square and PCA. The dimensionality reduction method to decrease the feature vectors dimensionality previously progress to classifier was proposed. The Chi-square and PCA tests provide more effective attributes for spam detection. This model enhances the accuracy by 4% and the F1 score by 20%. This method was limited to only a tiny dataset (Umer, et al., 2020).

The incorrect message concentrated on unique words, morphosyntactic resources, term sequence, word score, and recurrence of function was identified. The reduction of dimension was carried utilizing LSA and k-means algorithms. The model validates an extra homogeneous achievement among the metrics, distinguishing itself primarily for high precision with an improved efficacy than the other mentioned methods. This method requires reducing the total count of characteristics to achieve 86% accuracy and 94% precision (de Oliveira, et al., 2020).

A model that can detect and dispense fake news from OSNs was developed (Shrivastava, et al., 2020). A model employs differential equations to verify and block the users and thereby pass the information on OSNs. The latent and isolation method must be implemented to prevent social media from spreading rumours and spreading fake news. A model presented by the Author intends to recognise counterfeit posts on Facebook in a chrome location and also use countless Facebook functionalities to examine the user's behaviour through deep learning techniques (Sahoo, et al., 2021).

The incorrect posts recognising system(FakeBert) detects the incorrect posts on social media like WhatsApp, Twitter, Facebook, etc. with the BERT-based learning method by joining various Simultaneous frames of a single layer deep convolution neural network with varying kernel sizes and filters using BERT (Kaliyar, et al., 2021). The Researcher introduced an ensemble based deep learning model on labelling news on social media platforms as to which information is fake and which one is real using the dataset LIAR (Aslam, et al., 2021).

The Author planned a novel hybrid deep learning model for misinformation classifier that merges convolutional neural networks and recurrent neural networks via web-based media. The proposed model utilizes the capacity of the convolution neural organization to separate neighbourhood highlights (emotion detection, sign language recognition from video stream) and of the RNN-LSTM to identify deep constraints (sequential features) (Nasir, et al., 2021). Robotized methods for incorrect posts recognition on web-based media from a text mining point of view. The classification algorithm dependent on the convolution neural network (CNN), Long Short-Term Memory (LSTM), Bidirectional Encoder Representations from Transformers (BERT). On the Covid-19 Misinformation recognition dataset, this strategy has a better performance of 98.41 percentage. (Wani, et al., 2021). The Author presents a novel-based technique for programmed recognition of phony news on the Twitter stage. This methodology includes pairwise text input, word implanting, and etymological and network highlights (Mouratidis, et al., 2021). Detect fake news in Amharic language using deep learning techniques (Gereme, et al., 2021).

Programmed counterfeit news identification via online media with the dimensionality reduction LSA(latent semantic analysis). The ability of LSA(latent semantic analysis) is to extract the relationships between the words by sense (Giglou, et al., 2021). Dong et al. presented the Deep two-way semi-supervised learning where one way is for supervised(labelled) learning and another way is for unsupervised(unlabeled) learning to detect the fake information spreading on web-based media like Twitter, Facebook, Instagram, WhatsApp etc., using both machine learning methods like Naive Bayes, Decision Tree, Adaboost, Support Vector Machine and deep learning method bidirectional recurrent neural networks (Dong, et al., 2019). Nguyen et al. proposed the framework to identify the fake images shared over social media using CNN and BERT's deep learning techniques (Tuan, et al., 2021). Early warning on social media platform (Facebook) misinformation (Vicario, et al., 2019). They assessed the exhibition of five machine learning techniques and three deep learning models and two fake and real news datasets for fake news detection. Likewise, utilized Term Frequency (TF), Term frequency Inverse document frequency, and embedding represent the text data for machine learning and deep learning models (Jiang, et al., 2021). The Author proposed the model to expose the incorrect information on the social media platform make use of the technique CNN and furthermore contrast static word embedding with non-static word embedding to give the refreshing word installing in the preparation stage and this framework assessed on two ongoing datasets specifically LIAR and ISOT (Goldani, et al., 2021). The progression of feeling data in counterfeit news via online media utilises neural organizations (Ghanem, et al., 2021). Use container neural organizations to distinguish counterfeit data via online media (Goldani, et al., 2021). Bang, et al., (2021) intend to accomplish a strong model for the COVID-19 phony news identification task utilizing two datasets Fake-News CONVID-19 (FakeNews-19) and Tweets COVID-19 (Tweets-19). Das, et al., (2021) proposed the novel bogus data framework that consequently distinguishes whether the data is valid or genuine. Programmed bogus data discovery on Facebook utilizing ongoing datasets (Dewam, et al., 2017). The expectation of character via web-based media clients (Dandannavar, et al., 2018). Counterfeit news grouping using machine learning algorithm Naïve Bayes classifier (Granik, et al., 2017). An approach based on geometric deep learning for detecting fake news in online media (Monti, et al., 2019). An approach based on BERT for detecting fake news on social media. (Kula, et al., 2020), (Liu, et al., 2019), (Jwa, et al., 2019), (Mehta, et al., 2021).

Based on the above literature survey, the authors understand that most of the early work has been executed by researchers using Machine Learning techniques. The early work focused on finding a set of features that help separate fake news from legitimate information. And also, the models not adequately handled the missing/improper data from social media platforms such as Facebook, Twitter, etc. The processes of classification time will not be limited.

Consolidated Review Report

METHODOLOGY

The authors researched social media text mining and started assessing the most used social media platform and the kind of messages shared using it. The data collected from the various participants during the survey is taken as the primary data. We had collected data from 2425 individuals, and we focused mainly on two questions for this research.

The key question that helped us decide the platform we desired to research was 'Which is your favorite social media platform?' From the data collected from around 2500 users (2425 exact), the authors concluded that 1233 users spend their time regularly on Facebook. Thus, almost 50% of the people were chosen Facebook, which gave us our first answer: Facebook is the favorite social media platform.

The reference of it and the graph is shown below Fig.2.

After knowing from the previous survey question that Facebook was the most used social media platform, the authors decided to proceed with the following question: ' What type of messages do you usually share (videos, texts, images, memes, audio)?' Among the 1233 users who answered Facebook as their favorite platform, 691 responded that they shared texts, whereas 175 shared videos apart from images.

Based on the above survey data analysis, the authors understood that most users share text messages. Based on this understanding, we have considered text mining as the key to our study. Our data mining study will categorize the shared messages and block or filter fake and imitated text.

Fake News Detection System: FNDN-LSTM

The research on fake news detection on social media platforms using machine learning techniques has been a lot of exploration on the extensive range of the dataset. However, deep learning techniques for detecting fake news on social media and related works have yet to be fully evaluated. The proposed novel techniques introduce the combination of BERT and LSTM, which boost the performance of the fake news detection method (FNDN-LSTM).

The proposed framework of FNDN-LSTM based Model of Fake News Detection considers social media news datasets gathered from a particular platform. This data will be preprocessed using the TF BERT model. Once the data is preprocessed, it is important to choose the suitable significant features from the data that can provide the characteristics with which fake news was distinguished from the real ones. This process is known as feature selection. The selected features will be fed to this FNDN-LSTM

Table 1.

Title	Aim and Objectives	Methods	Limitation/ Drawbacks/ Future work	Year
(Kaliyar, et al., 2021)	A BERT based deep learning using convolution neural network	CNN, LSTM	Hybrid approach will be applying for both the binary as well as multiclass fake news data set.	2021
(Aslam, et al., 2021)	Evaluating information as true or false utilizing the LIAR dataset based on an ensemble deep learning model.	bi-LSTM-GRU	FND the usage of deep learning is still a brand-new topic and difficult; there is still a place for upgrading.	2021
(Nasir, et al., 2021)	Combines CNN and RNN for detecting fake information on social media.	CNN, LSTM, Word2vec	Generalization doesn't work well for specific data set.	2021
(Wani, et al., 2021)	False information in the form of text on social media can be detected automatically.	CNN, LSTM, BERT	The Author plans to expand on this work with a different dataset in the future.	2021
(Mouratidis, et al., 2021)	Detect the fake tweets on the Twitter platform.	Relu, sigmoid, Adam optimizer, one-hot function	Aim to put a different model configuration to the test.	2021
(Gereme, et al., 2021)	Detect fake news in Amharic language using deep learning techniques	CNN, MaxPooling, Relu	This work could be improved even more by expanding more data and BERT for word embedding.	2021
(Tuan, et al., 2021)	Framework to detect bogus pictures shared on online media	CNN, BERT	In the future, plan to use more than one image for fake news classification.	2021
(Sahoo, et al., 2021)	Deep learning techniques used to analyse the user account's behaviour.	LSTM, Bi-LSTM, GRU, Bi-GRU, Hybrid Approach, KNN, Decision tree, Logistic Regression, Naïve Bayes, Support Vector Machine (SVM)	It can be improved by analysing the features with different deep learning algorithms such as bidirectional LSTM, bidirectional GRU, and some hybrid approach based completely deep learning classifier for better decision making with more datasets.	2021
(Choudhary, et al., 2020)	Solution of fake news detection and classification	Decision Tree, Naïve Bayes, SVM (Support Vector Machine), and KNN	Want to work on huge functions and parameters to boost the overall model performance.	2020
(Huang, et al., 2020)	Fake news detection system using ensemble deep learning model based on self-adaptive harmony search algorithms and Text Analysis Using LIWC.	N-gram CNN, LSTM, depth LSTM and LIWC CNN	Grammar analysis needs to be richly researched and worth facts extracted from the preprocessing and need to grow fake news detection accuracy.	2020
(Kaliyar, et al., 2020)	The deep neural network automatically learns the unfair features for fake news classification through multiple hidden layers assembled in the deep neural network.	CNN, GloVe	Want a plan to consist of a bi-directional transformer encoder (BERT) for pre-training the model.	2020
(Ahmad, et al., 2020)	Automated classification of news articles by combining different machine learning algorithms.	stochastic gradient descent, K-nearest neighbor(KNN), support vector machine (SVM), logistic regression, linear support vector machine and decision tree	Destiny direction: 1) fake information detection on real time motion pictures. 2) perceive Key factors to lessen the spread of counterfeit information. 3) Graph theory and machine mastering techniques can be employed to categories the key sources worried in scattering incorrect records.	2020
(Zeng, et al., 2020)	A method designed to detect Fake News and Semantic Correlations between Text content and Images.	Image-enhanced Text Representation Learning, Word Embeddings and VGG Features.	A picture enhancing software programs like Photoshop and deep generative networks like GANs	2020
(Umer, et al., 2020)	Created a model that detects fake news articles automatically.	PCA, chi-Square, CNN and LSTM	Want to Validate with a large dataset and specific textual features and their combination will be examined to grow the overall performance.	2020
(de Oliveira, et al., 2020)	Focus on linguistic characteristics, grammatical resources, word pattern, term count, and frequency of specific expressions to identify fake content.	LSA and K-mean	Based on this distribution, the classifier produced an average result.	2020
(Shrivastava, et al., 2020)	Developed a model that will detect and block fake information.	Differential equation	The latent and isolation method needs to be implemented to prevent the social network from spreading rumors and fake news propagation.	2020
(Giglou, et al., 2020)	Automatic fake news detection on social media.	LSA	Add characteristic weighting for representations and use specific deep neural community models like RNN.	2020
(Vishwakarma, et al., 2019)	A model for analysing the veracity of the information on different online media platforms that is accessible in images has been proposed.	Optical Character recognition (OPR), Selenium	Text extraction should be tested for images with a large amount of text and improve the extraction process.	2019
(Zhang, et al., 2019)	Fake news detection for reducing the hazards posed by incorrect news consumption on online media.	Affinity Propagation (AP) and K-means clustering.	Deal with real-time news	2019
(Alzanin, et al., 2019)	Created the algorithm to detecting rumors in Arabic tweets	expectation-maximization (E-M)	Discover more powerful capabilities related to the content material of tweets, save you the unlabeled data from degrading the category accuracy	2019
(Dong, et al., 2019)	Semi-supervised learning for fake news detection on Twitter.	Naive Bayes, Decision Tree, Adaboost, Support Vector Machine, bidirectional	The authors intend to test the proposed model on other NLP tasks, such as sentiment analysis, in the future.	2019

continued on following page

Table 1. Continued

Title	Aim and Objectives	Methods	Limitation/ Drawbacks/ Future work	Year
(Vicario, et al., 2019)	Method for classifies fake information on social media.	logistic regression, Decision Trees, Linear Regression, K-Nearest Neighbors, Support Vector Machine, Neural Network Models	In order to make it simpler and easier, assume that all fake news comes from an unofficial news source.	2019
(Yadav, et al., 2019)	Analysis of the future buying behavior of the user using machine learning algorithms.	Naive Bayes algorithm and SVM	In order to extract event-related information from the news, it must be adequately performed.	2019
(Jang, et al., 2018)	Determine the root tweets about fake news and the significant differences in evolution patterns between real and fake news.	Text phylogeny and evolution tree analysis	Efforts need to be taken to perceive the chief traits of fake news and enhance the virtual space waft.	2018
(Pendyala, et al., 2018)	The framework employs statistical techniques to aid in the detection of veiled Web fraud attacks in social media.	Sentiment analysis, CUSUM detector	Misinformation containment was found to be NP-hard, and the proposed technique was not able to solve it. Hence accuracy needs to be improved using correlation analysis of some kind.	2018
(Wani, et al., 2018)	Detecting malicious or negative links within the communities of the users.	Decision Tree, SVM, and Naïve Bayes.	In future work, the Author extend this model for another platform and create a publicly available dataset	2018
(Inuwa-Dutse, et al., 2018)	Filter and delete unnecessary and irrelevant tweets	Maximum-Entropy (MaxEnt), Random Forest, Extremely Randomized Trees (ExtraTrees), C-Support Vector Classification (SVC5), Gradient Boosting and Multi-layer Perceptron (MLP).	Forming enclaves of spammers excessive-level statement that had to aim and explore.	2018
(Cardoso, et al., 2018)	Introduced several related works on spam detection and spam review detection.	Content based, Behavior based, information based and group spam detection	An analysis that uses new labelled datasets would be more robust.	2018

model of classification. This model characterizes fake news from real news. This FNDN-LSTM network's performance will be evaluated and compared with the state-of-art machine learning and deep learning classifiers.

Figure 1. Data Collection pattern by online

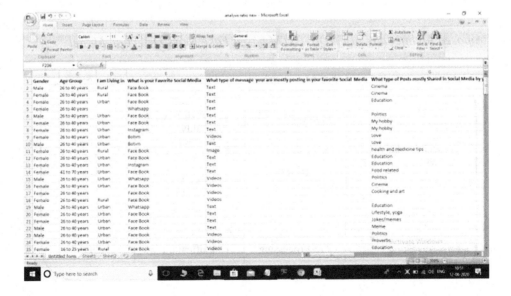

Dataset and Preprocessing

The benchmark dataset of fake news on social media is collected from the official website, whereas Fake News Corpus (https://github.com/several27/FakeNewsCorpus, https://codeload.github.com/thepana-cealab/covid19_twitter/zip/master), Getting Real About Fake News (https://www.kaggle.com/mrisdal/

Figure 2. Favorite social media

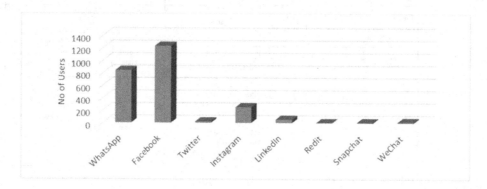

Figure 3. Type of messages posting on Facebook

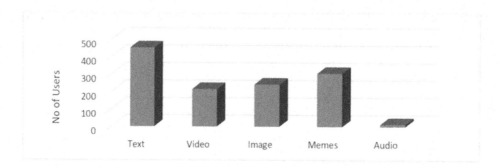

Figure 4. Proposed Architecture of FNDN-LSTM based Fake News Detection Model

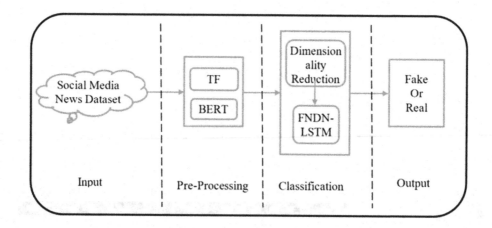

fake-news), Fake News Detection (https://www.kaggle.com/jruvika/fake-news-detection), News Dataset from TI-CNN (https://arxiv.org/abs/1806.00749). The Authors will extract the required Facebook data for this research from the collected dataset.

To fed the data into the classification (FNDN-LSTM) models, the data must be preprocessed using the NLP (Natural Language Processing) techniques. It helps to select the top relevant/important features and increase the performance of the model. Preprocessing is the data mining technique that converts the complex/imperfect and inconsistent unprocessed data into the machine intelligible pattern. It will be efficient for the process of classification. In order to perform these tasks, TF (Term Frequency) and BERT (Bidirectional Encoder Representations from Transformers) models will be combined and applied in this work for effective data preprocessing.

BERT

The architectures of BERT and other Transformer encoders have been effective on an assortment of errands in NLP (natural language processing). BERT models are typically pre-trained on an enormous corpus of text, then fine-tuned for explicit tasks (Kaliyar, et al., 2021). It combines the Mask Language Model (MLM) and Next Sentence Prediction (NSP). It is context-dependent and also the best method in NLP to understand heavy context texts. BERT model has been exposed the active in numerous NLP (natural language processing) responsibilities as well as text classification (Tuan, et al., 2021).

Term-Frequency

Term-Frequency is used to measure how frequently a term appears in documents and calculate the similarity between the document and the number of words that pop up. In the context of natural language processing, terms correspond to words or phrases, but they could also represent any tokens in text.TF is commonly used for information retrieval tasks (Jiang, et al., 2021).

Dimensionality Reduction Techniques

In the dimensionality reduction techniques, there are two types to play a role in text classification. They are feature selection and feature extraction. The most significant and applicable features are saved in feature selection methods, and the remaining features are rejected. A novel vector space with unique attributes is produced by changing the first vector space in feature extraction methods on the flip side. The features are summary in novel vector space. The dimensionality reduction methods aim to decrease the dimension of the features set to boost the model's performance and reduce the computational cost. For the text classification result, feature reduction has a boundless impression. Accordingly, to reduce the dimensions, it is very decisive to pick the perfect algorithm. Some of the frequent dimensionality reduction techniques are Term Frequency-Inverse Document Frequency (TF-IDF) Chi-Square Statistics (CHI), Latent Semantic Analysis (LSA), Gini Coefficient (GI), Information Gain (IG), Mutual Information and Principal Component Analysis (PCA). To expand the flexibility of the text classifier, Principal Component Analysis and Latent Semantic Analysis are two dimensionality reduction approaches used in Fake news detection (FNDN-LSTM) to reduce the features and boost the model's performance.

Principal Component Analysis (PCA)

The Principal Component Analysis (PCA) technique, which employs a linear transformation, is widely used to diminish the size of a feature set. The reduced dataset may contain the same or fewer features than the original datasets. The major components of the datasets are calculated using the covariance matrix. (Umer, et al., 2020). The PCA process is first to standardize the dataset; second, calculate the covariance matrix and compute the eigenvalues and eigenvectors. Finally, sort both eigenvalues and eigenvectors.

Latent Semantic Analysis (LSA)

A latent semantic analysis reduces the number of features while building up a prediction model. To decrease the cost of computational modelling, and in some cases, to improve the model's performance, it is necessary to cut back on the number of features. Statistical-based feature selection methods include assessing each input and target variable's connection utilizing statistics and choosing those input variables with a strong relation with target variables. Additionally, it is used to take into account the relationship between words based on their meaning and to reduce the impact of noise in the data as well as to find the hidden topics. Then these hidden topics help to classify similar documents (Giglou, et al., 2020). However, the selection of statistical measures relies upon the input and output features (de Oliveira, et al., 2020).

RNN-LSTM

This module is intended to classify a particular social media news dataset into fake news and real news. The selected features fed into the FNDN-LSTM model of classification. This model characterizes fake news from real news. A recurrent neural network is a strong neural network and is used for sequential data. It is obtained from the feedforward neural network. The RNN (Recurrent Neural Network) is similar to how the human brain operates and performs well with sequential data compared to other algorithms.

CONCLUSION

In the present state of media Platforms, incorrect information is spreading more quickly than the speed of light. The idea is to Identify and reduce or block the imitated text among the public. This article aims to propose a solution to detect the spreading of fake news. By developing this false information detecting system, the problems behind the imitated text will be controlled and rumors will be blocked. This research proposes a novel FNDN-LSTM model of fake information and real information from the social media news datasets. The LSTM unit of the proposed NN model is a memory extension unit. It permits the user to employ a large dataset for processing without degrading the performance of the network. LSTM also has the advantage of overcoming the gradient explosion problem, thereby exhibiting accurate classification. Thus, this model can classify efficiently, conserve memory usage and consume less time for training. Thus, the study assists appropriate guidelines on the fake news detection model(FNDN-LSTM) on social media.

REFERENCES

Ahlers, D. (2006). News consumption and the new electronic media. *The Harvard International Journal of Press/Politics, 11*(1), 29–52. doi:10.1177/1081180X05284317

Ahmad, I., Yousaf, M., Yousaf, S., & Ahmad, M. O. (2020). Fake News Detection Using Machine Learning Ensemble Methods. *Complexity, 2020*, 2020. doi:10.1155/2020/8885861

Ahmad, I., Yousaf, M., Yousaf, S., & Ahmad, M. O. (2020). Fake News Detection Using Machine Learning Ensemble Methods. *Complexity*.

Ahmed, H., Traore, I., & Saad, S. (2017, October). Detection of online fake news using N-gram analysis and machine learning techniques. In *International Conference on Intelligent, Secure, and Dependable Systems in Distributed and Cloud Environments* (pp. 127-138). Springer.

Alzanin, S. M., & Azmi, A. M. (2019). Rumor detection in Arabic tweets using semi-supervised and unsupervised expectation–maximization. *Knowledge-Based Systems, 185*, 104945.

Aslam, N., Ullah Khan, I., Alotaibi, F. S., Aldaej, L. A., & Aldubaikil, A. K. (2021). Fake Detect: A Deep Learning Ensemble Model for Fake News Detection. *Complexity*.

Bang, Y., Ishii, E., Cahyawijaya, S., Ji, Z., & Fung, P. (2021). *Model Generalization on COVID-19 Fake News Detection.* arXiv preprint arXiv:2101.03841.

Cardoso, E. F., Silva, R. M., & Almeida, T. A. (2018). Towards automatic filtering of fake reviews. *Neurocomputing, 309*, 106–116. doi:10.1016/j.neucom.2018.04.074

Choudhary, A., & Arora, A. (2020). Linguistic Feature Based Learning Model for Fake News Detection and Classification. *Expert Systems with Applications*, 114171.

Dandannavar, P. S., Mangalwede, S. R., & Kulkarni, P. M. (2018, December). Social Media Text-A Source for Personality Prediction. In *2018 International Conference on Computational Techniques, Electronics and Mechanical Systems (CTEMS)* (pp. 62- 65). IEEE.

Das, S. D., Basak, A., & Dutta, S. (2021). *A Heuristic-driven Uncertainty based Ensemble Framework for Fake News Detection in Tweets and News Articles.* arXiv preprint arXiv:2104.01791.

de Oliveira, N. R., Medeiros, D. S., & Mattos, D. M. (2020). A sensitive stylistic approach to identify fake news on social networking. *IEEE Signal Processing Letters, 27*, 1250–1254.

Dewan, P., & Kumaraguru, P. (2017). Facebook Inspector (FbI): Towards automatic real-time detection of malicious content on Facebook. *Social Network Analysis and Mining, 7*(1), 15.

Dong, X., Victor, U., Chowdhury, S., & Qian, L. (2019). *Deep Two-path Semisupervised Learning for Fake News Detection.* arXiv preprint arXiv:1906.05659.

García, S. A., García, G. G., Prieto, M. S., Moreno Guerrero, A. J., & Rodríguez Jiménez, C. (2020). The Impact of Term Fake News on the Scientific Community. Scientific Performance and Mapping in Web of Science. *Social Sciences, 9*(5), 73. doi:10.3390ocsci9050073

Gereme, F., Zhu, W., Ayall, T., & Alemu, D. (2021). Combating Fake News in "Low-Resource" Languages: Amharic Fake News Detection Accompanied by Resource Crafting. *Information, 2021*(12), 20.

Ghafari, S. M., Yakhchi, S., Beheshti, A., & Orgun, M. (2018, November). Social context-aware trust prediction: methods for identifying fake news. In *International Conference on Web Information Systems Engineering* (pp. 161-177). Springer.

Ghanem, B., Ponzetto, S. P., Rosso, P., & Rangel, F. (2021). *FakeFlow: fake news detection by modeling the flow of affective information.* arXiv preprint arXiv:2101.09810.

Giglou, H. B., Razmara, J., Rahgouy, M., & Sanaei, M. (2020). LSACoNet: A Combination of Lexical and Conceptual Features for Analysis of Fake News Spreaders on Twitter. CLEF.

Goldani, M. H., Momtazi, S., & Safabakhsh, R. (2021). Detecting fake news with capsule neural networks. *Applied Soft Computing, 101*, 106991.

Goldani, M. H., Safabakhsh, R., & Momtazi, S. (2021). Convolutional neural network with margin loss for fake news detection. *Information Processing & Management, 58*(1), 102418.

Granik, M., & Mesyura, V. (2017, May). Fake news detection using naive Bayes classifier. In *2017 IEEE First Ukraine Conference on Electrical and Computer Engineering (UKRCON)* (pp. 900-903). IEEE.

Huang, Y. F., & Chen, P. H. (2020). Fake news detection using an ensemble learning model based on self-adaptive harmony search algorithms. *Expert Systems with Applications, 159*, 113584.

Inuwa-Dutse, I., Liptrott, M., & Korkontzelos, I. (2018). Detection of spam-posting accounts on Twitter. *Neurocomputing, 315*, 496–511. doi:10.1016/j.neucom.2018.07.044

Islam, M. S., Islam, M. A., Hossain, M. A., & Dey, J. J. (2016, December). Supervised approach of sentimentality extraction from bengalifacebook status. In *2016 19th International Conference on Computer and Information Technology (ICCIT)* (pp. 383- 387). IEEE.

Jang, S. M., Geng, T., Li, J. Y. Q., Xia, R., Huang, C. T., Kim, H., & Tang, J. (2018). A computational approach for examining the roots and spreading patterns of fake news: Evolution tree analysis. *Computers in Human Behavior, 84*, 103–113. doi:10.1016/j.chb.2018.02.032

Jiang, T., Li, J. P., Haq, A. U., Saboor, A., & Ali, A. (2021). A Novel Stacking Approach for Accurate Detection of Fake News. *IEEE Access: Practical Innovations, Open Solutions, 9*, 22626–22639.

Jin, Z., Cao, J., Zhang, Y., Zhou, J., & Tian, Q. (2016). Novel visual and statistical image features for microblogs news verification. *IEEE Transactions on Multimedia, 19*(3), 598–608. doi:10.1109/TMM.2016.2617078

Jwa, H., Oh, D., Park, K., Kang, J. M., & Lim, H. (2019). exBAKE: Automatic fake news detection model based on bidirectional encoder representations from transformers (bert). *Applied Sciences (Basel, Switzerland), 9*(19), 4062.

Kaliyar, R. K., Goswami, A., & Narang, P. (2021). FakeBERT: Fake news detection in social media with a BERT-based deep learning approach. *Multimedia Tools and Applications, 80*(8), 11765–11788.

Kaliyar, R. K., Goswami, A., Narang, P., & Sinha, S. (2020). FNDNet–a deep convolutional neural network for fake news detection. *Cognitive Systems Research*, *61*, 32–44.

Kula, S., Choraś, M., & Kozik, R. (2020, September). Application of the BERT-Based Architecture in Fake News Detection. In *Conference on Complex, Intelligent, and Software Intensive Systems* (pp. 239-249). Springer.

Lazer, D. M., Baum, M. A., Benkler, Y., Berinsky, A. J., Greenhill, K. M., Menczer, F., Metzger, M. J., Nyhan, B., Pennycook, G., Rothschild, D., Schudson, M., Sloman, S. A., Sunstein, C. R., Thorson, E. A., Watts, D. J., & Zittrain, J. L. (2018). The science of fake news. *Science*, *359*(6380), 1094–1096. doi:10.1126cience.aao2998 PMID:29590025

Lin, K. C., Wu, S. H., Chen, L. P., Ku, T., & Chen, G. D. (2014, August). Mining the user clusters on Facebook fan pages based on topic and sentiment analysis. In *Proceedings of the 2014 IEEE 15th International Conference on Information Reuse and Integration (IEEE IRI 2014)* (pp. 627-632). IEEE.

Liu, C., Wu, X., Yu, M., Li, G., Jiang, J., Huang, W., & Lu, X. (2019, August). A two-stage model based on bert for short fake news detection. In *International Conference on Knowledge Science, Engineering and Management* (pp. 172-183). Springer.

Mehta, D., Dwivedi, A., Patra, A., & Kumar, M. A. (2021). A transformer-based architecture for fake news classification. *Social Network Analysis and Mining*, *11*(1), 1–12.

Mhamdi, C., Al-Emran, M., & Salloum, S. A. (2018). Text mining and analytics: A case study from news channels posts on Facebook. In *Intelligent Natural Language Processing: Trends and Applications* (pp. 399–415). Springer.

Monti, F., Frasca, F., Eynard, D., Mannion, D., & Bronstein, M. M. (2019). *Fake News Detection on Social Media using Geometric Deep Learning*. arXiv preprint arXiv:1902.06673.

Mouratidis, D., Nikiforos, M. N., & Kermanidis, K. L. (2021). Deep Learning for Fake News Detection in a Pairwise Textual Input Schema. *Computation*, *9*(2), 20.

Nasir, J. A., Khan, O. S., & Varlamis, I. (2021). Fake news detection: A hybrid CNN-RNN based deep learning approach. *International Journal of Information Management Data Insights*, *1*(1), 100007.

Pendyala, V. S., Liu, Y., & Figueira, S. M. (2018). A framework for detecting injected influence attacks on microblog websites using change detection techniques. *Development Engineering*, *3*, 218–233. doi:10.1016/j.deveng.2018.08.002

Sahoo, S. R., & Gupta, B. B. (2021). Multiple features based approach for automatic fake news detection on social networks using deep learning. *Applied Soft Computing*, *100*, 106983.

Shrivastava, G., Kumar, P., Ojha, R. P., Srivastava, P. K., Mohan, S., & Srivastava, G. (2020). Defensive modeling of fake news through online social networks. *IEEE Transactions on Computational Social Systems*, *7*(5), 1159–1167.

Sutskever, I., Vinyals, O., & Le, Q. V. (2014). Sequence to sequence learning with neural networks. In Advances in neural information processing systems (pp. 3104-3112). Academic Press.

Tanwani, N., Kumar, S., Jalbani, A. H., Soomro, S., Channa, M. I., & Nizamani, Z. (2017, November). Student opinion mining regarding educational system using facebook group. In *2017 First International Conference on Latest trends in Electrical Engineering and Computing Technologies (INTELLECT)* (pp. 1-5). IEEE.

Tuan, N. M. D., & Minh, P. Q. N. (2021). *Multimodal Fusion with BERT and Attention Mechanism for Fake News Detection.* arXiv preprint arXiv:2104.11476.

Umer, M., Imtiaz, Z., Ullah, S., Mehmood, A., Choi, G. S., & On, B. W. (2020). Fake news stance detection using deep learning architecture (cnn-lstm). *IEEE Access: Practical Innovations, Open Solutions, 8*, 156695–156706.

Vicario, M. D., Quattrociocchi, W., Scala, A., & Zollo, F. (2019). Polarization and fake news: Early warning of potential misinformation targets. *ACM Transactions on the Web, 13*(2), 1–22.

Vishwakarma, D. K., Varshney, D., & Yadav, A. (2019). Detection and veracity analysis of fake news via scrapping and authenticating the web search. *Cognitive Systems Research, 58*, 217–229. doi:10.1016/j.cogsys.2019.07.004

Wang, W. Y. (2017). *"Liar, liar pants on fire": A new benchmark dataset for fakenews detection.* arXiv preprint arXiv:1705.00648.

Wang, Y., Wang, L., Yang, Y., & Lian, T. (2021). SemSeq4FD: Integrating global semantic relationship and local sequential order to enhance text representation for fake news detection. *Expert Systems with Applications, 166*, 114090.

Wani, A., Joshi, I., Khandve, S., Wagh, V., & Joshi, R. (2021). *Evaluating Deep Learning Approaches for Covid19 Fake News Detection.* arXiv preprint arXiv:2101.04012.

Wani, M. A., & Jabin, S. (2018). *Mutual clustering coefficient-based suspicious-link detection approach for online social networks. Journal of King Saud University.*

Wong, J. (2016). *Almost all the traffic to fake news sites is from Facebook, new data show.* The Medium.

Yadav, R., Kumar, A. V., & Kumar, A. (2019). News-based supervised sentiment analysis for prediction of futures buying behaviour. *IIMB Management Review, 31*(2), 157–166. doi:10.1016/j.iimb.2019.03.006

Zeng, J., Zhang, Y., & Ma, X. (2020). Fake news detection for epidemic emergencies via deep correlations between text and images. *Sustainable Cities and Society*, 102652.

Zhang, C., Gupta, A., Kauten, C., Deokar, A. V., & Qin, X. (2019). Detecting fake news for reducing misinformation risks using analytics approaches. *European Journal of Operational Research, 279*(3), 1036–1052. doi:10.1016/j.ejor.2019.06.022

Zhou, C., Neubig, G., Gu, J., Diab, M., Guzman, P., Zettlemoyer, L., & Ghazvininejad, M. (2020). *Detecting hallucinated content in conditional neural sequence generation.* arXiv preprint arXiv:2011.02593.

Chapter 13
Word Embedding Techniques for Sentiment Analyzers:
A Review

Upendar Rao Rayala
Rajiv Gandhi University of Knowledge and Technology, Nuzvid, India

Karthick Seshadri
iD https://orcid.org/0000-0002-5658-141X
National Institute of Technology, Tadepalligudem, India

ABSTRACT

Sentiment analysis is perceived to be a multi-disciplinary research domain composed of machine learning, artificial intelligence, deep learning, image processing, and social networks. Sentiment analysis can be used to determine opinions of the public about products and to find the customers' interest and their feedback through social networks. To perform any natural language processing task, the input text/comments should be represented in a numerical form. Word embeddings represent the given text/sentences/words as a vector that can be employed in performing subsequent natural language processing tasks. In this chapter, the authors discuss different techniques that can improve the performance of sentiment analysis using concepts and techniques like traditional word embeddings, sentiment embeddings, emoticons, lexicons, and neural networks. This chapter also traces the evolution of word embedding techniques with a chronological discussion of the recent research advancements in word embedding techniques.

INTRODUCTION

Sentiment analysis makes use of structural, syntactical and semantic information present in the text along with statistical metrics to analyze, process, induce and deduce subjective texts with affective or emotional information (Tumasjan, A., Sprenger, T. O., Sandner, P. G. & Welpe, I. M., 2010). Sentiment analysis has started to focus on the classification of a given text/sentence/word/emotion with coarse grained binary sentiment classification with two polarity labels as positive and negative. Later most research studies

DOI: 10.4018/978-1-7998-8061-5.ch013

focus on more fine-grained sentiment analysis instead of simple binary sentiment classifications. Recent studies focus on dimensional sentiment analysis, which allows a user to extract more specific opinions/ sentiments for a given text/word/sentence. Though there are many methods and techniques proposed in different aspects still accurate sentiment classification and inference is a challenging task as it must work across different contexts from micro blog posts to large text corpora.

The accuracy of sentiment analyzers can be improved only when words of the given text/sentence/ post are presented in low dimensional numerical values (vectors) which describe the relationships (Syntactic, Semantic and Sentimental) among the words/text/sentences/posts. One hot encoding is a popular encoding technique to represent the words of the natural language in the form of word vectors. One hot encoding overcomes the drawbacks of integer encoding by establishing syntactic and semantic relationships among words of the natural language. Due to the sparseness of one hot encoding, a heavy memory footprint is typically needed to store the one-hot vectors of a given document / text.

To overcome the limitations of one hot encoding technique, context-based *word embeddings* were introduced to represent the words in low dimensional dense vectors which can be used to perform many natural language processing tasks. Some of the popular context-based word embedding techniques includes Word2Vec, Global Vectors (GloVe). However, the context-based embeddings can be similar for words having opposite sentiment polarities (for instance, good and bad, happy and sad).Hence context-based word embeddings are as such not sufficient for sentiment inference.

To handle these problems, *sentiment embeddings* were introduced, in which researchers incorporated sentiment-related information as a part of the word embedding and modified the contextual word vectors. These sentiment embeddings are inferred using training corpora labeled with appropriate sentiments, which can be used to guide the training process of learning dissimilar word vector representations for words having opposite polarities. Some of the popular sentiment embeddings are Hybrid Ranking (HyRank), Multi-prototype Topic and Sentiment Word enriched Word Embeddings (M-TSWE) (Ren, Y., Zhang, Y., Zhang, M. & Ji, D.., 2016).and word vector refinement using sentiment lexicons (Yu, L.-C., Wang, J., Lai, K. R. & Zhang, X., 2018). M-TSWE requires a corpus manually annotated with sentiment polarities; M-TSWE optimizes a suitable objective function to refine the embeddings such that their positions in the vector space mimic the underlying sentiment polarities implied. Thereby, the words which express similar sentiments are moved closer in the word embedding space away from the words with dissimilar sentiment polarities.

Emoticon embedding is a method to improve the accuracy of sentiment inference, especially in micro blog posts, wherein emoticons encode concise affective information. When combining emoticons and words into an emoticon space, it can help to identify polarity, subjectivity and emotion in micro blog environments. Some of the popular emoticon-based word embeddings are Emotion Space Model (ESM) and Emoticon Smoothed Language Model (ESLAM) (Liu, K.-L., Li, W.-J. & Guo, M.., 2012). *Dimensional sentiment analysis* is yet another method to enhance the accuracy of sentiment inference by improving the valence and arousal space scores of the lexicon words in a given text/sentence/post.

This chapter discusses various embedding techniques that can be employed for constructing better models for sentiment analysis like basic word embedding techniques, sentiment embedding techniques, and emoticon space embedding techniques and also traces the evolution of word embedding techniques in a chronological order.

As word embeddings have a significant impact on the performance of sentiment analyzers and allied NLP applications; it is justified to perform a review of the contemporary word embedding techniques and the recent research findings about their impact on different sentiment analysis related tasks. This survey has to perform periodically to keep the readers updated regarding the recent developments in the rapidly changing sentiment analysis and word embedding domains.

FUNDAMENTAL WORD EMBEDDING TECHNIQUES

Most of machine learning algorithms and advanced deep learning structures are not capable of understanding raw text. They all require numerical values as input to perform supervised or unsupervised tasks. Hence there is a dire need of technique which converts the given text information into numbers. Word embedding is a popular technique to learn the words representation of the text into real numbers in the form of vectors. For words used in similar context, should have the similar vector representation. Generally, vector space models and Hyper-space Analogue to Language (HAL) methods are used to represent words in a text. HAL is a semantic space model, where it captures the statistical interdependency information among the words using word co-occurrence statistical information (Azzopardi, L., Girolami, M. A. & Crowe, M. K.., 2005). Neural Network Language Model (NNLM) (Bengio, Y., Ducharme, Ré., Vincent, P. & Janvin, C., 2003) uses a joint probability function to represent each word as a distributed vector based on the sequence of previous words. The authors of NNLM experimented on both brown corpus (1,181,041 words) and Associated Press (AP) news corpus (14 million words) with a vocabulary of size of 16,383 and 17, 964 respectively. NNLM outperformed the back-off n-gram models and modified Kneser Ney models. However, it is observed that the NNLM model consumes high computational complexity and memory especially while calculating the conditional probability estimates. A unified deep neural network architecture (Collobert, R., Weston, J., Bottou, Lé., Karlen, M., Kavukcuoglu, K. & Kuksa, P..,2011) was later proposed to perform multiple tasks like chunking, POS tagging, named entity recognition, semantic role labeling and learning language models. Deep layers of NN maintain look-up tables to store the learned features from the words. The unified deep neural network architecture was evaluated based on standard benchmark tasks like POS tagging by Toutanova et al. (2003), chunking by Sha and Pereira (2003), named entity recognition by Ando and Zhang (2005), and semantic role labeling task by Koomen et al. (2005). Given model outperformed on all tasks compared to above mentioned benchmark systems. However, training through the unified NN model is computationally quite expensive,

A revolutionary change was brought into the field of natural language processing (T., Chen, K., Corrado, G. & Dean, J.., 2013a) by predicting the distributed vector representations of the context words and centralized words using a single layer neural network architecture. This model works based on the premise that words in similar contexts tend to have similar vector representations. A demerit of this approach is that words with opposite polarities tend to have similar vector representations, which is detrimental especially to the performance of Sentiment analysis tasks. Subsequently, the negative sampling method was used to train a neural model (Mikolov et al.,2013b) to obtain better word embeddings. In another study, the linear bag of contexts of Mikolov was replaced by arbitrary syntactic contexts. It was observed that this replacement helped the model in realizing a better retrieval performance for inferring the top five most similar words, over the Mikolov's skip-gram model with negative sampling. Pennington, J., Socher, R. & Manning, C. D., (2014) introduced a global log bi-linear regression model (GloVe) by taking advantage of both matrix factorization methods and local window-based contexts methods. Pennington argued that though skip-gram model performed better on word analogy task, it does not use global statistical information effectively. Most of the later studies use the above-mentioned models as the baseline models and enhanced the word embeddings generated through these models by considering semantic lexicons, synonyms, antonyms, and sub-words information (Faruqui, M., Dodge, J., Jauhar, S. K., Dyer, C., Hovy, E. & Smith, N. A., 2015; Kiela, D., Hill, F. & Clark, S., 2015; Kim, J. K., de Marneffe, M. C. & Fosler-Lussier, E., 2016; Nikola Mrksic et al., 2016;,Bojanowski, P., Grave, E., Joulin, A. & Mikolov, T.., 2016). Typically, word embeddings capture the contextual, co-occurrence and statistical characteristics of a word using a neural model. A Summary of the seminal word embedding techniques is illustrated in Table 1.

Table 1. Summary of Fundamental Word Embedding Techniques

S. no.	Authors	Description of Method/Model	Data Sets Used	Models Compared With
1	Bengio, Y., Ducharme, Ré., Vincent, P. & Janvin, C.., 2003	Neural network language model (NNLM) was introduced to develop word embeddings for each word based on previous words. A statistical language model is used to model the joint distribution of words in a sequence of words using the n-gram technique.	Brown corpus, Associated press news	MLP (Multi-Layer Perceptron), Kneser Ney backoff
2	Collobert, R., Weston, J., Bottou, Lé., Karlen, M., Kavukcuoglu, K. & Kuksa, P.., 2011	The Authors expanded the idea of Bengio et al., 2003 by considering the succeeding contexts along with the preceding contexts. Here a statistical language model is used to model the likelihood of the succeeding word based on the context of a word.	WSJ (Wall street journal data), Reuters, Wikipedia data	Suffix2, Gazetteer
3	, T., Chen, K., Corrado, G. & Dean, J., 2013	Mikolov et al. propose to use CBOW (Continuous bag of words) and Skip-gram models that uses a one-layer neural model to compute the word embeddings from large datasets. Here CBOW model takes the input as surrounding words and predicts the central word, whereas Skip-gram model takes the input as the central key word and predicts the surrounding contextual words based on the window size.	Internal Google news data set	Negative sampling, hierarchical softmax with frequency-based Huffman codes
4	Levy, O. & Goldberg, Y.., 2014	As the above cited methods inferred embeddings using a topological window of words, they fail to capture relations based on arbitrary contexts (here the context words need not be surrounding words). Hence, Levy at al. proposed computing dependency-based word embeddings where word embeddings are learnt based on an arbitrary context of words by collapsing prepositions along with object into a single word. For example, consider the following sentence "Australian scientist discovers stars with Telescope". In this statement preposition "with" merged with the object "Telescope". Hence, it is used to find the appropriate surrounding words for a given centralized word.	English Wikipedia, Giga word	Continuous Bag of Words (CBOW)
5	Pennington, J., Socher, R. & Manning, C. D., 2014	The proposed model is trained by optimizing an objective function based on minimizing the sum of squared errors between the prediction and the ground truths in the training set. The features utilized by the model include both global word concordance and local contextual information.	CoNLL-2003(NER), Wikipedia, ACE-2003	Word2Vec: CBOW and Skip-gram
6	Faruqui, M., Dodge, J., Jauhar, S. K., Dyer, C., Hovy, E. & Smith, N. A., 2015	The model proposed uses both distributional vector representations and semantic lexicons like WordNet. Word embeddings of the semantically linked words in semantic lexicons, are adjusted so that these words can have similar vector representations. This readjustment therefore enhances the performance of subsequent NLP tasks.	WMT-11, Wikipedia	CBOW, SG, PPDB, SYN-REL(Syntactic Relations)
7	Kiela, D., Hill, F. & Clark, S., 2015	Experimented on finding similarity or relatedness for downstream applications (synonym detection and document classification) of NLP by introducing specialized semantic spaces. Specialized semantic spaces learned for similarity task (synonym detection) using corpus and thesaurus (collection of synonyms) whereas relatedness task semantic spaces learned using corpus and physiological association norms. Learning canine for a word dog is synonym detection task and relating dog and cat is a relatedness task.	SimLex-999, MEN, MyThes, USF free association norms	Skip-gram, Fit-norms, Joint-norms, Retrofit-norms
8	Kim, J.-K., deMarneffe, M.-C. & Fosler-Lussier, E., *2016*	Pre-trained word vectors produced by word2vec are adjusted with the help of semantic lexicon ordering information (semantic lexicon words can be ordered by valence/arousal score, where valence and arousal score used as indicator for assessing the opinion/sentiment of the given text) in addition to the synonym and antonym related information provided by the semantic lexicons.	WordNet synset, Word intensity orders, Indirect question-answer pairs (IQAP)	GloVe, CBOW, Paragram
9	Bolukbasi, T., Chang, K.-W., Zou, J. Y., Saligrama, V. & Kalai, A. T., *2016*	Focused on gender bias in word embeddings and proposed an algorithm which removes the gender bias while generating the embeddings from the given corpus.	Google News	w2vNEWS and the GloVe web-crawl
10	Nikola Mrksic *et al.*, 2016	The proposed model modifies the word vectors generated by popular word embedding models like word2vec based on the synonyms and antonyms information provided by semantic lexicons. This modification is done in such a way that question and answer systems are capable of distinguishing semantically different words from conceptually related words. (e.g., *cheaper* and *costly*).	Restaurants, Tourist Information	Glove, Paragram-SL999
11	Bojanowski, P., Grave, E., Joulin, A. & Mikolov, T., 2016	The model learnt character level information using a bag of n-gram characters (uses morphology), where character level sub-words are learnt to produce the valid vector representation for out of vocabulary words.	Wikipedia data set	Gurevych -GUR350, Zesch and Gurevych - ZG222 WS353, RW WS353 (Rare Word data set), RG65

SENTIMENT BASED WORD EMBEDDINGS

A demerit of learning word embeddings based on contextual information is that words expressing opposite sentiments may have embeddings that are nearby in the vector space inferred. This demerit will not impact NLP applications relying on semantics in the text; however, this tendency limits the application of contextual word embeddings for inferring sentiments. (L Chih Yu et al, 2018) assessed the similarity of words in the Affective Norms of English Words (ANEW) Lexicon, using pre-trained word vectors of the Wor2Vec model, and found that around 30% of words have opposite sentiment polarities among the top 10 semantically similar words. Most of the neural network language-based models produce generic word embeddings, which are arguably suitable in performing a majority of the sentiment analysis tasks. However, specific custom-optimized word embeddings are required to perform sentimental analysis tasks requiring a high degree of accuracy. In this regard (R. Lebret, J. Legrand, and R. Collobert, 2013) a frequency-based word embedding model was developed in which a word co-occurrence matrix stores the probability distribution of each word given a sequence of words. As the word co-occurrence statistics are discrete in nature, similarity between words is calculated using the Hellinger distance. The dimensionality of the word co-occurrence matrix is reduced by using the principal component analysis (PCA).

Amidst the information explosion of the present era, neural network-based models are perceived as promising in inferring deep structural information at character/word/sentence/document levels, which may be leveraged in performing NLP tasks. The recent research trend is to encode and incorporate sentiment information within the word embedding itself, instead of augmenting it as auxiliary information. Such embeddings models include the following: DCNN (Kalchbrenner, N., Grefenstette, E. & Blunsom, P., 2014), CNN with multiple kernels (Poria, S., Cambria, E. & Gelbukh, A. F., 2015), LSTM architecture along with RNN (Wang, X., Liu, Y., Sun, C., Wang, B. & Wang, X., 2015; Palangi et al., 2016), CNN architecture with two channels (Lan, M., Zhang, Z., Lu, Y. & Wu, J.., 2016), CNN with LSTM architecture (Park, C. C., Kim, Y. & Kim, G., 2018), and a handful of models that use existing frameworks to refine the word embeddings to factor-in the sentiments. (Ren, Y., Zhang, Y., Zhang, M. & Ji, D.., 2015; Labutov and Lipson, 2018; Yu, L.-C., Wang, J., Lai, K. R. & Zhang, X.., 2018).

The models proposed by (Chen, T., Xu, R., He, Y. & Wang, X., 2017), make use of divide and conquer strategy to infer word-sense and topic sense aware embeddings (Zhao, R. & Mao, K.., 2017). Fine grained differences in terms of architecture, hyper parameters, and additional fine-tuning logic have been observed among the above-mentioned models. Xingliang M. et al., 2019 proposed to embed external lexical knowledge information into word embedding models to produce hybrid word vectors, to infer sentiment aware embeddings. Abhishek K. et al., 2019 proposed a two-layer multitasking attention model, in which Bi-LSTM encoder output will be used for an emotion-aware sentiment analysis task. Emotion-aware sentiment analysis can be performed by using two attention (word attention and sentence attention) layers one each for encoding sentiment and emotion. Semantically similar words are identified using a distributional thesaurus, in the word attention layer to find a task-specific word representation. Recent studies using sentiment embeddings focus on inferring both syntactic/semantic information and sentiment information such that no two words of opposite sentiment polarity have similar vector representation. A Summary of such sentiment word embedding techniques is presented in Table2.

EMOTICON BASED WORD EMBEDDINGS

Table 2. Summary of Techniques on Sentiment Word Embeddings

S. no.	Authors	Description of Method/Model	Datasets used	Models compared with
1	R. Lebret, J. Legrand, and R. Collobert, 2013	Proposed to learn the word embeddings using principal component analysis and word co-occurrence matrix. The authors also experimented and showed that traditional word embeddings must be fine-tuned to perform a specific NLP task.	NER-Dataset (Named Entity Recognition), IMDB movie review dataset	H-PCA, E-PCA, Low Rank Multi View Learning (LR-MVL), CW, Turian, Hierarchical Log-Bilinear Model (HLBL)
2	Kalchbrenner, N., Grefenstette, E. & Blunsom, P., 2014	Developed a Dynamic Convolutional Neural Network (DCNN) model which enhances the performance of emotional semantic synthesis by learning the sentence structure.	movie reviews (Socher et al., 2013b), TREC dataset (Li and Roth, 2002)	Max-TDNN, NBoW and DCNN
3	Dos Santos, C. N. & Gatti, M., 2014	The neural model used here comprises of two layers that leverages morphological and semantic features expressed by characters and words respectively to infer sentiments.	Stanford Twitter Sentiment corpus (STS), Movie reviews (SSTb)	SCNN, CharSCNN, RNTN (Socher et al., 2013b), MV-RNN (Socher et al., 2013b), RNN (Socher et al., 2013b), NB (Socher et al., 2013b), SVM (Socher et al., 2013b)
4	Poria, S., Cambria, E. & Gelbukh, A. F., 2015	Designed a novel approach to extract features from short texts. The authors used a deep CNN to extract features from text and used multiple kernels learning (MKL) to classify heterogeneous data.	Morency et al. (2011). The dataset,	Unimodal, Unimodal3-way
5	Wang, X., Liu, Y., Sun, C., Wang, B. & Wang, X., 2015	Proposed a model composed of LSTM along with RNN architecture to capture the sentiments of twitter data. Compared DCNN and RNN-TLT (trainable lookup table) models with LSTM on the Twitter dataset. They found that DCNN and RNN-TLT outperformed other models like SVM, MNB, MAXENT, NBoW, RAE.	Twitter Sentiment corpus (STS)	Speriosu et al. (2011), Saif et al. (2012a), Lek and Poo (2013)
6	Ren, Y., Zhang, Y., Zhang, M. & Ji, D., 2016	This model uses the frameworks proposed by R. Collobert et al, 2011 and Tang et al., listed in Table.1 to learn multiple word vectors for polysemous words by leveraging the M-TSWE embeddings. Here authors generate the embeddings using local contexts, sentiment information and topic distribution of tweets.	SemEval 2013,	C&W, TSWE (Topic and Sentiment-Enriched Word Embedding), SSWE,
7	Lan, M., Zhang, Z., Lu, Y. & Wu, J., 2016	Developed a model based on convolutional neural networks consisting of two channels. These two channels are used to extract the semantic and sentiment information separately; later these two channels were combined to generate sentiment word vectors (SWV) using three different methods: mixed (SWV-M), combined (SWV-C) and hybrid (SWV-H).	SemEval2013	Sentiment Word Vectors – Hybrid (SWV-H), CBOW, LDA
8	Tang, D., Wei, F., Qin, B., Yang, N., Liu, T. & Zhou, M., 2016	Focused on a supervised learning of sentiment embeddings from tweets by considering the contextual and sentimental features of the words in the tweets. Here authors make use of the model proposed by R. Collobert et al, 2011 listed in Table 1.	SemEval, Rotten Tomatoes	Collobert and Weston (C&W), Sentiment Embedding –Prediction (SE-Pred), SE-rank, SE-HyPred, SE-HyPred-Lex, word2vec
9	Palangi et al., 2016	Proposed a deep sentence embedding method which uses the recurrent neural networks along with long short-term memory cells to store and keep track of the longer sequence of words in a sentence. For each word, features are extracted sequentially from the given sentence and are projected into semantic vectors; thereby the model captures the entire information of a particular sentence.	Query-document pairs	Long Short-Term Memory (LSTM), Recurrent Neural Network (RNN)
10	Chen, T., Xu, R., He, Y. & Wang, X., 2017	Proposed sentiment classification model for sentences, in which a divide and conquer strategy is used to divide the given sentences into different types such as positive and negative. The authors then performed the sentimental analysis separately on each sentence type to improve the performance of the classification model.	Stanford sentiment Treebank (SST), customer review dataset	CNN, Recursive Neural Tensor Network (RNTN), Dynamic Convolutional Neural Network (DCNN), NBSVM,
11	Zhao, R. & Mao, K., 2017	Designed a word sense model composed of two parts: general sense and topic sense. General sense of the word can be learned from large corpus of the data. Topic sense can be learned from task specific corpus. Finding single word vector for a particular word in different context does not provide the accurate information. Topic sense polysemous word embeddings consider different representations in different contexts for expressing multiple meanings in different contexts. Hence the proposed model focuses on semantic composition of words rather than a comprehension of the words.	Google News dataset, Movie Review Dataset, Subjectivity Dataset, Customer review dataset, Question classification dataset	Naïve Bayes SVM (NBSVM), Multinomial Naïve Bayes (MNB), CNN-variants, Recurrent Neural Networks, Long Short-Term Memory (LSTM), Gated Recurrent Unit (GRU), AdaSent

continued on following page

Table 2. Continued

S. no.	Authors	Description of Method/Model	Datasets used	Models compared with
12	Park, C. C., Kim, Y. & Kim, G., 2018	Proposed a model named Coherence Recurrent Convolutional Network (CRCN) which uses the convolution neural network along with the Bi-LSTM technique to know the description for photo stream. Bi-directional LSTM used to model stream of the images in both backward and forward direction, so that the model captures the previous and next sentence information, to maintain the flow of text content between sentences.	Unstructured blog posts (both posts and images)	CNN+LSTM, CNN+RNN, Modality biased &Factored 3-way Log Bi-Linear model (MLBL-F & MLBL-B) Log Bi-Linear Model (LBL), GloMatch, 1NN, Dynamic Time Wrapping (DTW) +1NN, Recursive Cortical Network (RCN) +BRNN, Coherent Recurrent Convolutional Networks (CRCN) +Bi-directional Recurrent Neural Network (BRNN), CRCN+BRNN+L2 (Regularization), CRCN+BRNN +ReLU, CRCN+Bi-directional LSTM (BLSTM)+L2, CRCN+BLSTM+ReLU+L2
13	Maas, A. L., Daly, R. E., Pham, P. T., Huang, D., Ng, A. Y. & Potts, C., *2018*	This model is learnt using a semi-supervised approach to infer sentiment using a hand-crafted labeled corpora with the help of predictor functions and also learned semantic information from an unlabeled data with help of probabilistic document model.	IMDB, Pang and Lee Movie Review Dataset	Bag of Words, Latent Dirichlet Allocation (LDA), Support Vector Machine (SVM)
14	Labutov and Lipson, 2018	Introduced quick method to adjust/ improve the existing semantic word vectors by using a model which was learnt using movie review corpora by optimizing the predictive accuracy of the model with respect to polarities of the sentiments expressed in the review dataset.	IMDB, Pang and Lee Movie Review Dataset	Hierarchical log-bilinear model (HLBL), C&B, LSA (Latent semantic analysis)
15	Yu, L. C., Wang, J., Lai, K. R. & Zhang, X., 2018	Proposed a word vector refinement model which refines the word vectors in such a way that sentimentally similar words must be close to each other where sentimentally dissimilar words must be away from each other in the vector space. E-ANEW lexicon was used to rank the words which are nearer to the target word with a lower value and the words which have an opposite sentiment polarity with a higher value. For each nearest neighbor, an intensity score difference is calculated with respect to the target word and a rank is assigned based on the intensity score difference. Further, reciprocal rank of the words will be used as a weight parameter in the objective function to calculate the minimized distance between the target and its top-k nearest neighbors.	SemEval2013, Sentiment Tree Bank	Word2Vec, GloVe, HyRank, M-TSWE, SWV-H
16	Xingliang Mao et al., 2019	The authors felt that learning distributed word vector representation developed from the corpus is not enough to learn high quality word representations, to enhance the performance of word embedding models, it is proposed to use external emotional information can be embedded into word embedding models to do emotional analysis effectively.	Natural Language Processing and Chinese Computing (NLPCC) dataset, Weibo DataSet	Experimented on three models SVM, Decision Tree and Gradient boost classification models by providing semantic vectors developed through Word2Vec and hybrid vectors generated using author proposed model. Proposed model has given best performance compared to existing word embedding models.
17	Abhishek Kumar et al, 2019	Introduced two attention-layers neural network architecture to do sentiment analysis through emotional analysis. Proposed model includes Bi-LSTM and external knowledge to build meaningful word representations. Here distributional thesaurus as external resource.	SemEval2016	Significant results obtained on SemEval2016 Task 6

Although several research works have been carried out on the micro blog posts, still it is a non-trivial challenge to extract contextual information to analyze the sentiment of post(s). Most of the existing sentiment analysis research works treated emoticons as noisy statements or redundant indicators of similar sentiments. However, these emoticons contain clear emotional meanings, which not only can improve the emotional expression of subjective texts, but also add emotional responses to the objective texts (Yang, G., He, H. & Chen, Q., 2019). Sentiment classification performance can be improved, when emoticons are embedded in the vector space along with word embeddings. While embedding emoticons into the vector space typically only the top influential emoticons are considered. Derks, D., Bos, A. E. R. &Von Grumbkow, J. (2007) experimented to identify the role of emoticons in the internet messaging applications and discussed that the usage of emoticons to amplify verbal communication. Brand image analysis done through twitter blog posts (Jansen, B. J., Zhang, M., Sobel, K. & Chowdury, A., 2009), in which authors found that around 20% of the twits contain brand information. Around 150,000 posts were considered for this study, which can be used to find relationships among brand image popularity

Table 3. Summary of Emoticon based word embeddings

S. no.	Author(s)	Proposed model	Datasets used	Findings/Results
1	Derks, D., Bos, A. E. R. & von Grumbkow, J., 2007	Discussed the influence of social context on the usage of emoticons in the current era of internet communication.	Valence score considered for the classification of emoticons	Experimented on just 158 students to know the emoticons used by students based on the context.
2	Jansen, B. J., Zhang, M., Sobel, K. & Chowdury, A., 2009	Authors inferred the opinions of customers regarding a brand through online micro-blog postings. Summize tool is used to collect brand information tweets from twitter.	Twitter API	Developed a system to know any brand's sentiment and the system facilitated monitoring the brand value with considerable ease.
3	Andranik et al., 2010	In this article, authors discussed how online micro blog political companion tweets affect the offline political landscape. The authors used a Linguistic Inquiry and Word Count (LIWC) model to infer whether a tweet expresses positive, negative or neutral sentiments. LIWC is a software analysis tool popularly used by psychology departments to find the emotional, cognitive, structural analysis of the given texts/posts.	Twitter API	Found that tweets 'sentiment closely mimics the voter's political preference and sentiments expressed by party profiles reflect the similarity of the political partnerships.
4	Pak and Patrik, 2010	This article discussed the opinion mining and sentimental analysis on micro blog posts. The authors explained the way to crawl the corpus automatically and also developed a sentiment classification technique to classify posts into positive, negative and neutral categories using a statistical linguistic analysis on the corpus.	Twitter API dataset	Model performed well for bigrams compared to unigram and trigram of posts during sentimental classification of posts.
5	Zhao, J., Dong, L., Wu, J. & Xu, K., 2012	Developed a system named MoodLens for sentimental analysis for Chinese tweets that uses the Weibo API and a fast Naïve Bayes classifier with the help of graphical emoticons.	Weibo API	Generated sentiment labels for tweets using a Bayesian approach
6	Liu, K. L., Li, W. J. & Guo, M., 2012	Proposed a method called Emoticon Smoothed Language Model (ESLAM) by combining both handpicked labeled data and emoticon based labeled data into a single framework to design a better model for inferring sentiments. While the model was trained using manual labeled data, the emoticon based noisy labeled data was used in smoothing the model learnt.	Sanders Corpus	Outperformed the fully distant-supervised Language model.
7	Michael Sejr Schlichtkrull,, 2015	Explored emoticon-emotion associations with help of Principal Component Analysis (PCA) and K-nearest neighbor algorithms. The emoticons are mapped onto the distributional space using PCA. The intuition behind using K-nearest neighbor method is to place similar emoticons near one another in the vector space.	SentiSense Dataset	A model capable of capturing the semantics of textual emoticons, thereby providing an interpretation beyond the binary sentiment labels.
8	Jiang, F., Liu, Y., Luan, H. B., Sun, J., Zhu, X., Zhang, M. & Ma, S., 2015	The authors proposed a model to infer emotions and polarities of sentiments in micro-blog posts	NLP&CC 2013	Both supervised and unsupervised methods have been used for micro-blog sentiment analysis with the help of emoticons.
9	Xia, R., Jiang, J. & He, H.., 2017	Most of the statistical algorithms and deep neural algorithms are normally trained on independent data sets. Models which are learned through past experience may not perform well for handling new tasks. So, the authors proposed a distantly supervised lifelong learning framework to find the sentiments expressed by social media data, where size of the social media data varied for every second. To learn sentiments from such kind of data is typically a challenging task. In this approach, data was divided into different sections according to time intervals and single sentiment was inferred for each section of data.	Twitter dataset (SemEval, Chinese Weibo dataset	Outperformed the following models: Point wise Mutual Information Sentiment Orientation (PMI-SO) Lexicon, Naïve Bayes, Logistic Regression

based on company, products and services offered. Some researchers have used micro blog posts to infer the public opinion about the government policies, and political influence (Andranik et al., 2010). Similarly, few authors (Zhao, J., Dong, L., Wu, J. & Xu, K.., 2012; Liu, K. L., Li, W. J. & Guo, M., 2012) utilize emoticons for smoothening the model which is constructed based on manually labeled data. Xia, R., Jiang, J. & He, H. (2017) proposed a distantly supervised lifelong learning framework to infer sentiments from the streaming data generated through social networks. A summary of Emoticon based word embedding techniques is presented in Table 3.

EVOLUTION OF WORD EMBEDDINGS

In natural language processing, for any task to be performed on a given text, first the words of the given text must be converted into a distributed numerical representation (also called as word vectors). When the words are represented in the form of word vectors, the machine becomes capable of understanding the semantics, associations, and contexts of the words. Several seminal and significant research works were carried out on word embeddings during the last two decades.

The typical procedure followed to infer word embeddings using various models like Word2Vec is outlined below.

Step1: Collect the data from online or offline data repositories.
Step2: Preprocess the collected data.
Step3: Create word pairs (target word, context word) based on the context-window.
Step4: Train a neural network model to predict the context word for a given word.
Step5: Extract the weights from the input layer.

The extracted weights from the input layer will act as the distributed vector for a target word. We consider the following sentence:

Dasaratha is the King of the Ayodhya Kingdom

In practice, stop words like prepositions, articles, and conjunctions are removed during the preprocessing stage. After preprocessing, this sentence consists of fourwords. Now word pairs will be created based on the contextual window size. if the window size is two, then the following word pairs are inferred from the sentence: (Dasaratha, King), (King, Dasaratha), (King, Ayodhya), (Ayodhya, King), (Ayodhya, Kingdom), and (Kingdom, Ayodhya). Similarly, word pairs will be created for the entire corpus. Then a unique number is assigned for each word in the vocabulary in the lexicographic order. For instance, Ayodhya:0, Dasaratha:1, King:2 and Kingdom:3. The obtained word pairs will be used to create a one hot encoded matrix for both the target words and context words. X represents the target word's encoded matrix, Y represents the context words' matrix, and m denotes the vocabulary size and then denotes the number of word pairs.

$$X = \begin{bmatrix} 0 & 1 & 0 & 0 \\ 0 & 0 & 1 & 0 \\ 0 & 0 & 1 & 0 \\ 1 & 0 & 0 & 1 \\ 1 & 0 & 0 & 0 \\ 0 & 0 & 0 & 1 \end{bmatrix} . Y = \begin{bmatrix} 0 & 0 & 1 & 0 \\ 0 & 1 & 0 & 0 \\ 1 & 0 & 1 & 1 \\ 0 & 0 & 1 & 0 \\ 1 & 0 & 0 & 0 \\ 0 & 0 & 1 & 0 \end{bmatrix} .$$

n x m is the dimensionality of the matrices X and Y. X will be supplied as the input to the neural network model, where the model consists of three layers: input layer, hidden layer and output layer. Hidden layer of the model is used to represent the dimension of word embedding. If the hidden layer consists of four units, then each input will be connected via four weights. After completion of the training, the input weights extracted for each word will be considered as its distributed word vector. The input weights are corrected through back propagation by minimizing the error between the predicted output and context word.

Word embeddings are classified into two major categories namely, frequency-based models and prediction-based models. Examples of frequency-based methods are Latent Semantic Analysis (LSA), HAL, LR-MVL, Hellinger PCA and GloVe. Popular prediction-based word embeddings are Word2Vec, FastText, ELMO and BERT. In this section, we discuss seminal frequency-based and prediction-based word embeddings.

ONE HOT VECTOR

Many machine learning algorithms can't operate on labeled data directly like color, place, pets, animal type etc,. In general, categorical labels may be encoded as numerical values, for example consider the categorical attribute color having red, green and blue values which are represented in the following numerical form "red" as 1, "green" as 2 and "blue" as 3. This kind of representation (Figure1) (integer encoding/ label encoding) may produce a natural ordering among the values of the categorical attribute; however, the model which is trained on this data leads to poor performance or unexpected results. If we label the countries as per alphabetical order like India as '1', Nepal as '2', Srilanka as '3' and, then trained model captures the relationship among the countries with high probabilities as follows: India<Nepal<Srilanka. This is not desirable. One hot encoding was introduced to overcome the limitations of integer encoding. However, it is not suitable for categorical data with a high dimensionality, due to the quick proliferation in the size of the feature vector space. Further, such encodings are not suitable for finding associations among the words due to the sparsity exhibited by the vector space. Figure 1 illustrates such an encoding scheme.

Vector Space Model

Vector Space Model (VSM) is a representation of textual information as vectors. VSM issued in NLP for representing the words of text in a distributed vector space, to encode the semantics and infer relationships between pairs of words. This renders the computation of predictions by generalization, which

Figure 1. One hot encoding

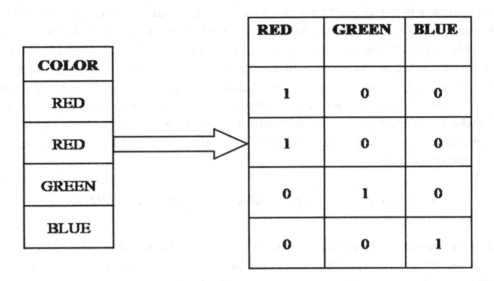

is typically done by calculating vector similarity, as a supervised classification problem. To capture the meaning of a group of words occurring together, two popular matrix designs used are the word-document matrix and window-based word-word matrix.

Word-document matrix: in this vector representation method, terms represent the rows and documents are represented as columns. Let $|V| \times D$ .be the size of the word-document matrix, where |v| represents size of the vocabulary and d denotes number of documents. We illustrate the word-document matrix with a simple example. Consider the following three statements to construct the word-document matrix:

D1: Rama married Seeta.
D2: Rama and Laxman are brothers.
D3: Laxman went to forest along with Rama and Seeta.

Table 4. Word-document matrix

Documents Terms	D1	D2	D3
Rama	1	1	1
Seeta	1	0	1
Married	1	0	0
Laxman	0	1	1
Brothers	0	1	0
Forest	0	0	1

In word-document matrix listed in Table 4, where each cell M[i,j] denotes presence of word in corresponding document or not. If given term presented in the document, then frequency of that term will be assigned to that cell and 0 used for absence of the word. Generally, term-document matrix is used to represent the relation between words and documents with a bag of words model. Entries of term-document matrix filled in two ways, one is frequency count method (mentioned in Table 4) and another one is TF-IDF. However, the matrix representations assigns a higher score for common words like "is", "are", "I", "We" etc,. Hence, to overcome this drawback of these representations, TF-IDF measure was introduced which assigns a higher score for important words and a lower score for common words. TF-IDF is a numerical static to assign weight according to usage of a particular word in a given document. TF-IDF is defined as follows:

$$TF - IDF = TermFrequency(TF) \times InverseDocumentFrequency(IDF).$$ (1)

Where, TF represents the frequency of a term in a document. Inverse Document Frequency (IDF) is computed as log $(n/(df + 1))$, where n is the number of documents and df is the number of occurrences of the term t across the documents.

Window based word-word matrix: It is also known as the co-occurrence matrix where the frequency of occurrence of a word in the vicinity of another word is measured. For example, considering a window size of 3, we measure the number of times a word appearing in the vicinity (range of i-3 to i+3) of the target word indexed at the ith position.

Table 5. Word-word window based matrix

Vocabulary	Rama	Seeta	Laxman	Brothers	Forest	...
Rama	1	1	1	0	1	
Seeta	2	0	1	0	0	
Married	2	1	0	0	0	
Laxman	1	1	1	1	1	
Brothers	0	0	2	0	1	
Forest	1	0	1	0	0	
...						

The word-word window based matrix shown in Table 5, where each cell i.e., M[i,j] indicates the frequency of occurrence of a word in a given fixed contextual window. Co-occurrence matrix does not provide the word vector representation directly; however, co-occurrence matrix can factorized by using principle component analysis (PCA) and latent semantic analysis (LSA) methods.

Latent Semantic Analysis

Latent Semantic Analysis is a bag of words method of embedding documents into a vector space. Each word of vocabulary represented with a unique axis in the vector space. Let M be a matrix composed of d documents and t terms. Every column of W represents the document vector. Latent Semantic Index-ing (LSI) takes the matrix M and transforms M through Singular Value Decomposition (SVD) into the following form UWV^T, where U and V are left, and right singular matrices and W is a diagonal matrix. W contains sorted Eigen values in the decreasing order. Left singular matrix is MM^T and right singular matrix is M^TM. The main objective of LSI is to place the given term-document into a semantic space, such that documents which are related are co-located in the semantic space (Seshadri, K. & Iyer, K. V.., 2010). The main drawback of latent semantic analysis is that it is computationally heavy and also demands a heavy memory requirement.

Word2Vec: CBOW and Skip-gram

Word2vec is a prediction-based word embedding model devised by, T., Chen, K., Corrado, G. & Dean, J.in 2013, which is considered as a seminal research for developing NLP applications. . There are mainly two novel new log linear models proposed for representing the words in continuous real values in the form of vectors, namely continuous of bag of word model (CBOW) and Skip-gram model.

Figure 2. Continuous Bag of Words Model (CBOW)

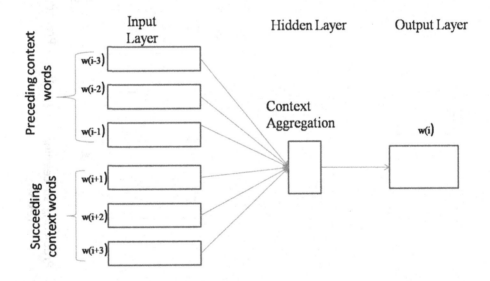

CBOW:

In the CBOW model, the mean of the word embeddings of a word's contextual words is used to train a log linear model to predict the word. As the contextual words are averaged and considered as a feature, the order in which the context words appear bears no impact on the prediction and hence the name "Bag of Words" in CBOW. Training complexity of CBOW model is given by equation (2).

$$Q = N * D + D * \lg(V) \ .$$
(2)

Skip-gram:

Skip-gram model uses a log-linear supervised model which can predict the contextual words of centralized word. It can be observed that Skip-gram model performs the opposite function as that of the CBOW model. The training complexity of skip-gram model is given equation (3).

$$Q = C * \left(D + D * \lg\left(V\right)\right).$$
(3)

Where C is the maximum distance between any pair of words, D is the dimensionality of the projection layer; V denotes the size of the vocabulary. The architecture of the skip-gram model is as shown in Figure3 (referred from Mikolov et al. 2013).

Figure 3. Architecture of the skip-gram model

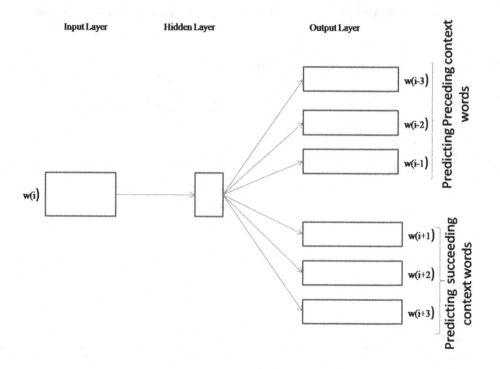

Global Vectors (GloVe)

Glove is yet another embedding technique for words proposed by Penington et al. in the year 2014. Word2Vec model predicts the words within a contextual window. It works purely on the local context of the words, whereas GloVe model leverages the advantages of both the local context window methods and global matrix factorization-based methods. Hence GloVe overcomes the demerits of the window-based embedding techniques that leverages just the local context and overlooks considering the global word concordance statistics. Penington et al. experimented on the word analogy task, in which when the number of negative samples is increased beyond ten, both the CBOW and Skip-gram models of Word-2Vec underperformed compared to the GloVe model. When the GloVe model is compared with CBOW model, the CBOW model exhibited better performance for few initial iterations; however, the GloVe model exhibited an exponentially better performance than CBOW after certain number of iterations. Similarly, GloVe model was observed to significantly outperform the Skip-gram model.

Embeddings from Language Model

Embeddings from language model (ELMo) (Peters, M et al., 2018) uses a Bi-LSTM to learn the embedding of a word by providing more importance to the context of the word. It is a layered neural model which consists of a forward pass in which the network models the relationship between a word and its successors and a backward pass in which the network learns the correlation between the word and its predecessors. The embedding for a word is generated by aggregating the internal states of the Bi-LSTM layers in a way that is sensitive to the NLP task being performed. The model generalizes well to unseen test samples, as it uses both contextual features and morphological features at the character-level. ELMo is predominantly used as a pre-trained helper model to enhance the efficiency of other models for tasks like Q&A and IR systems.

Bi-directional Encoders Representations from Transformers

Bi-directional Encoders Representations from Transformers (BERT) (Devlin, J., Chang, M.-W., Lee, K. & Toutanova, K., 2018) is an embedding technique proposed by researchers from Google that produces dynamic embeddings to address polysemous contexts of a word using encoder-decoder architecture. BERT also effectively facilitates transfer learning and can be used as a pre-trained model to enhance the accuracy of other NLP tasks. For instance, we consider the following sentences.

1. I like Cafe.
2. I like to code in Cafe.

Traditional Word2Vec model produces the same vector for word "Cafe" for both the contexts mentioned above, whereas BERT produces different distributed word vectors for word "Cafe" based on the context.

Attention Mechanism: Figure 4 depicts an encoder-decoder architecture which employs LSTM and RNNs to obtain the sentence embeddings from the last layer of the encoder unit and the sentence embedding this obtained is fed to the decoder unit which reconstructs the word embeddings of the sentence one by one. However, if the sentence is large, these results in a reconstruction error as word embeddings may not be dependent on the whole sentence. To address this problem Bahdanau, D., Cho, K. & Bengio, Y. (2015) proposed to employ the attention mechanism using which a word embedding can be made to depend on only the relevant sections of the sentence on which it is dependent.

There are two variants of BERT reported in the literature namely, BERT-Base and BERT-Large. BERT-Base consists of 12 encoding layers stacked on top of each other, whereas BERT-Large contains 24 layers of encoders.

Figure 4. Encoder-decoder architecture

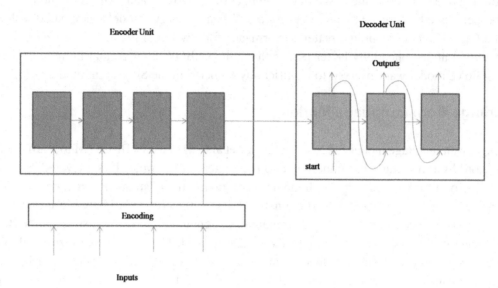

RESEARCH PROSPECTS

This survey presented the preliminaries required to comprehend the concept of word embeddings and how these embeddings can be inferred for a particular language. This chapter also presents seminal approaches to fine tune these embeddings for a specific NLP task. Researchers may adapt the techniques outlined in this survey, to develop custom embeddings for a target language. Though significant research focus has been given to word embeddings, still there are certain challenges to be addressed like handling polysemy, developing generic word embeddings for multiple NLP tasks and inferring cross lingual word embeddings from monolingual embeddings. If researchers succeed in inferring cross-lingual embeddings, then multiple NLP tasks can be efficiently performed in various regional languages.

CONCLUSION

Inferring word embeddings is an interesting and challenging task in NLP. Word embeddings play a vital role in various applications requiring natural language processing tasks like sentimental analysis, named entity recognition, synonym detection, text/document classification, word analogy, image captioning, etc,. To develop appropriate word embeddings for an NLP task, researchers attempt to leverage the syntactic, semantic, sentimental and contextual information among the words using various models. Word concordance-based methods and prediction-based methods (using different neural networks architectures) were employed by researchers in the past two decades to infer word embeddings. These models generate similar distributed vector representation for similar words; so that the resultant metric space may be used subsequently for performing NLP tasks. This chapter presented a survey on various word embedding techniques which can use syntactic structure, semantics, emoticons, sentimental and contextual information of the words to find word, phrase and sentence level sentiments. This chapter also discussed some of the seminal research advancements in word embedding techniques in a chronological order.

REFERENCES

Azzopardi, L., Girolami, M. A., & Crowe, M. K. (2005). Probabilistic hyperspace analogue to language. In R. A. Baeza-Yates, N. Ziviani, G. Marchionini, A. Moffat & J. Tait (Eds.), SIGIR (pp. 575-576). ACM. doi:10.1145/1076034.1076135

Bahdanau, D., Cho, K., & Bengio, Y. (2014). *Neural Machine Translation by Jointly Learning to Align and Translate.* arxiv:1409.0473.

Bengio, Y., Ducharme, R., Vincent, P., & Janvin, C. (2003). A Neural Probabilistic Language Model. *Journal of Machine Learning Research, 3,* 1137–1155.

Bojanowski, P., Grave, E., Joulin, A. & Mikolov, T. (2016). Enriching Word Vectors with Subword Information. *CoRR,* abs/1607.04606.

Bolukbasi, T., Chang, K.-W., Zou, J. Y., Saligrama, V., & Kalai, A. T. (2016). Man is to Computer Programmer as Woman is to Homemaker? Debiasing Word Embeddings. In D. D. Lee, M. Sugiyama, U. von Luxburg, I. Guyon & R. Garnett (Eds.), NIPS (pp. 4349-4357). Academic Press.

Chen, T., Xu, R., He, Y., & Wang, X. (2017). Improving sentiment analysis via sentence type classification using BiLSTM-CRF and CNN. *Expert Systems with Applications, 72,* 221–230. doi:10.1016/j.eswa.2016.10.065

Collobert, R., & Weston, J., Bottou, L., Karlen, M., Kavukcuoglu, K., & Kuksa, P. (2011). Natural Language Processing (Almost) from Scratch. *Journal of Machine Learning Research, 12,* 2493–2537.

Derks, D., Bos, A. E. R., & von Grumbkow, J. (2007). Emoticons and social interaction on the Internet: The importance of social context. *Computers in Human Behavior, 23*(1), 842–849. doi:10.1016/j.chb.2004.11.013

Devlin, J., Chang, M.-W., Lee, K., & Toutanova, K. (2018). *BERT: Pre-training of Deep Bidirectional Transformers for Language Understanding.* arxiv:1810.04805.

dos Santos, C. N., & Gatti, M. (2014). Deep Convolutional Neural Networks for Sentiment Analysis of Short Texts. In J. Hajic & J. Tsujii (Eds.), COLING (pp. 69-78). ACL.

Faruqui, M., Dodge, J., Jauhar, S. K., Dyer, C., Hovy, E., & Smith, N. A. (2014). Retrofitting Word Vectors to Semantic Lexicons. *Proceedings of NAACL 2015.*

Jansen, B. J., Zhang, M., Sobel, K., & Chowdury, A. (2009). Micro-blogging as online word of mouth branding. In D. R. O. Jr., R. B. Arthur, K. Hinckley, M. R. Morris, S. E. Hudson & S. Greenberg (Eds.), CHI Extended Abstracts (pp. 3859-3864). ACM. doi:10.1145/1520340.1520584

Jiang, F., Liu, Y., Luan, H.-B., Sun, J., Zhu, X., Zhang, M., & Ma, S. (2015). Microblog Sentiment Analysis with Emoticon Space Model. *J. Comput. Sci. Technol., 30*(5), 1120–1129. doi:10.100711390-015-1587-1

Kalchbrenner, N., Grefenstette, E. & Blunsom, P. (2014). A Convolutional Neural Network for Modelling Sentences. *CoRR,* abs/1404.2188.

Kiela, D., Hill, F., & Clark, S. (2015). Specializing Word Embeddings for Similarity or Relatedness. In L. Màrquez, C. Callison-Burch, J. Su, D. Pighin & Y. Marton (Eds.), EMNLP (pp. 2044-2048). The Association for Computational Linguistics. doi:10.18653/v1/D15-1242

Kim, J.-K., de Marneffe, M.-C., & Fosler-Lussier, E. (2016). Adjusting Word Embeddings with Semantic Intensity Orders. In P. Blunsom, K. Cho, S. B. Cohen, E. Grefenstette, K. M. Hermann, L. Rimell, J. Weston & S. W. Tau Yih (Eds.), Rep4NLP@ACL (pp. 62-69). Association for Computational Linguistics. doi:10.18653/v1/W16-1607

Kumar, A., Ekbal, A., Kawahara, D., & Kurohashi, S. (2019). Emotion helps Sentiment: A Multi-task Model for Sentiment and Emotion Analysis. IJCNN, 1-8.

Labutov, I., & Lipson, H. (2013). Re-embedding words. ACL, (2), 489-493.

Lan, M., Zhang, Z., Lu, Y., & Wu, J. (2016). Three Convolutional Neural Network-based models for learning Sentiment Word Vectors towards sentiment analysis. IJCNN, 3172-3179.

Lebret, Legrand, & Collobert. (2013). *Is deep learning really necessary for word embeddings?* Idiap, Tech. Rep.

Levy, O., & Goldberg, Y. (2014). Dependency-Based Word Embeddings. In *Proceedings of the 52nd Annual Meeting of the Association for Computational Linguistics (*Volume 2*: Short Papers)* (pp. 302-308). Association for Computational Linguistics.

Liu, K.-L., Li, W.-J., & Guo, M. (2012). Emoticon Smoothed Language Models for Twitter Sentiment Analysis. *AAAI Press.*

Maas, A. L., Daly, R. E., Pham, P. T., Huang, D., Ng, A. Y., & Potts, C. (2011). Learning Word Vectors for Sentiment Analysis. In *Proceedings of the 49th Annual Meeting of the Association for Computational Linguistics: Human Language Technologies* - Volume 1 (pp. 142-150). Association for Computational Linguistics.

Mao, X., Chang, S., Shi, J., Li, F., & Ronghua, S. (2019). Sentiment-Aware Word Embedding for Emotion Classification. *Applied Sciences (Basel, Switzerland), 9*(7), 1334. doi:10.3390/app9071334

Mikolov, T., Chen, K., Corrado, G., & Dean, J. (2013). *Efficient Estimation of Word Representations in Vector Space.* arxiv:1301.3781.

Mrksic, N., Séaghdha, D. Ó., Thomson, B., Gasic, M., Rojas-Barahona, L. M., Su, P.-H., Vandyke, D., Wen, T.-H., & Young, S. J. (2016). Counter-fitting Word Vectors to Linguistic Constraints. In K. Knight, A. Nenkova & O. Rambow (Eds.), HLT-NAACL (pp. 142-148). The Association for Computational Linguistics.

Pak, A., & Paroubek, P. (2010). Twitter as a Corpus for Sentiment Analysis and Opinion Mining. Academic Press.

Palangi, H., Deng, L., Shen, Y., Gao, J., He, X., Chen, J., Song, X., & Ward, R. K. (2016). Deep Sentence Embedding Using Long Short-Term Memory Networks: Analysis and Application to Information Retrieval. *IEEE/ACM Transactions on Audio, Speech, and Language Processing, 24*(4), 694–707. doi:10.1109/TASLP.2016.2520371

Park, C. C., Kim, Y., & Kim, G. (2018). Retrieval of Sentence Sequences for an Image Stream via Coherence Recurrent Convolutional Networks. *IEEE Transactions on Pattern Analysis and Machine Intelligence, 40*(4), 945–957. doi:10.1109/TPAMI.2017.2700381 PMID:28475047

Pennington, J., Socher, R., & Manning, C. D. (2014). Glove: Global Vectors for Word Representation. In EMNLP (pp. 1532-1543). Academic Press.

Peters, M. E., Neumann, M., Iyyer, M., Gardner, M., Clark, C., Lee, K., & Zettlemoyer, L. (2018). Deep contextualized word representations. *NAACL 2018*.

Poria, S., Cambria, E., & Gelbukh, A. F. (2015). Deep Convolutional Neural Network Textual Features and Multiple Kernel Learning for Utterance-level Multimodal Sentiment Analysis. In L. Màrquez, C. Callison-Burch, J. Su, D. Pighin & Y. Marton (Eds.), EMNLP (pp. 2539-2544). The Association for Computational Linguistics. doi:10.18653/v1/D15-1303

Ren, Y., Zhang, Y., Zhang, M., & Ji, D. (2016). Improving Twitter Sentiment Classification Using Topic-Enriched Multi-Prototype Word Embeddings. In D. Schuurmans & M. P. Wellman (Eds.), AAAI (pp. 3038-3044). AAAI Press.

Schlichtkrull. (2015). *Learning Affective Projections for Emoticons on Twitter*. In CogInfoCom, 6th IEEE international conference on Cognitive Info communications, Gyor, Hungary.

Seshadri, K., & Iyer, K. V. (2010). Parallelization of a dynamic SVD clustering algorithm and its application in information retrieval. *Software, Practice & Experience, 40*(10), 883–896. doi:10.1002pe.987

Tang, D., Wei, F., Qin, B., Yang, N., Liu, T., & Zhou, M. (2016). Sentiment Embeddings with Applications to Sentiment Analysis. *IEEE Transactions on Knowledge and Data Engineering, 28*(2), 496–509. doi:10.1109/TKDE.2015.2489653

Tumasjan, A., Sprenger, T. O., Sandner, P. G., & Welpe, I. M. (2010). Predicting Elections with Twitter: What 140 Characters Reveal about Political Sentiment. In W. W. Cohen & S. Gosling (Eds.), *ICWSM. The AAAI Press*.

Wang, J., Yu, L.-C., Lai, K. R., & Zhang, X. (2020). Tree-Structured Regional CNN-LSTM Model for Dimensional Sentiment Analysis. *IEEE/ACM Transactions on Audio, Speech, and Language Processing, 28*, 581–591. doi:10.1109/TASLP.2019.2959251

Wang, X., Liu, Y., Sun, C., Wang, B., & Wang, X. (2015). Predicting Polarities of Tweets by Composing Word Embeddings with Long Short-Term Memory. ACL, (1), 1343-1353.

Xia, R., Jiang, J., & He, H. (2017). Distantly Supervised Lifelong Learning for Large-Scale Social Media Sentiment Analysis. *IEEE Transactions on Affective Computing, 8*(4), 480–491. doi:10.1109/TAFFC.2017.2771234

Yang, G., He, H., & Chen, Q. (2019). Emotion-Semantic-Enhanced Neural Network. *IEEE/ACM Transactions on Audio, Speech, and Language Processing, 27*(3), 531–543. doi:10.1109/TASLP.2018.2885775

Yu, L.-C., Wang, J., Lai, K. R., & Zhang, X. (2018). Refining Word Embeddings Using Intensity Scores for Sentiment Analysis. *IEEE/ACM Transactions on Audio, Speech, and Language Processing, 26*(3), 671–681. doi:10.1109/TASLP.2017.2788182

Zhao, J., Dong, L., Wu, J., & Xu, K. (2012). MoodLens: an emoticon-based sentiment analysis system for chinese tweets. In Q. Yang, D. Agarwal & J. Pei (Eds.), KDD (pp. 1528-1531). ACM. doi:10.1145/2339530.2339772

Zhao, R., & Mao, K. (2017). Topic-Aware Deep Compositional Models for Sentence Classification. *IEEE/ACM Transactions on Audio, Speech, and Language Processing*, 25(2), 248–260. doi:10.1109/TASLP.2016.2632521

Chapter 14
Sentiment Time Series Analysis on US Economic News

Vikas Kumar
Maulana Azad National Institute of Technology, India

Sri Khetwat Saritha
Maulana Azad National Institute of Technology, India

ABSTRACT

In the internet world we will have a lot of information, public opinions, and researchers' comments on the economy of a country, but it will be very difficult to analyze these opinions. Analysis of these opinions is very important to know how the economy of a country does change and to predict the economy of the country. Sentiment analysis does analysis of public opinion in the textual form, and it provides either of positive, neutral or negative sentiments of the textual comment given on the economy. Sometimes, sentiment analysis may not develop a model for better prediction and judgement of public opinion. In this chapter, the authors proposed a method that integrates sentiment analysis with the time series. They proposed a method to create a domain-specific lexicon to calculate the sentiment of the textual opinions over the economic dataset. This chapter implements the sentiment time series model on economic news by using the lexicon-based approach based on built-in lexicons and domain-specific lexicon.

INTRODUCTION

In the world of social media, people can easily post their comments, thoughts, and their opinions regarding economic news and one can easily find a lot of opinions, suggestions, comments on the economy of a country. The economy of a country includes several areas like IT sectors, Public sector areas, educational areas, healthcare, safety areas, arms sector. All these areas involve a large scale to build a better economy of the country.

The comments, posts, and suggestions related to economic news on social media are increasing day by day and it would be very difficult to analyze the posts manually. There is a need to analyze the people's opinion towards economic news automatically i.e., finding what percentage of people are supporting

DOI: 10.4018/978-1-7998-8061-5.ch014

the current situation of the economy and what percent of people are against the current situation of the economy.

Sentiment analysis is a method that takes textual comments as input and predicts the sentiments of the textual contents as positive, negative, or neutral. But sentiment analysis may not be able to build a better model for the data that changes over time, i.e., sentiment analysis may not result in better prediction when the public opinion changes according to time and different scenarios.

In time series, the input data is ordered in the sequence of chronological at different timestamps. Time series analysis analyses the metadata of time series data and it observes, estimates, and studies the statistical regularity of the data in the long period of the change process. Building a sentiment model with time series can result in better predictions of sentiment development over time.

In this paper, a sentiment time series model aggregates the calculated sentiment of public opinions into time series is proposed. The proposed model results in better sentiment predictions on the data that sentiments change over time series. A built-in lexicon to calculate the sentiment of the textual opinions of the economic dataset is being used. The built-in lexicon consists of a collection of words related to all areas that have sentiment polarity i.e., the lexicon is built in consideration of generalized concepts. Using the built-in lexicon, the system takes more time to calculate the sentiment. So, to reduce the time complexity of the system, a domain-specific lexicon is built and words in the lexicon have a sentiment polarity in the range [-1,1]

BACKGROUND

A lot of information and public opinions related to any specific topic are available on social media. To achieve better results of sentiment models, there is a need to research sentiment analysis. In recent years, public opinions are changing over time. Let's look into the example of the stock market, people post their suggestions or comments based on stock prices that change over time. Research on sentiment analysis along with time series data is a hot topic to research. It is important to build an application on sentiment time-series data that grasp public opinion and development.

The sentiments expressed by football fans over the time on Twitter while watching the game were analyzed by (Samah & Abdulmotaleb, 2018). They created a domain-specific lexicon to analyze the sentiments by applying various machine learning algorithms and their results showed that domain-specific sentiment classifiers are effective in analyzing the fans' sentiment during the match.

A forecast model to predict the price of stocks in the share market based on investors' sentiment was built by (Rui Ren & Desheng Dash Wu, 2018). The authors collected the investors' comments over the internet. They applied Support Vector Machine algorithms to calculate the sentiment and forecasted the stock price range. The resultant model would help the investors to decide to invest in the stock market.

Sentiment time series method to analyze the sentiment of the online text collected from a Chinese microblog platform called Sina Weibo was proposed by (Lei Li et al, 2019). They implemented an effective time and user dual attention mechanism to analyze and judge the information of the public opinions on real-time series data.

To calculate US EPU (Economic Policy Uncertainty) index, a lexicon-based approach was proposed by (David et al, 2020). They collected US economic news from various US magazines and newspapers, later they built a model which calculated the EPU index based on the sentiment of public opinion based on economic news.

A framework for sentiment engineering was introduced to design a model for forecasting purposes (David et. Al, 2019). In this, they used elastic net regularization to select the sparse data-driven and calculated the sentiment values from the textual information to forecast the economic growth of the US.

From the above literature, a better analysis of public opinion and judgment is very important to build a robust application. As public opinion changes over time, one should consider their sentiments that change over time and situation. Hence, research on sentiment analysis with time series data is important to build a model that results in better sentiment predictions. In this paper, a model which predicts the gross domestic product (GDP) of the US, based on the US economic news data set is proposed. The model is implemented by using the lexicon-based approach on bi-gram language models. It determines how the gross domestic product (GDP) of the U.S country does change over different (time) periods by predicting the GDP of the U.S country over the collected public opinions from different social networking sites like Twitter.

PROPOSED METHOD & APPROACH

Following are the steps which are used for an experimental system

Create a corpus of texts with quantifiable features
Create an economic-based lexicon and use it to calculate textual sentiment
Aggregate the computed sentiment scores based on document level into time series
An estimate prediction model based on sentiment scores
Evaluate performance and accuracy of the created model

The above steps of the workflow are followed to implement the sentiment time series on the U.S. economic news performance dataset. Figure 1, shows the flow design for computing the sentiments.

Figure 1. Flow Design for Computing the Sentiments

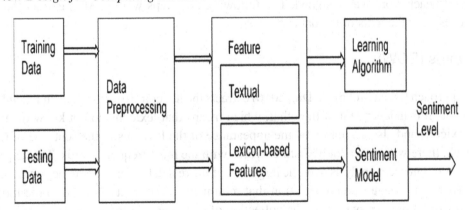

Unprocessed Data and Data Preprocessing

In the proposed model, texts were collected from the newspaper, magazine of the US country along with the date, relevance of the economy, and many other attributes. Collected data can have URL, HTML tags, web-related elements to remove all web-related elements preprocessing was performed on the collected textual data by applying regular expression on the text. All unnecessary attributes which do not make any meaningful existence with other important attributes in the dataset were removed. The text in the processed dataset contains a set of text in sorted order with the timestamp. The dataset contains 2135 documents with 624 positive documents, 284 negative documents, and 1227 neutral documents. Attributes of the processed dataset are id, date, texts, economy, and non-economy.

Feature Extraction

Features are very significant in analyzing the sentiments of the texts. Extracting good features from the dataset to achieve the better accuracy of the model. One should always have prior knowledge and information about the features of the dataset to create a better model. Feature extraction can be achieved by applying the POS (Part of Speech) tagging, a bag of words (BOW) approach, and n-gram approach. In this paper, feature extraction was achieved by applying the regular expressions on texts in the dataset. The economy and non-economy features were extracted by considering the relevant attribute of the dataset. Every document is associated with the binary features through binary or numerical values $w_{n,t}^k$ ϵ [0,1]. Here the binary features are represented by k = 1, ..., K. economy, non-economy, and other extracted features are binary features. Binary features represent which documents of the processed dataset belong to which feature of the dataset.

Economic-Specific Lexicon

An economic-specific lexicon is created to calculate the sentiment of the document-based texts of the US economic news dataset. To create a domain-specific lexicon, a word list from the dataset was extracted and polarity to each word was assigned. The following two steps were used to extract the sentiment/polarity words from the texts of the dataset.

Bag of Words (BOW)

The BOW approach (Doaa Mohey El-Din, 2016) extracts the lexicons from the texts independently. Each extracted lexicon is independent of the other, which means that lexicons do not know the positions of the other lexicons and also do not know the appearance of the lexicons in the sentence of the texts. In this approach, there will have a lot of distinct words with the most frequent words. This approach takes more time to do sentiment analysis over the large size of the real data. Term frequency-inverse document frequency (tf-idf) is a feature representation that minimizes the weight assigned to the most frequent words (stop words) that are present in the collection of documents. Term frequency (tf) is the number of occurrences of the term in the document. Inverse document frequency (idf) is the logarithmic inverse fraction of the documents in which the term presents in the documents. idf can be defined as,

$$idf\left(t\right) = log\left(\frac{|d|}{df\left(t\right)}\right)$$

|d| refers to number of documents in the processed dataset. df(t) refers to the number of documents containing the term t. idf(t) is the inverse document frequency of the term t.

The tf-idf is calculated as the product of the term frequency (tf) and inverse document frequency (idf) of the term. It is expressed as,

$$tf - idf\left(t\right) = tf\left(t\right) * log\left(\frac{|d|}{df\left(t\right)}\right)$$

tf(t) is the term frequency of the term t. tf-idf increases the weight of the rarely appeared words and it reduces the weight of the stop words. Based on the tf-idf we can append the term in the list of the lexicons to be used in the sentiment analysis.

POS (Part of Speech)

The process of tagging part of the speech (such as noun, adjective, verb, adverb, and so on) of a word in a sentence is known as POS (part of speech) tagging. In the proposed model, POS tagging is used to extract the words from the sentence of the document. Following are steps used to append the sentimental words in the lexicon list:

Step 1: Numbers are removed from the text as the numbers does not contain sentiment polarity
Step 2: Symbols, special characters are removed from the texts
Step 3: Tokenize the texts into sentences and apply POS tagging to the tokenized words of the sentence.
Step 4: Extract adjective words from the tagger and append them into the list of lexicons
Step 5: Convert words from the list of lexicons into lowercase
Step 6: Remove duplicates from the list of lexicons
Step 7: Remove stop words from the list of lexicons

By performing the above steps, a list of lexicons useful for the sentiment analysis is built. Later sentiment score of each lexicon is calculated with the list containing the economy dataset.

Domain-Specific Sentiment Calculation

The sentiment score of each lexicon from the list of lexicons is calculated. In the list of lexicons, each lexicon will be in lowercase and will be distinct. The Sentiment Score of each word can be calculated as,

$$Score\left(w_i\right) = \left(posCount\left(w_i\right) - negCount\left(w_i\right)\right) * idf\left(w_i\right)$$

Sentiment score of word w_i is the subtraction of its positive score by its negative score and then multiplied by its inverse document frequency idf (w_i). posCount (w_i) can be calculated as,

$$posCount(w_i) = \frac{freq(w_i, posDocs)}{N(posDocs)}$$

$freq(w_i, posDocs)$ is the number of occurrences of the word w$_i$ in the positive documents of the corpus. N(posDocs) is the number of positive documents that can have the word wi.
negCount(wi) can be calculated as,

$$negCount(w_i) = \frac{freq(w_i, negDocs)}{N(negDocs)}$$

idf(wi) is the inverse document frequency of the term wi. It can be computed as,

$$idf(w_i) = log\left(\frac{n}{df(w_i)}\right)$$

$df(w_i)$ refers to the number of available documents in which the word wi appears. Here, n refers to the total number of available documents of both positive documents and negative documents.
So that, each word in the list of lexicons will be assigned with sentiment polarity in the range [-1, 1]. Negative polarity shows the negative sentiment, positive polarity shows the positive sentiment and zero shows the neutral sentiment. In this domain-specific lexicon, each word will have sentiment polarity between -1 to 1 in decimal representation. This domain-specific lexicon is different from built-in lexicon as the sentiment value of lexicons in built-in lexicons is either -1 or 1.

SENTIMENT COMPUTATION AND AGGREGATION

Following built-in lexicons is used to calculate the sentiment of the document from the corpus of the economic dataset. The sentiment polarity of the document is calculated using the lexicon-based approach on the built-in lexicons.

Loughran McDonald (Loughran and McDonald 2011)
Henry (Henry 2008)

The built-in lexicon contains a list of words with sentiment polarity, the +1 value refers to the positive sentiment of the word and the -1 value refers to the negative sentiment of the word. The lexicon contains two columns named x and y. x column consists of the distinct sentiment words and y column contains the sentiment polarity of the corresponding words.
The sentiment of the document using a lexicon-based approach on the domain-specific lexicon is calculated. To analyze the sentiments, each document is assigned some sentiment values. A document consists of one or more than one sentence. To calculate the sentiment of the document, the documents are

decomposed into sentences. The Sum of the sentiment of sentences inside the document is the sentiment of the document. There are three ways of lexicon-based approaches for calculating the sentiments. They are

Uni-gram Approach

It is a simple method where the sentiment can be computed as a weighted sum of the score of all the terms that appear in the lexicon and it does not care about the order, position, and context of words appearing in the sentences. It contains only a bag of words without any metadata.

Bi-gram Approach

In the bi-gram approach, the word which appears before the detected/found word is evaluated. For example, consider the evaluation of the word "not" in "not good". In the proposed sentiment time series analysis model, a bi-gram approach to compute the sentiment value/score is used. This approach considers the positioning of the words appearing in the sentences and also includes the context of the words in the sentences. By applying this approach the proposed model will get better results compared to the uni-gram approach.

Cluster Approach

The calculation of sentiment of the document is also done based on the cluster approach. Figure 2, shows the general framework of computing sentiment of the textual information.

Figure 2. General Framework to Compute the Sentiment Analysis

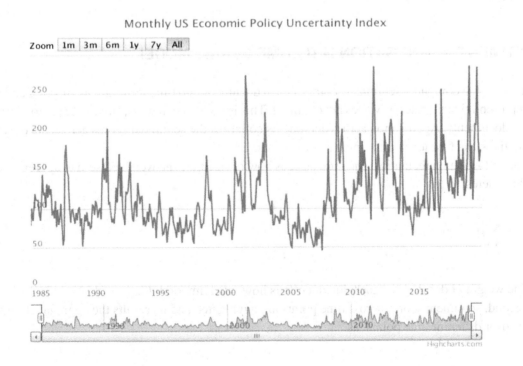

Sentiment Calculation

A bi-gram approach to calculate the sentiment of the document is applied. The sentiment score of each document $d_{n,t}$ can be calculated as the sum of the adjusted sentiment values/scores of all its uni-grams. The adjustment defines a method to apply the weights to every word based on the position of the word in the document and to adjust for the presence of the valence-shifting words. The sentiment is calculated by using the following formula

$$s_{n,t}^{\{l\}} \cong \sum_{i=1}^{Q_d} w_i v_i s_{i,n,t}^{\{l\}}$$

For each lexicon $l = 1, \ldots., L$. Q_d refers to the total number of uni-grams in the document. The score $s_{n,t}^{\{l\}}$ is the calculated sentiment score of the unigram i from document $d_{n,t}$ based on lexicon l. When the term is not present in the lexicon then $s_{n,t}^{\{l\}}$ becomes zero. A valence shifter v_i is used to shift the value of the preceding uni-gram i-1. The weights w_i defines the aggregation of computed sentiment scores within a document. The values vi and wi are specific to each document $d\_(n,t)$.

The obtained scores are then multiplied by the feature weights. By doing so, the sentiment values into lexicon-specific and feature-specific sentiment are found. It can define as,

$$s_{n,t}^{\{l,k\}} \cong s_{n,t}^{\{l\}} w_{n,t}^k$$

where k is the index to denote the feature. Whether the document does not belong to the feature, then the value of $s_{n,t}^{\{l,k\}}$ becomes zero.

SENTIMENT AGGREGATION INTO TIME SERIES MODEL

In this step, the computed sentiment scores of each document into time series are aggregated and different representative time series values are obtained. This is done in two ways, first, aggregation is applied across documents. Aggregation across documents collapses the sentiment scores across the documents within the same frequency into single sentiment scores.

The following mathematical equation defines how to calculate the weighted sum to aggregate across the documents.

$$s_t^{\{l,k\}} \cong \sum_{n=1}^{N_t} \theta_n s_{n,t}^{\{l,k\}}$$

The weight θ defines that each document n is how much important at time t.

Second, sentiment scores across time points are aggregated and its results the aggregated sentiment scores over different time points, as

$$s_u^{\{l,k,b\}} \cong \sum_{t=t_\tau}^{u} b_t \, s_t^{\{l,k\}}$$

Here $t_\tau \cong u - \tau + 1$. The different schemes of the time weighting b = 1, . . ., B work with the different values for b_t to make the time series to be smooth in different ways with a time lag of τ. The number of calculated time series is equal to the product of the number of lexicons, the number of used features, and the number of used different schemes of the time weighting. The group of time series values contains both the same information in various ways (various aggregation schemes, same features, and different lexicons) and the different features.

MODEL

After calculating sentiment with time series, it results in the sentiment in the time series variable equation. The reference equation will be fit in the regression equation. The regression equation can be expressed as linear regression.

$$y_{u+h} = \delta + \gamma^T x_u + \beta_1 s_u^1 + \ldots + \beta_p s_u^p + \ldots + \beta_p s_u^p + \epsilon_{u+h}$$

y_{u+h} is the target variable in the linear regression and h > 0. Let $s_u \cong \left(s_u^1, \ldots, s_u^p \right)^T$ encapsulate all calculated textual sentiment variables and $\beta \cong (\beta_1, \ldots, \beta_p)^T . x_u$ is another variable at time u and γ is the associated parameter vector.

The above linear regression equation contains the high dimension of the number of predictors relative to potential multicollinearity, and the number of observations. Both high dimension and multicollinearity create a problem to ordinary least squares (OLS) regression.

Elastic Net Regression over the LASSO and Ridge regressions to penalize the regression using the elastic net regularization used. Ridge regression penalizes the summation of the square of the regression coefficient and it adds this penalty to the least square term to have low variance. The Least Absolute Shrinkage and Selection Operator (LASSO) also penalizes the absolute size of the regression coefficients.

Regularization reduces the coefficient of the least important variables towards zero. It optimizes the ordinary least squares, or it optimizes likelihood functions that include a penalty component. The elastic net regression equation can be expressed as,

$$min_{\delta, \gamma, \beta} \left\{ \frac{1}{N} \sum_{u=\tau}^{T} \left(y_{u+h} - \delta - \gamma^T x_u - \beta^T s_u \right)^2 + \lambda \left[\pm \| \beta \|_1 + (1 - \pm) \| \beta \|_2^2 \right] \right\}$$

The tilde denotes standardized variables, and ||.||p is the Lp- norm. The re-scaled estimates of the coefficients of the model for the sentiment scores are in β. The β is usually a sparse vector that depends on the severity of the shrinkage.

The variable or parameter $0 <= \alpha <= 1$ explains the value of elastic net regularization over the Ridge and LASSO regularization. If $\alpha = 0$ then it behaves as Ridge regularization and if $\alpha = 1$ then it behaves as LASSO regularization.

If the parameter $\lambda >= 0$ then it defines the which level of regularization. if $\lambda = 0$, then the problem reduces to OLS (ordinary least square) estimation. The both two parameters α and λ are very important to drive this penalized regression.

RESULTS AND DISCUSSION

Dataset Description

The US economic performance news dataset to experiment with the sentiment time series model using either or both built-in lexicons and economic-specific lexicons are used. The US economic performance news dataset contains the news article headlines, and a short, bolded excerpt of the sentences from the US magazines, newspapers, and the attendant articles. It also contains the US economic indicator to indicate the U.S. economy's health as it decides whether the sentence belongs to the economic news or not. If the sentence comes under the economy then it indicates the U.S. economy's health, and then it indicates in a range of 1-9 on a scale, with 1 refers to negative, and 9 refers to positive. This dataset contains 5015 numbers of documents, each document may contain multiple sentences. It has multiple attributes as date, relevance, economy indication, article id, texts, and many attributes.

Execute the Prediction Model

The U.S. EPU index (Baker, S.R. et. al, 2016) as the actual target value of the gross domestic product of the US economy is used. The U.S. EPU index is used to execute the created prediction model for the US economy news performance dataset. Below Figure 3 shows the US EPU index value over time.

Figure 3. U.S. EPU Index Vs Time Plot

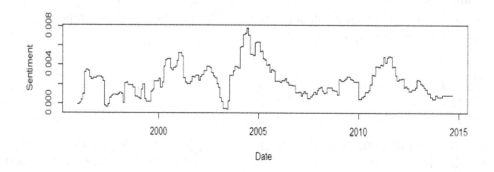

Sentiment Measure vs Time Based on Built-in lexicon

The sentiment prediction model is executed based on the built-in lexicons and the domain-specific lexicon using the lexicon approach and it is found that the predicted output is very close to the EPU index value. Figure 4, shows the graph of positive sentiment measures over time series from 1985 to 2015 on the US economic news dataset.

Figure 4. Positive Sentiment Measure Vs Time Based on Built-in Lexicon

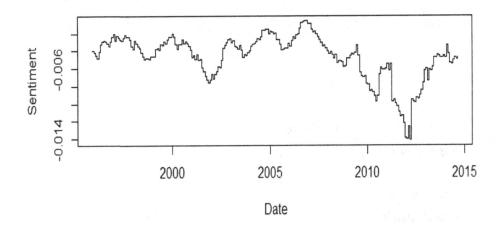

Figure 5, shows the negative sentiment measures over time series from 1985 to 2015 on the U.S. economic news dataset.

Sentiment Measure vs Time Based on Domain-Specific Lexicon

The sentiment time series model based on the domain-specific lexicon is executed. A graph of sentiment measures over time series from 1985 to 2010 on the U.S. economic news dataset is shown in Figures 6 (a) and 6 (b). The graph shows how the economy changes over the period from 1985 to 2010. The sentiments measures were calculated on different combinations of features, time series, and aggregation schemas.

EVALUATION METRICS

There are many ways to calculate the accuracy and measure the performance of the prediction model. It discusses below as,

Figure 5. Negative Sentiment Measure Vs Time Based on Built-in Lexicon

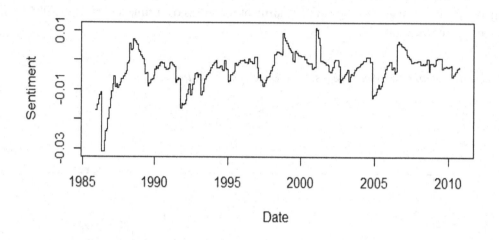

$$Accuracy = \frac{number\ of\ correct\ predictions}{total\ number\ of\ predictions}$$

$$Precision = \frac{true\ positive}{actual\ results}$$

Figure 6. Plot of sentiment measure vs time

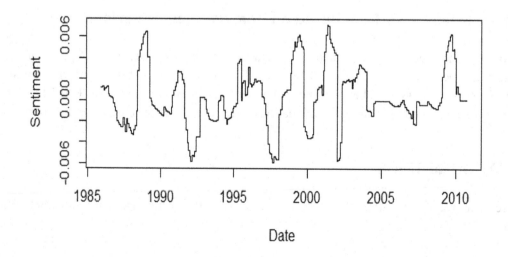

$$Recall = \frac{true\ positive}{predicted\ results}$$

$$F_1 = 2 * \frac{precision * recall}{precision + recall}$$

Apart from the above measures, root mean square error (rmse) and root mean square log error for the sentiment prediction is also calculated

Evaluation of Prediction Model Based On Built-In Lexicon

A sentiment prediction model for time series textual data based on built-in lexicons using the lexicon-based approach is created. On executing the prediction model, the root mean square error (rmse) is calculated, and then the root mean square log error (rmsle) for the different created model is calculated.

The rmse value of the Gaussian model on the Bayesian information criterion (BIC) is 33.79661 and rmsle value is 0.2956669. For Akaike Information Criterion (AIC) Gaussian model, rmse value is 33.54866 and rmsle value is 0.2932552. For Cp gaussian model, rmse value is 33.53415 and rmsle value is 0.2927885. For cv linear regression model (gaussian model), rmse value is 33.7857 and rmsle value is 0.2968078.

On executing the binomial logistic model the rmse value obtained is 2.199024. And later execute the multinomial logistic model and the accuracy of the model is calculated. rmse value obtained for this model is 2.389503 and rmsle value is 1.060157.

The binomial logistic regression model gives better accuracy with the least rmse value 2.199024 and better results among the other regression models for the US economic news dataset to forecast the gross domestic product of the US country.

Evaluation of Prediction Model Based On Domain-Specific Lexicon

The sentiment prediction model based on domain (economic) specific lexicon for the time series data is implemented. After creating the model, the model to find the accuracy of the model is executed. The root mean square error (rmse) and rmsle for the different created model is calculated.

The rmse value for the Gaussian model on the Bayesian information criterion (BIC) is 36.32198 and root mean square log error (rmsle) is 0.3213786. For Akaike Information Criterion (AIC) linear regression model (gaussian model), rmse value is 35.15316 and rmsle value is 0.3079765. For Cp linear regression model, rmse value is 35.3224 and rmsle value is 0.3098074. For cv linear regression model (gaussian model), rmse value is 36.40833 and rmsle value is 0.3222552.

The cross-validation (cv) technique to test the model for the binomial logistic regression model is used, it results in the rmse value as 2.535962. The cross-validation (cv) technique for the multinomial logistic regression model and its root mean square error (rmse) value is 1.045809 and the rmsle value is 0.5921674.

The multinomial logistic regression model gives better accuracy and better predictions among the other regression models for the US economic news performance dataset to forecast the gross domestic product (GDP) of the US country.

Finding the Best Model

There is a model confidence set package in R that finds the best model to get better results from the model. (Hansen et al., 2011) present the paper on the model confidence set package in which the author develops the model confidence set procedure to construct the set of best models. This procedure will consist of a sequence of tests on each different model and then check the null hypothesis of the equal predictive ability (EPA). The model would be selected for the list of superior models if the null hypothesis of equal predictive ability is not rejected at a certain confidence level. And if the null hypothesis of EPS is rejected then the model would be treated as the worst model for the specific dataset. Equal predictive ability can be calculated for the loss function of the model.

In the proposed model, a set of superior models among the several different models using the model confidence set procedure is considered. The MCS package in Rstudio using the R programming language is utilized. Different models of gaussian, logistic binomial, and logistic multinomial were created and tested different groups of models. Let look into the following experiment. Different models of linear regression (gaussian regression) were created and the MCS procedure is executed to find the set of superior models. It results in the following output.

Output 1. Result of executing different model on linear regression

```
###############################
Superior Set Model created :
Rank_M v_M MCS_M Rank_R v_R MCS_R Loss
m1 2 -1.0337838 1.0000 1 -0.2298879 1.0000 1037.515
m2 4 1.6206751 0.1744 4 1.9182971 0.1816 1189.690
m3 3 0.6440312 0.7430 3 0.9185994 0.7546 1130.541
m4 1 -1.0803901 1.0000 2 0.2298879 0.9948 1051.246
p-value :
[1] 0.1744
###############################
```

The above output only shows the set of superior models that satisfy the null hypothesis of equal predictive ability. During the execution of MCS procedure, it removes the worst model that doesn't satisfy the null hypothesis of EPA.

CONCLUSION

In this paper, a sentiment time series to forecast the gross domestic product of the US country based on the sentiment indices of the US economic news performance dataset is proposed. Built-in lexicons to implement the sentiment time series prediction model based on the lexicon approach are used. It was found that the logistic binomial regression model gives the best result or accuracy among the different regression models.

Also implemented the same model by using the domain-specific lexicon. In that approach, firstly economic-based lexicon was created and used this lexicon to calculate the textual sentiment of the economic dataset. By doing so, it reduces the time complexity of the system to compute the textual sentiment. It was found that multinomial logistic regression models give better accuracy and performance among different regression models for the economic news dataset. In this paper, an implementation of sentiment time series by using the lexicon-based approach on the domain-specific lexicons is shown.

Using the built-in lexicon to implement the prediction model, the binomial model gives the best accuracy. And using the domain-specific lexicon, the multinomial model gives the best accuracy among the different models.

FUTURE SCOPE

Researchers can analyze the emotions of people when they post their own opinions during the economic changes over the time points. Researchers can also work on semantic features and contextual features for increasing the sentiment prediction model performance.

REFERENCES

Aloufi, S., & Saddik, A. E. (2018). Sentiment Identification in Football-Specific Tweets. *IEEE Access: Practical Innovations, Open Solutions, 6*, 78609–78621. doi:10.1109/ACCESS.2018.2885117

Ardia, D., Bluteau, K., Borms, S., & Boudt K. (2018). *Scientometrics: An integrated framework for textual sentiment time series aggregation and prediction. version 0.4.* Academic Press.

Ardia, D., Bluteau, K., Borms, S., & Boudt, K. (2020). *The R Package sentometrics to Compute.* Aggregate and Predict with Textual Sentiment.

Ardia, D., Bluteau, K., & Boudt, K. (2019). Questioning the News about Economic Growth: Sparse Forecasting Using Thousands of News-Based Sentiment Values. *International Journal of Forecasting, 35*(4), 1370–1386. doi:10.1016/j.ijforecast.2018.10.010

Arnold, T. (2017). A Tidy Data Model for Natural Language Processing Using cleanNLP. *The R Journal, 9*(2), 1–20. doi:10.32614/RJ-2017-035

Baker, S. R., Bloom, N., & Davis, S. J. (2016). Measuring economic policy uncertainty. *The Quarterly Journal of Economics, 131*(4), 1593–1636. doi:10.1093/qje/qjw024

Benoit, K., Watanabe, K., Wang, H., Nulty, P., Obeng, A., Muller, S., & Matsuo, A. (2018). quanteda: An R Package for the Quantitative Analysis of Textual Data. *Journal of Open Source Software, 3*(30), 774. doi:10.21105/joss.00774

Bernardi, M., & Catania, L. (2014). *The Model Confidence Set package for R.* Academic Press.

Dowle, M., & Srinivasan, A. (2019). *data.table: Extension of 'data.frame'.* R Package Version 1.12.8.

Feinerer, I., Hornik, K., & Meyer, D. (2008). Text Mining Infrastructure in R. *Journal of Statistical Software, 22*(5), 1–54.

Feuerriegel, S., & Pr̈ollochs, N. (2019). *SentimentAnalysis: Dictionary–Based Sentiment Analysis.* R Package Version 1.3.3.

Gagolewski, M. (2020). *stringi: Character String Processing Facilities*. R Package Version 1.4.5.

Hansen, P. R., Lunde, A., & Nason, J. M. (2011). The model confidence set. *Econometrica, 79*(2), 453–497. doi:10.3982/ECTA5771

Henry. (2008). Are investors influenced by how earnings press releases are written? *Journal of Business Communication, 45*, 363-407.

Hoerl, A. E., & Kennard, R. W. (1970). Ridge regression: Biased estimation for nonorthogonal problems. *Technometrics, 12*(1), 55–67. doi:10.1080/00401706.1970.10488634

Li, L., Wu, Y., Zhang, Y., & Zhao, T. (2019). Time+User Dual Attention Based Sentiment Prediction for Multiple Social Network Texts With Time Series. *IEEE Access: Practical Innovations, Open Solutions, 7*, 17644–17653. doi:10.1109/ACCESS.2019.2895897

Loughran, T., & McDonald, B. (2011). When is a liability not a liability? Textual analysis, dictionaries, and 10-Ks. *The Journal of Finance, 66*(1), 35–65. doi:10.1111/j.1540-6261.2010.01625.x

Ren, R., Wu, D. D., & Liu, T. (2019). Forecasting Stock Market Movement Direction Using Sentiment Analysis and Support Vector Machine. *IEEE Systems Journal, 13*(1), 760–770. doi:10.1109/JSYST.2018.2794462

Taboada, M., Brooke, J., Tofiloski, M., Voll, K., & Stede, M. (2011). Lexicon-Based Methods for Sentiment Analysis. *Computational Linguistics, 37*(2), 267–307. doi:10.1162/COLI_a_00049

Tibshirani, R. (1996). Regression Shrinkage and Selection via the LASSO. *Journal of the Royal Statistical Society. Series B. Methodological, 58*(1), 267–288. doi:10.1111/j.2517-6161.1996.tb02080.x

Wang, X., Mccallum, A., & Wei, X. (2007). Topical N-Grams: Phrase and Topic Discovery, with an Application to Information Retrieval. *Proceedings - IEEE International Conference on Data Mining, ICDM*, 697-702. 10.1109/ICDM.2007.86

Zou, H., & Hastie, T. (2005). Regularization and variable selection via the elastic net. *Journal of the Royal Statistical Society. Series B. Methodological, 67*(2), 301–320. doi:10.1111/j.1467-9868.2005.00503.x

Compilation of References

Import.io. (2019). *Web Data Extraction Basics – The Difference Between Surface Web, Deep Web and Dark Web*. https://www.import.io/post/the-difference-between-surface-web-deep-web-and-dark-web/

YaunE. (n.d.). Retrieved from: https://eric-yuan.me/rnn1/

LearningD. (n.d.). Retrieved from: https://deeplearning4j.org/lstm

Tweak Library Team. (2020). *What Is The Difference Between Dark Web, Deep Web and Surface Web?* https://tweak-library.com/what-is-the-difference-between-dark-web-deep-web-and-surface-web/

The size of the World Wide Web (The Internet). (2021). https://www.worldwidewebsize.com/

Hermann, K. M., Kocisky, T., Grefenstette, E., Espeholt, L., Kay, W., Suley-man, M., & Blunsom, P. (2015). Teaching machines to read and comprehend. In *Advances in Neural Information Processing System*. NIPS.

Khelghati, M., Hiemstra, D., & Keulen, M. V. (2013). Deep web entity monitoring. *Proc. 22nd Int. Conf. World Wide Web Companion*, 377–382.

Boughammoura, R., & Omri, M. N. (2017). Querying deep web data bases without accessing to data. *2017 13th International Conference on Natural Computation, Fuzzy Systems and Knowledge Discovery (ICNC-FSKD)*, 597-603. 10.1109/FSKD.2017.8393338

Krizhevsky, Sutskever, & Salakhutdinov. (n.d.). *Dropout: A simple way to prevent neural networks from overfitting*. Academic Press.

Bergman, M. K. (2001). The Deep Web: Surfacing hidden value. *The Journal of Electronic Publishing*, 7(1). Advance online publication. doi:10.3998/3336451.0007.104

Tan, M., Santos, C. D., Xiang, B., & Zhou, B. W. (2015). LSTM-based deep learning models for non-factoid answer selection. arXiv preprint arXiv:1511.04108.

Lewandowski, D. (2005). Web searching, search engines, and information retrieval. *Information Services & Use*, 25(3-4), 137–147. doi:10.3233/ISU-2005-253-402

Finklea, K. (2015). *Dark Web*. Accessed March 28, 2021. https://www.fas.org/sgp/crs/misc/R44101. pdf

Tor vs. VPN: What They Do and which is Better. (n.d.). Accessed March 28, 2021. https://www.pandasecurity.com/en/mediacenter/privacy/tor-vs-vpn/

Lewandowski, D., & Mayr, P. (2006). Exploring the academic invisible web. *Library Hi Tech*, 24(4), 529–539. doi:10.1108/07378830610715392

Johnson, J. (2021). *Worldwide digital population as of January 2021*. Statista. www.statista.com/statistics/617136/digital-population-worldwide/

SemEval-2015 Task 3: Answer Selection in Community Question Answering. (n.d.). Retrieved from: https://alt.qcri.org/semeval2015/task3

Bhatia, Chaudhary, & Dey. (2020). *Opinion Mining in Information Retrieval*. Springer Brief.

Bhatia, S. (2020). A Comparative Study of Opinion Summarization Techniques. *IEEE Transactions on Social Computational Systems*, *18*(November), 1–8. doi:10.1109/TCSS.2020.3033810

Król, K. (2019). Geoinformation in the Invisible Resources of the Internet. *Geomatics, Landmanagement and Landscape*, *3*, 53–66. doi:10.15576/GLL/2019.3.53

He, B., Patel, M., Zhang, Z., & Chang, K. C. C. (2007). Accessing the deep web: A survey. *Communications of the ACM*, *50*(5), 94–101. doi:10.1145/1230819.1241670

Raghavan, S., & Garcia-Molina, H. (2001). Crawling the Hidden Web. *Proceedings of the 27th International Conference on Very Large Data Bases*, 129–138.

Tran, Tran, Vu, Nguyen, & Pham. (2015). *JAIST: Combining multiple features for Answer Selection in Community Question Answering*. . doi:10.18653/v1/S15-2038

Anuradha & Juneja. (2015). Dynamic Query Processing for Hidden Web Data Extraction. *2015 2nd International Conference on Computing for Sustainable Global Development (INDIACom)*, 1352-1356.

Hou, Tan, Wang, Zhang, Xu, & Chen. (2015). *HITSZ-ICRC: Exploiting Classification Approach for Answer Selection in Community Question Answering*. . doi:10.18653/v1/S15-2035

Ferrara, Fiumara, & Baumgartner. (2010). *Web Data Extraction, Applications and Techniques: A Survey*. Tech. Report.

Nicosia, Filice, No, Saleh, Mubarak, Gao, Nakov, Martino, Moschitti, Darwish, Màrquez, Joty, & Magdy. (2015). *QCRI: Answer Selection for Community Question Answering – Experiments for Arabic and English*. . doi:10.18653/v1/S15-2036

Xiaoqiang, Hu, Lin, Xiang, & Wang. (2015). *ICRC-HIT: A Deep Learning based Comment Sequence Labeling System for Answer Selection Challenge*. . doi:10.18653/v1/S15-2037

Yang, T., & Gerasoulis, A. (2014). Web Search Engines: Practice and Experience. In Computing Handbook (3rd ed.). Chapman & Hall/CRC Press.

Castillo, C. (2005). Effective web crawling. *ACM SIGIR Forum, 39*(1), 55-56. 10.1145/1067268.1067287

Fan, H., Ma, Z., Li, H., Wang, D., & Liu, J. (2019). Enhanced answer selection in CQA using multi-dimensional features combination. *Tsinghua Science and Technology*, *24*(3), 346–359. doi:10.26599/TST.2018.9010050

Mikolov, T., Sutskever, I., Chen, K., Corrado, G. S., & Dean, J. (2013). *Distributed rep- resentations of words and phrases and their compositionality*. Advances in Neural Information Processing Systems. NIPS.

Sharma & Sharma. (2010). Deep Web Information Retrieval Process: A Technical Survey. *International Journal of Information Technology & Web Engineering, 5*(1), 1-22.

Akilandeswari, J., & Gopalan, N. P. (2008). An Architectural Framework of a Crawler for Locating Deep Web Repositories Using Learning Multi-Agent Systems. *Proceedings of the 2008 Third International Conference on Internet & Web Applications and Services*, 558-562. 10.1109/ICIW.2008.94

Feng, M., Xiang, B., Glass, M., Wang, L., & Zhou, B. (2015). Applying deep learning to answer selection: A study and an open task. *IEEE Automatic Speech Recognition and Understanding Workshop (ASRU)*. 10.1109/ASRU.2015.7404872

Bastien, F., Lamblin, P., Pascanu, R., Bergstra, J., Goodfellow, I. J., Bergeron, A., Bouchard, N., & Bengio, Y. (2012). Theano: new features and speed improvements. *Deep Learning and Unsupervised Feature Learning NIPS 2012 Workshop*.

Sharma & Sharma. (2011). Search Engine: A Backbone for Information Extraction in ICT Scenario. *International Journal of ICTHD, 3*(2), 38-51.

Abdullah, M. F., & Ahmad, K. (2013). The mapping process of unstructured data to structured data. In *International Conference on Research and Innovation in Information Systems (ICRIIS)*. IEEE. 10.1109/ICRIIS.2013.6716700

Adams, B., & Mckenzie, G. (2018). Crowdsourcing the character of a place: Character-level convolutional networks for multilingual geographic text classification. *Trans. GIS, 22*(2), 394–408. HTTPS://DOI.ORG/10.1111/TGIS.12317

Adelani, D. I., Mai, H., Fang, F., Nguyen, H. H., Yamagishi, J., & Echizen, I. (2020). Generating Sentiment-Preserving Fake Online Reviews Using Neural Language Models and Their Human- and Machine-Based Detection. In L. Barolli, F. Amato, F. Moscato, T. Enokido, & M. Takizawa (Eds.), *Advanced Information Networking and Applications. AINA 2020. Advances in Intelligent Systems and Computing* (Vol. 1151, pp. 1341–1354). Springer. doi:10.1007/978-3-030-44041-1_114

Agarwal, A., Xie, B., Vovsha, I., Rambow, O., & Passonneau, R. J. (2011). Sentiment analysis of Twitter data. In *Proceedings of the Workshop on Language in Social Media (LSM 2011)* (pp. 30-38). Academic Press.

Agbonifo, O. C., & Akinsete, M. (2020). Development of an Ontology-Based Personalised E-Learning Recommender System *International Journal of Computer, 38*(1), 102–112.

Aggarwal, D. (2009). Role of e-Learning in a developing country like India. *Proceedings of the 3rd national conference; INDIACom-2009 computing for nation development*.

Ahlers, D. (2006). News consumption and the new electronic media. *The Harvard International Journal of Press/Politics, 11*(1), 29–52. doi:10.1177/1081180X05284317

Ahmad, I., Yousaf, M., Yousaf, S., & Ahmad, M. O. (2020). Fake News Detection Using Machine Learning Ensemble Methods. *Complexity, 2020*, 2020. doi:10.1155/2020/8885861

Ahmed, H., Traore, I., & Saad, S. (2017, October). Detection of online fake news using N-gram analysis and machine learning techniques. In *International Conference on Intelligent, Secure, and Dependable Systems in Distributed and Cloud Environments* (pp. 127-138). Springer.

Ahmed, M. E., Rabin, M. R. I., & Chowdhury, F. N. (2020). *COVID-19: Social Media Sentiment Analysis on Reopening*. ArXiv.

Akamai (2017). *The state of online retail performance*. https://www.soasta.com/wp-content/uploads/2017/04/Stateof-Online-Retail-Performance-Spring-2017.pdf

Alami, N., Meknassi, M., & En-nahnahi, N. (2019). Enhancing unsupervised neural networks based text summarization with word embedding and ensemble learning. *Expert Systems with Applications, 123*, 195–211. doi:10.1016/j.eswa.2019.01.037

Alamoodi, A. H., Zaidan, B. B., Zaidan, A. A., Albahri, O. S., Mohammed, K. I., Malik, R. Q., ... Alaa, M. (2020). Sentiment analysis and its applications in fighting COVID-19 and infectious diseases: A systematic review. *Expert Systems with Applications, 114155*. Advance online publication. doi:10.1016/j.eswa.2020.114155 PMID:33139966

Alexa. (2018a). *Alexa: Keyword research, competitive analysis, & website ranking.* http://www.alexa.com

Alexa. (2018b). *Top Sites in Tanzania.* https://www.alexa.com/topsites/countries/TZ

Alguliyev, R. M., Aliguliyev, R. M., Isazade, N. R., Abdi, A., & Idris, N. (2019). COSUM: Text summarization based on clustering and optimization. *Expert Systems: International Journal of Knowledge Engineering and Neural Networks, 36*(1), 1–17. doi:10.1111/exsy.12340

Ali Ahmed, G. H., & Kovacs, L. (2020). Ontology Domain Model for E-Tutoring System. *Journal of Software Engineering & Intelligent Systems, 5*(1).

Almana, A., & Mirza, A. A. (2013). The Impact of Electronic Word of Mouth on Consumers' Purchasing Decisions. *International Journal of Computers and Applications, 82*(9), 23–31. doi:10.5120/14145-2286

Alonazi, M., Beloff, N., & White, M. (2020). Perceptions towards the adoption and utilization of m-government services: A study from the citizens' perspective in Saudi Arabia. In E. Ziemba (Ed.), *Information Technology for Management: Current Research and Future Directions* (pp. 3–26). Springer. doi:10.1007/978-3-030-43353-6_1

Aloufi, S., & Saddik, A. E. (2018). Sentiment Identification in Football-Specific Tweets. *IEEE Access: Practical Innovations, Open Solutions, 6*, 78609–78621. doi:10.1109/ACCESS.2018.2885117

Alqurashi, E. (2017). Micro Learning: A Pedogogical Approach for technology integration. *The Turkish Online Journal of Educational Technology*, 942–947.

Al-Sakran, H., & Almutairi, M. (2021). Usability and accessibility assessment of Saudi Arabia mobile e-Government websites. *IEEE Access: Practical Innovations, Open Solutions, 9*, 48254–48275. doi:10.1109/ACCESS.2021.3068917

Alshahwan, N., & Harman, M. (2012). State aware test case regeneration for improving web application test suite coverage and fault detection. *Proceedings of the 2012 International Symposium on Software Testing and Analysis*, 45-55. 10.1145/2338965.2336759

Altemeier, W. A. (1997). Just tell me what I need to know. *Pediatric Annals, 26*(2), 74–76. doi:10.3928/0090-4481-19970201-03 PMID:9121844

Alvaro, N., Conway, M., Doan, S., Lofi, C., Overington, J., & Collier, N. (2015). Crowdsourcing Twitter annotations to identify first-hand experiences of prescription drug use. *Journal of Biomedical Informatics, 58*, 280–287. doi:10.1016/j.jbi.2015.11.004 PMID:26556646

Al-Zaman, M. S. (2020). COVID-19-related fake news in social media. MedRxiv, 1–12. doi:10.1101/2020.07.06.20147066

Alzanin, S. M., & Azmi, A. M. (2019). Rumor detection in Arabic tweets using semi-supervised and unsupervised expectation–maximization. *Knowledge-Based Systems, 185*, 104945.

Alzate, M., Arce-Uriza, M., & Cebollada, J. (2021). Online Reviews and Product Sales: The Role of Review Visibility. *Journal of Theoretical and Applied Electronic Commerce Research, 16*(4), 638–669. doi:10.3390/jtaer16040038

Amasha, M. A., Areed, M. F., Alkhalaf, S., Abougalala, R. A., Elatawy, S. M., & Khairy, D. (2020). The future of Internet of Things (IoTs) and Context-Aware Technology in E-Learning. *ICEIT 2020: Proceedings of the 2020 9th International Conference on Educational and Information Technology*, 114-123.

Amin, S., Uddin, M. I., Zeb, M. A., Alarood, A. A., Mahmoud, M., & Alkinani, M. H. (2020). Detecting Dengue/Flu Infections Based on Tweets Using LSTM and Word Embedding. *IEEE Access: Practical Innovations, Open Solutions, 8*, 189054–189068. doi:10.1109/ACCESS.2020.3031174

Anderson, P. (2007). What is Web 2.0? Ideas, technologies and implications for education. *Technology & Standards Watch*, 2-56.

Anderson, W. E. (1998). Customer Satisfaction and Word of Mouth. *Journal of Service Research*, *1*(1), 5–17. doi:10.1177/109467059800100102

Andrews, G., Cuijpers, P., Craske, M. G., Mcevoy, P., & Titov, N. (2010). Computer Therapy for the Anxiety and Depressive Disorders Is Effective, Acceptable and Practical Health Care : A Meta-Analysis. *PLoS One*, *5*(10), e13196. Advance online publication. doi:10.1371/journal.pone.0013196 PMID:20967242

Annareddy, S., & Tammina, S. (2019, December). A Comparative Study of Deep Learning Methods for Spam Detection. In *2019 Third International conference on I-SMAC (IoT in Social, Mobile, Analytics and Cloud)(I-SMAC)* (pp. 66-72). IEEE. 10.1109/I-SMAC47947.2019.9032627

Annie, C.S., Choy, J.Y, Krishna, M., & Alex, L. (2017). Intention to use m-Government services: Does age, gender and education matter? *International Journal of e-business and e-Government Studies*, *9*(2).

Anusudha, R. S., Krishnendu, R., & Krishnan, P. (2021). Education at the crossroads: Digitalization of Education in India During an Age of Pandemic. *Psychology and Education Journal, 58*(3). Doi:10.17762/pae.v58i3.3878

Apoki, U. C. (2020). A Model of a weighed Agent System for Personalised E-Learning Curriculum. In Communications in Computer and Information Science (Vol. 1126). Springer.

Ardia, D., Bluteau, K., Borms, S., & Boudt K. (2018). *Scientometrics: An integrated framework for textual sentiment time series aggregation and prediction. version 0.4.* Academic Press.

Ardia, D., Bluteau, K., Borms, S., & Boudt, K. (2020). *The R Package sentometrics to Compute.* Aggregate and Predict with Textual Sentiment.

Ardia, D., Bluteau, K., & Boudt, K. (2019). Questioning the News about Economic Growth: Sparse Forecasting Using Thousands of News-Based Sentiment Values. *International Journal of Forecasting*, *35*(4), 1370–1386. doi:10.1016/j.ijforecast.2018.10.010

Arnold, T. (2017). A Tidy Data Model for Natural Language Processing Using cleanNLP. *The R Journal*, *9*(2), 1–20. doi:10.32614/RJ-2017-035

Arnquist, M. D. (2020). *The Role of the Technical Communicator in the Corporate eLearning Industry.* Retrieved from the University of Minnesota Digital Conservancy, https://hdl.handle.net/11299/213219

Arshey, M., & KS, A. V. (2020). An optimization-based deep belief network for the detection of phishing e-mails. *Data Technologies and Applications*.

Arslan, Y., Küçük, D., & Birtürk, A. (2018). Twitter sentiment analysis experiments using word embeddings on datasets of various scales. In *International Conference on Applications of Natural Language to Information Systems* (pp. 40-47). 10.1007/978-3-319-91947-8_4

Arsovic, B., & Stefanovic, N. (2020). E-learning based on the adaptive learning model: Case study in Serbia. *Sadhana*, *45*, 266. https://doi.org/10.1007/s12046-020-01499-8

Aslam, N., Ullah Khan, I., Alotaibi, F. S., Aldaej, L. A., & Aldubaikil, A. K. (2021). Fake Detect: A Deep Learning Ensemble Model for Fake News Detection. *Complexity*.

Astono, A. D. (2021). The Effect of Reputation and Competence on Costumer Loyalty Through Costumer Trust. *International Journal of Global Accounting, Management, Education, and Entrepreneurship*, *1*(2), 90–99.

Aubert, B. A., & Hamel, G. (2001). Adoption of smart cards in the medical sector: The Canadian experience. *Social Science & Medicine*, *53*(7), 879–894. doi:10.1016/S0277-9536(00)00388-9 PMID:11522135

Axelsson, K., & Melin, U. (2012). Citizens' Attitudes towards Electronic Identification in a Public E-Service Context – An Essential Perspective in the eID Development Process. In *Pro JavaScript Performance: Monitoring and Visualization*. Apress. doi:10.1007/978-3-642-33489-4_22

Azzi, I. (2020). Approach Based on Artificial Neural Network to Improve Personalisation in Adaptive E-Learning System. In Advances in Intelligent Systems and Computing (Vol. 1076). Springer.

Azzopardi, L., Girolami, M. A., & Crowe, M. K. (2005). Probabilistic hyperspace analogue to language. In R. A. Baeza-Yates, N. Ziviani, G. Marchionini, A. Moffat & J. Tait (Eds.), SIGIR (pp. 575-576). ACM. doi:10.1145/1076034.1076135

Bagui, S., Nandi, D., Bagui, S., & White, R. J. (2019, June). Classifying phishing email using machine learning and deep learning. In *2019 International Conference on Cyber Security and Protection of Digital Services (Cyber Security)* (pp. 1-2). IEEE. 10.1109/CyberSecPODS.2019.8885143

Bahdanau, D., Cho, K., & Bengio, Y. (2014). *Neural Machine Translation by Jointly Learning to Align and Translate.* arxiv:1409.0473.

Baker, Q. B., Shatnawi, F., Rawashdeh, S., Al-Smadi, M., & Jararweh, Y. (2020). Detecting epidemic diseases using sentiment analysis of arabic tweets. *Journal of Universal Computer Science*, *26*(1), 50–70.

Baker, S. R., Bloom, N., & Davis, S. J. (2016). Measuring economic policy uncertainty. *The Quarterly Journal of Economics*, *131*(4), 1593–1636. doi:10.1093/qje/qjw024

Balahur, A., Turchi, M., Steinberger, R., Ortega, J. M. P., Jacquet, G., Küçük, D., Zavarella, V., & El Ghali, A. (2014). Resource creation and evaluation for multilingual sentiment analysis in social media texts. In *Proceedings of the Language Resources and Evaluation Conference (LREC)* (pp. 4265-4269). Academic Press.

Balmer, J., & Greyser, S. (2006). Integrate corporate identity, corporate branding, corporate communications, corporate image and corporate reputation. *European Journal of Marketing*, *40*(7/8), 730–741. doi:10.1108/03090560610669964

Balodis, K., & Deksne, D. (2019). FastText-based intent detection for inflected languages. *Information (Basel)*, *10*(5), 161. doi:10.3390/info10050161

Banane, M., & Belangour, A. (2020). Towards a New Scalable Big Data System Semantic Web Applied on Mobile Learning. *International Journal of Interactive Mobile Technologies.*, *14*(1), 126–140. https://doi.org/10.3991/ijim.v14i01.10922

BandaJ. M.TekumallaR.WangG.YuJ.LiuT.DingY.ChowellG. (2020). A large-scale COVID-19 twitter chatter dataset for open scientific research - An international collaboration. *ArXiv*. doi:10.5281/zenodo.3766929

Bang, Y., Ishii, E., Cahyawijaya, S., Ji, Z., & Fung, P. (2021). *Model Generalization on COVID-19 Fake News Detection.* arXiv preprint arXiv:2101.03841.

Baralis, E., Cagliero, L., Mahoto, N., & Fiori, A. (2013). GraphSum: Discovering correlations among multiple terms for graph-based summarization. *Information Sciences*, *249*, 96–109. doi:10.1016/j.ins.2013.06.046

Bariso, E. U. (2010). Personalised elearning in further education. *Technology-Supported Environments for Personalised Learning: Methods and Case Studies*, 109-127.

Basheer, S., Bhatia, S., & Sakri, S. B. (2021). Computational Modeling of Dementia Prediction Using Deep Neural Network: Analysis on OASIS Dataset. *IEEE Access: Practical Innovations, Open Solutions*, *9*, 42449–42462. doi:10.1109/ACCESS.2021.3066213

Basiri, M. E., Abdar, M., Cifci, M. A., Nemati, S., & Acharya, U. R. (2020). A novel method for sentiment classification of drug reviews using fusion of deep and machine learning techniques. *Knowledge-Based Systems*, *198*, 105949. doi:10.1016/j.knosys.2020.105949

Bengio, Y., Ducharme, R., Vincent, P., & Janvin, C. (2003). A Neural Probabilistic Language Model. *Journal of Machine Learning Research*, *3*, 1137–1155.

Bennani, S., Maalel, A., & Ghezala, H. B. (2020). AGE-Learn: Ontology-Based Representation of personalized Gamification in E-Learning. *Procedia Computer Science*, *176*, 1005–1014.

Benoit, K., Watanabe, K., Wang, H., Nulty, P., Obeng, A., Muller, S., & Matsuo, A. (2018). quanteda: An R Package for the Quantitative Analysis of Textual Data. *Journal of Open Source Software*, *3*(30), 774. doi:10.21105/joss.00774

Bernardi, M., & Catania, L. (2014). *The Model Confidence Set package for R.* Academic Press.

Berry, M., & Linoff, G. (2004). *Data Mining Techniques. For Marketing, Sales and Costumer Relationship Management*. Wiley Publishing.

Bhagat, S., & Joshi, P. (2019). Evaluation of accessibility and accessibility audit methods for e-Governance Portals. *ICEGOV2019: Proceedings of the 12th International Conference on Theory and Practice of Electronic Governance*, 220–226. 10.1145/3326365.3326394

Bigne, E., Ruiz, C., & Sanz, S. (2005). The Impact of Internet User Shopping Patterns and Demographics on Consumer Mobile Buying Behavior. *Journal of Electronic Commerce Research*, *6*(3), 193–209.

Blattberg, R. C., & Briesch, R. A. (2012). Sales Promotion. In Ö. Özer & R. Phillips (Eds.), *The Oxford Handbook of Pricing Management* (pp. 585–619). Oxford University Press.

Blended. (2020). *Washable Cotton Face Mask Reusable Made in the USA*. https://www.walmart.com/ip/Washable-Cotton-Face-Mask-Reusable-Made-in-the-USA/625326064

Bojanowski, P., Grave, E., Joulin, A. & Mikolov, T. (2016). Enriching Word Vectors with Subword Information. *CoRR*, abs/1607.04606.

Boje, D. (2018). *Organizational Research: Storytelling in Action*. Routledge. doi:10.4324/9781315205854

Bolukbasi, T., Chang, K.-W., Zou, J. Y., Saligrama, V., & Kalai, A. T. (2016). Man is to Computer Programmer as Woman is to Homemaker? Debiasing Word Embeddings. In D. D. Lee, M. Sugiyama, U. von Luxburg, I. Guyon & R. Garnett (Eds.), NIPS (pp. 4349-4357). Academic Press.

Bordoloi, R., Das, P., & Das, K. (2020). Lifelong learning opportunities through MOOCs in India. *Asian Association of Open Universities Journal, 15*(1), 83-95. doi:10.1108/aaouj-09-2019-0042

Boytchev, P., & Boytcheva, S. (2020). Gamified Evaluation in Game-Based Learning. In A. Lopata, R. Butkienė, D. Gudonienė, & V. Sukackė (Eds.), Information and Software Technologies. ICIST 2020. Communications in Computer and Information Science (Vol. 1283). Springer. https://doi.org/10.1007/978-3-030-59506-7_24.

Brenes, D. J., Gayo-Avello, D., & Pérez-González, K. (2009). Survey and evaluation of query intent detection methods. In *Proceedings of the 2009 Workshop on Web Search Click Data* (pp. 1-7). 10.1145/1507509.1507510

Briciu, V.-A., & Briciu, A. (2019). Web 1.0 and Web 2.0 Variations of Identity Characteristics of Official Place Brands Websites. In A.-D. Bibiri, C. Grădinaru, E. Grosu, A. Mironescu, R. Patraș (Eds.), Exploring the Digital Turn (pp. 307-324). "Alexandru Ioan Cuza" University of Iași Publishing House.

Briciu, V.-A., & Briciu, A. (2020b). COVID-19 Influence and Future Perspectives of Artificial Intelligence on the Labour Market. *BRAIN. Broad Research in Artificial Intelligence and Neuroscience, 11*(2Sup1), 21-28.

Briciu, V.-A., & Briciu, A. (2021). Social Media and Organizational Communication. In M. Khosrow-Pour (Ed.), Encyclopedia of Organizational Knowledge, Administration, and Technology (pp. 2609-2624). IGI Global. doi:10.4018/978-1-7998-3473-1.ch180

Briciu, V.-A., Briciu, A., & Găitan, Ş-M. (2020). Impression Management through Websites: An Analysis of the Romanian Banking Industry. In *Strategic Innovative Marketing and Tourism. Springer Proceedings in Business and Economics* (pp. 417-424). Springer.

Briciu, A., & Briciu, V.-A. (2020). Participatory Culture and Tourist Experience: Promoting Destinations through YouTube. In A. Kavoura, E. Kefallonitis, & P. Theodoridis (Eds.), *Strategic Innovative Marketing and Tourism. Springer Proceedings in Business and Economics* (pp. 425–433). Springer. doi:10.1007/978-3-030-36126-6_47

Briciu, A., & Briciu, V.-A. (2020a). Designing the Virtual Product Experience: Learnings from Shenzhen, China and the ESUN Solutions. In A. Kavoura, E. Kefallonitis, & P. Theodoridis (Eds.), *Strategic Innovative Marketing and Tourism. Springer Proceedings in Business and Economics* (pp. 435–442). Springer. doi:10.1007/978-3-030-36126-6_48

Briciu, A., Briciu, V.-A., & Pilipinschi, A.-M. (2017). A Website Brand Analysis of Romanian Companies from Automotive Industry. *Bulletin of the Transilvania University of Brasov, 10*(59), 133–142.

Briciu, V.-A., Mircea, I., & Briciu, A. (2020). Communication and Entrepreneurship in Romania: Dissimulation of First Impression in 30 Seconds. In A. Masouras, G. Maris, & A. Kavoura (Eds.), *Entrepreneurial Development and Innovation in Family Businesses and SMEs* (pp. 22–38). IGI Global. doi:10.4018/978-1-7998-3648-3.ch002

Briciu, V.-A., Rezeanu, C.-I., & Briciu, A. (2020). Online Place Branding: Is Geography 'Destiny' in a 'Space of Flows' World? *Sustainability, 12*(10), 4073. doi:10.3390u12104073

Brookfield, S. D. (2009). Self-Directed Learning. In R. Maclean & D. Wilson (Eds.), *International Handbook of Education for the Changing World of Work*. Springer.

Brooks, L., & Persaud, A. (2015). Comparing local e-government websites in Canada and the UK. In Lecture Notes in Computer Science: Vol. 9248. *Electronic Government. EGOV 2015*. Springer. doi:10.1007/978-3-319-22479-4_22

Buil, I., de Chernatony, L., & Martinez, E. (2011). Examining the role of advertising and sales promotion in brand equity creation. *Journal of Business Research, 66*(1), 115–122. doi:10.1016/j.jbusres.2011.07.030

Burton, R. M. (2018). Hawthorne effect, the. In M. Augier & D. J. Teece (Eds.), *The Palgrave Encyclopedia of Strategic Management*. Palgrave Macmillan. doi:10.1057/978-1-137-00772-8_316

Cagliero, L., Garza, P., & Baralis, E. (2019). ELSA: A multilingual document summarization algorithm based on frequent itemsets and latent semantic analysis. *ACM Transactions on Information Systems, 37*(2), 1–33. doi:10.1145/3298987

Cai X., Li S., Feng G. (2020). Evaluating the performance of government websites: An automatic assessment system based on the TFN-AHP methodology. *Journal of Information Science, 46*(6), 760-775.

Calin, R. A. (2018). Virtual Reality, Augmented Reality and mixed Reality- trends in pedagogy. *Social Sciences and Education Research Review., 5*(1), 169–179.

Cardoso, E. F., Silva, R. M., & Almeida, T. A. (2018). Towards automatic filtering of fake reviews. *Neurocomputing, 309*, 106–116. doi:10.1016/j.neucom.2018.04.074

Carlbring, P., Andersson, G., Cuijpers, P., Riper, H., & Hedman-Lagerlöf, E. (2018). Internet-based vs. face-to-face cognitive behavior therapy for psychiatric and somatic disorders : An updated systematic review and meta-analysis. *Cognitive Behaviour Therapy*, *6073*(1), 1–21. doi:10.1080/16506073.2017.1401115 PMID:29215315

Carmeli, A., & Tishler, A. (2005). Perceived Organizational Reputation and Organizational Performance: An Empirical Investigation of Industrial Enterprises. *Corporate Reputation Review*, *8*(1), 13–30. doi:10.1057/palgrave.crr.1540236

Cascella, M., Rajnik, M., Cuomo, A., Dulebohn, S. C., & Di Napoli, R. (2021). Features, Evaluation, and Treatment of Coronavirus (COVID-19). StatPearls Publishing.

Casillas, A., Pérez, A., Oronoz, M., Gojenola, K., & Santiso, S. (2016). Learning to extract adverse drug reaction events from electronic health records in Spanish. *Expert Systems with Applications*, *61*, 235–245. doi:10.1016/j.eswa.2016.05.034

CDT, & infoDev. (2007). *E-Government Handbook: Accessibility*. Retrieved June 19, 2007, from https://www.cdt.org/egov/handbook/accessibility.shtml

Chakraborty, K., Bhatia, S., Bhattacharyya, S., Platos, J., Bag, R., & Hassanien, A. E. (2020). Sentiment Analysis of COVID-19 tweets by Deep Learning Classifiers—A study to show how popularity is affecting accuracy in social media. *Applied Soft Computing*, *97*, 106754. doi:10.1016/j.asoc.2020.106754 PMID:33013254

Chalmeta, R. (2005). Methodology for costumer relationship mangement. *Journal of Systems and Software*, *79*(7), 1015–1024. doi:10.1016/j.jss.2005.10.018

Chamorro, Miranda, Rodrigo, & González. (2001). A new web assessment Index: Spanish universities analysis. *Internet Research*, *11*(3), 226-234.

Chee, C. H., Jaafar, J., Aziz, I. A., Hasan, M. H., & Yeoh, W. (2019). Algorithms for frequent itemset mining: A literature review. *Artificial Intelligence Review*, *52*(4), 2603–2621. doi:10.100710462-018-9629-z

Chelcea, S. (2004). *Metodologia cercetării sociologice. Metode cantitative şi calitative* [Sociological research methodology. Quantitative and qualitative methods] (2nd ed.). Economic Publishing House.

Chen, E. T. (2008). Successful E-Learning in Corporations. Communications of the IIMA, 8(2).

Chen, G., Ye, D., Cambria, E., Chen, J., & Xing, Z. (2017). *Ensemble Application of Convolutional and Recurrent Neural Networks for Multi-Label Text Categorization*. Academic Press.

Cheng, Q., Li, T. M., Kwok, C. L., Zhu, T., & Yip, P. S. (2017). Assessing suicide risk and emotional distress in Chinese social media: A text mining and machine learning study. *Journal of Medical Internet Research*, *19*(7), 1–10. doi:10.2196/jmir.7276 PMID:28694239

Chen, H., Yin, C., Li, R., Rong, W., Xiong, Z., & David, B. (2020). Enhanced learning resource recommendation based on online learning style model. *Tsinghua Science and Technology*, *25*(3), 348–356.

Chen, L., Li, W., Chen, H., & Geng, S. (2019). Detection of Fake Reviews: Analysis of Sellers Manipulation Behavior. *Sustainability*, *11*(4802), 1–13. doi:10.3390u11174802

Chen, T., Xu, R., He, Y., & Wang, X. (2017). Improving sentiment analysis via sentence type classification using BiLSTM-CRF and CNN. *Expert Systems with Applications*, *72*, 221–230. doi:10.1016/j.eswa.2016.10.065

Chen, Y., Fay, S., & Wang, Q. (2011). The Role of Marketing in Social Media: How Online Consumers Reviews Evolve. *Journal of Interactive Marketing*, *25*(2), 85–94. doi:10.1016/j.intmar.2011.01.003

Chetty, G., Bui, H., & White, M. (2019, December). Deep learning based spam detection system. In *2019 International Conference on Machine Learning and Data Engineering (iCMLDE)* (pp. 91-96). IEEE. 10.1109/iCMLDE49015.2019.00027

Choi, S., Lee, J., Kang, M. G., Min, H., Chang, Y. S., & Yoon, S. (2017). Large-scale machine learning of media outlets for understanding public reactions to nation-wide viral infection outbreaks. *Methods (San Diego, Calif.)*, *129*, 50–59. doi:10.1016/j.ymeth.2017.07.027 PMID:28813689

Chong, A., Li, B., Ngai, E., Ch'ng, E., & Lee, F. (2016). Predicting online product sales via online reviews, sentiments, and promotion strategies. *International Journal of Operations & Production Management*, *36*(4), 358–383. doi:10.1108/IJOPM-03-2015-0151

Choudhary, A., & Arora, A. (2020). Linguistic Feature Based Learning Model for Fake News Detection and Classification. *Expert Systems with Applications*, 114171.

Chweya, R., Ajibade, S. S. M., Buba, A. K., & Samuel, M. (2020). IoT and Big Data Technologies: Oppurtunities and Challenges for Higher Learning. *International Journal of Recent Technology and Engineering*, *9*(2).

Çoban, Ö., Özel, S. A., & İnan, A. (2021). Deep learning-based sentiment analysis of Facebook data: The case of Turkish users. *The Computer Journal*, *64*(3), 473–499. doi:10.1093/comjnl/bxaa172

Collobert, R., & Weston, J., Bottou, L., Karlen, M., Kavukcuoglu, K., & Kuksa, P. (2011). Natural Language Processing (Almost) from Scratch. *Journal of Machine Learning Research*, *12*, 2493–2537.

Conneau, A., Schwenk, H., Barrault, L., & Lecun, Y. (2017). Very Deep Convolutional Networks for Text Classification. In *Proceedings of the 15th Conference of the European Chapter of the Association for Computational Linguistics*. Association for Computational Linguistics. 10.18653/v1/E17-1104

Constantinides, E., & Holleschovsky, N. I. (2016). Impact of Online Products on Purchasing Decisions. In *Proceedings of the 12th International Conference on Web Information Systems and Technologies* (vol. *1*, pp. 271-278). Scitepress – Science and Technology Publications, Lda. 10.5220/0005861002710278

Constantinides, E., & Fountain, S. (2008). Web 2.0: Conceptual foundations and marketing issues. *Special Issues Papers*, *9*(3), 231–244. doi:10.1057/palgrave.dddmp.4350098

Corbell, J. R., Kahn, B. H., & Corbell, M. E. (Eds.). (2020). *Microlearning in the digital age: The design and delivery of learning snippets*. Routledge.

Cormode, G., & Krishnamurthy, B. (2008). Key differences between Web 1.0 and Web 2.0. *First Monday*, *13*(6), 1–21. doi:10.5210/fm.v13i6.2125

Corneli, J., & Danoff, C. J. (2011). Paragogy: Synergizing individual and organizational learning. *1st International Conference on Learning Analytics and Knowledge*.

Cornelissen, J. P. (2008). *Corporate Communication. A guide to Theory and Practice*. SAGE Publications.

Crouch, C. H., & Mazur, E. (2001). Peer instruction: Ten years of experience and results. *American Journal of Physics*, *69*(9), 970–977.

Cui, G., Lui, H. K., & Guo, X. (2012). The Effect of Online Consumer Reviews on New Product Sales. *International Journal of Electronic Commerce*, *17*(1), 39–57. doi:10.2753/JEC1086-4415170102

Czerwinska, M. (2020). Use of Web 2.0 Tools by Polish Health Portals. *Informatyka Automatyka Pomiary w Gospodarce i Ochronie Srodowiska*, *10*(4), 77–82. doi:10.35784/iapgos.2398

Daher, J. B., Brun, A., & Boyer, A. (2018). Multi-source data mining for e-learning. *7th International Symposium "From Data to Models and Back (DataMod)" 2018*. arXiv:2009.08791 [cs.DB]

Dandannavar, P. S., Mangalwede, S. R., & Kulkarni, P. M. (2018, December). Social Media Text-A Source for Personality Prediction. In *2018 International Conference on Computational Techniques, Electronics and Mechanical Systems (CTEMS)* (pp. 62- 65). IEEE.

Das, S. D., Basak, A., & Dutta, S. (2021). *A Heuristic-driven Uncertainty based Ensemble Framework for Fake News Detection in Tweets and News Articles.* arXiv preprint arXiv:2104.01791.

Daughtery, T., Eastin, S., & Bright, L. (2008). Exploring Consumer Motivations for Creating User-Generated Content. *Journal of Interactive Advertising, 8*(2), 16–25. doi:10.1080/15252019.2008.10722139

Davazdahemami, B., & Delen, D. (2019). The confounding role of common diabetes medications in developing acute renal failure: A data mining approach with emphasis on drug-drug interactions. *Expert Systems with Applications, 123,* 168–177. doi:10.1016/j.eswa.2019.01.006

de Oliveira, N. R., Medeiros, D. S., & Mattos, D. M. (2020). A sensitive stylistic approach to identify fake news on social networking. *IEEE Signal Processing Letters, 27,* 1250–1254.

Dede, J., & Forster, A. (2021). Automatic Content Curation for Online Learning Materials. *Conference: SIGCSE '21: The 52nd ACM Technical Symposium on Computer Science Education.* DOI: 10.1145/3408877.3439601

Dellarocas, C., Zhang, X., & Awad, F. (2007). Exploring the value of online product reviews in forecasting sales: The case of motion pictures. *Journal of Interactive Marketing, 21*(4), 23–45. doi:10.1002/dir.20087

Demertzi, V., & Demertzis, K. (2020). *A Hybrid Adaptive Educational eLearning project based on Ontologies Matching and Recommendation System.* arXiv:2007.14771

Demertzi, V., & Demertzis, K. (2020). *An Adaptive Educational eLearning System based on Semantics, Ontologies Matching and Recommendation system.* Available: https://arvix.org/abs/2007.14771

Dennhardt, S. (2014). *User Generated Content and its Impact on Branding. How Users and Communities Create and Manage Brands in Social Media.* Springer Gabler. doi:10.1007/978-3-658-02350-8

Derks, D., Bos, A. E. R., & von Grumbkow, J. (2007). Emoticons and social interaction on the Internet: The importance of social context. *Computers in Human Behavior, 23*(1), 842–849. doi:10.1016/j.chb.2004.11.013

Devlin, J., Chang, M.-W., Lee, K., & Toutanova, K. (2018). *BERT: Pre-training of Deep Bidirectional Transformers for Language Understanding.* arxiv:1810.04805.

Devlin, J., Chang, M., Lee, K., & Toutanova, K. (2019). BERT: Pre-Training of Deep Bidirectional Transformers for Language Understanding. *Proceedings of the 2019 Conference of the North American Chapter of the Association for Computational Linguistics: Human Language Technologies, 1,* 4171–4186. 10.18653/v1/N19-1423

Dewan, P., & Kumaraguru, P. (2017). Facebook Inspector (FbI): Towards automatic real-time detection of malicious content on Facebook. *Social Network Analysis and Mining, 7*(1), 15.

Dey, K., Shrivastava, R., & Kaushik, S. (2018). Topical stance detection for Twitter: A two-phase LSTM model using attention. In *European Conference on Information Retrieval* (pp. 529-536). Springer. 10.1007/978-3-319-76941-7_40

Dieng, A. B., Wang, C., Gao, J., & Paisley, J. (2017). TopicRNN: A Recurrent Neural Network with Long-Range Semantic Dependency. *Proceedings of International Conference on Learning Representations.* arXiv:1611.01702 [cs.CL].

Ding, J., Li, Y., Ni, H., & Yang, Z. (2020). Generative Text Summary Based on Enhanced Semantic Attention and Gain-Benefit Gate. *IEEE Access: Practical Innovations, Open Solutions, 8,* 92659–92668. doi:10.1109/ACCESS.2020.2994092

Dingli, A., & Mifsud, J. (2011). USEFul: A framework to mainstream web site usability through automated evaluation. *International Journal of Human-Computer Interaction*, *2*(1).

Dixit, R. K., Yalagi, P. S., & Nirgude, M. A. (2012). Breaking the walls of classroom through Micro learning: Short burst of learning. *Journal of Physics: Conference Series*, *1854*(1), 012018.

Doh, S. J., & Hwang, J. S. (2009). How Consumers Evaluate eWOM Messages. *Cyberpsychology & Behavior*, *12*(2), 193–197. doi:10.1089/cpb.2008.0109 PMID:19072076

Dolasinski, M. J., & Reynolds, J. (2020). Microlearning: A new learning model. *Journal of Hospitality & Tourism Research (Washington, D.C.)*, *44*(3). doi:10.1177/1096348020901579

Dong, X., Victor, U., Chowdhury, S., & Qian, L. (2019). *Deep Two-path Semisupervised Learning for Fake News Detection*. arXiv preprint arXiv:1906.05659.

dos Santos, C. N., & Gatti, M. (2014). Deep Convolutional Neural Networks for Sentiment Analysis of Short Texts. In J. Hajic & J. Tsujii (Eds.), COLING (pp. 69-78). ACL.

Doupé, A., Cui, W., Jakubowski, M., Peinado, M., Kruegel, C., & Vigna, D. (2013). deDacota: Toward preventing server-side XSS via automatic code and data separation. *Proceedings of the 2013 ACM SIGSAC Conference on Computer & Communications Security*.

Dowle, M., & Srinivasan, A. (2019). *data.table: Extension of 'data.frame'*. R Package Version 1.12.8.

Doychev, E., Stoyanova-Doycheva, A., Stoyanov, S., Glushkova, T., & Ivanova, V. (2020). An IoT Virtual eLearning Space. *Transactions on Computational Collective Intelligence*, *XXXV*, 148–169.

Dutta, S., Das, A. K., Bhattacharya, A., Dutta, G., Parikh, K. K., Das, A., & Ganguly, D. (2019). Community detection based tweet summarization. *Advances in Intelligent Systems and Computing, 813*(September), 797–808. doi:10.1007/978-981-13-1498-8_70

Dwivedi, Y. K. (2020). Impact of COVID-19 pandemic on information management research and practice: Transforming education, work and life. *International Journal of Information Management*, *55*, 102211.

Edo-Osagie, O., De La Iglesia, B., Lake, I., & Edeghere, O. (2020). A scoping review of the use of Twitter for public health research. *Computers in Biology and Medicine*, *122*(May), 103770. doi:10.1016/j.compbiomed.2020.103770 PMID:32502758

Esuli, A., Moreo, A., Sebastiani, F., & Cambria, E. (2020). Cross-lingual sentiment quantification. *IEEE Intelligent Systems*, *35*(3), 106–114. doi:10.1109/MIS.2020.2979203

Fakespot. (2020). https://www.fakespot.com/about-us

Fakespot. (2020a). https://www.fakespot.com/product/think-ink-face-mask-10-1-5-1-1-1-cotton-mask-with-elastic-strap-washable-face-mask

Fakespot. (2020b). https://www.fakespot.com/walmart/4pcs-set-unisex-face-mask-paris-letters-print-protect-reusable-comfy-washable-made-in-usa

Faruqui, M., Dodge, J., Jauhar, S. K., Dyer, C., Hovy, E., & Smith, N. A. (2014). Retrofitting Word Vectors to Semantic Lexicons. *Proceedings of NAACL 2015*.

Feinerer, I., Hornik, K., & Meyer, D. (2008). Text Mining Infrastructure in R. *Journal of Statistical Software*, *22*(5), 1–54.

Feldman, R. (2013). Techniques and applications for sentiment analysis. *Communications of the ACM, 56*(4), 82–89. doi:10.1145/2436256.2436274

Felfernig, A., Friedrich, G., Jannach, D., & Zanker, M. (2015). Constraint-Based Recommender Systems. In F. Ricci, L. Rokach, & B. Shapira (Eds.), *Recommender Systems Handbook*. Springer.

Feuerriegel, S., & Pr"ollochs, N. (2019). *SentimentAnalysis: Dictionary–Based Sentiment Analysis*. R Package Version 1.3.3.

Flanagin, A. J., & Metzger, M. J. (2013). Trusting expert-versus user generated ratings online: The role of information volume, valence, and consumer characteristics. *Computers in Human Behavior, 29*(4), 1626–1634. doi:10.1016/j.chb.2013.02.001

Fleuren, W. W. M., & Alkema, W. (2015). Application of text mining in the biomedical domain. *Methods (San Diego, Calif.), 74*, 97–106. doi:10.1016/j.ymeth.2015.01.015 PMID:25641519

Fong, E. M., & Chung, W. Y. (2013). Mobile cloud-computing-based healthcare service by noncontact ECG monitoring. *Sensors (Basel), 12*(12), 16451–16473. doi:10.3390131216451 PMID:24316562

Frohlich, K., Nieminen, M., & Pinomaa, A. (2020). Factors influencing the adoption of m-Government: Perspectives from a Namibian marginalised community. In R. Zitouni, M. Agueh, P. Houngue, & H. Soude (Eds.), *e-Infrastructure and e-Services for Developing Countries. AFRICOMM 2019. Lecture Notes of the Institute for Computer Sciences, Social Informatics and Telecommunications Engineering* (Vol. 311). Springer. doi:10.1007/978-3-030-41593-8_17

Gagolewski, M. (2020). *stringi: Character String Processing Facilities*. R Package Version 1.4.5.

Gambhir, M., & Gupta, V. (2017). Recent automatic text summarization techniques: A survey. *Artificial Intelligence Review, 47*(1), 1–66. doi:10.100710462-016-9475-9

Ganapathi, J. (2019). User-Generated Content's Impact on the Sustainability of Open Educational Resources. *Open Praxis, 11*(2), 211-225.

Garcia, M. B., Revano, T. F., Habal, B. G. M., Contreras, J. O., & Enriquez, J. B. R. (2018, November). A pornographic image and video filtering application using optimized nudity recognition and detection algorithm. In *2018 IEEE 10th International Conference on Humanoid, Nanotechnology, Information Technology, Communication and Control, Environment and Management (HNICEM)* (pp. 1-5). IEEE. 10.1109/HNICEM.2018.8666227

García, S. A., García, G. G., Prieto, M. S., Moreno Guerrero, A. J., & Rodríguez Jiménez, C. (2020). The Impact of Term Fake News on the Scientific Community. Scientific Performance and Mapping in Web of Science. *Social Sciences, 9*(5), 73. doi:10.3390ocsci9050073

Gashaw, Y., & Liu, F. (2018). Performance evaluation of frequent pattern mining algorithms using web log data for web usage mining. *Proceedings - 2017 10th International Congress on Image and Signal Processing, BioMedical Engineering and Informatics, CISP-BMEI 2017*, 1–5. 10.1109/CISP-BMEI.2017.8302317

Gefen, D., Karahanna, E., & Straub, D. W. (2003). Inexperience and Experience with Online Stores: The Importance of TAM and Trust. *IEEE Transactions on Engineering Management, 50*(3), 307–321. doi:10.1109/TEM.2003.817277

Gereme, F., Zhu, W., Ayall, T., & Alemu, D. (2021). Combating Fake News in "Low-Resource" Languages: Amharic Fake News Detection Accompanied by Resource Crafting. *Information, 2021*(12), 20.

Ghafari, S. M., Yakhchi, S., Beheshti, A., & Orgun, M. (2018, November). Social context-aware trust prediction: methods for identifying fake news. In *International Conference on Web Information Systems Engineering* (pp. 161-177). Springer.

Ghanem, B., Ponzetto, S. P., Rosso, P., & Rangel, F. (2021). *FakeFlow: fake news detection by modeling the flow of affective information.* arXiv preprint arXiv:2101.09810.

Giannakis-Bompolis, C., & Boutsouki, C. (2014). Customer Relationship Management in the Era of Social Web and Social Customer: An Investigation of Customer Engagement in the Greek Retail Banking Sector. *Procedia: Social and Behavioral Sciences, 148*, 67–78. doi:10.1016/j.sbspro.2014.07.018

Giglou, H. B., Razmara, J., Rahgouy, M., & Sanaei, M. (2020). LSACoNet: A Combination of Lexical and Conceptual Features for Analysis of Fake News Spreaders on Twitter. CLEF.

Giurgiu, L. (2017). Microlearning an evolving elearning trend. Scientific Bulletin – Nicolae Balcescu Land Forces Academy, 22(1), 18-23.

Godes, D., & Mayzlin, D. (2004). Using Online Conversations to Study Word-of-Mouth Communication. *Marketing Science, 23*(4), 545–560. doi:10.1287/mksc.1040.0071

Goga, M. (2015). A Recommender for Improving the Student Academic Performance. *Procedia: Social and Behavioral Sciences, 180*, 1481–1488.

Goldani, M. H., Momtazi, S., & Safabakhsh, R. (2021). Detecting fake news with capsule neural networks. *Applied Soft Computing, 101*, 106991.

Goldani, M. H., Safabakhsh, R., & Momtazi, S. (2021). Convolutional neural network with margin loss for fake news detection. *Information Processing & Management, 58*(1), 102418.

Gopalakrishnan, V., & Ramaswamy, C. (2017). Patient opinion mining to analyze drugs satisfaction using supervised learning. *Journal of Applied Research and Technology, 15*(4), 311–319. doi:10.1016/j.jart.2017.02.005

Gossling, Z. H., Hall, M., Martin-Rios, C., Ram, Y., & Grotte, P. (2018). A cross country comparison of accommodation manager perspectives on online review manipulation. *Current Issues in Tourism, 22*(14), 1744–1763. doi:10.1080/13683500.2018.1455171

Goyal, A., Gupta, V., & Kumar, M. (2018). Recent named entity recognition and classification techniques: A systematic review. *Computer Science Review, 29*, 21–43. doi:10.1016/j.cosrev.2018.06.001

Granik, M., & Mesyura, V. (2017, May). Fake news detection using naive Bayes classifier. In *2017 IEEE First Ukraine Conference on Electrical and Computer Engineering (UKRCON)* (pp. 900-903). IEEE.

Griffiths, S., Wong, M. S., Kwok, C. Y. T., Kam, R., Lam, S. C., Yang, L., Yip, T. L., Heo, J., Chan, B. S. B., Xiong, G., & Lu, K. (2019). Exploring Bluetooth Beacon Use Cases in Teaching and Learning: Increasing the Sustainability of Physical Learning Spaces. *Sustainability, 11*, 4005. https://doi.org/10.3390/su11154005

Gupta, S. D., Saha, S., & Das, S. K. (2021, February). SMS Spam Detection Using Machine Learning. *Journal of Physics: Conference Series, 1797*(1), 012017. doi:10.1088/1742-6596/1797/1/012017

Gupta, V., & Lehal, G. S. (2010). A Survey of Text Summarization Extractive techniques. *Journal of Emerging Technologies in Web Intelligence, 2*(3), 258–268. doi:10.4304/jetwi.2.3.258-268

Hall, M., Frank, E., Holmes, G., Pfahringer, B., Reutemann, P., & Witten, I. H. (2009). The WEKA data mining software: An update. *SIGKDD Explorations, 11*(1), 10–18. doi:10.1145/1656274.1656278

Hansen, P. R., Lunde, A., & Nason, J. M. (2011). The model confidence set. *Econometrica, 79*(2), 453–497. doi:10.3982/ECTA5771

Harasim, L. (2006). A History of E-learning: Shift Happened. In J. Weiss, J. Nolan, J. Hunsinger, & P. Trifonas (Eds.), *The International Handbook of Virtual Learning Environments*. Springer.

Harous, S., El Menshawy, M., Serhani, M. A., & Benharref, A. (2018). Mobile health architecture for obesity management using sensory and social data. *Informatics in Medicine Unlocked, 10*(December), 27–44. doi:10.1016/j.imu.2017.12.005

Hasan, L. (2009). *Usability Evaluation Framework for E-commerce Websites in Developing Countries* (Doctoral Thesis). Loughborough University.

Hase, S., & Kenyon, C. (Eds.). (2013). *Self-determined learning: Heutagogy in action*. Bloomsbury Academic.

Hashemi, H. B., Asiaee, A., & Kraft, R. (2016). Query intent detection using convolutional neural networks. In *International Conference on Web Search and Data Mining, Workshop on Query Understanding*. Academic Press.

Hassan, N., Amer, A., & Sawsan, A. (2021). A review of website evaluation using web diagnostic tools and data envelopment analysis. *Bulletin of Electrical Engineering and Informatics*.

He, K., Zhang, X., Ren, S., & Sun, J. (2016). Identity mappings in deep residual networks. doi:10.1007/978-3-319-46493-0_38

He, K., Zhang, X., Ren, S., & Sun, J. (2016). Deep Residual Learning for Image Recognition. *Proceedings of The IEEE Computer Society Conference on Computer Vision and Pattern Recognition (CVPR)*. 10.1109/CVPR.2016.90

Hendradi, P. (2020). Artificial Intelligence Influence in Education 4.0 to Architecture Cloud based E-Learning System. *International Journal of Artificial Intelligence Research, 4*(1). doi:10.29099/ijair.v4i1.109

Henry. (2008). Are investors influenced by how earnings press releases are written? *Journal of Business Communication, 45*, 363-407.

Herath, D., & Jayaratne, L. (2017). A personalized web content recommendation system for E-learners in E-learning environment. In *2017 National Information Technology Conference (NITC)*. IEEE.

He, S., Hollenbeck, B., & Proserpio, D. (2021). The Market for Fake Reviews. *Munich Personal RePEc Archive, 105507*, 1–47.

HESLB. (2006). *Annual report, 2005 – 2006*. Higher Education Students' Loans Board.

Hiremath, B. N., & Patil, M. M. (2020). Enhancing Optimized Personalized Therapy in Clinical Decision Support System using Natural Language Processing. *Journal of King Saud University - Computer and Information Sciences*. doi:10.1016/j.jksuci.2020.03.006

Hochreiter, S., & Schmidhuber, J. (1997). Long Short-term Memory. *Neural Computation, 9*(8), 1735–1780. doi:10.1162/neco.1997.9.8.1735 PMID:9377276

Hoerl, A. E., & Kennard, R. W. (1970). Ridge regression: Biased estimation for nonorthogonal problems. *Technometrics, 12*(1), 55–67. doi:10.1080/00401706.1970.10488634

Hofstede, G. (1981). *Culture and organisations*. McGraw-Hill.

Hoic-Bozic, N., Mornar, V., & Boticki, I. (2009). A Blended Learning Approach to Course Design and Implementation. *IEEE Transactions on Education, 52*(1), 19–30.

Hoogendoorn, M., Berger, T., Schulz, A., Stolz, T., & Szolovits, P. (2017). Predicting Social Anxiety Treatment Outcome Based on Therapeutic Email Conversations. *IEEE Journal of Biomedical and Health Informatics, 21*(5), 1449–1459. doi:10.1109/JBHI.2016.2601123 PMID:27542187

Hrastinski, S. (2008). Asynchronous and synchronous e-learning. *EDUCAUSE Quarterly, 31*(4), 51–55.

Hsu, B. (2020). Comparison of Supervised Classification Models on Textual Data. *Mathematics, 8*(5), 851. Advance online publication. doi:10.3390/math8050851

Huang, Y. F., & Chen, P. H. (2020). Fake news detection using an ensemble learning model based on self-adaptive harmony search algorithms. *Expert Systems with Applications, 159*, 113584.

Humayun, M. (2020). Blockchain-Based secure framework for e-learning during COVID-19. *Indian Journal of Science and Technology, 13*(12), 1328–1341. https://doi.org/10.17485/IJST/v13i12.152

Hu, N., Bose, I., Koh, N., & Liu, L. (2012). Manipulation of online reviews: An analysis of ratings, readability, and sentiments. *Decision Support Systems, 52*(3), 674–684. doi:10.1016/j.dss.2011.11.002

Hu, N., Koh, N. S., & Reddy, S. K. (2014). Ratings Lead you to the Product Reviews Help You Clinch it? The Dynamics and Impact of Online Review Sentiments on Product Sales. *Decision Support Systems, 57*, 42–53. doi:10.1016/j.dss.2013.07.009

Inuwa-Dutse, I., Liptrott, M., & Korkontzelos, I. (2018). Detection of spam-posting accounts on Twitter. *Neurocomputing, 315*, 496–511. doi:10.1016/j.neucom.2018.07.044

Iqbal, S., Ahmad, S., Bano, B., Akkour, K., Alghamdi, M. A. A., & Alothri, A. M. (2021). A Systematic Review: Role of Artificial Intelligence During the COVID-19 Pandemic in the Healthcare System. *International Journal of Intelligent Information Technologies, 17*.

Irsoy, O., & Cardie, C. (2014). Deep Recursive Neural Networks for Compositionality in Language. *Advances in Neural Information Processing Systems, 27*, 2096–2104.

Ishengoma, F., Mselle, L., & Mongi, H. (2019). Power distance and user's behavior towards the adoption of m-Government services in Tanzania: A web analytics study. *International Journal of Open Information Technologies, 7*(9).

Ishengoma, F., Mselle, L., & Mongi, H. (2018). Critical success factors towards the adoption of m-Government services in Tanzania. A conceptual framework. *The Electronic Journal on Information Systems in Developing Countries, 85*(1), e12064. doi:10.1002/isd2.12064

Islam, M. S., Islam, M. A., Hossain, M. A., & Dey, J. J. (2016, December). Supervised approach of sentimentality extraction from bengalifacebook status. In *2016 19th International Conference on Computer and Information Technology (ICCIT)* (pp. 383- 387). IEEE.

Ismail, H. M., Belkhouche, B., & Harous, S. (2019). Framework for Personalized Content Recommendations to Support Informal Learning in Massively Diverse Information Wikis. *IEEE Access: Practical Innovations, Open Solutions, 7*, 172752–172773.

Jain, A. K., & Gupta, B. B. (2021). A survey of phishing attack techniques, defence mechanisms and open research challenges. *Enterprise Information Systems*, 1–39. doi:10.1080/17517575.2021.1896786

Jain, A. K., Yadav, S. K., & Choudhary, N. (2020). A Novel Approach to Detect Spam and Smishing SMS using Machine Learning Techniques. *International Journal of E-Services and Mobile Applications, 12*(1), 21–38. doi:10.4018/IJESMA.2020010102

Jain, S., Jain, A. K., & Singh, S. P. (2020). A Multilayer Deep Learning Framework for Auto-content Tagging. *Advanced in Intelligent Systems and Computing, 1141*, 609–619. doi:10.1007/978-981-15-3383-9_55

Jain, V. K., & Kumar, S. (2018). Effective surveillance and predictive mapping of mosquito-borne diseases using social media. *Journal of Computational Science*, *25*, 406–415. doi:10.1016/j.jocs.2017.07.003

Jalilvand, M. R., Esfahani, S., & Samiei, N. (2011). Electronic word-of-mouth challenges and opportunities. *Procedia Computer Science*, *3*, 42–46. doi:10.1016/j.procs.2010.12.008

Jang, S. M., Geng, T., Li, J. Y. Q., Xia, R., Huang, C. T., Kim, H., & Tang, J. (2018). A computational approach for examining the roots and spreading patterns of fake news: Evolution tree analysis. *Computers in Human Behavior*, *84*, 103–113. doi:10.1016/j.chb.2018.02.032

Jansen, B. J., Zhang, M., Sobel, K., & Chowdury, A. (2009). Micro-blogging as online word of mouth branding. In D. R. O. Jr., R. B. Arthur, K. Hinckley, M. R. Morris, S. E. Hudson & S. Greenberg (Eds.), CHI Extended Abstracts (pp. 3859-3864). ACM. doi:10.1145/1520340.1520584

Janssen, M., Wimmer, M. A., Moe, C. E., & Flak, L. S. (Eds.). Electronic Government. Lecture Notes in Computer Science, 7443.

Jelodar, H., Wang, Y., Orji, R., & Huang, H. (2020). Deep sentiment classification and topic discovery on novel coronavirus or COVID-19 online discussions: NLP using LSTM recurrent neural network approach. *IEEE Journal of Biomedical and Health Informatics*, *24*(10), 2733–2742. doi:10.1109/JBHI.2020.3001216 PMID:32750931

Jiang, S., Wu, W., Tomita, N., Ganoe, C., & Hassanpour, S. (2020). Multi-ontology refined embeddings (MORE): A hybrid multi-ontology and corpus-based semantic representation for biomedical concepts. *ArXiv*, 1–25.

Jiang, F., Liu, Y., Luan, H.-B., Sun, J., Zhu, X., Zhang, M., & Ma, S. (2015). Microblog Sentiment Analysis with Emoticon Space Model. *J. Comput. Sci. Technol.*, *30*(5), 1120–1129. doi:10.100711390-015-1587-1

Jiang, T., Li, J. P., Haq, A. U., Saboor, A., & Ali, A. (2021). A Novel Stacking Approach for Accurate Detection of Fake News. *IEEE Access: Practical Innovations, Open Solutions*, *9*, 22626–22639.

Ji, G., Li, C., North, M., & Liu, J. (2016). Staking reputation on stakeholders: How does stakeholders' Facebook engagement help or ruin a company's reputation. *Public Relations Review*, *43*(1), 1–10.

Jiménez-Zafra, S. M., Martín-Valdivia, M. T., Molina-González, M. D., & Ureña-López, L. A. (2019). How do we talk about doctors and drugs? Sentiment analysis in forums expressing opinions for medical domain. *Artificial Intelligence in Medicine*, *93*, 50–57. doi:10.1016/j.artmed.2018.03.007 PMID:29685725

Jin, Z., Cao, J., Zhang, Y., Zhou, J., & Tian, Q. (2016). Novel visual and statistical image features for microblogs news verification. *IEEE Transactions on Multimedia*, *19*(3), 598–608. doi:10.1109/TMM.2016.2617078

John, B., Baulch, B., & Wickramasinghe, N. (2020). A Sentiment Analysis of the 2014-15 Ebola Outbreak in the Media and Social Media. In Handbook of Research on Optimizing Healthcare Management Techniques (p. 11). Academic Press.

Jordan, J. (2020). Recommending Learning Videos for MOOCS and flipped classrooms. Advances In Practical Applications of Agents, Multi-Agent Systems, and Trustworthiness. The PAAMS Collection. PAAMS 2020. Lecture Notes in Computer Science, Vol.12092. Springer.

Jung, T., Tom Dieck, M. C., Lee, H., & Chung, N. (2020). Moderating role of long-term orientation on augmented reality adoption. *International Journal of Human-Computer Interaction*, *36*(3), 239–250.

Jupin, J. A., Sutikno, T., Ismail, M. A., Mohamad, M. S., Kasim, S., & Stiawan, D. (2019). Review of the machine learning methods in the classification of phishing attack. *Bulletin of Electrical Engineering and Informatics*, *8*(4), 1545–1555. doi:10.11591/eei.v8i4.1344

Jwa, H., Oh, D., Park, K., Kang, J. M., & Lim, H. (2019). exBAKE: Automatic fake news detection model based on bidirectional encoder representations from transformers (bert). *Applied Sciences (Basel, Switzerland)*, *9*(19), 4062.

Kacen, J., Hess, J., & Chiang, W. (2013). Bricks or Clicks? Consumer Attitudes toward Traditional Stores and Online Stores. *Global Economics and Management Review*, *18*(1), 12–21. doi:10.1016/S2340-1540(13)70003-3

Kalaharsha, P., & Mehtre, B. M. (2021). *Detecting Phishing Sites—An Overview.* arXiv preprint arXiv:2103.12739.

Kalchbrenner, N., Grefenstette, E. & Blunsom, P. (2014). A Convolutional Neural Network for Modelling Sentences. *CoRR*, abs/1404.2188.

Kalchbrenner, N., Grefenstette, E., & Blunsom, P. (2014). A Convolutional Neural Network for Modelling Sentences. In *Proceedings of 52nd Annual Meeting of The Association for Computational Linguistics.* Association for Computational Linguistics. 10.3115/v1/P14-1062

Kaliyar, R. K., Goswami, A., & Narang, P. (2021). FakeBERT: Fake news detection in social media with a BERT-based deep learning approach. *Multimedia Tools and Applications*, *80*(8), 11765–11788.

Kaliyar, R. K., Goswami, A., Narang, P., & Sinha, S. (2020). FNDNet–a deep convolutional neural network for fake news detection. *Cognitive Systems Research*, *61*, 32–44.

Karkin, N., & Janssen, M. (2014). Evaluating websites from a public value perspective: A review of Turkish local government websites. *International Journal of Information Management*, *34*(3), 351–363. doi:10.1016/j.ijinfomgt.2013.11.004

Kausar, S. (2020). Paper-Mining Smart Learning Analytics Data Using Ensemble Analytics Data Using Ensemble Classifiers. *International Journal of Emerging Technologies in Learning.*, *15*, 81–102.

Keller, K. L. (2010). Mastering the Marketing Communication Mix: Micro and Macro Perspectives on Integrated Marketing Communication Programs. *Journal of Marketing Management*, *17*(7-8), 819–847. doi:10.1362/026725701323366836

Khalid, A. (2017). Automated usability evaluation of e-learning websites in Saudi Arabia. *5th International Conference of Advanced Computer Science & Information Technology*, 1-10. 10.5121/csit.2017.70801

Khanna, S., Tiwari, B., Das, P., & Das, A. (2020). A Comparative Study on Various Text Classification Methods. *Computational Intelligence in Pattern Recognition*, 539-549.

Khan, S., & Alqahtani, S. (2020). Big Data Application and its Impact on Education. *International Journal of Emerging Technologies in Learning*, *15*(17), 36–46.

Kiela, D., Hill, F., & Clark, S. (2015). Specializing Word Embeddings for Similarity or Relatedness. In L. Màrquez, C. Callison-Burch, J. Su, D. Pighin & Y. Marton (Eds.), EMNLP (pp. 2044-2048). The Association for Computational Linguistics. doi:10.18653/v1/D15-1242

Kilimci, Z. H., & Akyokus, S. (2018). Deep Learning- And Word Embedding-Based Heterogeneous Classifier Ensembles for Text Classification. *Complexity*, *2018*, 1–10. Advance online publication. doi:10.1155/2018/7130146

Kim, J.-K., de Marneffe, M.-C., & Fosler-Lussier, E. (2016). Adjusting Word Embeddings with Semantic Intensity Orders. In P. Blunsom, K. Cho, S. B. Cohen, E. Grefenstette, K. M. Hermann, L. Rimell, J. Weston & S. W. Tau Yih (Eds.), Rep4NLP@ACL (pp. 62-69). Association for Computational Linguistics. doi:10.18653/v1/W16-1607

Kim, Y. (2014). Convolutional Neural Networks for sentence classification. In *Proceedings of the 2014 Conference on Empirical Methods in Natural Language Processing (EMNLP).* Association for Computational Linguistics. 10.3115/v1/D14-1181

Kim, J. K., Tur, G., Celikyilmaz, A., Cao, B., & Wang, Y. Y. (2016). Intent detection using semantically enriched word embeddings. In *IEEE Spoken Language Technology Workshop (SLT)* (pp. 414-419). 10.1109/SLT.2016.7846297

Kim, Y., Jernite, Y., Sontag, D., & Rush, A. M. (2016). Character-Aware Neural Language Models. *Proceedings of Thirtieth AAAI Conference on Artificial Intelligence.*

King, S. F., & Burgess, T. F. (2008). Understanding succes and failure in costumer relationship management. *Industrial Marketing Management, 37*(4), 421–431. doi:10.1016/j.indmarman.2007.02.005

Klasnja Milicevic, A., Vesin, B., & Ivanovic, M. (2018). Social tagging strategy for enhancing e-learning experience. *Computers & Education, 118,* 166–181.

Knowles, M. S. (1975). *Self-directed learning: a guide for learners and teachers.* Cambridge Books.

Knowles, M. S., Holton, E. F., & Swanson, R. A. (1998). *The adult learner.* Gulf Publishing.

Korfiatis, N., Barriocanal-Garcia, E., & Sanchez, S. (2012). Evaluating content quality and helpfulness of online products reviews: The interplay of review helpfulness vs. review content. *Electronic Commerce Research and Applications, 11*(3), 205–217. doi:10.1016/j.elerap.2011.10.003

Korkontzelos, I., Nikfarjam, A., Shardlow, M., Sarker, A., Ananiadou, S., & Gonzalez, G. H. (2016). Analysis of the effect of sentiment analysis on extracting adverse drug reactions from tweets and forum posts. *Journal of Biomedical Informatics, 62,* 148–158. doi:10.1016/j.jbi.2016.06.007 PMID:27363901

Kous, K., & Polančič, G. (2021). An empirical investigation of the accessibility of official European tourism websites. In C. Eusébio, L. Teixeira, & M. Carneiro (Eds.), *ICT Tools and Applications for Accessible Tourism* (pp. 169–195). IGI Global. doi:10.4018/978-1-7998-6428-8.ch008

Kowsari, K., Brown, D. E., Heidarysafa, M., Meimandi, K. J., Gerber, M. S., & Barnes, L. E. (2007). HDLTex: Hierarchical Deep Learning for Text Classification. In *Proceedings of 2017 16th Ieee International Conference on Machine Learning and Applications (ICMLA).* IEEE.

Kowsari, K., Meimandi, K. J., Heidarysafa, M., Mendu, S., Barnes, L., & Brown, D. (2019). Text Classification Algorithms: A Survey. *Information (Basel), 10*(4), 150. doi:10.3390/info10040150

Krauss, C. (2018). *Time-dependent recommender systems for the prediction of appropriate learning objects* (Doctoral thesis). Technische Universitat Berlin.

Küçük, D., & Can, F. (2018). *Stance detection on tweets: An SVM-based approach.* arXiv preprint arXiv:1803.08910.

Küçük, D., & Can, F. (2019). *A tweet dataset annotated for named entity recognition and stance detection.* arXiv preprint arXiv:1901.04787.

Küçük, D., & Steinberger, R. (2014). Experiments to improve named entity recognition on Turkish tweets. arXiv preprint arXiv:1410.8668. doi:10.3115/v1/W14-1309

Küçük, D. (2017). Stance detection in Turkish tweets. In *Proceedings of the International Workshop on Social Media World Sensors (SIDEWAYS) of ACM Hypertext Conference.* Prague, Czech Republic: ACM.

Küçük, D., Arıcı, N., & Küçük, D. (2017). Named entity recognition in Turkish: Approaches and issues. In *International Conference on Applications of Natural Language to Information Systems* (pp. 176-181). Springer.

Küçük, D., & Can, F. (2020). Stance detection: A survey. *ACM Computing Surveys, 53*(1), 1–37. doi:10.1145/3369026

Küçük, D., & Can, F. (2021). Stance detection: Concepts, approaches, resources, and outstanding issues. *Proceedings of the 44th International ACM SIGIR Conference on Research and Development in Information Retrieval.*

Kukharenko, V., & Syrotenko, N. (2014). Open On-line Course "Content Curator". *Education and Information Technologies*. Advance online publication. doi:10.14308/ite000511

Kula, S., Choraś, M., & Kozik, R. (2020, September). Application of the BERT-Based Architecture in Fake News Detection. In *Conference on Complex, Intelligent, and Software Intensive Systems* (pp. 239-249). Springer.

Kumar, A., Ekbal, A., Kawahara, D., & Kurohashi, S. (2019). Emotion helps Sentiment: A Multi-task Model for Sentiment and Emotion Analysis. IJCNN, 1-8.

Kwok, S., & Uncles, M. (2002). Sales Promotion Effectiveness: The Impact of Culture at an Ethnic-Group Level. *School of Marketing Working Paper, 2*(4), 1-37.

Labutov, I., & Lipson, H. (2013). Re-embedding words. ACL, (2), 489-493.

Lai, C. H., Liu, D. R., & Lin, S. R. (2018). Document recommendation with implicit feedback based on matrix factorization and topic model. *2018 IEEE International Conference on Applied System Invention (ICASI)*, 62-65. doi: 10.1109/ICASI.2018.8394337

Lalitha, T. B., & Sreeja, P. S. (2020). Personalised Self-Directed Learning Recommendation System. *Procedia Computer Science, 171*, 583–592.

Lamsal, R. (2020). Design and analysis of a large-scale COVID-19 tweets dataset. *Applied Intelligence*, (October). Advance online publication. doi:10.100710489-020-02029-z

Lam, T. Y., & Dongol, B. (2020). A Blockchain enabled e-learning platform. *Interactive Learning Environments*, 1–23. doi:10.1080/10494820.2020.1716022

Lan, M., Zhang, Z., Lu, Y., & Wu, J. (2016). Three Convolutional Neural Network-based models for learning Sentiment Word Vectors towards sentiment analysis. IJCNN, 3172-3179.

Lan, Z., Chen, M., Goodman, S., Gimpel, K., Sharma, P., & Soricut, R. (2020). ALBERT: A Lite Bert for Self-Supervised Learning of Language Representations. *Proceedings of ICLR.*

Lappas, T., Sabnis, G., & Valkanas, G. (2016). The Impact of Fake Reviews on Online Visibility: A Vulnerability Assessment of the Hotel Industry. *Information Systems Research, 27*(4), 940–961. doi:10.1287/isre.2016.0674

Lara, J. A., Aljawarneh, S., & Pamplona, S. (2020). Special issue on the current trends in E-learning system. *Journal of Computing in Higher Education, 32*, 1–8. https://doi.org/10.1007/s12528-019-09235-w

Larochelle, H., Bengio, Y., Louradour, J., & Lamblin, P. (2009). Exploring Strategies for Training Deep Neural Networks. *Journal of Machine Learning Research, 10*(1).

Lazer, D. M., Baum, M. A., Benkler, Y., Berinsky, A. J., Greenhill, K. M., Menczer, F., Metzger, M. J., Nyhan, B., Pennycook, G., Rothschild, D., Schudson, M., Sloman, S. A., Sunstein, C. R., Thorson, E. A., Watts, D. J., & Zittrain, J. L. (2018). The science of fake news. *Science, 359*(6380), 1094–1096. doi:10.1126cience.aao2998 PMID:29590025

Lebret, Legrand, & Collobert. (2013). *Is deep learning really necessary for word embeddings?* Idiap, Tech. Rep.

Lenzi, A., Maranghi, M., Stilo, G., & Velardi, P. (2019). The social phenotype: Extracting a patient-centered perspective of diabetes from health-related blogs. *Artificial Intelligence in Medicine, 101*(September), 101727. doi:10.1016/j.artmed.2019.101727 PMID:31813490

Le, Q., & Mikolov, T. (2014). Distributed Representations of Sentences and Documents. *Proceedings of the 31st International Conference on Machine Learning, 32*(2), 1188–1196.

Levy, M. (2009). Web 2.0 implications on Knowledge management. *Journal of Knowledge Management, 13*(1), 120–134. doi:10.1108/13673270910931215

Levy, O., & Goldberg, Y. (2014). Dependency-Based Word Embeddings. In *Proceedings of the 52nd Annual Meeting of the Association for Computational Linguistics (*Volume 2*: Short Papers)* (pp. 302-308). Association for Computational Linguistics.

Li, C. (2019). A Blockchain System for E-Learning Assessment and Certification. *IEEE International Conference on Smart Internet of Things (SmartIoT).* doi:10.1109/SmartIoT.2019.00040

Li, L., Wu, Y., Zhang, Y., & Zhao, T. (2019). Time+User Dual Attention Based Sentiment Prediction for Multiple Social Network Texts With Time Series. *IEEE Access: Practical Innovations, Open Solutions, 7,* 17644–17653. doi:10.1109/ACCESS.2019.2895897

Li, M., Huang, L., Tan, H. C., & Wei, K. (2013). Helpfulness of online product reviews as seen by costumers: Sources and context features. *International Journal of Electronic Commerce, 17*(4), 101–136. doi:10.2753/JEC1086-4415170404

Lin, K. C., Wu, S. H., Chen, L. P., Ku, T., & Chen, G. D. (2014, August). Mining the user clusters on Facebook fan pages based on topic and sentiment analysis. In *Proceedings of the 2014 IEEE 15th International Conference on Information Reuse and Integration (IEEE IRI 2014)* (pp. 627-632). IEEE.

Lin, C.-Y. (2004). ROUGE: A Package for Automatic Evaluation of Summaries. *Association for Computational Linguistics Anthology, 34*(12), 1213–1220. doi:10.1253/jcj.34.1213

Lingwood, J., Farran, E. K., Courbois, Y., & Blades, M. (2020). Investigating route learning, metacognition, and beacon-based strategies using virtual environments. *European Review of Applied Psychology, 70*(4), 100570.

Lin, H., Jia, J., Qiu, J., Zhang, Y., Shen, G., Xie, L., Tang, J., Feng, L., & Chua, T. S. (2017). Detecting stress based on social interactions in social networks. *IEEE Transactions on Knowledge and Data Engineering, 29*(9), 1820–1833. doi:10.1109/TKDE.2017.2686382

Littlejohn, A., Falconer, I., & Mcgill, L. (2008). Characterising effective eLearning resources. *Computer Education, 50*(3), 757–771.

Liu, B. (2010). Sentiment analysis and subjectivity. Handbook of natural language processing, 2(2010), 627-666.

Liu, B., & Lane, I. (2016). Attention-based recurrent neural network models for joint intent detection and slot filling. arXiv preprint arXiv:1609.01454. doi:10.21437/Interspeech.2016-1352

Liu, Y., Ott, M., Goyal, N., Du, J., Joshi, M., Chen, D., Levy, O., Lewis, M., Zettlemoyer, L., & Stoyanov, V. (2019). RoBERT: A Robustly Optimized Bert Pretraining Approach. arXiv:1907.11692v1.

Liu, C., Wu, X., Yu, M., Li, G., Jiang, J., Huang, W., & Lu, X. (2019, August). A two-stage model based on bert for short fake news detection. In *International Conference on Knowledge Science, Engineering and Management* (pp. 172-183). Springer.

Liu, K.-L., Li, W.-J., & Guo, M. (2012). Emoticon Smoothed Language Models for Twitter Sentiment Analysis. *AAAI Press.*

Liu, S., & Lee, I. (2019). Extracting features with medical sentiment lexicon and position encoding for drug reviews. *Health Information Science and Systems, 7*(1), 11. Advance online publication. doi:10.100713755-019-0072-6 PMID:31168364

Livari, N., Sharma, S., & Venta-Olkkonen, L. (2020). Digital transformation of everyday life- How COVID-19 pandemic transformed the basic education of the young generation and why information management research should care? *International Journal of Information Management*, *55*, 102183.

Liwen, V., & Rongbin, Y. (2013). Web traffic and organisation performance measures: Relationships and data sources examined. *Journal of Informetrics*, *7*(3), 699–711. doi:10.1016/j.joi.2013.04.005

Lloret, E., Plaza, L., & Aker, A. (2018). The challenging task of summary evaluation: An overview. *Language Resources and Evaluation*, *52*(1), 101–148. doi:10.100710579-017-9399-2

Losey, D. P., McDonald, C. G., Battaglia, E., & O'Malley, M. K. (2018). A review of intent detection, arbitration, and communication aspects of shared control for physical human–robot interaction. *Applied Mechanics Reviews*, *70*(1), 010804. doi:10.1115/1.4039145

Loughran, T., & McDonald, B. (2011). When is a liability not a liability? Textual analysis, dictionaries, and 10-Ks. *The Journal of Finance*, *66*(1), 35–65. doi:10.1111/j.1540-6261.2010.01625.x

Maas, A. L., Daly, R. E., Pham, P. T., Huang, D., Ng, A. Y., & Potts, C. (2011). Learning Word Vectors for Sentiment Analysis. In *Proceedings of the 49th Annual Meeting of the Association for Computational Linguistics: Human Language Technologies* - Volume 1 (pp. 142-150). Association for Computational Linguistics.

Mackey, T., Purushothaman, V., Li, J., Shah, N., Nali, M., Bardier, C., Liang, B., Cai, M., & Cuomo, R. (2020). Machine Learning to Detect Self-Reporting of Symptoms, Testing Access, and Recovery Associated With COVID-19 on Twitter: Retrospective Big Data Infoveillance Study. *JMIR Public Health and Surveillance*, *6*(2), e19509. doi:10.2196/19509 PMID:32490846

Mackiewicz, J. (2010). The Co-Construction of Credibility in Online Product Reviews. *Technical Communication Quarterly*, *19*(4), 403–426. doi:10.1080/10572252.2010.502091

Madani, Y., Erritali, M., Bengourram, J., & Sailhan, F. (2019). Social Collaborative Filtering Approach for Recommending Courses in an E-learning Platform. *Procedia Computer Science*, *151*, 1164–1169.

Makino, Y., & Klyuev, V. (2015). Evaluation of web vulnerability scanners. *The 8th IEEE International Conference on Intelligent Data Acquisition and Advanced Computing Systems: Technology and Applications*.

Makkar, A., & Kumar, N. (2020). An efficient deep learning-based scheme for web spam detection in IoT environment. *Future Generation Computer Systems*, *108*, 467–487. doi:10.1016/j.future.2020.03.004

Malaquias, F. & Júnior, R. (2021). The use of m-government applications: Empirical evidence from the smartest cities of Brazil. *Information Technology & People*. ahead-of-print. doi:10.1108/ITP-05-2020-0346

Malbon, J. (2012). Taking Fake Online Consumer Reviews Seriously. *Journal of Consumer Policy*, *36*(2), 139–157. doi:10.100710603-012-9216-7

Mallick, C., Das, A. K., Dutta, M., Das, A. K., & Sarkar, A. (n.d.). *Graph-BasedTextSummarizationUsing ModifiedTextRank.pdf*. Springer Singapore. doi:10.1007/978-981-13-0514-6

Mao, X., Chang, S., Shi, J., Li, F., & Ronghua, S. (2019). Sentiment-Aware Word Embedding for Emotion Classification. *Applied Sciences (Basel, Switzerland)*, *9*(7), 1334. doi:10.3390/app9071334

Marsault, B., Gigot, F., & Jagorel, G. (2020). *Sms Spam Detection*. Text Analysis And Retrieval 2020 Course Project Reports, 42.

Martin, J., Bohuslava, J., & Igor, H. (2018). Augmented Reality in Education 4.0. *2018 IEEE 13th International Scientific and Technical Conference on Computer Sciences and Information Technologies (CSIT), 2018*, 231-236. doi: 10.1109/STC-CSIT.2018.8526676

Mata, F., Torres-Ruiz, M., Zagal, R., Guzman, G., Moreno-Ibarra, M., & Quintero, R. (2018). A cross-domain framework for designing healthcare mobile applications mining social networks to generate recommendations of training and nutrition planning. *Telematics and Informatics, 35*(4), 837–853. doi:10.1016/j.tele.2017.04.005

Mateos, J. Jong, & Timothy. (2021). The impact of mobile ICT on national productivity in developed and developing countries. *Information & Management, 58*(3). doi:10.1016/j.im.2021.103442

Maurya, S., & Jain, A. (2020). Deep learning to combat phishing. *Journal of Statistics and Management Systems, 23*(6), 945–957. doi:10.1080/09720510.2020.1799496

Mayzlin, D., Dover, Y., & Chevalier, J. (2012). Promotional Reviews. An Empirical Investigation of Online Review Manipulation. *NBER Working Paper Series, 104*(8), 1-49.

McKechnie, S. (1992). Consumer Buying Behaviour in Financial Services: An Overview. *International Journal of Bank Marketing, 10*(5), 4–12. doi:10.1108/02652329210016803

Mehta, D., Dwivedi, A., Patra, A., & Kumar, M. A. (2021). A transformer-based architecture for fake news classification. *Social Network Analysis and Mining, 11*(1), 1–12.

Melnyk, R., Snyder, M. M., & Verner, A. (2020). Towards the Development of A Classification Model for Technical Documents in Knowledge Discovery System. *Issues in Information Systems, 21*, 67–72.

Mentsiev, A. U., Magomaev, T. R., & Dauletukaeva, K. D. (2020). The impact of big data on the development of education. *Journal of Physics: Conference Series, 1691*(1), 012181.

Merriam, S. B. (2001). Andragogy and Self-Directed Learning: Pillars of Adult Learning Theory. In S. B. Merriam (Ed.), *The new update on adult learning theory. New Directions for Adult and Continuing Education, No. 89.* Jossey-Bass. Springer.

Mhamdi, C., Al-Emran, M., & Salloum, S. A. (2018). Text mining and analytics: A case study from news channels posts on Facebook. In *Intelligent Natural Language Processing: Trends and Applications* (pp. 399–415). Springer.

Mihart, C. (2012). Impact of Integrated Marketing Communication on Consumer Behavior. Effect on Consumer Decision-Making Process. *International Journal of Marketing Studies, 4*(2), 121–129. doi:10.5539/ijms.v4n2p121

Mihelis, G., Grigoroudis, E., Siskos, Y., Politis, Y., & Malandrakis, Y. (2001). Customer satisfaction measurement in the private bank sector. *European Journal of Operational Research, 130*(2), 347–360. doi:10.1016/S0377-2217(00)00036-9

Mikolov, T., Chen, K., Córrado, G., & Dean, J. (2013). Efficient Estimation of Word Representations in Vector Space. arxiv preprint arxiv:1301.3781.

Mikolov, T., Chen, K., Corrado, G., & Dean, J. (2013). *Efficient Estimation of Word Representations in Vector Space.* arxiv:1301.3781.

Minaee, S. Kalchbrenner, Cambria, E., Nikzad, N., Chenaghlu, M., & Gao, J. (2020). Deep learning based text classification: A comprehensive review. arxiv:2004.03705 [cs.cl], 1.

Mishra, R., Bian, J., Fiszman, M., Weir, C. R., Jonnalagadda, S., Mostafa, J., & Del, G. (2014). Text summarization in the biomedical domain : A systematic review of recent research. *Journal of Biomedical Informatics, 52*, 457–467. doi:10.1016/j.jbi.2014.06.009 PMID:25016293

Mishra, S., & Soni, D. (2020). Smishing Detector: A security model to detect smishing through SMS content analysis and URL behavior analysis. *Future Generation Computer Systems*, *108*, 803–815. doi:10.1016/j.future.2020.03.021

Mohammad, S., Kiritchenko, S., Sobhani, P., Zhu, X., & Cherry, C. (2016a). A dataset for detecting stance in tweets. In *Proceedings of the Tenth International Conference on Language Resources and Evaluation (LREC'16)* (pp. 3945-3952). Academic Press.

Mohammad, S. M., Sobhani, P., & Kiritchenko, S. (2017). Stance and sentiment in tweets. *ACM Transactions on Internet Technology*, *17*(3), 1–23. doi:10.1145/3003433

Mohammad, S., Kiritchenko, S., Sobhani, P., Zhu, X., & Cherry, C. (2016b). Semeval-2016 task 6: Detecting stance in tweets. In *Proceedings of the 10th International Workshop on Semantic Evaluation (SemEval-2016)* (pp. 31-41). 10.18653/v1/S16-1003

Moharm, K., & Eltahan, M. (2020). The role of big data in improving e-learning transition. *IOP Conference Series. Materials Science and Engineering*, *885*(1), 012003.

Mohd Kamal, M. A., Adnan, A. H. M., Azamri, N. M., Idris, K. B., Zuraimi, N. A., & Yusof, M. N. (2019). Video-based learing as an Education 4.0 technique for blended learning in flipped classrooms. Proc. of the International Invention, Innovative & Creative (InIIC) Conference (series 2/2019), 17-27.

Moh, M., Moh, T. S., Peng, Y., & Wu, L. (2017). On adverse drug event extractions using twitter sentiment analysis. *Network Modeling and Analysis in Health Informatics and Bioinformatics*, *6*(1), 1–12. doi:10.100713721-017-0159-4

Mondal, B., Patra, O., Mishra, S., & Patra, P. (2020). A course recommendation system based on grades. *2020 International Conference on Computer Science, Engineering and Applications (ICCSEA)*, 1-5.

Monsalve-Pulido, J. (2020). Autonomous recommender system architecture for virtual learning environments. In Applied Computing and Informatics. Elsevier.

Monti, F., Frasca, F., Eynard, D., Mannion, D., & Bronstein, M. M. (2019). *Fake News Detection on Social Media using Geometric Deep Learning.* arXiv preprint arXiv:1902.06673.

Moradi, M. (2018b). *Concept-based single- and multi-document biomedical text summarization Concept-based single- and multi-document biomedical text summarization.* Milad Moradi Department of Electrical and Computer Engineering Language : Farsi Abstract.

Moradi, M. (2018a). CIBS: A biomedical text summarizer using topic-based sentence clustering. *Journal of Biomedical Informatics*, *88*(November), 53–61. doi:10.1016/j.jbi.2018.11.006 PMID:30445218

Moradi, M., & Ghadiri, N. (2017). Quantifying the informativeness for biomedical literature summarization: An itemset mining method. In *Computer Methods and Programs in Biomedicine* (Vol. 146). doi:10.1016/j.cmpb.2017.05.011

Moradi, M., & Ghadiri, N. (2018). Different approaches for identifying important concepts in probabilistic biomedical text summarization. *Artificial Intelligence in Medicine*, *84*, 101–116. doi:10.1016/j.artmed.2017.11.004 PMID:29208328

Morgan, C., Liu, D., & Carter, L. (2018). Impact of citizens' privacy concerns on e-Government adoption. In *Proceedings of the 19th Annual International Conference on Digital Government Research: Governance in the Data Age*. ACM.

Morze, N., Varchenko-Trotsenko, L., Terletska, T., & Smyrnova-Trybulska, E. (2021). Implementation of adaptive learning at higher education institutions by means of Moodle LMS. *Journal of Physics: Conference Series*, *1840*(1), 012062.

Mouratidis, D., Nikiforos, M. N., & Kermanidis, K. L. (2021). Deep Learning for Fake News Detection in a Pairwise Textual Input Schema. *Computation*, *9*(2), 20.

Mrksic, N., Séaghdha, D. Ó., Thomson, B., Gasic, M., Rojas-Barahona, L. M., Su, P.-H., Vandyke, D., Wen, T.-H., & Young, S. J. (2016). Counter-fitting Word Vectors to Linguistic Constraints. In K. Knight, A. Nenkova & O. Rambow (Eds.), HLT-NAACL (pp. 142-148). The Association for Computational Linguistics.

Mtingwi, J. E. (2015). Mobile Government in African Least Developed Countries (LDCs): Proposed Implementing Framework. *Proceedings of IST-Africa*, 1-14.

Müller, C., Hornung, D., Hamm, T., & Wulf, V. (2015). Measures and tools for supporting ICT appropriation by elderly and non-tech-savvy persons in a long-term perspective. In *ECSCW 2015: Proceedings of the 14th European Conference on Computer Supported Cooperative Work*. Springer. 10.1007/978-3-319-20499-4_14

Muniasamy, A., & Alasiry, A. (2020). Deep learning: The impact on future eLearning. *International Journal of Emerging Technologies in Learning*, *15*(1), 188–199. https://doi.org/10.3991/ijet.v15i01.11435

Nabizadeh, A. H. (2020). Learning Path Personalization and Recommendation Methods: A Survey of the State-Of-The-Art. *Expert Systems with Applications*, *159*, 113596.

Nabizadeh, A. H., Goncalves, D., Gama, S., Jorge, J., & Rafsanjani, H. N. (2020). Adaptive learning path recommender approach using auxiliary learning objects. *Computers & Education*, *147*, 103777.

Narayanan, S. P. (2016). A holistic approach to lowering latency in geo-distributed web applications. *Open Access Dissertations*, 834.

Nasir, J. A., Khan, O. S., & Varlamis, I. (2021). Fake news detection: A hybrid CNN-RNN based deep learning approach. *International Journal of Information Management Data Insights*, *1*(1), 100007.

Negash, S., & Wilcox, M. V. (2008). E-Learning Classifications: Differences and Similarities. Handbook of Distance Learning for Real-Time and Asynchronous Information Technology Education.

Nejati, J., & Balasubramanian, A. (2016). An in-depth study of mobile browser performance. *Proceedings of the 25th International Conference on World Wide Web (WWW '16)*, 1305-1315. 10.1145/2872427.2883014

Nilashi, M., & Ibrahim, O., & Ithnin, N. (2014). Hybrid recommendation approaches for multi-criteria collaborative filtering. *Expert Systems with Applications*, *41*(8), 3879–3900.

O'Flaherty, J., & Philips, C. (2015). The Use of Flipped Classrooms in Higher Education: A Scoping Review. *Internet and Higher Education*, *25*, 85–95.

Odunlami, I., & Ofoegbu, O. (2011). Effect of Marketing Communication in Promoting Organisational Sales. A Case Study of Sunshine Company. *Journal of Emerging Trends in Economics and Management Science*, *2*(5), 408–412.

Ojo, A., & Rizun, N. (2019). Enabling deeper linguistic-based text analytics - Construct development for the criticality of negative service experience. *IEEE Access: Practical Innovations, Open Solutions*, *7*, 169217–169256. doi:10.1109/ACCESS.2019.2947593

Ortigosa, A., Martín, J. M., & Carro, R. M. (2014). Sentiment analysis in Facebook and its application to e-learning. *Computers in Human Behavior*, *31*, 527–541.

Otto, J., & Wagner, W. (2004). Analysis of Online Customer Review. *Journal of Business & Economics Research*, *2*(10), 17–22.

Oussous, A., Benjelloun, F. Z., Lahcen, A. A., & Belfkih, S. (2018). Big Data technologies: A survey. *Journal of King Saud University – Computer and Information Sciences, 30*, 431–448.

Ouyang, F., & Jiao, P. (2021). Artificial intelligence in education: The three Paradigms. *Computers and Education: Artificial Intelligence, 2.* doi:10.1016/j.caeai.2021.100020

Ozdamil, F., & Cavus, N. (2011). Basic elements and Characteristics of mobile learning. *Procedia: Social and Behavioral Sciences, 28,* 937–942.

Padmavathy, P., & Pakkir Mohideen, S. (2020). An efficient two-pass classifier system for patient opinion mining to analyze drugs satisfaction. *Biomedical Signal Processing and Control, 57,* 101755. doi:10.1016/j.bspc.2019.101755

Pai, R. R., & Alathur, S. (2018). Assessing mobile health applications with twitter analytics. *International Journal of Medical Informatics, 113,* 72–84. doi:10.1016/j.ijmedinf.2018.02.016 PMID:29602436

Pak, A., & Paroubek, P. (2010). Twitter as a Corpus for Sentiment Analysis and Opinion Mining. Academic Press.

Pakkala, H., Presser, K., & Christensenc, T. (2012). Using Google analytics to measure visitor statistics: The case of food composition websites. *International Journal of Information Management, 32*(6), 504–512. doi:10.1016/j.ijinfomgt.2012.04.008

Palangi, H., Deng, L., Shen, Y., Gao, J., He, X., Chen, J., Song, X., & Ward, R. K. (2016). Deep Sentence Embedding Using Long Short-Term Memory Networks: Analysis and Application to Information Retrieval. *IEEE/ACM Transactions on Audio, Speech, and Language Processing, 24*(4), 694–707. doi:10.1109/TASLP.2016.2520371

Pant, H. V., Lohani, M. C., & Pande, J. (2021). *MOOCs in Higher Education: Current Trends in India and Developed Countries.* Ubiquitous Technologies for Human Development and Knowledge Management. doi:10.4018/978-1-7998-7844-5.ch004

Paramythis, A., & Loidl-Reisinger, S. (2004). Adaptive Learning Environments and e-Learning Standards. *Electronic Journal of e-Learning, 2*(1), 181–194.

Park, C. C., Kim, Y., & Kim, G. (2018). Retrieval of Sentence Sequences for an Image Stream via Coherence Recurrent Convolutional Networks. *IEEE Transactions on Pattern Analysis and Machine Intelligence, 40*(4), 945–957. doi:10.1109/TPAMI.2017.2700381 PMID:28475047

Park, C.-H., & Kim, Y.-G. (2003). Identifying key factors affecting consumer purchase behavior in an online shopping context. *International Journal of Retail & Distribution Management, 31*(1), 16–29. doi:10.1108/09590550310457818

Park, S., & Nicolau, J. L. (2015). Asymmetric effects of online consumer reviews. *Annals of Tourism Research, 50,* 67–83. doi:10.1016/j.annals.2014.10.007

Pauwels, K., Erguncu, S., & Yildirim, G. (2013). Winning hearts, minds and sales: How marketing communication enters the purchase process in emerging and mature markets. *International Journal of Research in Marketing, 30*(1), 57–68. doi:10.1016/j.ijresmar.2012.09.006

Peat, J., & Helland, K. (2004). *The competitive advantage of online versus traditional education.* University of Tennessee. ERIC Document Reproduction Service No. ED492477.

Pelkmann, D., Tharwat, A., & Schenck, W. (2020). How to Label? Combining Experts' Knowledge for German Text Classification. *7th Swiss Conference on Data Science (Sds),* 61-62. 10.1109/SDS49233.2020.00023

Pendyala, V. S., Liu, Y., & Figueira, S. M. (2018). A framework for detecting injected influence attacks on microblog websites using change detection techniques. *Development Engineering, 3,* 218–233. doi:10.1016/j.deveng.2018.08.002

Pennington, J., Socher, R., & Manning, C. (2014). GloVe: global vectors for word representation. In *Proceedings of the 2014 Conference on Empirical Methods in Natural Language Processing (EMNLP)*. Association for Computational Linguistics. 10.3115/v1/D14-1162

Pennington, J., Socher, R., & Manning, C. D. (2014). Glove: Global Vectors for Word Representation. In EMNLP (pp. 1532-1543). Academic Press.

Peters, M. E., Neumann, M., Iyyer, M., Gardner, M., Clark, C., Lee, K., & Zettlemoyer, L. (2018). Deep contextualized word representations. *NAACL 2018*.

Peters, M., Neumann, M., Iyyer, M., Gardner, M., Clark, C., Lee, K., & Zettlemoyer, L. (2018). Deep Contextualized Word Representations. *Proceedings of the 2018 Conference of the North American Chapter of the Association for Computational Linguistics: Human Language Technologies, 1*, 2227–2237. 10.18653/v1/N18-1202

Platt, J. (1998). Fast training of support vector machines using sequential minimal optimization. In B. Schoelkopf, C. Burges, & A. Smola (Eds.), Advances in Kernel Methods - Support Vector Learning. Academic Press.

Plaza, L., Díaz, A., & Gervás, P. (2011). A semantic graph-based approach to biomedical summarisation. *Artificial Intelligence in Medicine, 53*(1), 1–14. doi:10.1016/j.artmed.2011.06.005 PMID:21752612

Plessis, C., Angelopulo, G., & Plessis, D. (2012). A conceptual framework of corporate online communication: A marketing public relations (MPR) perspectives. *South African Journal of Communication Theory and Research, 32*(2), 241–263.

Poon, J. (2013). Blended learning: An institutional approach for enhancing students' learning experiences. *Journal of Online Learning and Teaching, 9*(2), 271–288.

Popovac, M., Karanovic, M., Sladojevic, S., Arsenovic, M., & Anderla, A. (2018, November). Convolutional neural network based SMS spam detection. In *2018 26th Telecommunications Forum (TELFOR)* (pp. 1-4). IEEE. 10.1109/TELFOR.2018.8611916

Poria, S., Cambria, E., & Gelbukh, A. F. (2015). Deep Convolutional Neural Network Textual Features and Multiple Kernel Learning for Utterance-level Multimodal Sentiment Analysis. In L. Màrquez, C. Callison-Burch, J. Su, D. Pighin & Y. Marton (Eds.), EMNLP (pp. 2539-2544). The Association for Computational Linguistics. doi:10.18653/v1/D15-1303

Poulos, M., Korfiatis, N., & Papavlassoouolos, S. (2020). Assessing stationary in web analytics: A study of bounce rates. *Expert Systems, 37*(3).

Purohit, H., Dong, G., Shalin, V., Thirunarayan, K., & Sheth, A. (2015). Intent classification of short-text on social media. In *Proceedings of IEEE International Conference on Smart City/SocialCom/SustainCom* (pp. 222-228). 10.1109/SmartCity.2015.75

Qazi, U., Imran, M., & Ofli, F. (2020). GeoCoV19: A Dataset of Hundreds of Millions of Multilingual COVID-19 Tweets with Location Information. *ArXiv*, 1–3.

Rabahallah, K., Mahdaoui, L., & Azouaou, F. (2018). MOOCs Recommender System Using Ontology and Memory-based Collaborative Filtering. *20th International Conference on Enterprise Information Systems*.

Radev, D. R., Jing, H., Styś, M., & Tam, D. (2004). Centroid-based summarization of multiple documents. *Information Processing & Management, 40*(6), 919–938. doi:10.1016/j.ipm.2003.10.006

Rafique, S., Humayun, M., Hamid, B., Abbas, A., Akhtar, M., & Iqbal, K. (2015). Web application security vulnerabilities detection approaches: A systematic mapping study. *IEEE/ACIS 16th International Conference on Software Engineering, Artificial Intelligence, Networking and Parallel/Distributed Computing (SNPD)*, 1-6. 10.1109/SNPD.2015.7176244

Raghupathi, D., Yannou, B., Farel, R., & Poirson, E. (2015). Customer sentiment appraisal from user-generated product reviews: A domain independent heuristic algorithm. *International Journal on Interactive Design and Manufacturing, 9*(3), 201–211. doi:10.100712008-015-0273-4

Rahman, A. (2016). Cloud based E-Learning, security threats and security measures. *Indian Journal of Science and Technology, 9*(48), 1–8.

Rahman, N., & Borah, B. (2020). Improvement of query-based text summarization using word sense disambiguation. *Complex & Intelligent Systems, 6*(1), 75–85. doi:10.100740747-019-0115-2

Rajesh, M., Illayaraja, K., & Kalaiselvi, R. (2018). Emerging Trends of E-Learning in India. *Shanlax International Journal of Commerce, 6*(S1), 52-29. zenodo.1438190 doi:10.5281/

Rajeswari, B., & Nisha, S. S. (2018). *Web Page Prediction Using Web Mining.* Academic Press.

Raju, C., Philipsy, E., Chacko, S., & Suresh, L. P. (2018). *Mining Techniques.* Academic Press.

Rani, M., Nayak, R., & Vyas, O. P. (2015). An Ontology-based Adaptive Personalized E-learning System, Assisted by Software Agents on Cloud Storage. *Knowledge-Based Systems, 90*, 33–48.

Ray, A., Bala, P. K., & Dwivedi, Y. K. (2020). Exploring barriers affecting usage intentions: an NLP-based multi-method approach. *Behaviour & Information Technology.* doi:10.1080/0144929X.2020.1849403

Ray, A., Bala, P. K., & Dwivedi, Y. K. (2020). Exploring Values affecting e-Learning adoption from the user-generated-content: A Consumption-value-theory perspective. *Journal of Strategic Marketing.* doi:10.1080/0965254X.2020.1749875

Razzaque, A., & Hamdan, A. (2020). Internet of Things for Learning Styles and Learning Outcomes Improve e-Learning: A Review of Literature. *Joint European-US Workshop on Applications of Invariance in Computer Vision*, 783-791.

Reddick, C. G., & Zheng, Y. (2018). Online privacy protection in Chinese city Governments: An analysis of privacy statements. In L. Alcaide Muñoz & M. Rodríguez Bolívar (Eds.), *International E-Government Development.* Palgrave Macmillan. doi:10.1007/978-3-319-63284-1_5

Redondo, T., & Sandoval, A. M. (2016). Text Analytics: The Convergence of Big Data and Artificial Intelligence. *International Journal of Interactive Multimedia and Artificial Intelligence, 3*(6), 57–64. doi:10.9781/ijimai.2016.369

Reimers, G. (2015). Learner Generated Content - Fostering and Valuing User Generated Content in eLearning using Social Feedback. Doctoral Consortium - DCCSEDU, 3-7.

Ren, Y., Zhang, Y., Zhang, M., & Ji, D. (2016). Improving Twitter Sentiment Classification Using Topic-Enriched Multi-Prototype Word Embeddings. In D. Schuurmans & M. P. Wellman (Eds.), *AAAI* (pp. 3038-3044). AAAI Press.

Ren, R., Wu, D. D., & Liu, T. (2019). Forecasting Stock Market Movement Direction Using Sentiment Analysis and Support Vector Machine. *IEEE Systems Journal, 13*(1), 760–770. doi:10.1109/JSYST.2018.2794462

Reyes-Menedez, A., Saura, J., & Filipe, F. (2019). The importance of behavioral data to identify online fake reviews for tourism businesses: A systematic review. *PeerJ. Computer Science, 5*, e219. doi:10.7717/peerj-cs.219 PMID:33816872

Rinaldi, A. M., Russo, C., & Tommasino, C. (2021). A semantic approach for document classification using deep neural networks and multimedia knowledge graph. *Expert Systems with Applications, 169*, 114320. doi:10.1016/j.eswa.2020.114320

Rindova, V., Williamson, I., Petkova, A., & Sever, J. (2005). Being good or being known: An empirical examination of the dimensions, antecedents and consequences of organizational reputation. *Academy of Management Journal, 48*(6), 2–42. doi:10.5465/amj.2005.19573108

Rivero-Albarran, D. (2018). Design of a Recommender System for Intelligent Classrooms Based on Multiagent Systems. In Advances in Intelligent Systems and Computing (Vol. 721). Springer.

Robson, K., Bredican, J., Farshid, M., & Humphrey, S. (2013). Making Sense of Online Consumer Reviews: A Methodology. *International Journal of Market Research*, *55*(4), 521–537. doi:10.2501/IJMR-2013-046

Rodrigues, U. M., & Xu, J. (2020). Regulation of COVID-19 fake news infodemic in China and India. *Media International Australia*, *177*(1), 125–131. doi:10.1177/1329878X20948202

Ru, B., Li, D., Hu, Y., & Yao, L. (2019). Serendipity - A Machine-Learning Application for Mining Serendipitous Drug Usage from Social Media. *IEEE Transactions on Nanobioscience*, *18*(3), 324–334. doi:10.1109/TNB.2019.2909094 PMID:30951476

Rukmana, A. A., & Mulyanti, B. (2020). Internet of Things (IoT): Web learning for smart school system. *IOP Conference Series. Materials Science and Engineering*, *830*(3), 032042.

Saha, I., Sarma, D., Chakma, R. J., Alam, M. N., Sultana, A., & Hossain, S. (2020, August). Phishing Attacks Detection using Deep Learning Approach. In *2020 Third International Conference on Smart Systems and Inventive Technology (ICSSIT)* (pp. 1180-1185). IEEE. 10.1109/ICSSIT48917.2020.9214132

Sahoo, S. R., & Gupta, B. B. (2021). Multiple features based approach for automatic fake news detection on social networks using deep learning. *Applied Soft Computing*, *100*, 106983.

Salehi, M., & Kamalabadi, I. N. (2013). Hybrid recommendation approach for learning material based on sequential pattern of the accessed material and the learner's preference tree. *Knowledge-Based Systems*, *48*, 57–69.

Salehi, M., & Kmalabadi, I. N. (2012). A hybrid attribute-based recommender system for e-learning material recommendation. *IERI Procedia*, *2*, 565–570.

Salminena, J., Yoganathan, V., Corporand, J., Jansena, B. J., & Junga, S. (2019). Machine learning approach to auto-tagging online content for content marketing efficiency: A comparative analysis between methods and content type. *Journal of Business Research*, *101*, 203–217. doi:10.1016/j.jbusres.2019.04.018

Samuel, J., Ali, G. G. M. N., Rahman, M. M., Esawi, E., & Samuel, Y. (2020). COVID-19 public sentiment insights and machine learning for tweets classification. *Information (Switzerland)*, *11*(6), 1–23. doi:10.3390/info11060314

Samuel, J., Rahman, M. M., Ali, G. G. M. N., Samuel, Y., Pelaez, A., Chong, P. H. J., & Yakubov, M. (2020). Feeling Positive about Reopening? New Normal Scenarios from COVID-19 US Reopen Sentiment Analytics. *IEEE Access: Practical Innovations, Open Solutions*, *8*, 142173–142190. doi:10.1109/ACCESS.2020.3013933

Sánchez-Torres, J., Arroyo, X., Varon, S., & Sánchez-Alzate, J. (2021). Adoption of e-government in Colombia: The importance of government policy in citizens' use of e-government. *An International Journal of Electronic Government*, *17*(2), 220–236. doi:10.1504/EG.2021.114577

Sarrab, M., Elgamel, L., & Aldabbas, H. (2012). Mobile Learning (m-learning) and educational environments. *International Journal of Distributed and Parallel Systems, 3*(4).

Sattarov, A. R., & Khaitova, N. F. (2019). Mobile learning as new forms and methods of increasing the effectiveness of education. *European Journal of Research and Reflection in Educational Sciences*, *7*(12), 1169–1175.

Schiavone, A. & Paternò, F. (2015). An extensible environment for guideline-based accessibility evaluation of dynamic web applications. In *Universal Access in the Information Society* (vol. 14, pp. 111-132). . doi:10.100710209-014-0399-3

Schlegel, D. (2015). *Deep Machine Learning on Gpu*. University of Heidelber-Ziti.

Schlichtkrull. (2015). *Learning Affective Projections for Emoticons on Twitter.* In CogInfoCom, 6th IEEE international conference on Cognitive Info communications, Gyor, Hungary.

Semberecki, P., & Maciejewski, H. (n.d.). Deep learning methods for subject text classifification of articles. *Proceedings of the Federated Conference on Computer Science and Information Systems*, 11, 357-360. doi:10.15439/2017F414

Semerádová, T., & Weinlich, P. (2020). Using Google Analytics to Examine the Website Traffic. In *Website Quality and Shopping Behavior.* Springer. doi:10.1007/978-3-030-44440-2_5

Seshadri, K., & Iyer, K. V. (2010). Parallelization of a dynamic SVD clustering algorithm and its application in information retrieval. *Software, Practice & Experience*, *40*(10), 883–896. doi:10.1002pe.987

Shahabadi, M. M., & Uplane, M. (2015). Synchronous and asynchronous learning styles and academic performance of e-learners. *Procedia: Social and Behavioral Sciences*, *176*(20), 129–138.

Shareef, M., Dwivedi, Y., Laumer, S., & Archer, N. (2016). Citizens' adoption behavior of mobile government (mGov): A cross-cultural study. *Information Systems Management*, *33*(3), 268–283. doi:10.1080/10580530.2016.1188573

Sheshasaayee, A., & Malathi, S. (2017). Impact and consequences of BIG DATA in e-learning. *2017 International Conference on Innovative Mechanisms for Industry Applications (ICIMIA)*, 726-729. doi: 10.1109/ICIMIA.2017.7975560

Shi, D. (2020). A learning path recommendation model based on a multidimensional knowledge graph framework for e-learning. *Knowledge-Based Systems*, *193*, 105618.

Shirazi, H., Haefner, K., & Ray, I. (2017, August). Fresh-phish: a framework for auto-detection of phishing websites. In 2017 IEEE international conference on information reuse and integration (IRI) (pp. 137-143). IEEE. doi:10.1109/IRI.2017.40

Shrivastava, G., Kumar, P., Ojha, R. P., Srivastava, P. K., Mohan, S., & Srivastava, G. (2020). Defensive modeling of fake news through online social networks. *IEEE Transactions on Computational Social Systems*, *7*(5), 1159–1167.

Shu, K., Sliva, A., Wang, S., Tang, J., & Liu, H. (2017). Fake news detection on social media: A data mining perspective. *SIGKDD Explorations*, *19*(1), 22–36. doi:10.1145/3137597.3137600

Siddiqui, S. T., Alam, S., Khan, Z. A., & Gupta, A. (2019). Cloud-Based E-Learning: Using Cloud Computing Platform for an Effective E-Learning. In S. Tiwari, M. Trivedi, K. Mishra, A. Misra, & K. Kumar (Eds.), Smart Innovations in Communication and Computational Sciences. Advances in Intelligent Systems and Computing (Vol. 851). Springer., https://doi.org/10.1007/978-981-13-2414-7_31.

Simonyan, K., & Zisserman, A. (2015). Very Deep Convolutional Networks for Large-Scale Image Recognition. *Proceedings of 3rd International Conference on Learning Representations, ICLR- Conference Track Proceeding*, 1409-1556.

Skinner, B. F. (1961). Teaching machines. *Scientific American*, *205*(3), 90–112.

Sleeper, M., Consolvo, S., & Staddon, J. (2014). Exploring the benefits and uses of web analytics tools for non-transactional websites. In *Proceedings of the Conference on Designing Interactive Systems: Processes, Practices, Methods, and Techniques.* Springer. 10.1145/2598510.2598555

SmartMunk. (2020). *Text mining software.* https://www.smartmunk.com/en/text-mining-software/

Sobhani, P., Mohammad, S., & Kiritchenko, S. (2016). Detecting stance in tweets and analyzing its interaction with sentiment. In *Proceedings of the Fifth Joint Conference on Lexical and Computational Semantics* (pp. 159-169). 10.18653/v1/S16-2021

Sonowal, G. (2020). Detecting Phishing SMS Based on Multiple Correlation Algorithms. *SN Computer Science*, *1*(6), 1–9. doi:10.100742979-020-00377-8 PMID:33163974

Souabi, S., Retbi, A., Idrissi, M. K., & Bennani, S. (2020). Toward a Recommendation-Oriented Approach Based on Community Detection Within Social Learning Network. In M. Ezziyyani (Ed.), Advanced Intelligent Systems for Sustainable Development (AI2SD'2019). AI2SD 2019. Advances in Intelligent Systems and Computing (Vol. 1102). Springer. https://doi.org/10.1007/978-3-030-36653-7_22.

Souabi, S., Retbi, A., Idrissi, M. K., & Bennani, S. (2020). A Recommendation Approach in Social Learning Based on K-Means Clustering. *2020 International Conference on Intelligent Systems and Computer Vision (ISVC)*, 1-5. doi: 10.1109/ISCV49265.2020.9204203

Southworth, J. H., Flanigan, J. M., & Knezek, G. (1981). *Computers in education: international multimode electronic conferencing.* The Printout.

Soykan, E. U., Bagriyanik, M., & Soykan, G. (2021). Disrupting the power grid via EV charging: The impact of the SMS Phishing attacks. *Sustainable Energy, Grids and Networks*, 100477.

Sundaram, D. S., Mitra, K., & Webster, C. (1998). Word-of-Mouth Communication: A Motivational Analysis. *Advances in Consumer Research. Association for Consumer Research (U. S.)*, *25*, 527–531.

Sutskever, I., Vinyals, O., & Le, Q. V. (2014). Sequence to sequence learning with neural networks. In Advances in neural information processing systems (pp. 3104-3112). Academic Press.

Swan, K. (2003). Learning effectiveness Online: what the research tells us. In J. Bourne & J. C. Moore (Eds.), *Elements of Quality Online Education, Practice and Direction.* Needham, MA: Sloan Center for Online Education.

Taboada, M., Brooke, J., Tofiloski, M., Voll, K., & Stede, M. (2011). Lexicon-Based Methods for Sentiment Analysis. *Computational Linguistics*, *37*(2), 267–307. doi:10.1162/COLI_a_00049

Tai, S., Socher, R., & Manning, C. D. (2015). Improved Semantic Representations from Tree-Structured Long Short-Term Memory Networks. *Proceedings of the 53rd Annual Meeting of the Association for Computational Linguistics and the 7th International Joint Conference on Natural Language Processing*, *1*, 1556–1566. 10.3115/v1/P15-1150

Tang, D., Wei, F., Qin, B., Yang, N., Liu, T., & Zhou, M. (2016). Sentiment Embeddings with Applications to Sentiment Analysis. *IEEE Transactions on Knowledge and Data Engineering*, *28*(2), 496–509. doi:10.1109/TKDE.2015.2489653

Tang, K. Y., Chang, C. Y., & Hwang, G. J. (2021). Trends in artificial intelligence-supported e-learning: A systematic review and co-citation network analysis (1998-2019). *Interactive Learning Environments*. Advance online publication. doi:10.1080/10494820.2021.1875001

Tanwani, N., Kumar, S., Jalbani, A. H., Soomro, S., Channa, M. I., & Nizamani, Z. (2017, November). Student opinion mining regarding educational system using facebook group. In *2017 First International Conference on Latest trends in Electrical Engineering and Computing Technologies (INTELLECT)* (pp. 1-5). IEEE.

Tarus, J. K., Niu, Z., & Mustafa, G. (2018). Knowledge-based Recommendation: A review of ontology-based recommender systems for e-learning. *Artificial Intelligence Review*, *50*, 21–48.

Taulé, M., Martí, M. A., Rangel, F. M., Rosso, P., Bosco, C., & Patti, V. (2017). Overview of the task on stance and gender detection in tweets on Catalan independence at IberEval 2017. In *2nd Workshop on Evaluation of Human Language Technologies for Iberian Languages, IberEval 2017* (Vol. 1881, pp. 157-177). CEUR-WS.

Tayarani-N., M.-H. (2020). Applications of Artificial Intelligence in Battling Against Covid-19: A Literature Review. *Chaos, Solitons, and Fractals*, *110338*. Advance online publication. doi:10.1016/j.chaos.2020.110338 PMID:33041533

Thai-Nghe, N., Drumond, L., Krohn-Grimberghe, A., & Schmidt-Thieme, L. (2010). Recommender system for predicting student performance. *Procedia Computer Science, 1*, 2811–2819.

Tharwat. A. (2020). Classification Assessment Methods. *Applied Computing and Informatics, 17*(1).

The United Republic of Tanzania. (2004). *Higher Education Students Loans Board (HELBS) Act, 2004.* URT.

Think Ink. (2020). *Think Ink Face Mask (10/1, 5/1, 1/1) Cotton Mask with Elastic Strap Washable Face Mask.* https://www.amazon.co.uk/Think-Ink-Cotton-Elastic-Washable/dp/B086QTXY9Y/ref=mp_s_a_1_1?dchild=1&keywords=think+ink+face+mask&qid=1591548206&quartzVehicle=3514-1426&replacementKeywords=ink+face+mask&sprefix=think+inc+face+&sr=8-1

Tibshirani, R. (1996). Regression Shrinkage and Selection via the LASSO. *Journal of the Royal Statistical Society. Series B. Methodological, 58*(1), 267–288. doi:10.1111/j.2517-6161.1996.tb02080.x

Timoshenko, A., & Hauser, J. (2018). Identifying Customer Needs from User-Generated Content. *Marketing Science, 38*(1), 1–20. doi:10.1287/mksc.2018.1123

Tuan, N. M. D., & Minh, P. Q. N. (2021). *Multimodal Fusion with BERT and Attention Mechanism for Fake News Detection.* arXiv preprint arXiv:2104.11476.

Tumasjan, A., Sprenger, T. O., Sandner, P. G., & Welpe, I. M. (2010). Predicting Elections with Twitter: What 140 Characters Reveal about Political Sentiment. In W. W. Cohen & S. Gosling (Eds.), *ICWSM. The AAAI Press.*

Tutkan, M., Ganiz, M. C., & Akyokuş, S. (2016). Helmholtz principle based supervised and unsupervised feature selection methods for text mining. *Information Processing & Management, 52*(5), 885–910. doi:10.1016/j.ipm.2016.03.007

Umer, M., Imtiaz, Z., Ullah, S., Mehmood, A., Choi, G. S., & On, B. W. (2020). Fake news stance detection using deep learning architecture (cnn-lstm). *IEEE Access: Practical Innovations, Open Solutions, 8*, 156695–156706.

Utz, S., Kerkhof, P., & van den Bos, J. (2012). Consumers rule: How consumer reviews influence perceived trustworthiness of online stores. *Electronic Commerce Research and Applications, 11*(1), 49–58. doi:10.1016/j.elerap.2011.07.010

Venkatesh, V., & David, F. R. (2000). A Theoretical Extension of the Technology Acceptance Model: Four Longitudinal Field Studies. *Management Science, 46*(2), 186–204. doi:10.1287/mnsc.46.2.186.11926

Verbert, K. (2012). Context-Aware Recommender Systems for Learning: A Survey and Future Challenges. *IEEE Transactions on Learning Technologies, 5*(4), 318–335.

Vicario, M. D., Quattrociocchi, W., Scala, A., & Zollo, F. (2019). Polarization and fake news: Early warning of potential misinformation targets. *ACM Transactions on the Web, 13*(2), 1–22.

Vishwakarma, D. K., Varshney, D., & Yadav, A. (2019). Detection and veracity analysis of fake news via scrapping and authenticating the web search. *Cognitive Systems Research, 58*, 217–229. doi:10.1016/j.cogsys.2019.07.004

Wakhu, S. M., Fuyuan, X., & Kakonge, J. O. (2020). Enhancing e/m-Government synergy in Kenya: citizens' perspectives on the driving factors for m-government diffusion. In G. Salvendy & J. Wei (Eds.), Lecture Notes in Computer Science: Vol. 12216. *Design, Operation and Evaluation of Mobile Communications. HCII 2020.* Springer. doi:10.1007/978-3-030-50350-5_11

Wang, J., Zhu, Z., & Caverlee, J. (2020). User Recommendation in Content Curation Platforms. *Conference: WSDM'20: The Thirteenth ACM International Conference on Web Search and Data Mining.* DOI: 10.1145/3336191.3371822

Wang, M., & Kang, M. (2006). Cybergogy for Engaged Learning: A Framework for Creating Learner Engagement through Information and Communication Technology. In *Engaged Learning with Emerging Technologies.* Academic Press.

Wang, T., Brede, M., Ianni, A., & Mentzakis, E. (2017). Detecting and characterizing eating-disorder communities on social media. *WSDM 2017 - Proceedings of the 10th ACM International Conference on Web Search and Data Mining*, 91–100. 10.1145/3018661.3018706

Wang, W. Y. (2017). *"Liar, liar pants on fire": A new benchmark dataset for fakenews detection.* arXiv preprint arXiv:1705.00648.

Wang, X., Liu, Y., Sun, C., Wang, B., & Wang, X. (2015). Predicting Polarities of Tweets by Composing Word Embeddings with Long Short-Term Memory. ACL, (1), 1343-1353.

Wang, D., Zhu, S., & Li, T. (2013). SumView: A Web-based engine for summarizing product reviews and customer opinions. *Expert Systems with Applications*, *40*(1), 27–33. doi:10.1016/j.eswa.2012.05.070

Wang, F., Fong, J., & Kwan, R. (Eds.). (2010). *Research on hybrid learning models: Advanced tools, technologies, and applications*. Information Science Reference.

Wang, J., Yu, L.-C., Lai, K. R., & Zhang, X. (2020). Tree-Structured Regional CNN-LSTM Model for Dimensional Sentiment Analysis. *IEEE/ACM Transactions on Audio, Speech, and Language Processing*, *28*, 581–591. doi:10.1109/TASLP.2019.2959251

Wang, X., Mccallum, A., & Wei, X. (2007). Topical N-Grams: Phrase and Topic Discovery, with an Application to Information Retrieval. *Proceedings - IEEE International Conference on Data Mining, ICDM*, 697-702. 10.1109/ICDM.2007.86

Wang, Y., Lu, X., & Tan, Y. (2018). Impact of product attributes on customer satisfaction: An analysis of online reviews for washing machines. *Electronic Commerce Research and Applications*, *29*, 1–11. doi:10.1016/j.elerap.2018.03.003

Wang, Y., & Rodgers, S. (2011). Electronic Word of Mouth and Consumer Generated Content: From Concept to Application. In M. S. Eastin, T. Daugherty, & N. M. Burns (Eds.), *Handbook of Research on Digital Media and Advertising: User Generated Content Consumption* (pp. 212–231). Information Science Reference.

Wang, Y., Wang, L., Yang, Y., & Lian, T. (2021). SemSeq4FD: Integrating global semantic relationship and local sequential order to enhance text representation for fake news detection. *Expert Systems with Applications*, *166*, 114090.

Wani, A., Joshi, I., Khandve, S., Wagh, V., & Joshi, R. (2021). *Evaluating Deep Learning Approaches for Covid19 Fake News Detection.* arXiv preprint arXiv:2101.04012.

Wani, M. A., & Jabin, S. (2018). *Mutual clustering coefficient-based suspicious-link detection approach for online social networks. Journal of King Saud University.*

Weiss, A., Anderson, E., & MacInnis, J. (1999). Reputation Management as a Motivation for Sales Structure Decisions. *Journal of Marketing*, *63*(4), 74–89. doi:10.1177/002224299906300407

Weitzl, W. (2017). *Measuring Electronic Word-of-Mouth Effectiveness.* Springer Gabler. doi:10.1007/978-3-658-15889-7

Weld, H., Huang, X., Long, S., Poon, J., & Han, S. (2021). *A survey of joint intent detection and slot-filling models in natural language understanding.* arXiv preprint arXiv:2101.08091.

Wong, J. K., Oladinrin, O. T., Ho, C. M., Guilbert, E., & Kam, R. (2018). Assessment of video-based e-learning in a construction measurement course. *International Journal of Construction Management*, 1-7. doi:10.1080/15623599.2018.1435152

Wong, J. (2016). *Almost all the traffic to fake news sites is from Facebook, new data show.* The Medium.

World Economic Forum (WEF). (2017). Global Gender Gap Report. WEF.

World Health Organization. (2020). *Advice on the use of masks in the context of COVID-19: interim guidance.* WHO.

Wu, T., & Gu, C. (2015). Metadata-based method for online learning resources recommendation. *ICIC Express Letters. An International Journal of Research and Surveys., 6*(11), 2929–2935.

Xia, C., Zhang, C., Yan, X., Chang, Y., & Yu, P. S. (2018). Zero-shot user intent detection via capsule neural networks. arXiv preprint arXiv:1809.00385. doi:10.18653/v1/D18-1348

Xia, H., An, W., Li, J., & Zhang, Z. (2020). Outlier knowledge management for extreme public health events: Understanding public opinions about COVID-19 based on microblog data. *Socio-Economic Planning Sciences, 100941*(July), 100941. doi:10.1016/j.seps.2020.100941 PMID:32921839

Xiao, Y., & Cho, K. (2016). Efficient Character-Level Document Classification by Combining Convolution and Recurrent Layers. arxiv:1602.00367.

Xia, R., Jiang, J., & He, H. (2017). Distantly Supervised Lifelong Learning for Large-Scale Social Media Sentiment Analysis. *IEEE Transactions on Affective Computing, 8*(4), 480–491. doi:10.1109/TAFFC.2017.2771234

Xue, J., Chen, J., Chen, C., Zheng, C., Li, S., & Zhu, T. (2020). Public discourse and sentiment during the COVID 19 pandemic: Using latent dirichlet allocation for topic modeling on twitter. *PLoS ONE, 15*(9), 1–23. doi:10.1371/journal.pone.0239441

Xue, J., Chen, J., Hu, R., Chen, C., Zheng, C., Liu, X., & Zhu, T. (2020). Twitter discussions and emotions about COVID-19 pandemic: a machine learning approach. *ArXivLabs*. Retrieved from http://library1.nida.ac.th/termpaper6/sd/2554/19755.pdf

Xue, W., Zhou, W., Li, T., & Wang, Q. (2017). MTNA: A Neural Multi-Task Model for Aspect Category classification and Aspect Term Extraction on Restaurant Reviews. In *Proceedings of the Eighth International Joint Conference on Natural Language Processing.* Asian Federation of Natural Language Processing.

Xu, R., Zhou, Y., Wu, D., Gui, L., Du, J., & Xue, Y. (2016). Overview of nlpcc shared task 4: Stance detection in Chinese microblogs. In *Natural Language Understanding and Intelligent Applications* (pp. 907–916). Springer. doi:10.1007/978-3-319-50496-4_85

Xu, Y., Yen, D., Lin, B., & Chou, D. (2002). Adopting costumer relationship management technology. *Industrial Management & Data Systems, 102*(8), 442–452. doi:10.1108/02635570210445871

Yadav, S., Ekbal, A., Saha, S., & Bhattacharyya, P. (2019). Medical sentiment analysis using social media: Towards building a patient assisted system. *LREC 2018 - 11th International Conference on Language Resources and Evaluation,* 2790–2797.

Yadav, A., & Vishwakarma, D. K. (2020). Sentiment analysis using deep learning architectures: A review. *Artificial Intelligence Review, 53*(6), 4335–4385. doi:10.100710462-019-09794-5

Yadav, R., Kumar, A. V., & Kumar, A. (2019). News-based supervised sentiment analysis for prediction of futures buying behaviour. *IIMB Management Review, 31*(2), 157–166. doi:10.1016/j.iimb.2019.03.006

Yang, G., He, H., & Chen, Q. (2019). Emotion-Semantic-Enhanced Neural Network. *IEEE/ACM Transactions on Audio, Speech, and Language Processing, 27*(3), 531–543. doi:10.1109/TASLP.2018.2885775

Yang, S., & Hong, S. (2009). Effects of Reputation, Relational Satisfaction and Costumer-Company Identification on Positive Word-of-Mouth Intenstions. *Journal of Public Relations Research, 21*(4), 381–403. doi:10.1080/10627260902966433

Yao, J., Wan, X., & Xiao, J. (2017). Recent advances in document summarization. *Knowledge and Information Systems*, *53*(2), 297–336. doi:10.100710115-017-1042-4

Yarandi, M., Jahankhani, H., & Tawil, A. (2013). A Personalized Adaptive e-learning approach based on semantic web technology. *Webology, 10*(2).

Yayli, A., & Bayram, M. (2012). E-WOM: The effects of online consumer reviews on purchasing decisions. *International Journal of Internet Marketing and Advertising*, *7*(1), 1–13.

Yerima, S. Y., Alzaylaee, M. K., Shajan, A., & P, V. (2021). Deep Learning Techniques for Android Botnet Detection. *Electronics (Basel)*, *2021*(10), 519. doi:10.3390/electronics10040519

Yi, L., Zhou, Q., Xiao, T., Qing, G., & Mayer, I. (2020). Conscientiousness in Game-Based Learning. *Simulation & Gaming*, *51*(5), 712–734. doi:10.1177/1046878120927061

Yolchuyeva, S., Németh, G., & Gyires-Tóth, B. (2020). *Self-attention networks for intent detection*. arXiv preprint arXiv:2006.15585.

Yu, J., Zha, Z. J., Wang, M., & Chua, T. S. (2011). Aspect Ranking: Identifying Important Product Aspects from Online Consumer Reviews. In *Proceedings of the 49th Annual Meeting of the Association for Competitional Linguistic* (pp. 1496-1505). Association for Computational Linguistics.

Yu, L.-C., Wang, J., Lai, K. R., & Zhang, X. (2018). Refining Word Embeddings Using Intensity Scores for Sentiment Analysis. *IEEE/ACM Transactions on Audio, Speech, and Language Processing*, *26*(3), 671–681. doi:10.1109/TASLP.2017.2788182

Zain, S. (2020). *Digital transformation trends in education*. Future Directions in Digital Information.

Zeng, J., Zhang, Y., & Ma, X. (2020). Fake news detection for epidemic emergencies via deep correlations between text and images. *Sustainable Cities and Society*, 102652.

Zhang, X., Zhao, J., & LeCun, Y. (2015). Character-Level Convolutional Networks for Text Classification. In *Proceedings of the 28th International Conference on Neural Information Processing Systems (NIPS'15)*. Advances in Neural Information Processing Systems.

Zhang, Z., Brun, A., & Boyer, A. (2020). New Measures for Offline Evaluation of Learning path Recommenders. In Addressing Global Challenges and Quality Education. Springer International Publishing.

Zhang, C., Gupta, A., Kauten, C., Deokar, A. V., & Qin, X. (2019). Detecting fake news for reducing misinformation risks using analytics approaches. *European Journal of Operational Research*, *279*(3), 1036–1052. doi:10.1016/j.ejor.2019.06.022

Zhang, L., Hall, M., & Bastola, D. (2018). Utilizing Twitter data for analysis of chemotherapy. *International Journal of Medical Informatics*, *120*, 92–100. doi:10.1016/j.ijmedinf.2018.10.002 PMID:30409350

Zhang, L., Wang, S., & Liu, B. (2018). Deep learning for sentiment analysis: A survey. *Wiley Interdisciplinary Reviews. Data Mining and Knowledge Discovery*, *8*(4), e1253. doi:10.1002/widm.1253

Zhang, X., Zeng, Y., Jin, X. B., Yan, Z. W., & Geng, G. G. (2017, December). *Boosting the phishing detection performance by semantic analysis. In 2017 IEEE international conference on big data (big data)*. IEEE.

Zhao, J., Dong, L., Wu, J., & Xu, K. (2012). MoodLens: an emoticon-based sentiment analysis system for chinese tweets. In Q. Yang, D. Agarwal & J. Pei (Eds.), KDD (pp. 1528-1531). ACM. doi:10.1145/2339530.2339772

Zhao, R., & Mao, K. (2017). Topic-Aware Deep Compositional Models for Sentence Classification. *IEEE/ACM Transactions on Audio, Speech, and Language Processing*, *25*(2), 248–260. doi:10.1109/TASLP.2016.2632521

Zhou, C., Neubig, G., Gu, J., Diab, M., Guzman, P., Zettlemoyer, L., & Ghazvininejad, M. (2020). *Detecting hallucinated content in conditional neural sequence generation.* arXiv preprint arXiv:2011.02593.

Zhou, C., Sun, C., Liu, Z., & Lau, F. C. M. (2015). A C-LSTM Neural Network for Text Classification. arxiv preprint arxiv:1511.08630.

Zhou, P., Qi, Z., Zheng, S., Xu, J., Bao, H., & Xu, B. (2016).Text Classification Improved by Integrating Bidirectional Lstm with Two-Dimensional Max Pooling. *Proceedings of COLING 2016, the 26th International Conference on Computational Linguistics: Technical Papers, The COLING 2016 Organizing Committee*, 3485–3495.

Zhuang, M., Cui, G., & Peng, L. (2018). Manufactured opinions: The effect of manipulating online product reviews. *Journal of Business Research*, *87*, 24–35. doi:10.1016/j.jbusres.2018.02.016

Zhu, E., Ju, Y., Chen, Z., Liu, F., & Fang, X. (2020). DTOF-ANN: An Artificial Neural Network phishing detection model based on Decision Tree and Optimal Features. *Applied Soft Computing*, *95*, 106505. doi:10.1016/j.asoc.2020.106505

Zhu, X., Sobihani, P., & Guo, H. (2015). Long Short-Term Memory Over Recursive Structures. *Proceedings of the 32nd International Conference on Machine Learning*, *37*, 1604–1612.

Zou, H., & Hastie, T. (2005). Regularization and variable selection via the elastic net. *Journal of the Royal Statistical Society. Series B. Methodological*, *67*(2), 301–320. doi:10.1111/j.1467-9868.2005.00503.x

Zubiaga, A., Aker, A., Bontcheva, K., Liakata, M., & Procter, R. (2018). Detection and resolution of rumours in social media: A survey. *ACM Computing Surveys*, *51*(2), 1–36. doi:10.1145/3161603

About the Contributors

Aakanksha Sharaff is working as an Assistant Professor in Department of Computer Science & Engineering at National Institute of Technology Raipur Chhattisgarh India. She has completed her schooling, graduation and postgraduation with Honours. She has teaching experience of more than 9 years. She has published more than 51 research papers in reputed International Journals and Conferences. She has been granted with five international patents. She has edited a book on "Data Science and its Application" with CRC, Taylor and Francis. She contributes to various conferences as Session Chairs, Invited/Keynote Speakers in various national and international workshops and conferences. She is active technical reviewer of leading International journals of IEEE, ACM, Springer, IGI and Elsevier etc. Dr. Sharaff has supervised 50+ undergraduate and 5+ postgraduate projects. Currently she is guiding five Ph.D. scholars. Her research areas focus mainly on Data Science, Text Analytics, Sentiment Analysis, Information Retrieval, Soft Computing, Artificial Intelligence, Machine and Deep Learning.

G. R. Sinha is Adjunct Professor at International Institute of Information Technology (IIIT) Bangalore and currently deputed as Professor at Myanmar Institute of Information Technology (MIIT) Mandalay Myanmar. He obtained his B.E. (Electronics Engineering) and M.Tech. (Computer Technology) with Gold Medal from National Institute of Technology Raipur. He received his Ph.D. in Electronics & Telecommunication Engineering from Chhattisgarh Swami Vivekanand Technical University Bhilai. He has published 227 research papers in various international and national journals and conferences. He has authored 06 Books including Biometrics published by Wiley India, a subsidiary of John Wiley and Medical Image Processing published by Prentice Hall of India. He has also published 05 Edited books as Editor, such as Cognitive Science-Two Volumes (Elsevier), Optimization Theory (IOP) and Biometrics (Springer). He is active reviewer and editorial member of more than 12 Reputed International Journals such IEEE Transactions on Image Processing, Elsevier Computer Methods and Programs in Biomedicine, Springer Journal of Neural Computing and Applications, etc.

Surbhi Bhatia, PMP®, completed her doctorate from Banasthali Vidyapith, India and is currently working in the College of Computer Sciences and Information Technology, King Faisal University, Saudi Arabia. With over 8 years of academic experience, she has authored 41 papers in conferences, edited books and reputed SCI journals with impact factor and has 9 patents, published and granted from USA, Australia, and India in her list. She has authored 2 books and edited 7 books from Springer, Elsevier, and Wiley. She has been awarded 2 funded research project grants from the Deanship of Scientific Research at King Faisal University and from the Ministry of Education, Saudi Arabia. Her research interests include machine learning, sentiment analysis, and information retrieval.

* * *

Arabela Briciu is Associate Professor at the Department of Social Sciences and Communication, Faculty of Sociology and Communication, Transilvania University of Braşov, Romania. She has a PhD in Communication and her research and teaching interests are oriented towards political communication, electoral debates, public sphere and political image, brand management, corporative identity and Social Media.

Victor-Alexandru Briciu Associate Professor at the Department of Social Sciences and Communication, Faculty of Sociology and Communication, Transilvania University of Braşov, Romania. He received his PhD in 2015 in Mass Communication Studies Field of Research, from University of Bucharest, Faculty of Journalism and Communication. His research and teaching interests are oriented towards communication, public relations campaigns and strategies, branding, online branding strategies and his scientific activity produced in the last years was disseminated through several books and book chapters, more than 10 academic journal articles, more than 25 international and national conferences. He's been involved in projects and grants investigating online place branding strategies and communication through Social Media.

Siddharth Chaurasia is a dual master's in computer science. He received his MTech degree from BITS Pilani, India, in System Software, and MCA degree from BHU, Varanasi, India. Presently, he is pursuing his Doctoral degree in the Department of Computer Science at the University of Lucknow, India. He has been in the field of Information Technology for more than 16 years and is currently working as a Data Scientist. His research interests include artificial intelligence and data mining. He is particularly interested in the field of machine learning and its application to the field of finance.

Supriya Gupta received her Bachelor's degree in Information Technology from CSVTU Technical University, chhatisgarh, India in 2012 and M.Tech. in Computer Science and Engineering from RTMNU Nagpur, India in 2014. She is currently pursuing PhD degree in Computer Science and Engineering at National Institute of Technology Raipur, Raipur, India. Her research interests include Data Analytics ,Data Mining, Biomedical data Analysis.

Fredrick Ishengoma holds a Bachelor of Science in Information and Communication Technology Management (ICTM) from Mzumbe University, Tanzania and Masters of Engineering in Computer and Information Engineering from Daegu University, South Korea. Fredrick Ishengoma currently serves as a lecturer at the College of Informatics and Virtual Education, The University of Dodoma, Tanzania. has participated in a number of ICT4D projects and published more than 15 research papers in international journals and conferences. His research interests include technology adoption, social dimensions of ICT, e/m-Government Information and blockchain technology and ICT4D. He is a member of IEEE and ACM computer societies.

D. Kishan is working as Associate Professor in Department of Civil Engineering, MANIT, Bhopal Area of research in Geo and Geoenvironmental Engineering.

Dilek Küçük, PhD, is an associate professor and chief researcher at the Energy Institute of TÜBİTAK Marmara Research Center (MRC). She is also the leader of Power Systems Information Technologies Group at the institute. Her group is the recipient of best research group award of TÜBİTAK MRC for the year 2017. She has obtained her B.S., M.S. and Ph.D. degrees all from Middle East Technical University in Ankara (Turkey), in 2003, 2005, and 2011, respectively. Between May 2013 and May 2014, she has studied as a post-doctoral researcher at European Commission's Joint Research Centre in Italy. Her research interests include energy informatics, data mining, social media analysis, natural language processing, and database applications in engineering domains. She is the author or co-author of 16 papers published at SCI-indexed journals, in addition to more than 35 papers presented at international conferences.

Puneet Misra is an Assistant Professor of Computer Science in the Department of Computer Science at the University of Lucknow, Lucknow, U.P., India. He received bachelor's degree (1995) in Physics and Maths and a dual Master's degree in Electronics and Computer Applications, and a Ph.D. degree (2003) from the University of Lucknow. He is currently engaged in research areas that includes Soft computing, Artificial Intelligent Systems, human-computer interaction and issues related to cybercrime and its prevention policies, etc.

Naresh Kumar Nagwani (PhD, Senior Member IEEE) is Associate Professor at National Institute of Technology Raipur (NIT Raipur). He has more than 50 research papers into his credit. He is also having industrial experience of more than 3 years with Persistent Systems Limited, where he was the part of software development team and developed data analytics software such as SPSS and Transaction Processing System. He is also Sun certified Java programmer and Sun certified web component developer. He is active reviewer of more than 10 reputed International Journals in his research areas, such as IEEE Transactions, Elsevier Journals, Springer Journals etc. He has teaching and research experience of 13 years. He has delivered more than 10 Keynote/Invited Talks and Chaired many Technical Sessions in National and International Workshops and Conferences. Dr Nagwani has Supervised Four (04) PhD Scholars, 8 M. Tech. Scholars and has been Supervising 08 more PhD Scholars. His research interest includes Text Mining, Software Repositories Mining and Big Data Analytics.

Sreeja P. S. is an Assistant Professor (SG) in the Department of Computer Applications, HITS, Padur. She completed her MCA from Bharathidasan University, M.Phil. (Computer Applications), and Ph.D. from College of Engineering, Anna University, Chennai. She has got the first rank in M.Phil. and received a UGC-BSR fellowship for her research. She received Honorary Rosalind Membership from London Journal Press for her significant research work. She has many International journal and conference publications to her credit and derived 60+ citations. Her research interests include Artificial Intelligence, Text Mining, and Natural Language Processing, Cognitive Poetics.

Allenki Ramya is currently working as a software engineer in UnitedHealthGroup. She got graduated in Computer Science from National Institute of Technology, Raipur.

Cristian-Laurenţiu Roman is a communication and public relations practitioner and an online customer's reviews enthusiast. He also has a B.A. degree in Communication and Public Relations (from 2020), the Faculty of Sociology and Communication, Transilvania University of Brasov.

Saritha S. K. is working as Assistant Professor in the Department of Computer Science and Engineering Area of research Information Retrieval, Machine Learning, Natural Language Processing, Quantum Machine Learning.

Rakhi Seth is a Temporary Faculty in the Department of Computer Science & Engineering (CSE) at the National Institute of Technology Raipur (NITR) India. She has been actively involved in research activities leading to Data Science research and related areas. She worked as Assistant Professor previously in different universities and colleges. She holds a Degree of Master of Technology from Chhattisgarh Swami Vivekananda Technical University (CSVTU), and a Bachelor of Engineering Degree from CSVTU as well. She has received a gold medal in the Post-Graduation program Master of Technology (2015). She has completed a Bachelor of Engineering (2012) as a second branch topper. Her research areas focus mainly on Data Science, Sentiment Analysis, Recommender Systems, Machine and Deep Learning.

Lalitha T. B. is a research scholar in the Department of Computer Applications, HITS, Padur. She has completed her MCA from SRM University with distinction. She has worked in WIPRO technologies for 5 years before pursuing full time Ph.D. She has multiple conference publications to her credit. She received best scholar award from international research awards on new science innovations organized by SFS. Her research interests include machine learning, artificial intelligence, smart learning, natural language processing.

Steni Mol T. S. is pursuing PhD in the Computer Science Department of the Hindustan Institute of Technology and Science, India. This research involves the challenge and solutions of Text Mining, Natural Language Processing and Artificial Intelligence. She holds a Bachelor Degree in computer science (2011) at Nesamony Memorial Christian College, Manonmaniam Sundaranar University, India and a Master of Degree in Computer Application (2014) at School of Communication & Management Studies Cochin, Mahatma Gandhi University, India.

Arun Yadav is a research scholar in Department of Computer Science, University of Lucknow. His research area involves use of Machine Learning in the health care space.

Saneh Yadav is an Assistant Professor, Computer Science and Engineering, K. R. Mangalam University, Gurugram, Haryana, India.

Index

H

healthcare 45, 72-73, 77-78, 81-84, 86-87, 136, 253
hidden web 50, 52, 58-59, 62, 66-68, 70, 220
hybrid learning 170, 174, 186

I

influence 33, 81, 92-94, 96, 98-100, 102, 105, 108, 118-119, 125, 128, 130, 134, 148, 158, 182, 188, 191, 194, 197, 199-200, 205, 231, 241
Information Retrieval 2, 45, 50, 52, 69-71, 207-208, 215, 227, 250-251, 268
intent detection 206-208, 213-217
itemset mining 140, 143, 149, 151-152

L

latest trends 166, 168, 176, 179, 232
lexicon 76, 87, 233-234, 237, 253-260, 263-267
likes 105, 109
loading time 117, 121, 124, 128-130, 134, 139
Long Short-Term Memory 28, 46, 48-49, 157, 218, 222, 250-251
LSTM 26, 34-36, 39, 42-43, 49, 85-86, 153, 157-159, 161-162, 164, 215, 218, 221-223, 228, 237, 247

M

machine learning 1-3, 13, 26-27, 29-30, 33, 37, 39, 44-45, 47-49, 72-73, 75, 82, 85-88, 155, 163, 166, 174-175, 179, 206, 208, 210, 213, 222-223, 225, 229, 233, 235, 242, 249, 254
manipulate 7, 197, 199-200, 205
manipulation 188, 196, 199-203
marketing communication 90, 93-94, 106-107
MAUVE 117, 121-122, 132
Message Length 22-23, 28

N

Naïve Bayes 13, 15, 25, 33, 39-41, 220, 222
Natural Language Processing 31, 47-48, 72-73, 86, 140, 156-157, 204, 207, 215, 227, 231, 233-235, 241, 248-249, 267
negative reviews 90-91, 100, 103-104, 195, 199
non-authentic 188, 197, 205
non-authentic online reviews 188, 197
number of requests 121, 124, 128-130, 134, 139

O

online shops 91
online store 99-101, 109
Organic Search Results 139
organizational reputation 90, 93, 96, 106-107

P

page size 117, 121, 124, 128-130, 134, 139
penalized regression 253, 262
pooling 18, 25, 28, 35, 49, 160
privacy 71, 73, 121, 124, 130, 132-134, 137-138
probabilistic language models 233
public opinion 241, 253-255
Punctuation Count 22-23, 28
purchase decision 91-92, 94, 97-100, 102, 105, 188, 190, 192, 194-195, 197, 199-200
purchasing decision 109, 192

Q

qualitative 90-91, 106, 109, 134, 144, 169
Quantitative measure 109

R

rating 100-104, 108, 195-198, 205
recommendation system 4, 166, 174, 177, 179, 181-184

S

security 26-27, 30, 121-122, 124, 130-134, 136-137, 185
self-approval 98, 195, 205
Self-Directed Learning 166, 172-173, 180, 182-183
SemEval-2015 154, 161, 164
sentiment analysis 1-2, 12, 27, 35-36, 73-74, 77, 83, 85-88, 108-109, 151, 155, 184, 204, 206-208, 213-217, 231-235, 237, 239, 249-257, 259, 267-268
sentiment prediction 253, 263, 265, 267-268
sentiments 74-77, 80-82, 91, 98-99, 106, 196, 202, 204-205, 234, 237, 239, 241, 248, 253-256, 258-259, 263
sentrometrics 253
social media 27, 30-31, 43, 72-76, 78, 80-88, 91, 93, 105-106, 125, 151, 168, 193-194, 201-202, 206-208, 214-223, 226, 228-231, 251, 253-254
social media analysis 206-207

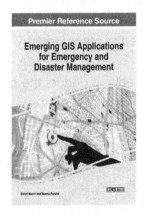
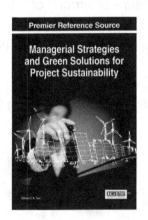

IGI Global Author Services

Providing a high-quality, affordable, and expeditious service, IGI Global's Author Services enable authors to streamline their publishing process, increase chance of acceptance, and adhere to IGI Global's publication standards.

Benefits of Author Services:

- **Professional Service:** All our editors, designers, and translators are experts in their field with years of experience and professional certifications.

- **Quality Guarantee & Certificate:** Each order is returned with a quality guarantee and certificate of professional completion.

- **Timeliness:** All editorial orders have a guaranteed return timeframe of 3-5 business days and translation orders are guaranteed in 7-10 business days.

- **Affordable Pricing:** IGI Global Author Services are competitively priced compared to other industry service providers.

- **APC Reimbursement:** IGI Global authors publishing Open Access (OA) will be able to deduct the cost of editing and other IGI Global author services from their OA APC publishing fee.

Author Services Offered:

English Language Copy Editing
Professional, native English language copy editors improve your manuscript's grammar, spelling, punctuation, terminology, semantics, consistency, flow, formatting, and more.

Scientific & Scholarly Editing
A Ph.D. level review for qualities such as originality and significance, interest to researchers, level of methodology and analysis, coverage of literature, organization, quality of writing, and strengths and weaknesses.

Figure, Table, Chart & Equation Conversions
Work with IGI Global's graphic designers before submission to enhance and design all figures and charts to IGI Global's specific standards for clarity.

Translation
Providing 70 language options, including Simplified and Traditional Chinese, Spanish, Arabic, German, French, and more.

Hear What the Experts Are Saying About IGI Global's Author Services

*"Publishing with IGI Global has been **an amazing experience** for me for sharing my research. The **strong academic production** support ensures quality and timely completion."* – **Prof. Margaret Niess, Oregon State University, USA**

*"The service was **very fast, very thorough, and very helpful** in ensuring our chapter meets the criteria and requirements of the book's editors. I was **quite impressed and happy** with your service."* – **Prof. Tom Brinthaupt, Middle Tennessee State University, USA**

Learn More or Get Started Here:

For Questions, Contact IGI Global's Customer Service Team at cust@igi-global.com or 717-533-8845

IGI Global
PUBLISHER of TIMELY KNOWLEDGE
www.igi-global.com

Printed in the United States
by Baker & Taylor Publisher Services